Hebrew Bible Summaries
The Five Books of Moses

A summary & Outline of the Commands & Events discussed in the five books of Moses, in accordance to the weekly Torah portion

Compiled by Rabbi Yaakov Goldstein
Co-author: Shayna Goldstein

Shulchanaruchharav.com
Shulchan/Tablearuchharav.com is a state of the art Halacha website that contains the largest English database of detailed Halacha available on the web. As part of this site a special Hebrew Bible database has been established to help the learner research any part of the Five Books of Moses and have it available on his fingertips. For further information visit our site at

www.shulchanaruchharav.com

Please support us!
Our website is available free of charge and is dependent on Donors like you! Please contact the above email to become a partner in our holy work!

Foreword

Acknowledgement:

First and foremost, I give thanks to the Almighty who has blessed me to be able to compile this work. I thank my wife, My Eishes Chayil, Shayna, who took a very active role in preparing this book for print, copyediting each and every Portion to verify its accuracy and consistency. A special thanks to Rabbi Roberto Szerer and his wife who have graciously given their support throughout the course of the writing of this book. The merit of the masses rests on their shoulders. I also thank Rabbi/Dr. Kenneth Trestman and his wife for their monthly support throughout the course of the writing of this book, as well as each and every member of shulchanaruchharav.com who with their support fulfill the dictum of the Sages "If there is flour [$] there is Torah" and allowed me the time to write this book.

The intent and format of the book:

Many scholarly and academic books of translations and explanations of the Chumash have been printed and made available to the English-speaking public. The intent of this book is not to serve as a translation of the text found in scripture, or as a depiction of every detail mentioned in scripture, which has already been done justice to in the various works currently available. It certainly does not take the place of learning Chumash in the Hebrew original which connects oneself and one's soul to the Holy words of the Torah as said by G-d, in Lashon Hakodesh. The purpose of this book is to serve as a tool to review the weekly Portion, and a quick reference guide of reminders for the topics discussed in the weekly portion. This will serve the many individuals who need to give over a presentation on a topic in the Portion, otherwise known as a Dvar Torah, as a reminder of the topics that they could discuss. It will help fathers on the Shabbat table have a reference of ideas to talk about regarding the Portion. It will help children review and prepare for tests. It saves them the time of fishing through the entire weekly portion to find a subject and prevents them from feeling overwhelmed by the material. It will also help those learning Chitas or Chok LeIsrael to have a quick summary of the Torah portion of that day. While the book is not a translation of the verses, we tried as much as possible to keep the original wording of the text when writing the chosen segments. This is mainly due to the fact that various verses of scripture contain different ways of interpretation, as brought in the commentaries, and when not necessary, we did not formulate the summary in accordance to a specific commentator, but simply dictated the words of the Torah. However, in mitigating circumstances, we chose one of the commentaries out of the many commentaries, most notably Rashi, to help us summarize a certain matter properly and clearly. In majority of cases, these additional commentaries have been added to the brackets. Often, certain words in the scripture are debated as to their meaning, and in such a case we usually went with the translation of Rashi, and the English term used by the scholarly translations of the Chumash.

The importance of learning Chumash and being an expert in its content:

Chumash is not just the holiest book of the Jewish religion, containing the actual words of G-d, but it is the basis of all Jewish law and theology. Thus, we find that the Talmud and Codifiers rule that it is a Biblical obligation upon every male Jew to study the Chumash until he becomes an expert in its content. This is included in the positive command of Torah learning. This book will IY"H help Jews world over to fulfill this basic Biblical command and become an expert in the content of all of the Parshiyot of the Torah. A thorough article on this subject feature's in the introduction.

About the author:

Rabbi Yaakov Goldstein is the director of Shulchan/Tablearuchharav.com, the world's leading web-based Halacha database, and is the director of the Home Study Semicha Program. Rabbi Goldstein received Semicha from Rabbi Schneur Zalman Labkowski of the Tomchei Temimim headquarters in 2005 and served as a chaplain in the Lotar/Kalatz and K9 unit of the IDF from years 2005-2008. There he dealt with various Halachic issues relating to soldiers in his unit. Since then he has become a certified Shochet, and taught classes in Halacha and Chassidus in the Jerusalem area. Rabbi Goldstein currently lives with his wife Shayna and nine children in Tzfas, Israel in which he serves through his classes to spread the knowledge of Torah to the public.

The following is a list of other subjects currently available in print:

*All books are available for purchase on Shulchan/Tablearuchharav.com & Amazon.com

1. *The Chassidishe Portion-Torah Or-Likkutei Torah*
2. *Topics in Practical Halacha Vol. 1*
3. *Topics in Practical Halacha Vol. 2*
4. *Awaking like a Jew*
    a. *Awaking like a Jew-Workbook*
5. *The Laws of Tzitzis*
6. *The laws & Customs of Rosh Chodesh*
7. *The laws & Customs of Pesach*
8. *Between Pesach & Shavuot*
9. *The laws & Customs of Shavuot*
10. *The Laws & Customs of the Three Weeks*
11. *The Laws of Rosh Hashanah*
12. *The Laws & Customs of Yom Kippur*
13. *The Laws of Purim*
14. *A Semicha Aid for Learning the Laws of Shabbat Vol. 1*
15. *A Semicha Aid for Learning the Laws of Shabbat Vol. 2*
16. *The Laws of Shabbat Volume 3*
17. *The Laws and Customs of Erev Shabbat and Motzei Shabbat*
    a. *The laws of Shabbat-Workbook*
18. *A Semicha aid for learning the laws of Basar Bechalav*
    a. *Basar Bechalav-Workbook*
19. *A Semicha aid for learning the laws of Taaruvos*
    a. *Taaruvos-Workbook*
20. *A Semicha aid for learning the laws of Melicha*
    a. *Melicha-Workbook*

Subscription:

To subscribe to our websites mailing list please visit shulchanaruchharav.com
The subscription is free and includes a weekly Mamar in English from Torah Or/Likkutei Torah, a daily Halacha via email and/or WhatsApp, and updates on Halachic sections as they become available.

Table of Contents

Introduction

1. The intent of the book:

Many scholarly and academic books of translations and explanations of the Chumash have been printed and made available to the English-speaking public. The intent of this book is not to serve as a translation of the text in scripture, or as a depiction of every detail mentioned in scripture, which has already been done justice to in the various works currently available. The intent of this book is to serve as a general outline and summary of the topics that are discussed in each Portion together with their crucial details. Since I was a small child, I have always taken interest in the weekly Portion, as do many, and used various scholarly books that translate and explain the Portion. However, I felt that amongst all the available English [and even Hebrew] literature, there is one very basic non-particularly scholarly work that is fundamentally needed, and that is a basic summary and outline of the events in the Portion. How many of us sit through the weekly Torah reading in synagogue on Shabbat but have no knowledge of its content? How many of us have sat by our Shabbat table wanting to say something over on the Portion, but can't seem to remember its content to help us choose a topic of discussion? How many of us need to prepare a Shabbat speech for our synagogue and community but can't seem to remember the topics of discussion that we can choose from. How many of us have children who need to study for a Portion test but are too overwhelmed by the amount of material required to review. Sitting and flipping through a Chumash with or without a translation, is a long and mentally tiring task, which can exhaust too much of our time and energy. How great would it be to have a general summary and outline with topics and subtopics available in front of us as a quick reference and reminder of what the Portion speaks about? Well, its finally here; an outline and summary of the entire Chumash, one Portion at a time, split in accordance to Aliyot, with an enumeration of the Mitzvot found in each Portion, the amount of verses it contains, and the weekly Haftorah. This work will help the layman and scholar alike in their preparation of the Portion, and in keeping one in tune with the Aliya just read in synagogue. This work will also help those learning their daily Chitas or Chok Leyisrael to have a quick summary of the Torah portion of that day. Last, but not least, this book will help Jews world over to fulfill one of the basic Biblical commands of Torah learning which includes an obligation upon all males to study and become an expert in the content of all of the Parshiyot of the Torah. A thorough article on this subject feature's next. It is my humble wish that the book will assist its readers in all the above and bring a day when the knowledge of G-d fills the entire earth like the water fills the seas.

2. Learning Chumash and Tanakh and being an expert in its content:[1]

It is a Biblical obligation upon every [male[2]] Jew to study the entirety of scripture, [the 24 books[3] of] Torah Nevi'im and Kesuvim[4], and know its content by heart.[5] This is included in the positive

---

[1] Admur Hilchos Talmud Torah 1:1, 4, 6; 2:1 and 9; O.C. 155:1; Kuntrus Achron 1:1; Michaber Y.D. 245:6; 246:4; Tur 245 and 246; Rambam Talmud Torah 1:7; Kiddushin 30a "Until when must one teach his child...Mikra which is Torah"; See Likkutei Sichos 36:16 [printed in synagoguechan Menachem 4:202]

[2] See Admur 1:14

[3] Michaber Y.D. 246:4 "24 books"

[4] Admur 1:1, 4 and 6; 2:9; See Kuntrus Achron 1:1 "Also includes Nevi'im and Kesuvim....According to this there is no merit to the custom to not learn Nevi'im and Kesuvim"; Michaber Y.D. 245:6 "Entire scripture" and 246:4 "24 books"; Shach 245:5 that so is implied from Michaber ibid; Tur 245 and 246 "Torah, Nevi'im and Kesuvim"; Rambam Talmud Torah 1:7 and 12 "The entire scripture...The words of Kabalah are included in scripture"; See Bach 245:5 in length; Likkutei Sichos 36:16 footnote 38

Other opinions: Some Poskim rule it is not necessary to teach one's child Nevi'im and Kesuvim. [Rashi on Kiddushin ibid; See Bach ibid in length] Practically, we do not rule like Rashi, as stated in the above Poskim. [See Bach ibid; Kuntrus Achron ibid]

[5] Admur Hilchos Talmud Torah 2:2-3

command of Torah learning.[6] This is the first subject that a father is obligated to teach a child[7], as will be explained, and takes precedence over the study of all other subjects of Torah, including Jewish law.[8] [It is included in the Mitzvah of Torah Knowledge, although is not considered part of the main Mitzvah of Torah Knowledge.[9]] Those who are not accustomed to learning Torah, Nevi'im and Kesuvim, do not have upon whom to rely even if they learn the Talmud daily, as all of Tanakh must be studied and reviewed many times until one is an expert in all its content.[10] [In other words, one may not rely on the study of Talmud to gain expertise in Tanakh and fulfill the obligation of having knowledge in its content, and rather he must study the entire scripture of Tanakh from the original books in order to fulfill his obligation of Torah Knowledge in this subject.]

The required daily learning of Tanakh:[11] Although children are first taught Tanakh and only then proceed to study Mishneh and Talmud[12], an adult who has yet to learn and know the content of Tanakh, is not to schedule his learning time to first learn the entire Tanakh and only then proceed to Mishneh and Talmud.[13] Rather, an adult's daily[14] learning schedule is obligated to include

---

[6] See Admur and all Poskim ibid that it is part of the Mitzvah of Vishinantam Livanecha and Talmud Torah

[7] Admur 1:1

[8] Admur 2:9 "All this is aside for the reading of Tanach at set times, which has priority over everything."

[9] See Likkutei Sichos 36:16 footnote 38 and 45 that the study of the verses which relate the Mitzvos are included in the main Mitzvah of Yedias Hatorah, while the study of the remaining parts of scripture is similar to the obligation to study Agados, which is included in the Mitzvah of Yedias Hatorah, but is not the main Mitzvah. Accordingly, although its study is required, it does not push off the Mitzvah of getting married. See there in length.

[10] Admur Hilchos Talmud Torah 2:2-3 "According to all, in the start of one's learning one must study scripture every day and repeat it not just one or two or three times, but a great abundance of times, each person in accordance to his memorization capabilities, so he memorize it well."; Admur O.C. 155:1 "At this time one must learn the written Torah"; Admur Kuntrus Achron 1:1 "According to this there is no merit to the custom to not teach Nevi'im and Kesuvim, and what the Shach wrote…is inaccurate"; Bach ibid; Admur in 2:1-3 and O.C. 155:1 completely omits the allowance of Rama/Shach/Tosafus [brought in other opinions] to rely on the study of Talmud for one's knowledge of Tanach and he explicitly negates this opinion in Kuntrus Achron ibid saying in truth that even the Rama and Rabbeinu Tam agree that to begin with one must first study Tanach; See in great length glosses of Rav Ashkenazi on Kuntrus Achron 1 in Vol. 2 p. 890- 899

Other opinions and customs: Some Poskim rule it is not necessary to teach one's child Nevi'im and Kesuvim. [Rashi on Kiddushin ibid; See Bach ibid in length] This is the widespread custom today, to not learn Nevi'im and Kesuvim. [See Bach ibid in length; Shach ibid; Kuntrus Achron ibid] The Bach ibid completely negates this custom. However, some Poskim defend this custom saying that it is a Minhag Israel which is Torah and relies on the opinion of the Poskim [Rama 246:4; Tosafus Kiddushin 30a; Hagahos Maimanis; Rabbeinu Peretz on Hagahos Hasemak 105; Rabbeinu Yerucham 2] who rule that the Babylonian Talmud includes all parts of the Torah and Tanach, and hence this obligation of learning Tanach is fulfilled through the study of Talmud. [Shach Y.D. 246:5] Practically, Admur rules as follows: While this custom is correct from the aspect that the father does not need to hire a teacher to teach him all of Tanach when he is a child [Admur 1:6, unlike Bach ibid, See Kuntrus Achron 1:1] it is not correct from the perspective that there is no obligation to learn and be an expert in Tanach, and in truth one does not fulfill this obligation through the study of Talmud, unlike the Shach ibid. Admur novelizes and explains that even according to the above Poskim ibid who rule one fulfills his obligation of 1/3 learning of Tanach through studying Talmud, this only applies once he has studied all of Tanach and become an expert in it, memorizing all its content. However, until one has reached this level of knowledge in Tanach, all the above Poskim agree that one may not fulfill his obligation with simply learning Talmud. [Admur Kuntrus Achron ibid] In other words, everyone agrees that to fulfill the Mitzvah of Yedias Hatorah one must learn and become expert in all of Tanach, and it is only once this is accomplished that the Poskim discuss the Mitzvah of Vihagisa Bo Yomam Valayla, in which one can fulfill his 1/3 of Tanach through studying the Talmud. [See glosses of Rav Ashkenazi ibid] While this is the ruling of Admur, the widespread custom today is like the Shach's understanding. See Glosses of Rav Ashkenazi ibid who explains that perhaps according to the Shach ibid there is no obligation of Yedias Hatorah by Tanach and it is rather only an obligation for the sake of understanding Talmud [see also Admur 1:6 for a similar idea], however according to Admur ibid there is a complete obligation of Yedias Hatorah in Tanach in it of itself.

The reason: As the Talmud does not contain all the verses of Tanach and it is not in the correct order. It is hence impossible to fulfill one's Mitzvah of Yedias Hatorah of Tanach through studying Talmud. [See Glosses of Rav Ashkeanzi ibid] See other opinions!

[11] Admur Hilchos Talmud Torah 2:1

[12] See next part of this Halacha

[13] Admur 2:1

The reason: As only by children who are not mentally mature or knowledgeable enough to study Mishneh and Talmud do we first teach them the entire scripture for five years. However, an adult who has ability to also study Mishneh and Talmud is not allowed to spend his entire learning schedule first learning all of Tanach, as there is no telling how long he will live [and he has an obligation to study Mikra, Mishneh and Talmud]. [Admur ibid; See Kiddushin ibid]

[14] Admur Hilchos Talmud Torah 2:1 "Each and every day"; Michaber Y.D. 246:4; Tur 246; Tosafus 30a; Rambam 1:12; Kiddushin 30a "For daily"

Other opinions: Some Poskim rule one is to split the week to three subjects. [Rashi Kiddushin ibid] This means that one is to study two days Mikra, two days Mishneh, and two days Talmud. [Tosafus ibid in explanation of Rashi ibid]

three subjects, **Mikra** [i.e. Tanakh[15]], **Mishneh** [i.e. Halacha[16]] and **Talmud** [i.e. the reasons behind the Halachos[17]].[18] This is a Biblical obligation, received from Moses on Sinai.[19] Even one who is unable to study and remember a great amount of Torah, and is hence required to dedicate all his time to the study of practical Halacha, is required to also study Tanakh at the set times.[20] [Thus, one's daily learning schedule must include the study of scripture [i.e. Tanakh], in addition to the study of Halacha and Talmud.]

How much time must one dedicate daily for learning Tanakh:[21] Some Poskim[22] rule one must divide the amount of time he has available each day for Torah learning by three and dedicate exactly 1/3 of that time to the study of Tanakh. [Thus, if for example he has nine hours a day available for Torah learning, he is to study three hours Tanakh, three hours Mishneh, and three hours Talmud.[23]] Other Poskim[24], however, rule that one is not meant to divide the learning hours to three and give each subject the same amount of time, as Mishneh is more severe than Tanakh and requires more learning time, while Talmud is more severe than Mishneh, and require more learning time than it. Rather, one is to schedule his daily Torah learning in a way that he will complete all three subjects of Tanakh, Mishneh, and Talmud at the same time. Thus, each day he studies a little bit of Tanakh, even more of Mishneh, and even more of Talmud. Practically, it is good to suspect for this latter opinion.[25] [However, in Likkutei Torah[26] Admur implies that in the beginning of one's learning he should dedicate literally 1/3 of his time for learning Tanakh, until he is well versed in it.]

Until when must one have a daily study session in Tanakh?[27] Even if he has already completed the study of the entire scripture [i.e. Tanakh] one time he is required to repeat its study from the beginning several times, and learn it every day as stated above, until all its content is well versed

---

[15] Admur Hilchos Talmud Torah 2:1 only mentions Tanach as Mikra; See Kunrtus Achron 1:1 and all that was explained in the previous paragraph that even according to the Rama 246:4 and Rabbeinu Tam in Kiddushin 30a one may not rely on the study of Talmud which includes Mikra for his Tanach studies; Even in Likkutei Torah Vayikra 5c where Admur offers other alternatives for Mikra, he concludes that one is first obligated to learn and review the entire Tanach, and only afterwards move forward to studying the other subjects of Mikra [i.e. Agados, Zohar, Midrash].

Other alternatives of Mikra: **1)** Agados [Likkutei Torah Vayikra 5c]; **2)** Reading Zohar and other Sifrei Kabalah (without proper understanding) [Likkutei Torah Vayikra 5c; However, see Admur Hilchos Talmud Torah 2:1 who states "The wisdom of Kabalah is included in the 1/3 of Talmud"; See Likkutei Sichos 30:173 who makes the distinction between in depth learning of Kabalah which is like Talmud, and superficial learning which is like Mikra; See also Igros Kodesh 11:277]; **3)** Possibly also Midrash Raba [Likkutei Torah Vayikra 5c and Shir Hashirim 3c; However, Admur in Hilchos Talmud Torah 2:1 writes "The Pirush Hamikraos and Drashos and Hagados are included in the 1/3 of Mishneh." Admur in Shir Hashirim ibid differentiates between Midrash of Halachos which is part of Mishneh, and Midrash of stories which is part of Mikra.] As stated above, one is first obligated to learn and review the entire Tanach, and only afterwards move forward to studying the other subjects of Mikra. [Likkutei Torah ibid]

[16] Admur ibid

Other alternatives of Mishneh: Midrash [Admur ibid] of Halacha such as Sifra [Likkutei Torah Shir Hashirim 3c]

[17] Admur ibid

Other alternatives of Talmud: Kabbalah study [Admur ibid] that is in depth. [Likkutei Sichos 30:173]

[18] Admur Hilchos Talmud Torah 2:1; O.C. 155:1; Michaber Y.D. 246:4; Tur 246; Rambam Talmud Torah 1:11; Kiddushin 30a

[19] Kuntrus Achron 3:1 "This obligation is from the Sinai Tradition, as all the detailed laws of the oral Torah, which were received from generation to generation" See Kiddushin ibid that it is learned from the verse "Vishinantem Livanecha" that one should read it Veshilashtem. However, Admur ibid learns that this verse is a mere Asmachta.

[20] Admur Hilchos Talmud Torah 2:9; Vetzaruch Iyun as to the intent of Admur's ruling here regarding if such an individual is required to split his daily learning time to the three subjects of Tanach, Mishneh and Talmud. The following are the possibilities: 1) He is to study every day Tanach, plain Halacha, and the Mefarshim of Halacha until he becomes an expert in Tanach, in which case he spends all day studying practical Halacha and on occasion reviews Tanach. [See Admur 2:2] 2) He is to only study Halacha, and once in a while study Tanach. 3) He is to split his daily learning time to three and study Tanach daily, as stated in option 1, but only study those parts of Tanach that relate to the practical Mitzvos, and on occasion also study the other parts of Tanach. [See Admur 1:6] Vetzaruch Iyun!

[21] Admur Hilchos Talmud Torah 2:1-2

[22] 1st opinion in Admur 2:1; Michaber Y.D. 246:4; Rambam Talmud Torah 1:11

[23] Michaber ibid

[24] 2nd opinion in Admur 2:2; Darkei Moses 246:2; Ran Avoda Zara 5b; See Kuntrus Achron 1:1 that so is also the opinion of Tosafus Kiddushin 30a

[25] Admur ibid; Vetzaruch Iyun as to why this is considered a Chumra to suspect for the opinion of the Ran. [See Glosses of Rav Ashkeanzi ibid 2:186]

[26] Likkutei Torah Vayikra 5c; See Glosses of Rav Ashkenazi ibid 2:182-186

[27] Admur Hilchos Talmud Torah 2:2-3

and mAmoritezed in his mind.[28] [It is, however, not necessary to mAmoriteze the context word for word, as it is forbidden to recite the written Torah by heart.[29]] Once he has reviewed the Tanakh enough times to mAmoriteze its content, he is no longer required to have a daily session of studying Tanakh, and rather he is to only read it on occasion in order to prevent him from losing memory of its content.[30] [He may spend the remainder of his day studying Mishneh and Talmud.[31]]

The learning schedule for children:[32] Children, in the beginning of their study, are first taught Chumash. In previous times it was accustomed to teach them the entire Tanakh many times until age ten.[33] However, in today's times, the custom is no longer to teach children the entire Tanakh, and rather they are only taught Chumash.[34] Nevertheless, they are required to study, and repeat the study many times, of all the Parshiyot of the Torah which have the Mitzvot written in them, and are explained in the Talmud.

Summary:

It is a Biblical obligation upon every male Jew to have a daily study session in Tanakh [i.e. Torah, Nevi'im, and Kesuvim] and review it several times from the beginning until he becomes an expert in its content. One is to split his time of daily Torah study between the subjects of Tanakh, Mishneh [i.e. Halacha], and Talmud, dedicating some time to each subject. Nevertheless, one should dedicate more time daily to the study of Mishneh, and certainly to the study of Talmud, than to the study of Tanakh. Once one has become an expert in the content of Tanakh after studying it several times, he is no longer required to have a daily learning session in Tanakh, and is to simply review it on occasion to prevent lapse of memory.

The custom of Hassidim:

The Rebbe Rashab would recite Tanakh daily.[35] The Chassidim, even of mediocre status, were experts in Tanakh. They had a set custom to study a session of Tanakh upon folding their Tallis, in a way that they would complete it in its entirety every three months.[36]

---

[28] Admur Hilchos Talmud Torah 2:3 "According to all, in the start of one's learning one must study scripture every day and repeat it not just one or two or three times, but a great abundance of times, each person in accordance to his memorization capabilities, so he memorizes it well."

[29] See Admur Hilchos Talmud Torah 2:2 "As the written Torah may not be said by heart"; See Admur 49:1 for a dispute in this matter; Likkutei Torah Vayikra 30d that one should memorize the entire five books of Moses, and the implication there is to memorize the actual words. See Likkutei Sichos 14:237 that this statement of Admur in Likkutei Torah is referring to memorizing it in one's mind and not verbalizing with one's mouth. See Glosses of Rav Ashkenazi ibid 2:203 who explains that perhaps from the aspect of Talmud Torah it is not required to memorize the actual words, but for the sake of having the Shechina dwell within oneself the words must be memorized. However, from Likkutei Sichos ibid it is implied that the memorization of the actual words is part of the Mitzvah of Talmud Torah. See Hayom Yom 2nd of Nissan that the Rebbe Rashab would recite daily Tanach from memory.

[30] Admur 2:2; Michaber Y.D. 246:4; Rambam Talmud Torah 1:11

Other opinions: See Admur in Kuntrus Achron 1:1 that the intent of the ruling of Tosafus Kiddushin ibid [and the Rama 246:4 who rules like him], is that even after one has already finished learning and memorizing all the content of Tanach he is still obligated to learn Mikra daily, as the Talmud Kiddushin ibid states that "**Forever** one is to learn the three subjects…" However, at this stage they rule that it suffices to learn the Talmud, as the Talmud includes all three parts of the Torah. Admur 2:2 completely omits this opinion, thus ruling like the Rambam, and learning that even according to the Ran ibid there is no longer a requirement to learn Mikra/Tanach once one has completed his studies. However, see Admur in Likkutei Torah Vayikra 5c who implies that according to the Ran ibid one is to learn Mikra every day for his entire life, and so concludes Admur there that after the study of Tanach one is to study the other alternatives of Mikra daily.

[31] See Admur and Michaber ibid who write the above statement regarding one who finished learning and memorizing all the three subjects of Mikra, Mishneh and Talmud, however, in truth the same would apply if he finished Mikra first but did not yet finish Mishneh and Talmud. See Admur 2:3

[32] Admur Hilchos Talmud Torah 1:1

[33] Admur Hilchos Talmud Torah 1:6

[34] Admur Hilchos Talmud Torah 1:6; See Bach 145:5; Shach 246:5; Kuntrus Achron 1:1

The reason: As in previous times the written Tanach was unavailable with vowelization, and hence they had to be taught in school, however today that it is available in print, the children are only taught a small amount of Tanach [for about two years-Kuntrus Achron 1:1], as they are expected to learn it on their own when they get older. [Admur ibid]

[35] Hayom Yom 3rd Nissan

3. Background on the reading of the weekly Portion in synagogue [i.e. Keriat Hatorah]:

Moses established for the Jewish people that they are to read from the Torah scroll on Shabbat and Holidays.[37] [This reading is of Rabbinical status.[38]] The Sages of the Mishneh and Gemara chose the exact portion of the Torah that is read on each holiday.[39] However, according to most approaches, they did not establish what portions should be read on each Shabbat, and hence in previous times two different customs existed regarding this matter.[40] The widespread custom even in previous times was to read one Portion per week and arrange to finish the entire Chumash annually.[41] There were communities, however, who were accustomed to follow a triennial cycle and hence finish the entire Chumash every three years.[42] This was the custom of Jewry in Israel during Talmudic times.[43] Each Portion was thus split up to three parts, with each part being read in one week. This minority custom became extinct several generations ago[44] and hence the custom amongst all Jewry dating back many generations is to read one Portion per week and complete the reading of the entire Torah annually.[45] The set order of these Parshiyot, when to begin Bereishit, when to finish Zos Habracha, and which Parshiyot to connect, is based on the order suggested by Rav Sadia Gaon, as recorded in his Siddur Rasag.[46] Practically, the weekly Torah portion for each Shabbat has the full backing of all Minhagei Israel, Jewish customs, and it is hence forbidden to switch the Parshiyot and change the custom.[47] Furthermore, the Portion of each week has a special connection with the events and times of that week, and it is all arranged with Divine providence.[48] This book will G-d willing assist the reader in following along with the learning and reading of the weekly Torah portion, each week. To follow, we will give a general historic and Halachic background towards the different forms of divisions found in the Chumash, including the division of the Parshiyot.

---

[36] Hayom Yom 19th Adar Rishon

[37] Admur 282:1; 488:5; M"A 135:1; Rambam Tefila 12:1 "Moses"; Rif Megillah 4; Bava Kama 82a that the prophets in the times of Moses established it, See Kesef Mishneh ibid; Yerushalmi Megillah 4:1 "Moses"; Miseches Sofrim 10:1; Mishneh Megillah 31a regarding Yom Tov; See P"M 135 A"A 1

[38] P"M 135 A"A 1 that so is implied from Setimas Haposkim in 135 and 685; Tosafus Megillah 17b
Other opinions: Some Poskim rule that Kerias Hatorah on Shabbos is a Biblical obligation. [Bach 685 and that so is opinion of Rashi, brought and negated in P"M ibid]

[39] Admur ibid; Megillah ibid

[40] See Bach 685 "However, Moses did not establish the order of what should be read on Shabbos until Ezra came along." See Rambam 13:1-2 that the weekly Torah portion read on Shabbos is based on custom and not law, although Ezra established that certain Parshiyos are to be read at certain times, as brought in the Michaber 428 and 685. The fact that Ezra gave rules regarding certain Parshiyos and when they are to be read seems to prove that there was never an order of one set Portion per week, and rather every community could choose their order, so long as they follow the rules of Ezra. See Piskeiy Teshuvos 135:1
Other opinions: Some Poskim write that Moses established which Portion is to be read each Shabbos for all the Parshiyos of the Torah. [See Zohar Vayakhel p. 206b "It is forbidden to stop in a Portion that Moses did not stop, and it is forbidden to read a different weeks Portion on that Shabbos." M"A 282:1 explains that the intent of the Zohar is to say that one may not read another weeks Portion on Shabbos, and each Shabbos must have its designated Portion read. Thus, we see that Moses himself handed us a tradition of the start and end of each weekly Portion; Yeish Sechar Dinei Kerias Hatorah 6 [1600's] writes that Ezra Hasofer established all seven Aliyos of each Portion based on a tradition dating all the way back to Moses; Aruch Hashulchan 282:2 "Moses Rabbeinu established which Sedra should be read each Shabbos."; synagoguechan Hatahor 135:4 that even the double Parshiyos are a tradition of Moses from Sinai; See Piskeiy Teshuvos 135:1]

[41] Rambam ibid

[42] Rambam ibid; Testimony of Rav Binyamon Tudela regarding the Egyptian community; Manuscripts in Cairo Geniza; Some sources state that they split the Torah to 155 Parshiyos. Others say they split it to 167 Parshiyos, while others say it was split to 141 Parshiyos.

[43] Megillah 29b

[44] Some historians claim that this custom became extinct in the Geonic period. However, see Rambam ibid from whom it is clear that it existed in his times, and so in truth we found historical manuscripts from the Geniza Kahir which clearly prove that in the Rambam's time period there still existed Egyptian Jewish communities, known as Shamites, who followed the triennial cycle of Eretz Israel. According to the manuscript, pressure was placed on these communities to cease their practice although they did not heed the request and continued their practice, with some compromise at least until the 1600's.

[45] Aruch Hashulchan 282:3

[46] Siddur Rasag Hilchos Kerias Hatorah, printed by Mikitzei Nirdamim p. 363

[47] Zohar Parashat Vayakhel p. 369 [206b], brought in M"A 282:1, "One may not read the Portion of another week, this week."; M"A 282:1 in explanation of Zohar ibid; Aruch Hashulchan ibid "Chalila to switch one Portion for another"

[48] See Divrei Torah 9:93; Shlah Vayeishev; Rebbe in various Sichos

4. The divisions of the Parshiyot:

There are various forms of divisions found in Tanakh as it is published today, including verses, chapters, Sefarim, Parshiyot, and Aliyot. Interestingly, few of the above divisions are Biblically based, and rather have simply gained popularity throughout the generations as an organizational tool to divide the lengthy continuous text. We will now explore each one of these divisions and their source.

A. Verses:

All the verses [written in the five books of Moses] are a Halacha [i.e. tradition] from Moses from Sinai as to where they begin and end.[49] Nonetheless, we no longer retain exact knowledge as to the start and end points of all the verses that Moses received from Sinai.[50] However, for the most part, the verses printed in our Chumashim are accurate.[51]

Stopping in middle of reading a verse:[52] It is forbidden for one who is reading a verse to make a complete stop in the middle of the verse, and he is rather required to stop at the end of the verse in accordance to the tradition of Moses.

B. Chapters:

The division of the text of scripture into chapters can be found in all printed versions of the Tanakh available today, and so has been the case for hundreds of years. Nonetheless, going back in history, the chapter division of scripture is a fairly new development, and is not even attributed to the Rabbinate or Jewish clergyman but rather to an English bishop of the Catholic church known as Stephen Langton.[53] It is historically unclear as to why or how this Christian division found its way into the Jewish printing press, but fact remains that it has become accepted amongst the Jewish people and its Rabbinic leaders to adapt the chapter divisions within their Chumashim. Accordingly, the chapter division of the Chumash carries all the legitimacy of a Jewish custom and is to be respected as such.[54]

C. Chumashim-The five books of Moses:

It is universally accepted that the Chumash is divided into five books, known as the five books of Moses, containing the names 1) Bereishis; 2) Shemos; 3) Vayikra; 4) Bamidbar 5) Devarim. This division is mentioned in various places in the Talmud[55] which states "Chamisha Chumshei Torah/The five books of Torah." It is likely attributed to Moses himself.[56] Nonetheless, we do not have a Talmudic source which points at the areas of division of the five books, and where their start and end points are located. Thus, while the general division of the Chumash to five books has Talmudic basis, its names and groupings of Bereishis/Genesis, Shemos/Exodus, Vayikra/Leviticus, Bamidbar/Numbers and Devarim/Deuteronomy is not all found in the

---

[49] Admur 494:11; M"A 51:9; 282:1; 422:8; Taanis 27b; Megillah 22a; Brachos 12b regarding a Portion [See M"A 51:9]; Nedarim 37b; Tosafus Sukkah 38b; Rokeiach 319; Chasam Sofer 10; Rav Poalim 1:11; M"B 289:2 ; Siddur of Rav Raskin Miluim 14

[50] Admur 32:47; M"A 32:45; Kiddushin 30a

[51] One must conclude this to be the case as otherwise the law recorded in the Talmud and Poskim ibid to not stop in middle of a verse would have no relevance today.

[52] Poskim ibid; See our online article for the full details on this subject: https://shulchanaruchharav.com/halacha/stopping-in-the-middle-of-a-pasuk/

[53] See here: https://en.wikipedia.org/wiki/Stephen_Langton

[54] Likkutei Sichos 16 Yisro 4 footnote 40 "It is known the discussion regarding the chapter divisions of the Chumash. Whatever the case, these chapters are found in all the Chumashim of all the Jewish people for a number of generations, and a Jewish custom is Torah."

[55] Chagiga 14a; Megillah 15a and Rashi Megillah 29b; Nedarim 22b; Sanhedrin 44a; Yerushalmi Sanhedrin 10:1 [50b]; Sotah 5:6; Yalkut Shimoni Toldos Remez 111; Mishleiy Remez 944; The concept of Chumashim is mentioned in Megillah 27a

[56] See Mishneh Kesef of Rav Joseph Even Kasafi [1200's] p. 112 "We will never really know who was the first person to separate the Parshiyos and make the Torah into five parts, but most likely this was done by Moses himself."

Talmud.[57] Interestingly, a second opinion voiced in the Talmud[58] states that there are actually seven books, or seven divisions, in Chumash and not five.[59] This approach learns that the two verses of "Vayehi Binsoa Ha'aron" found in Parashat Beha'alosecha is its own book, and hence book four is Bamidbar/Numbers, book five is "Vayehi Binsoa", book six is "Vayehi Ha'am Kimisonanim," and book seven is Devarim/Deuteronomy.[60]

D. Parshiyot-The indentations of Pesucha and Setuma paragraphs:

Before analyzing the historical and Biblical status of the Parshiyot, we must first clarify that in truth, the term Parshiyot contains a distinct Halachic definition which is very different from the term Parshiyot that people use today to refer to the weekly Torah portion. The term Portion literally means paragraph, and indeed the Torah was split into a variety of paragraphs known as Pesuchos and Setumos, which represent two forms of indentation of a coming paragraph. The division of the paragraphs is a tradition from Moses on Sinai and contains Biblical status. In fact, a Torah scroll which is not written in accordance to the accepted tradition of Parshiyot is deemed invalid.[61] In total, there are 669 Parshiyot/paragraphs in the Torah.

Stopping in middle of reading a Portion: The Talmud[62] and Zohar[63] state that it is forbidden to stop in any Portion that Moses did not stop. Simply, this seems to mean that one who reads from the Torah [or Nevi'im and Kesuvim] may only stop at the end of a Pesucha and Setuma.[64] However, some Poskim[65] interpret this to refer not to the Parshiyot of Pesuchos and Setumos but to the weekly Portion.

E. Parshiyot-The 53 Torah portions:

The concept of an order of Parshiyot being read on a weekly basis on Shabbat is recorded in the Mishneh and Talmud.[66] However, the division of the Parshiyot into the 53[67] weekly Torah portions that we know of today, is not recorded in the Talmud and is possibly not of Biblical status. Historically, it is unclear as to when this division took place and as to who authored it.[68] Nonetheless, one thing is for certain, that since the times of Moses we have been reading from the Torah for the weekday, Shabbat, and Holiday Keriat Hatorah, and obviously some form of division had to be made in order to organize the portions of the scheduled reading. Thus, it is not historically unfounded to suggest the possibility that this division was already followed by Jews since the Torah was given on Sinai, and was established by Moses[69], and so is the understanding

---

[57] See Mishneh Menachos 4:3 who mentions Chumash Pikudin and Toras Kohanim; See Rav Menachem Kasher in Miluim Letorah Shleima 8:1

[58] Shabbos 116a "There are seven Sifrei Torah" Rashi ibid "The verses of Vayehi Binsoa Haron are their own Sefer, and it hence splits [Bamidbar] into three Sefarim."; Yalkut Shimoni Mishleiy Remez 944; See Zohar Mishpatim p. 119b

[59] This is derived from the verse Mishlei 9:1 "Chatzva Amudeha Shiva." [Yerushalmi ibid]

[60] Shabbos ibid

[61] See Rambam Hilchos Sefer Torah 7:11; Michaber Y.D. 275:1

[62] Brachos 12b [see however M"A 51:9]

[63] Zohar Parashat Vayakhel p. 369 [206b], brought in M"A 282:1, "It is forbidden for one who is reading the Torah to stop in [middle of] the Portion, even one word. One may only stop in a Portion that Moses stopped for the nation. One may not read the Portion of another week, this week."

[64] Rav Chaim Vital in Or Chama; See Piskeiy Teshuvos 138:3

[65] M"A ibid; Zohar Chaiy of Komrana Parashat Vayakhel ibid; Aruch Hashulchan 282:3

[66] Mishneh Megillah 29a and in Gemara 30b according to Rav Ami as explained in Rashi there; Megillah 31b regarding the order of the weekday reading

[67] The earliest sources record 53 Parshiyos, including Vezos Habracha. [Siddur Rasag Hilchos Kerias Hatorah, printed by Mikitzei Nirdamim p. 363; Zohar Vayakhel 206b; Tikkunei Zohar 19 p. 38a] However, in the list of Parshiyos known of today, there are 54 Parshiyos. [Aruch Hashulchan 282:2] One must conclude that there is one Portion that is not considered a real Portion and is meant to be attached to another Portion. The Chida in Dvash Lefi Mareches Pei 3 writes that Veata Titzaveh is really part of the Portion of Teruma. Others suggest that Nitzavim Vayeilech is really one Portion and so is the widespread accepted explanation.

[68] See Mishneh Kesef in next footnote

[69] See Mishneh Kesef of Rav Joseph Even Kasafi [1200's] p. 112 "We will never really know who was the first person to separate the Parshiyos and make the Torah into five parts, but most likely this was done by Moses himself."

of some Poskim.[70] Other Poskim[71] however learn that the Portion distribution was established by Ezra. Another approach is that the distribution is a mere custom that generated over the ages, not having been established by any one individual.[72] Thus, we find that during Talmudic times in Israel, they split the Torah to approximately 155 Parshiyot.[73] Practically, the first recorded source which mentions the distribution of the Torah into 53 Parshiyot is the Zohar.[74] The next earliest recorded source is in the Siddur of Rav Sadya Gaon [900 CE]. In his famous Siddur, known as Siddur Rasag, he writes[75] *"On each Shabbat we read 1/53 of the Torah, and this is called a Portion....we already stated that there are 53 Parshiyot...as is known the Torah includes 53 Parshiyot"*. A number of First Aliyahim[76] make mention of the 53 Parshiyot and their names. In conclusion, while the division of the 53 Parshiyot is not sourced in the Talmud, it is described as a known division by the Zohar, Rav Sadya Gaon and many First Aliyahim, likely dates back to the Talmud and possibly even to Biblical times and carries the full weight of a Jewish custom.

The division of the 53 portions: Regarding the start and end of each of the 53 Parshiyot as we know of today, we do not have a clearly written tradition. Rav Issachar of Susan [1500's] in his Sefer Ibur Shanim[77] writes this as follows *"Even in the Diaspora there are places which follow variant customs in the start and end points of the Parshiyot. Some divide Parashat Ki Sisa to two, while others end Parashat Vaeira in middle of the Portion and begin the next week from the middle of Vaeira. Other communities divide Parashat Mikeitz to two Parshiyot."* Rav Sadia Gaon in his Siddur attempts to make some organization of the Parshiyot, as to their start and end point, and in his words *"Regarding the remaining Parshiyot I want to make an order."* Nonetheless, it seems evident from the above sources, that the general Parshiyot which we know of today, were for the most part followed likewise in the Geonic times of Rav Sadya, and it is only in certain areas that the order was different.

The double Parshiyot: While there are 53 Parshiyot in the Torah there are only 51 weeks in a Jewish [non-Leap] year. In addition, the weekly portion is not read on any Shabbatim that coincide with Holidays. This created a surplus of Parshiyot over the available weeks in a year, and necessitated the joining together of certain Parshiyot, so the cycle can be completed within a year. The Geonim and First Aliyahim, including the Rasag, Machzor Vitri, Eshkol, Sefer Haibur, record various suggestions as to which Parshiyot should be connected. Practically, the accepted custom today is to connect some or all of the following Parshiyot to facilitate the completion of

---

[70] Some Poskim write that Moses established which Portion is to be read each Shabbos for all the Parshiyos of the Torah. [See Zohar Vayakhel p. 206b "It is forbidden to stop an area that Moses did not stop and it is forbidden to read a different weeks Portion."; M"A 282:1 understands the Zohar to refer to the [53] Parshiyos, and that on each Shabbos a designated Portion/Sedra is read, and this was received from Moses on Sinai. Yeish Sechar Dinei Kerias Hatorah 6 [1600's] writes that Ezra Hasofer established all seven Aliyos of each Portion based on a tradition dating all the way back to Moses; Aruch Hashulchan 282:2 "Moses Rabbeinu established which Sedra should be read each Shabbos."; synagoguechan Hatahor 135:4 that even the double Parshiyos are a tradition of Moses from Sinai; Piskeiy Teshuvos 135:1]

[71] See Bach 685 "However, Moses did not establish the order of what should be read on Shabbos until Ezra came along."

[72] See Rambam 13:1-2 that the weekly Torah portion read on Shabbos is based on custom and not law; See Megillah 29b that the custom of Jewry in Eretz Israel during Talmudic times was to follow a triennial cycle and hence finish the entire Chumash every three years. Some historians attribute the 53 Portion split to the Geonic or Talmud Savuraiy period. See, however, M"A 282:1 and Aruch Hashulchan 282:3 who seem to imply that everyone agrees to the split of 53 Parshiyos, however, in Eretz Israel, they held that it was permitted to split each Portion into three. Whatever the case, even if true that this division existed from the time of Sinai, the 53 Parshiyot distribution was not legally binding regarding the Torah reading and was not the universal practice, as evident from the fact that in Eretz Israel they split the Chumash into approximately 155/167 Parshiyos, thus completing it every three some years, unlike is done today.

[73] Some sources state that they split the Torah to 155 Parshiyos. Others say they split it to 167 Parshiyos, while others say it was split to 141 Parshiyos. Miseches Sofrim splits the Torah into 175 Parshiyos

[74] Zohar Vayakhel 206b; Tikkunei Zohar 19 p. 38a in play of the verse "Gan Naul Achosi Kallah"

[75] Siddur Rasag Hilchos Kerias Hatorah, printed by Mikitzei Nirdamim p. 363

[76] Rambam Ahavah Seder Tefilos Kol Hashana lists all 53 Parshiyos and their Haftora's; Rashi in Sefer Haorah "There are 53 Parshiyos in the Torah."; Machzor Vitri 2 Hilchos Kerias Hatorah 522; Abudarham; Eshkol 21; Sefer Haibur "There are 52 Parshiyos read every Shabbos annually."

[77] P. 33

the Torah reading cycle within one year. The exact number of Parshiyot that are connected in a given year, and their selection, is dependent on the factors mentioned above.

1. Vaykhel-Pekudei
2. Tazria-Metzora
3. Acharei-Kedoshim
4. Behar-Bechukotai
5. Matos-Maseiy
6. Chukas-Balak
7. Nitzavim-Vayelich

F. The names of the Parshiyot:

Just as the divisions of the 53 Parshiyot did not receive Talmudic mention, neither did their names, with exception to a few limited Parshiyot.[78] Several First Aliyahim[79], however, mention the names of all the 53 Parshiyot. Nonetheless, it is clear from the writings of these First Aliyahim that various customs existed regarding the names of the Parshiyot, and while the universal practice was to call it by one of the words mentioned in its opening sentence or paragraph, there were different customs regarding which word should be chosen as its name. For example, the Rasag in his Siddur, and the Rambam in his listing, refer to what is known today as Parashat Tazria as Parashat "Isha" and Parashat Metzora is referred to as Parashat "Vezos Tihyeh." Nonetheless, the Rasag also lists a number of names of Parshiyot which are followed likewise today, such as Vayakhel, Vezos Habracha, Vayeilech, Ha'azinu, Pekudei, Acharei Mos, Kedoshim. The full list can be found in the Rambam's Seder Tefilos Kol Hashanah [in end of Sefer Ahavah], and the vast majority of the Parshiyot retain the same name as we know of today. Thus, in conclusion, while not all of the names used today to refer to the Parshiyot were commonly used in previous times, such as in the Geonic era, for the most part the names are similar. Whatever the case, the fact that for over 1000 years the Parshiyot have received one universal name, is itself a matter of Divine providence and this is their name according to Torah.[80]

G. The Aliyot:[81]

Customarily, all Chumashim today contain stopping points for each Aliya; Levi, Israel, second Aliyah, third Aliyah, etc. Interestingly, the allocation of the grouping of verses that belong to each Aliya contains no source in Halachic literature, neither the Talmud or Poskim. Some Poskim[82] even attribute the distribution of Aliyot to the printers of the Chumashim and not to Rabbanim. While the Talmud and Poskim[83] provide certain rules and guidelines regarding the amount of verses each Aliya must contain and lists certain areas in which one may not end an Aliya, no distribution of Aliyot is recorded anywhere. Hence, ideally, one may stop wherever he wishes, so long as he abides by the Halachic restrictions, and so was done by some Gedolei Israel[84], claiming that the current distribution does not take into account all the Halachic and Zoharic requirements. Nonetheless, the widespread Jewish custom, which is Torah, is to stop by

---

[78] See Megillah 29b "Ata Titzaveh, Ki Sisa"; 31a "Vezos Habracha"; See Likkutei Sichos 5 Lech Lecha

[79] Rambam Ahavah Seder Tefilos Kol Hashana lists all 53 Parshiyos and their Haftora's; Machzor Vitri 2 Hilchos Kerias Hatorah 522; Abudarham; Eshkol 21

[80] Likkutei Sichos 5 Lech Lecha

[81] See Piskeiy Teshuvos 139:3

[82] Meoreiy Or Basar p. 156

[83] See Michaber 137:2 regarding that each Aliya must contain at least three verses; Michaber 138:1 that one may not end within three verses of a Setuma or Pesucha

[84] Gr"a in Maaseh Rav 132; Minchas Elazar 1:66; Piskeiy Teshuvos ibid

the end points of each Aliyah as written in the Chumash, and so is initially to be followed.[85] Nonetheless, different Chumashim contain different distribution points of Aliyot. The distribution of Aliyot in this Sefer is based on Chumash Torah Temima, which was followed by Russian Jewry, and is the Chabad custom until this day. It is beyond the scope of this book to research the hundreds of prints of Chumashim and their stop areas, and each community is to follow their custom. Accordingly, the subdivision of Aliya's as printed in this Sefer is subjective to one's community practice, and is not intended to cement in place their exact location.

5. The Haftora's:

The reading of the weekly Haftorah from the Prophets was established in the times of Antiochus due to a decree he initiated prohibiting the reading of the Chumash in synagogue. Ever since that time, the reading of Haftorah has remained a part of the weekly Torah reading, being read directly after the weekly portion.[86] In general, the Sages chose a portion of Navi that relates to the weekly portion. However, there exist a difference between Ashkenaz, Sefarad, and Yemenite customs regarding the exact location of the weeks Haftorah, and each community is to follow his custom. While this book does not delve into the content of the Haftora's, we have provided the reader the area in Tanakh from where the Haftorah is read each week. The locations provided are in accordance to the "Sefer Haftora's" that follow Chabad custom. It is beyond the scope of this book to research and note the particular Haftora's read by each community, and hence one may find discrepancies between their Chumash and community custom and that which is printed here.

6. The 613 Mitzvot:

Rebbe Simlaiy expounded:[87] There were 613 Mitzvot said over to Moses. 365 negative commands, corresponding to the days of the solar year, and 248 positive commands corresponding to the limbs of man. Rav Hamnuna stated: From where is this derived in the Torah? From the verse[88] "Torah Tziva Lanu Moses Morasha Kehilas Jacob," as the word Torah is the Gematria of 611. This means to say that Moses taught the Jewish people 611 commands, as the two commands of Anochi and Lo Yiyeh Lecha were said by G-d on Sinai. Starting in the Geonic period, attempts were made to list each of the 613 commands. In Geonic literature, this was composed in the form of songs, such as in the Sefer HaMitzvot of the Rasag. The Bahag [written in the end of the Geonic period] was the first to compile an actual list of all the 613 Mitzvot. This was followed by many Rishonim, such as the Rambam, Sefer Hachinuch, Semak and others. There are several discrepancies between the lists of the various Poskim, based on different viewpoints of understanding of what is to be viewed as a command and is to be included in the list.[89] In this Sefer we have provided a list of all the 613 Mitzvot, as they appear in each Portion. Our list follows the opinion of the Sefer Hachinuch, which based his list on that of the Rambam.

---

[85] See Shaar Hatziyon 138:1
[86] See Tosafus Yom Tov on Mishneh Megillah 3:4
[87] Makos 23b
[88] Devarim 33:4
[89] See Even Ezra in his Sefer Yesod Mora Shaar Hasheiyni

Bereishit/Genesis

Parashat Bereishit
Verses: 146 [Siman:אמצי״ה]
Haftorah: Isaiah 42:5-21[1]

Number of Mitzvot:
There is a total of **One** Mitzvah in Parashat Bereishis; **One** positive command and **Zero** negative commands. The following are the commands in the order listed by the Sefer Hachinuch.

1. **Mitzvah 1/Positive 1:** Peru Urevu. To multiply and have children

Chapter 1
First Aliyah

1. **Creation:**
   - G-d created the heaven and earth. At first, the world was Tohu and Vohu [i.e. Desolate]; in darkness, and the spirit of G-d rested over the water.
   - **Day 1:** On the first day, G-d created light, and separated between the light and darkness, and night and day.
   - **Day 2:** On the second day, G-d created the firmament which separated between the higher and lower waters and called it the sky.
   - **Day 3:** On the third day, G-d created land, having the water separate from the land and remain gathered only in the sea. G-d then commanded the earth to bring forth plants, vegetation, and fruits
   - **Day 4:** On the fourth day, G-d created luminaries to separate between night and day and to determine the time of festivals, days, and years. The sun for the day, the moon for the night, and the stars.
   - **Day 5:** On the fifth day, G-d created the birds, sea animals, and fish. G-d then commanded them to be fruitful and multiply.
   - **Day 6:** On the sixth day, G-d commanded the earth to sprout forth all the various animals and insects. G-d created mankind in his image, a male and female, to rule over all the other creatures of the earth. G-d blessed man and commanded him to have children and to rule all the creatures of the earth, the animals, birds, and fish. G-d told man and all the living creatures that all the produce of the earth is given to them to eat.

Chapter 2
   - **Day 7:** On the 7th day, G-d completed His work and rested from all His work. G-d blessed and sanctified the 7th day.

---

[1] So is followed by most Ashkenazi and Chabad communities. However, some Ashkenazi communities, as well as the Sephardim, read until verse 43:10.

Second Aliyah

2. Creation of man:

- The earth had not yet sprouted as there was no rain on the earth before man was created. G-d caused dew to ascend from the earth which moistened it to form man. G-d blew a soul into man, through his nostrils and man became a living being.
- Garden of Eden and the tree of knowledge: G-d planted a garden in Eden with many beautiful trees and fruits and placed man there to work it and guard it. A river left Eden to irrigate the garden and it split to four rivers. In the garden there was the tree of life and the tree of knowledge of good and evil and G-d commanded man that he may eat the fruit of all the trees, but he may not eat from the tree of knowledge lest he die.
- Adam's wife: G-d said it is not good for man to be alone and decided to make man a helpmate.
- Adam was given the rights of naming all the animals and creatures.

Third Aliyah

3. Creation of woman:

- Adam named all the animals but did not find a partner amongst them. G-d put Adam to sleep and extracted one of his ribs and then closed up the area. G-d built the rib into a woman. Adam named her Isha, being that she was taken from man.
- Adam and his wife were both naked and were not ashamed.

Chapter 3

4. The sin of the tree of knowledge:

- The sin: The snake, who was the most cunning of all creatures, approached the woman and asked her if she was told by G-d not to eat any of the fruits of the garden? She replied that they can eat from all the fruits except for the middle fruit tree of the garden from which they may not even contact, lest they die. The snake replied that in truth they will not die if they eat from it and will simply be like G-d and have knowledge of good and evil. She then had a lust for the fruit, desired it, and ate it, and then gave to her husband to also eat.
- G-d confronts them: Their eyes were opened; they suddenly realized that they were naked and took leaves from a fig tree to cover their extremities. They heard G-d walking around the garden and hid from Him in the garden amongst the trees. G-d called to Adam and said, "Where are you?" Adam replied that he hid from G-d because he is naked. G-d replied "Who told you that you are naked? Did you eat from the forbidden tree?" Adam replied that the woman gave him to eat from the fruits of the tree. The woman, upon being questioned, replied that she was tricked by the snake.

5. The punishments to the snake, woman, man:

- The snake's punishment: The snake was cursed to walk on its belly, eat only earth, and be cursed more than any creature all the days of its life. There will be hatred between you and the woman and her offspring. They will step on you and you will sting their heels.
- The woman's punishment: The woman was told that she will have difficulty in raising her children, and in pregnancy and births, and will desire her husband and will be ruled by him.

- The man's punishment: Adam was told that the earth would be cursed and will give forth food with difficulty, and that it will grow thorns and weeds. You will work by the sweat of your brow and die and be buried in the earth.

6. **Naming the woman/clothing:**
   - Adam named his wife Chava as she is the mother of all mankind.
   - G-d made clothing for Adam and Chava.

Fourth Aliyah

7. **Banishing man from the Garden of Eden:**
   - Due to worry that man may eat from the tree of life and live forever, G-d banished them from the Garden of Eden, and placed angels there as a guard, in the east side.

Chapter 4

8. **Birth of Cain/Abel:**
   - Adam knew his wife Chava and had a son whom he named Cain and then a son who he named Abel.
   - Abel worked as a shepherd while Cain worked in agriculture.

9. **Murder of Abel:**
   - The sacrificial offering After some time, Cain and Abel each brought an offering to G-d, Cain brought produce of the land and Abel brought from the best of his sheep. G-d accepted the offering of Abel but not of Cain. Cain was furious and was rebuked and encouraged by G-d to do the right thing.
   - The murder: Cain fought with Abel and killed him. G-d confronts Cain about the whereabouts of Abel and his murder. Cain is punished that the earth will not produce food for him and that he will wander the land. Cain is promised to live seven generations, and G-d placed a sign on him so he not be killed.
   - Cain moved to Nod.

10. **Offspring's of Cain:**
    - Cain had Hanoch who had children, and his children had children until the birth of Lemech.

Fifth Aliyah

- Lemech had two wives, and had Yaval and Yuval born from the wife called Adah.
- Yaval was a cattle farmer and Yuval innovated music.
- The second wife, Tzilah, had a son named Tuval Cain, who created metal and weaponry.
- The sister of Tuval Cain was Naamah.

Sixth Aliyah

11. **Death of Cain:**
    - Lemech pleads with his wives that they return to him [despite his accidental murder of Cain and Tuval-Cain]. He tells them that he will certainly live for 77 generations.

Chapter 5

12. Offspring of Adam:

- Adam knew his wife Chava and had a son whom he named Seth in place of his son Abel who was killed by Cain.
- Seth had a son named Enosh. Then people started to profane the name of G-d.
- Adam had Seth at age 130.
- Adam lived to the age of 930.
- The life and children of Seth.
- The life and children of Enosh
- The life and children of Keinon.
- The life and children of Mahalaleil.
- The life and children of Yared.
- The life and children of Hanoch. Hanoch lived a short life because he walked with G-d and G-d took him.

Seventh Aliyah

- The life and children of Metushalach.
- The life and children of Lemech. Lemech fathered Noah.
- At age 500, Noah fathered three sons, Sheim, Cham and Japheth.

Chapter 6

13. Depravity of society and G-d's wrath:

- Man began to multiply, and daughters were born. The sons of Elokim took daughters from whomever they wanted, including married women and fathered giants.
- G-d said that He will not judge man forever and he will give them 120 years to shape up. G-d saw that all man is doing is evil and he regretted their creation. G-d decided to wipe out all of humanity and animals.
- Noah found favor in the eyes of G-d.

Parashat Noah

Verses: 153 [Siman: בְּצַלְאֵל]
Haftorah: Isaiah 54:1-10[1]

Number of Mitzvot:
There are no Positive or Negative commands mentioned in Parashat Noah.

Chapter 7
First Aliyah

1. **Who is Noah?**
   - Noah was a righteous man, a pure man in his generation.
   - Noah had three children, Shem, Cham and Japheth.

2. **The depravity of the world:**
   - The world became depraved before G-d, and was filled with corruption. G-d took notice of this, as all the creations perverted their nature on the earth.
   - G-d told Noah that He has become fed up with the corruption of the world and that it will have to be destroyed.

3. **G-d instructs Noah to build an ark:**
   - G-d instructs Noah to build a wooden ark that is covered in tar. These instructions include the following:
     1) The Ark is to be 300 cubits [144 meters] long, 50 cubits wide [24 meters] and 30 cubits tall [14 meters].
     2) The Ark is to have a Tzohar [window] and is to be constructed with a pitched roof.
     3) It is to have three stories.
   - G-d said to Noah: The world will be flooded and all its creatures destroyed. I will make my covenant with you, and you and your wife and children and their families will survive on the Ark. You are to enter into the Ark a male and female creature of every species, animals, birds and insects. Gather food and store it in the Ark.
   - Noah followed the instructions of G-d in detail.

Second Aliyah

4. **The final instructions given days before the flood:**
   - G-d instructed Noah to bring himself and his family into the ark seven days before the flood.
   - Animals: Seven pairs of male and female animals and birds of every Kosher species is to enter the Ark. [Seven male and their wives.] From the impure animals take two of every species, a male and his wife.
   - The flood would last for 40 days and nights.
   - Noah was 600 years old at the time.

---

[1] So is followed by Sepharadi and Chabad communities. However, Ashkenazi communities read until verse 55:5.

- Noah did as he was instructed. He and his family, Noah and his wife, Sheim and Cham and Japheth and their three wives, entered the Ark. The animal pairs entered the Ark.

5. The flood:
- After the passing of seven days, on the 17th of the 2nd month [Marcheshvan] the torrential rain began and the depths of the earth began to shoot forth water. The rain lasted 40 days and nights.

Third Aliyah
- Fifteen cubits of water covered over even the highest mountains.
- All the living creatures on earth perished, besides for Noah and his family and the animals that remained with him.

Chapter 8
- The water recedes: The water remained on earth without receding for 150 days. It began to recede after 150 days. On the 17th of the 7th month [Iyar] the Ark landed on the mountain of Ararat. The peak of the mountains began to appear on the 1st of the 10th month [Av].
- Noah sends out a bird: 40 days later Noah opened the window of the ark and sent out the raven. The raven did not find land to rest on. He then sent out a dove, who returned to the ark after not finding dry land. Seven days later the dove was resent and the dove returned with an olive branch. He resent the dove seven days later and it did not return.
- The Ark is opened: On the first of the first month [Rosh Hashanah] the earth became free of water and Noah opened the cover of the Ark.
- The earth finally became dry on the 27th of the 2nd month [27th of Marcheshvan]

Fourth Aliyah
6. The survivors exit the Ark:
- G-d spoke to Noah and told him that he and his family, and all the living creatures, are to leave the Ark. They are to spread out on the land and multiply. Noah did as he was told, and him, his family, and all the living creatures, left the Ark.

7. The Sacrifices and G-d's blessings and promises:
- Noah built an altar and offered sacrifices to G-d from the Kosher animals and poultry. G-d smelled the scent and promised to never again to curse the earth, destroy all creations, or stop the seasons and celestial creations.

Chapter 9
- Command to have children: G-d blessed Noah and his children, that they should be fruitful and multiply.
- Inherent fear of humans: G-d stated that all animals will fear man.
- Permission to eat meat: G-d gave man permission to eat any living creature on earth.
- Prohibition against murder: Nonetheless, G-d warned them against committing murder against each other. "I will avenge the blood of man that is spilled by the hands of an animal, or by the hands of another human."

Fifth Aliyah

8. The covenant and rainbow:
- G-d makes a covenant with Noah and all future descendants, and all the living creatures, to never again bring a flood to destroy the earth.
- G-d designates the rainbow to be the sign of this covenant. It is positioned in the clouds between heaven and earth as a reminder to G-d of this covenant.

Sixth Aliyah

9. Noah gets drunk:
- The new world was established by the children of Noah who left the Ark.
- Noah degraded himself and planted a vineyard. He drank from the wine and became drunk and was unclothed within his tent. Cham, the father of Canaan, saw the nakedness of his father and told his two brother who were outside. Shem and Japheth took a garment and laid it upon their shoulders, walking backwards, and covered the nakedness of their father. They did not see their father's nakedness.
- <u>Noah curses Canaan</u>: Noah awoke from his drunken slumber and realized what his youngest son had done to him. He cursed Canaan that he should be a slave to the other two brothers, and blessed Japheth and Sheim.
- Noah lived after the flood for 350 years, his total years being 950 years.

Chapter 10

10. Offspring of Noah:
- The following are the offspring of Noah: Shem, Cham, and Japheth, and they had children after the flood. The following are the names of those children:
- **Japheth:**
    1) Gomer
        - Ashkenas
        - Rifas
        - Togarma
    2) Magog
    3) Maday
    4) Yavan
        - Elisha
        - Tarshish
        - Kitim
        - Dodanim
- From the above were created different nations, each according to their language and family.
    5) Tuval
    6) Meshech
    7) Tiras
- **Cham:**
    1) Kush
        - Seva
        - Chavila

- Savta
- Raama
- Sheba
- Dedan
- Nimrod.

<u>Who was Nimrod</u>: Nimrod became a mighty warrior on the earth. He was a mighty hunter before G-d. The start of his reign was in Babel, Erech, Accad, and Kalna in the land of Shinar. Ashur left from that land and built the city of Ninveh which is the great city, Rechovos Hair, Calah, and Resen.

2) Mitzrayim
  - Ludim
  - Anamim
  - Lahabim
  - Naphtuchim
  - Pasrusim
  - Kasluchim. The Phlishtim and Caphtorim came from them.
3) Put
4) Canaan
  - Tzidon
  - Ches
  - Jebusite
  - Amorite
  - Girgashi
  - Hivvite
  - Arki
  - Sini
  - Arvadi
  - Tzemari
  - Chamasi

- The Canaanite boundary extended from Tzidon to Gera, to Gaza, reaching Sodom, Amora, Adam and Tzvoyim.
- **Shem:**
  1) Eilam
  2) Ashur
  3) Arpachshad
     - Shalach
       o Ever
         o Peleg [see Seventh Aliyah for his descendants]
         o Yaktan
           o Almodad
           o Shalef
           o Tzarmaves
           o Yarach
           o Hadoram
           o Uzal

- o Dikla
- o Oval Abimale
- o Sheva
- o Ofer
- o Chavila
- o Yovav

4) Lud
5) Aram
- Utz
- Chul
- Geser
- Mash

Chapter 11
Seventh Aliyah

11. Tower of Babel:
- Building the tower: The entire earth spoke one language and was unified in words. When they migrated from the east they found a valley in the land of Shinar and settled there. Each man told his friend let us make bricks and build a city and tower whose top reaches the heavens. We will make for ourselves a name, lest we be dispersed throughout the earth.
- G-d confuses their language and disperses them: G-d descended to see the city and tower that they built. And said "They are one nation and language and this they have begun to do. Shall we not withhold them? Let us descend and confuse their languages, so that they should not understand each other's speech." G-d dispersed them throughout the entire earth and they stopped building the city.
- For this reason, the city is called Babel, as there G-d confused the language of man, and from there He dispersed them.

12. The descendants of Shem, the length of their lives and the birth of Abraham:
- Shem lived a total of 600 years.
- **Arpachshad** was born when Shem was 100 years old. He was born two years after the Mabul. He had Shalach at age 35. He lived a total of 438 years.
- **Shalach** had Ever at age 30. He lived a total of 433 years.
- **Ever** had Peleg at age 34. He lived a total of 464 years.
- **Peleg** had Reu at age 30. He lived a total of 239 years.
- **Reu** had Serug at age 32. He lived a total of 239 years.
- **Serug** had Nahor at age 30. He lived a total of 230 years.
- **Nahor** had Tarach at age 29. He lived a total of 148 years.
- **Terach** had Abraham, Nahor and Haran at age 70. He lived a total of 205 years.
- **Haran** had Lot. Haran died in the presence of his father in the land of Kasdim.
- Avram marries: Avram and Nahor got married. The wife of Avram was named Saraiy, and the wife of Nahor was named Milka. Milka and Yiska [i.e. Saraiy] were both the daughters of Haran. Saraiy was barren, she had no children.

- <u>Traveling to Haran:</u> Terach took his son Avram, his grandson Lot, and Saraiy his daughter in law and they traveled from Ur Kasdim towards the land of Canaan. They arrived in Haran and settled there. Terach passed away in Haran.

Parashat Lech Lecha
Verses: 126 [Siman: נמל"ו]
Haftorah: Isaiah 40:27-41:16

Number of Mitzvot:
There is a total of **One** Mitzvah in Parashat Noah. There is **One** positive command and Zero negative commands. The following are the commands in the order listed by the Sefer Hachinuch.
1. **Mitzvah 2/Positive 2:** Bris Mila. To circumcise a boy on the 8th day.

Chapter 12
First Aliyah

1. **Abraham travels to Eretz Canaan:**
   - G-d commands Abraham to leave his homeland to a land that he will be shown.
   - Abraham is blessed that through doing so, he will turn into a great nation and become famous. He will receive the power of blessing and curse.
   - Abraham was 75 years old at the time.
   - He left together with Lot, his nephew, and his wife Sarai, and all their followers, towards the land of Canaan.
   - Abraham arrived at the town of Shechem, known as Eilon Moreh.
   - G-d revealed Himself to Abraham there, and told him that his descendants will receive this land. Abraham built an altar in that area.
   - Abraham settled his tent on the mountain between Beth Ail and Ai and built an alter there.
   - Abraham continued traveling towards the south.

2. **Abraham travels to Egypt due to the famine:**
   - There was a famine in Eretz Canaan and Abraham went down towards Egypt, to settle there temporarily.
   - When they came close to Egypt, Abraham told his wife that he realized how beautiful she is and that when the Egyptians will see her, they will kill him, her husband, and let her live. He therefore asked Sarai to tell them that she is his sister, and thus he too will live.

Second Aliyah

3. **Abraham and Sarah in Egypt:**
   - When they arrived in Egypt, the Egyptians saw how beautiful she was, and the ministers of Pharaoh had her brought to Pharaoh. Pharaoh gave Abraham many cattle and slaves as a present.
   - G-d afflicted Pharaoh and his household with a great plague due to them taking Sarai. Pharaoh confronted Abraham saying that he should have told them that she is his wife, and not his sister. Sarai was then returned to Abraham.
   - Abraham and his wife were then escorted out of the country and traveled back to Israel, to the south of the country. He came back from Egypt with many cattle, gold and silver.

Chapter 13
Third Aliyah

4. **Lot separates from Abraham:**
    - Lot likewise had with him a lot of cattle, and together with the cattle of Abraham, there was not enough grazing land available for both of them. This caused their shepherds to quarrel. Abraham pleaded with Lot that they should not quarrel and rather Lot should travel in a separate direction.
    - Lot chose to travel towards the city of Sodom. The people of Sodom were very evil.
    - <u>G-d blesses Abraham with inheritance of Israel</u>: After Lots departure, G-d appeared to Abraham and reinsured him that his descendants will inherit all of the land of Canaan. G-d instructed Abraham to walk the land, in both its length and width to see how much he will be given. G-d promised Abraham that his descendants will be as many as the sand of the earth.
    - Abraham then settled in Elonei Mamrei, which is Hebron, and built an altar for G-d.

Chapter 14
Fourth Aliyah

5. **The battle of the 4 and 5 kings:**
    - Amrafel, the king of Shinar, Aryoch the king of Elasar, Kedarla'omer the king of Ailam, and Tidal the king of Goyim waged war with Bera the king of Sodom, Birsha the king of Amorah, Shinav the king of Admah, Shemaiver the king of Tzevoyim, and Bela the king of Tzoar. They waged war in the valley of Sidim, which is the dead sea.
    - For 12 years the five kings served Kedarla'omer and for 13 years they rebelled. In the 14th year, Kedarla'omer came with his three allies and waged war against them. The four kings overtook the five kings and their people fled.
    - Lot was taken captive during the war, and a certain fugitive came and informed Abraham of what occurred.
    - When Abraham heard this, he went out to wage war with members of his house, a total of 318, and he chased the four kings until Dan. He was successful in overcoming the four kings and drove them out until Damascus.
    - <u>King of Sodom/Malki Tzedek</u>: Abraham returned all the stolen property, and Lot and the people, back [to their homes]. The king of Sodom came to greet Abraham after the victory. Malki Tzedek, the king of Shaleim, came to greet Abraham and offered him bread and wine. He then gave praise to G-d for protecting Abraham.
    - Abraham gave him [i.e. Malki Tzedek] a tenth of all his possessions.

Fifth Aliyah

6. **The victory of the war and distribution of booty:**
    - The king of Sodom offered Abraham to keep the spoils, but return the people [to his nation]. Abraham refused to take any of the spoils, so people would not say that the king of Sodom made him wealthy. However, he did request payment for his people who joined him in battle.

Chapter 15

- G-d blesses Abraham with children: After the above occurrence, G-d appeared to Abraham and reassured him of his great reward. Abraham responded by saying that his reward is irrelevant as he has no heirs amongst his offspring who will inherit it. G-d then promised Abraham that he will have a child who will inherit him. He took Abraham outside and pointed towards the stars in heaven saying that his descendants will be as many as the stars of the sky.

Sixth Aliyah

7. The covenant of Bein Habetarim:

- Abraham requested from G-d a sign that in fact he would inherit the land of Canaan.
- Halving the animals: G-d instructed Abraham to take three calves, three goats, three rams, a dove, and a young bird. Abraham cut each one in half, with exception for the birds. A raven came to eat the carcasses and Abraham had to shoo him away.
- Vision of the Egyptian exile: Abraham fell into a deep sleep. In his sleep he felt a great darkness and fear. G-d then told Abraham that his children will be enslaved and oppressed for 400 years in a foreign nation. G-d promised to judge that nation and that the Jewish people will leave that nation with great wealth. You, Abraham, will die of good old age and return to your fathers in peace. After three generations of exile in Egypt, in the fourth generation, your children will return to inherit the land of Canaan.
- A great flame came and passed between the halved carcasses.
- Covenant to inherit the land to Abraham: On that day G-d made a covenant with Abraham to give the land to his descendants, from the river of Egypt until the great Euphrates river. The lands of Kini, Kenizi, Kadmoni, Hittite, Perizi, Refaim, Amori, Canaanite, Girgashite and Jebusite.

Chapter 16

8. Abraham marries Hagar:

- Sarai, who had not given birth to a child for Abraham, had a maid whose name was Hagar. She offered Abraham to marry her maid, so he have children and so she merits to have children through her. Abraham was given Hagar in marriage after settling in the land of Canaan for ten years. Hagar became pregnant right away and began to slight her master, Sarai, in her eyes.
- Hagar flees: Sarai was upset and confronted Abraham for being complacent towards the behavior of Hagar. As a result of the complaint, Abraham returned Hagar to Sarai, and she oppressed her to the point that she fled.
- Angel blesses Hagar: An angel found Hagar near a well in the desert. She told the angel that she was running away from her master Sarai. The angel told her to return to her master Sarai, and be subservient to her. The angel promised her that her children will be plenty and multiply to the point they are uncountable. He told her to call the son that she will have the name Ishmael. He will be a wild man, his hands reaching everywhere, and living everywhere.
- Ishmael is born: Hagar gave birth to a son for Abraham and Abraham called him Ishmael. Abraham was 86 years old at the time of the birth.

Chapter 17

9. Circumcision:

- At the age of 99, G-d appeared to Abraham and asked him to perform a covenant with Him.
- Avram becomes Abraham-Will become father of all nations: As a result, G-d promised that Abraham would become a father for all nations, and his name will be changed from Avram to Abraham in light of this position. He will have a multitude of offspring and many kings will sprout from him.

Seventh Aliyah

- Will inherit Israel: In merit of this Mitzvah, G-d will make a covenant with Abraham's descendants and be considered their G-d for eternity. They will be given the land of Canaan.
- Laws of circumcision: G-d requested that Abraham's descendants guard this covenant. What is the covenant? For every male to circumcise himself. The removal of the foreskin will be a sign and covenant between us and G-d. All household members are to be circumcised at eight days old. One who does not circumcise himself will be cut off from his nation, as he has denied My covenant.
- Saraiy becomes Sarah: G-d told Abraham to no longer call her by the name Sarai, as from now on Sarah is her name.
- Sarah is blessed with a child: G-d told Abraham that his wife Sarah will give birth to a son for him, and he will be blessed and become a great nation. Abraham fell to his face on the ground excited at the great news that he will have a child at 100 years old and his wife at 90 years old. Abraham exclaimed to G-d "If only Ishmael will live before you." G-d responded that Sarah will give him a son in exactly one year from now, and the covenant will continue with him. G-d told Abraham to name his son Isaac, and He will establish an everlasting covenant with his descendants.
- G-d told Abraham that from Ishmael will be born 12 princes.
- The circumcision: After G-d departed, Abraham took Ishmael and all of his household and circumcised them. Abraham was 99 years old at the time of his circumcision and Ishmael was 13 years old.

Parashat Vayeira
Verses: 147 [Siman: אמנון]
Haftorah: Kings 2 4:1-37[1]

Number of Mitzvot:
There are no Positive or Negative commands mentioned in Parashat Vayeira.

Chapter 18
First Aliyah

1. **Abraham receives guests:**
   - Abraham sat in the opening of the tent in the heat of the day when G-d visited him [on the third day after his circumcision]. Abraham noticed three people coming towards him and he ran to them from the entrance of his tent. Upon approaching them, Abraham bowed to the ground and asked them to come over and have some water, wash their feet, rest under the tree, and eat a fresh meal. The men acquiesced to his request.
   - The meal: Abraham rushed to his tent and asked Sarah to bake bread. Abraham then went on to tell the lad to prepare meat from a fresh slaughtered calf. Abraham served the guests butter and milk and the calf meat.

2. **Abraham and Sarah are blessed with children:**
   - The guest then asked Abraham as to the whereabouts of his wife and then promised them that they will have a son next year.
   - Sarah was already past menopause and Abraham was old, and she thus laughed at the suggestion that she could still bare a child. G-d asked Abraham as to why his wife laughed at the notion of her giving birth, as nothing is outside of G-d's hands.
   - G-d reassured Abraham that he will have a son.

Second Aliyah
   - Sarah denied having scorned with disbelief the blessing of children that she received.

3. **Abraham defends the city of Sodom:**
   - Abraham sees the guests walk off towards the city of Sodom.
   - G-d tells Abraham of his plan to destroy the five cities of the metropolitan of Sodom.
   - Abraham implores G-d to spare the city if there are righteous men in the city. G-d replies to Abraham that there are not even ten righteous men in the city.

Chapter 19
Third Aliyah

4. **The destruction of Sodom:**
   - Lot hosts the angels: Two angels arrived to Sodom and saw Lot sitting by the entrance of the city. Lot greeted the angels and invited them to come over to his home and bathe and

---

[1] So is followed by most Ashkenazi communities and Chabad. However, some Ashkenazi communities, as well as the Sepharadim read only until verse 4:23.

sleep. The people of Sodom surround the home and ask for the guests to be taken out. Lot offered the mob his daughters instead. The mob is stricken with blindness.

- Lot's escape: The angels take Lot, his wife, and his daughters out of the city. Lot requests not to go to Abraham, but rather to a nearby city that has few sins.

Fourth Aliyah

- The angels acquiesce to Lot's request and don't destroy this city. Lot arrives to Tzoar.
- The destruction of Sodom: G-d rained upon Sodom and Amora fire and brimstone, and turned over the city of Sodom and its neighboring cities.
- Lots wife: As they were fleeing from the city, Lots wife turned around and turned into a pillar of salt.
- Abraham viewed the aftermath of destruction of the city and saw smoke arising from that area.

5. Lot and his daughters:

- Lot and his daughters are afraid to remain in Tzoar and they thus move to the mountains.
- The daughters, fearing the end of mankind, gave their father wine and slept with him, for the sake of having offspring. They became pregnant and each had a child from their father. The older daughter gave birth to a son called Moab while the younger daughter gave birth to a son called Amon.

Chapter 20

6. Sarah is abducted by Abimelech:

- Abraham moves to the province of Abimelech and tells them that Sarah is his sister.
- Abimelech takes Sarah to be his wife.
- G-d came to Abimelech in a dream and warned him against touching Sarah, lest he die, as she is a married woman. Abimelech argues with G-d, saying that he is innocent, as he was told that she is his sister, and not married.
- Abimelech was forced to return Sarah to Abraham. Abraham was asked to pray for them [to be healed], and Abimelech severely warned his townspeople from touching Sarah.
- Abimelech confronted Abraham for misleading him, and in the end, Abimelech gave Abraham and Sarah cattle and money to compensate them for their suffering.
- Abraham davened for them to be healed, as all of their body cavities were sealed, and G-d answered his prayers.

Chapter 21

7. Sarah gives birth to Isaac:

- G-d remembers the promise she made to Sarah and she conceives.
- She gave birth to a son for Abraham, exactly a year from the previous year's prediction.
- Abraham named the son, Isaac, and circumcised him at eight days old, as he was commanded.

Fifth Aliyah

- Abraham was 100 years old at the time of birth.
- When Isaac was weaned at 24 months, Abraham and Sarah made a big feast.

8. **Ishmael and Hagar are expelled from the home:**
   - Ishmael was mischievous, and performed dangerous and forbidden activity.
   - Sarah asked Abraham to expel Ishmael and his mother from the home, and remove him from being his heir. Abraham was very distressed over this request. G-d reassures Abraham to listen to the request of his wife, and that his son Ishmael will be looked after. Ishmael will become a great nation with many descendants
   - <u>Angel saves Ishmael</u>: That morning Abraham sent off Ishmael and his mother with some bread and a flask of water. The water was quickly finished, and a sick Ishmael was placed under a bush, by his mother Hagar, who went to the side and cried in prayer. G-d heard their prayers and sent an angel to help them. Suddenly, a well appeared, from which Hagar gave Ishmael to drink.
   - They lived in the desert of Paran, and G-d was with the lad. Ishmael became an archer. His mother Hagar married him off to a girl from Egypt.

Sixth Aliyah

9. **Abraham and Abimelech make a treaty:**
   - After Abimelech saw all the Divine assistance Abraham received, he asked to make a treaty between him and his descendants and Abraham and his descendants. Abraham agreed to the treaty.
   - <u>The fight over the well</u>: Abraham then confronted Abimelech for letting his people steal his well. Abimelech denied any wrongdoing, saying that this is the first time he is hearing of the incident.
   - <u>The treaty</u>: Abraham took cattle and gave it to Abimelech and the two made a treaty. Abraham gave Abimelech seven sheep as a sign of ownership of his well. The area of the well became known as Beer-Sheba.
   - Abraham built a hotel from which he would spread the name of G-d

Chapter 22
Seventh Aliyah

10. **The offering of Isaac:**
   - After the above occurrences, G-d decided to test Abraham, and asked him to take his son Isaac to a certain mountain to be slaughtered like an offering.
   - Abraham did as he was told, and the next morning took with him Isaac, the lads, and wood and set forth for the destination to be revealed by G-d.
   - On the third day, Abraham got a glimpse of the area of destination. Abraham told the rest of his encampment to remain set in place and he and Isaac will travel alone. Abraham brought with him the wood, fire, and knife.
   - Isaac questioned his father as to the whereabouts of the lamb for the offering. Abraham replied that G-d will show them the lamb.
   - Upon arrival, Abraham built an altar, set up the wood, bound Isaac and placed him over the wood that was on the altar.
   - Abraham lifted his hand with knife, ready to slaughter his son. Suddenly, an angel appeared and told Abraham not to slaughter his son. Abraham then saw a ram stuck in the bushes and offered it as an offering instead of his son.
   - Abraham called this mountain, "G-d Yireh"

- An angel called out to Abraham a second time and blessed Abraham with an abundance of offspring and descendants.
- Abraham returned to the encampment and they made their way back to Beer-Sheba.

11. Abraham is told of the birth of Rebecca:
- Milkah, the daughter of Nahor, the brother of Abraham, had eight children. One of those children, Bethuel, had a daughter named Rebecca.

Parashat Chayeh Sarah
Verses: 105 [Siman: יהו״עד]
Haftorah: Kings 1 1:1-31

Number of Mitzvot:
There are no Positive or Negative commands mentioned in Parashat Chayeh Sarah.

Chapter 23
First Aliyah

1. **Sarah passes away:**
   - Sarah was 127 years old upon her passing.
   - Sarah passed away in Kiryat Araba, in Hebron.
   - Abraham mourned over her passing and came to eulogize her.

2. **Abraham purchases the Cave of Machpelah and buries Sarah:**
   - Abraham approaches the sons of Hes to purchase the Cave of Machpelah. The sons of Hes reply that he can bury Sarah wherever he wishes, without any protest.
   - Abraham bows to them [as a sign of greeting] and kindly rejects their offer. He asks to meet with the land owner of the Cave of Machpelah, Ephron the Hittite, in order to purchase it from him for its full price.
   - Ephron offers the field as a gift: Ephron offers Abraham to take the entire field, including the cave, as a present from him, without payment. Abraham once again kindly rejects the offer and asks to purchase the field for its full price. Ephron offers Abraham to purchase the land for 400 Shekel Kesef.
   - Abraham paid Ephron 400 silver Shekel of the best currency.

Second Aliyah
The fields, and its cave, and all its trees now belong to Abraham. Its sale was witnessed by all of the sons of Hes. Abraham then buried his wife Sara in the Cave of Machpelah, which is in Hebron.

Chapter 24
3. **Abraham appoints Eliezer to find a wife for his son Isaac:**
   - Abraham was old and was blessed with everything.
   - Abraham asked his servant Eliezer to place his hand under his thigh and swear that he would not take for his son Isaac as a wife, a woman from Canaan, and that rather he will take for him a wife from Abraham's family.
   - Eliezer asks Abraham if he should bring Isaac to his birthplace, in the event that the girl does not want to come to live in Eretz Canaan. Abraham replies with a stern warning to Eliezer that he is not to bring Isaac to his birthplace, and that G-d will send his angel before him to help him succeed in bringing back a wife for Isaac. If, however, you should prove unsuccessful, nevertheless, do not bring Isaac to that land.
   - Eliezer placed his hand under Abraham's thigh and swore to fulfill his request.

Third Aliyah

4. **The journey of Eliezer and the meeting of Rebecca by the well:**
   - Eliezer took with him ten camels and all the possessions of his master, and he travelled to Aram Naharayim, the city of Nahor.
   - By the approach of evening, upon arrival to the outskirts of the city, Eliezer kneeled the camels onto the ground, near the well. This was at the time that the people came to the well to draw water.
   - <u>The prayer of Eliezer</u>: Eliezer prayed to G-d, asking Him to assist him in his mission, and to arrange that the woman who would volunteer to give him and his camels to drink would be the one chosen to be the wife of Isaac.
   - <u>Rebecca</u>: As he finished speaking, Rebecca, the daughter of Bethuel, who was the nephew of Abraham, came out with a bucket of water. Rebecca was very pretty, and was still a virgin, not having been with any man.
   - <u>Rebecca draws water</u>: She proceeded to draw water from the well, and Eliezer ran towards her, asking her to give him some water to drink. Rebecca gave him to drink and then went ahead and gave his camels to drink until satiation. She went numerous times to the well to give all the camels water. Eliezer was astounded, waiting to see if his mission was accomplished or not.
   - <u>The presents given to Rebecca</u>: When the camels finished drinking, he went ahead and gave Rebecca gold nose rings and two gold bracelets.
   - <u>Asking to be hosted</u>: He asked Rebecca who her family is and if they can host him. She replied that she is the daughter of Bethuel, Son of Milcah and Nahor and that they have room to host him and his camels, and they have food for them all.
   - Eliezer bowed to G-d.

Fourth Aliyah

   - Eliezer thanks G-d for doing kindness for his master Abraham.
   - Rebecca ran to her mother and told her what happened.

5. **In the house of Bethuel:**
   - <u>Laban</u>: Rebecca's brother, Laban, ran to greet Eliezer upon seeing the jewelry that Eliezer gave her and hearing the story that she had to say. Laban invited Eliezer and his camels to come into their home. Laban gave food to the camels, and gave water for Eliezer and his men to wash their feet.
   - <u>Eliezer recounts the story</u>: They offered Eliezer a meal, but he refused to eat until he told his story. Eliezer told them that he is the servant of Abraham, who is very wealthy, and he had a son to whom he has given all of his possessions, for whom he sent me to find him a wife. Eliezer went on to retell the whole purpose of his travel and the prayer he said to G-d, and the ensuing episode.
   - <u>Asking permission to take Rebecca</u>: After telling them the story, Eliezer asked if they agree to give him Rebecca, otherwise he will look elsewhere to find a wife for Isaac. Laban and Bethuel replied that they agree, as it is not in their hands, but in the hands of G-d.

Fifth Aliyah

- <u>More presents given to Rebecca and family</u>: Eliezer took out gold and silver vessels and gave it to Rebecca, and gave presents to her brother and mother.

6. **Traveling back to marry Isaac:**
   - <u>Rebecca leaves home with Eliezer</u>: They ate and drank and in the morning Eliezer asked to be sent off. They replied that they wanted Rebecca to remain with them for some more time. Eliezer would not agree and asked for her to be sent off with him immediately. They asked Rebecca as to her opinion of going so suddenly and she acquiesced. They blessed Rebecca before she left that she should give birth to a great nation and overcome their enemies, and off they went on their journey.
   - <u>Isaac meets Rebecca</u>: In the meantime, Isaac had returned from a journey of his own and went to pray in the field. He lifted his eyes and saw camels coming towards him. Rebecca also lifted her eyes and saw Isaac, and she descended from the camel and asked who the man is. Eliezer replied that it is his master Isaac. Rebecca then placed a kerchief over her face. Eliezer told Isaac all that had occurred.
   - <u>Isaac and Rebecca get married</u>: Isaac marries Rebecca, loves her, and receives comfort for the death of his mother.

Chapter 25
Sixth Aliyah

7. **Abraham marries Keturah:**
   - Abraham marries Keturah and has six sons: Zimran, Yakshan, Medan, Midian, Yishbak, Shuach.
   - Abraham inherits all his property to Isaac but gives presents to the children of Keturah.

8. **Abraham passes away:**
   - Abraham passes away at age 175, at a good old age.
   - Isaac and Ishmael bury him in the Cave of Machpelah.
   - G-d blesses Isaac after Abraham's passing.

Seventh Aliyah

9. **The descendants of Ishmael:**
   - The verse lists the descendants of Ishmael.
   - Ishmael had a total of 12 sons.
   - Ishmael passed away at age 137.
   - They lived all together between Havilah and Shur, near Egypt.

Parashat Toldot
Verses: 106 [Siman: עֵלוֹ]
Haftorah: Malachi 1 1:1-2:7

Number of Mitzvot:
There are no Positive or Negative commands mentioned in Parashat Toldot.

First Aliyah

1. **The birth of Jacob and Esau:**
   - Abraham fathered Isaac. Isaac was 40 years old when he married Rebecca.
   - Rebecca's pregnancy: Rebecca was barren, and Isaac prayed for her to have a child, and Rebecca conceived. The fetuses were kicking inside of her womb and she went to search for G-d to find an answer to this phenomenon. G-d told her that she is carrying the heads of two nations, and the older one will serve the younger one.
   - The birth: Rebecca gave birth to twins. The first child came out a red head, full of hair, and he was named Esau. The next child came out grasping the heal of the first son, and he was named Jacob. Isaac was 60 years old at the time.
   - The kids grow up: The lads grew older, and Esau was a man of the field, a hunter, while Jacob was a simple man who sat in the tent of study. Isaac loved Esau, his hunter, while Rebecca loved Jacob.

2. **Esau sells his birthright:**
   - Elisa came back from the field exhausted and encountered his brother Jacob who had cooked a pot of lentils. Esau asked to be fed the pot of lentils, as he is very exhausted. Jacob agreed on condition that Esau sell him the birthright.
   - Esau agreed to the deal, claiming the firstborn obligations can be deadly, and it is thus a worthwhile exchange. Esau swore to Jacob and in exchange Jacob fed him bread and the lentils. Esau despised the right of the firstborn.

Chapter 26

3. **The famine:**
   - There was a famine in the land, and Isaac moved to the area of Abimelech.
   - G-d told Isaac not to descend to Egypt and to remain in the land that he is in.
   - G-d blesses Isaac with the blessings he gave Abraham, in merit of the fact that Abraham kept all of his Mitzvot.

Second Aliyah

4. **Isaac moves to the city of Abimelech:**
   - Isaac remained in Gerar, the land of Abimelech.
   - Rebecca's identity is disguised and then discovered: Upon being questioned by the city residents, Isaac replied that his wife Rebecca is really his sister, as she was very beautiful. After some time, Abimelech the king saw Isaac being intimate with his wife Rebecca. Abimelech confronted Isaac with his discovery, and complained that he was lied to about

her being Isaac's sister and not his wife. This could have caused the king to sin. Isaac replied that he felt no choice but to lie, as he feared for his life. Abimelech warned the public that anyone who lays hand on Isaac or his wife will be put to death.

- The blessing in the crop: Isaac plowed and planted the fields, and that year it produced one hundred-fold of produce.

Third Aliyah

- Isaac became very prosperous. He had flocks of cattle and sheep, which drew the jealousy of the Philistines.
- The sabotaging of the wells: All the wells that were dug by the servants of Abraham were filled with earth by the Philistines.
- Isaac is expelled: Abimelech asks Isaac to leave his land, as he has become too prosperous. Isaac proceeded to move to Nahal Gerar.

5. **The wells:**
   - Re-digging the old wells: Isaac re-dug the wells that were dug by his father, and closed up by the Philistines, and he named them the same names that his father had named.
   - The controversy on the new wells: They also dug a new well, and fresh water was found, which resulted in a dispute between the shepherds of Isaac and that of Gerar, each one claiming the water is his. Due to this dispute, the well was named Esek, which means to fight. Isaac dug another well, which also resulted in a fight, and it was thus named Sitnah, or harassment.
   - The well of peace: They moved from there and dug a third well, which did not result in a quarrel, and it was thus named Rehovot, being that G-d made space for them and provided them with plenty on the land.

Fourth Aliyah

6. **Isaac moves:**
   - From there, Isaac moved to Beer Sheva. G-d appeared to Isaac and blessed him.
   - Building an altar and another well: Isaac built an altar there, and encamped there, digging another well.

7. **The pact with Abimelech:**
   - Abimelech, and his general Fichol, came from Geror to greet Isaac and make a peace treaty with him, being that they saw G-d was with him.

Fifth Aliyah

- Isaac made a feast for them, and the next day they swore into the pact. Abimelech then departed back home.
- The wells of Beer Sheva: The servants of Isaac informed him that the new wells which were dug are flowing with water. The wells were named Shibah, and thus from there the city received the name Beer Sheva, until this very day.

8. **The wives of Esau:**
   - At 40 years old Esau married Yehudis the daughter of a Hittite and Basmas the daughter of a Hittite. These wives caused suffering to Isaac and Rebecca.

Chapter 27

9. The blessings-Isaac blesses Jacob who impersonates Esau:

- <u>Isaac instructs Esau to prepare to be blessed</u>: When Isaac became old, and his eyes had weakened, and he feared his days were coming, he asked for Esau to come before him, desiring to give him the blessings. Isaac asked Esau to first hunt for him a meal and make it into a delicacy and serve him the food. He will then bless him prior to his death.

- <u>Rebecca instructs Jacob to impersonate Esau</u>: Rebecca, who was positioned nearby, heard what Isaac asked of Esau, and Esau proceeded to do as he was asked. Rebecca informed Jacob about what Isaac had instructed Esau, and asked him to do as he instructs him. Rebecca asked Jacob to take for her two goats and she will prepare them into a delicacy, as his father enjoys. "You will then take the delicacy to your father, and he will eat, and bless you prior to his death." Jacob argued that Esau is hairy, while he is hairless, and his father will discover his impersonation of his brother, and he may get cursed and not blessed. Rebecca however was persistent and asked Jacob to do as instructed, and she will accept upon herself any curse that may result.

- <u>Rebecca prepares Jacob for the meeting</u>: Jacob brought his mother the goats, and she prepared the delicacy as Isaac enjoys. Rebecca dressed Jacob in the clothing of Esau, and placed the skins of goats on his arms and neck. She then sent Jacob with the bread and delicacies that she prepared.

- <u>Isaac suspects foul play and is reassured</u>: Jacob entered the room of Isaac and called for his father. Upon being asked, Jacob said "I am Esau your first-born son. Please stand and eat the food I prepared for you, as you requested in order to receive your blessing." Isaac was doubtful as to his identity and asked for him to come close, so he can feel him. He felt his arms and proclaimed "The voice is the voice of Jacob, while the hands are the hands of Esau.

- <u>Jacob is blessed</u>: Isaac then blessed Jacob, asked again for his identity, and ate the food and drink. He then blessed him. Isaac asked for Jacob to kiss him, and upon being kissed he smelled the scent of a G-dly blessed orchard, and he blessed him.

Sixth Aliyah

10. The content of the blessings

- The content of the blessings were as follows: G-d should bless you with:
    1) Dew of heaven.
    2) The fat of the land.
    3) Much grain.
    4) Much wine.
    5) The nations will serve you.
    6) You will be a master to your brother.
    7) Those who curse you will be cursed, and those who bless you will be blessed.

11. Esau returns and discovers the deception:

- <u>Esau returns with food</u>: As Isaac concluded the blessings, and Jacob exited the room, in walked Esau after completing his hunt. He also made delicacies and asked his father to get up and eat so he can be blessed.

- <u>Isaac realizes he was deceived by Jacob</u>: Isaac asked as to his identity, and he replied that he is Esau, your first-born son. Isaac became stricken with fright, and inquired who the imposter was who fed him earlier and received the blessings. Nonetheless, Isaac agreed for the blessings of the first person to remain steadfast.

- <u>Esau cries, and pleads to be blessed</u>: When Esau heard this, he let out a great cry and begged his father to also bless him. Isaac replied, that his brother connivingly took his blessing. Esau replied that his brother's name is Jacob, because he connivingly swindled him twice, first the right of the first born and now the blessings. Esau pleaded that his father leave him a blessing. Isaac replied that no blessings remain, as he has given everything over to Jacob, including that his brothers will serve him. Esau continued to plead for a blessing and raised his voice and cried.

- <u>Isaac blesses Esau</u>: Isaac blessed Esau that he will dwell in the fattest of the lands, and he will receive the dew of the heavens. "You will live by your sword, and serve your brother, although when he goes down, you will be able to remove his yoke from your neck."

12. Jacob is sent to Padan Aram:

- <u>Esau wants to kill Jacob</u>: Esau despised Jacob for what he did and conspired to kill him after Isaac's death.

- <u>Rebecca devises a plan to save Jacob</u>: Rebecca, who discovered Esau's scheme, informed Jacob of his brother's plans to murder him. She asked Jacob to run away to her brother Laban in Haran, and remain there until his brother's wrath subsides. Rebecca spoke to Isaac saying that she does not want Jacob to marry the daughters of the Hittites [and he should thus be sent to Haran].

Chapter 28

- <u>Isaac instructs Jacob to go to Padan-Aram to find a wife</u>: Isaac summoned Jacob, and blessed him, and instructed him not to take a daughter from the Canaanite nations. "Go to Padan-Aram, and take for yourself a wife from the daughters of Laban, your mother's brother. G-d will bless you, and you will multiply and become a nation. You will receive the blessings of Abraham"

Seventh Aliyah

- Isaac sent Jacob to Padan-Aram and Jacob obeyed the instructions of his father and mother and left.

13. Esau marries a third wife:

- Esau heard the instructions his father Isaac gave Jacob, and how he despised the daughters of Canaan. He thus married another wife, named Mahalat, the daughter of Ishmael, from the family of Abraham.

Parashat Vayeitzei
Verses: 148 [Siman: חלקי]
Haftorah:[1] Hosheia 11:7-12:14

Number of Mitzvot:
There are no Positive or Negative commands mentioned in Parashat Vayeitzei.

First Aliyah

1. **Jacob's dream:**
   - <u>Jacob sleeps during his journey to Haran</u>: Jacob departed from Beer Sheva and traveled towards Haran. [During his journey] he encountered the place [called Mount Hamoriah, or the Temple Mount] and slept there, being that the sun had set. He took stones from the area and placed them around his head and laid down to sleep.
   - <u>The dream, the angels, and the blessings from G-d</u>: Jacob had a dream. In the dream he saw a ladder reaching from the earth to the heavens, and there were angels ascending and descending from it. G-d was standing over Jacob and He said to him *"I am G-d the G-d of Abraham your father, and the G-d of Isaac. The land which you are resting on will be given to you and your descendants. Your descendants will multiply like the dust of the earth, and you will burst forth to all the directions of the world, the east, west, north and south. All the earth will bless themselves through you and your descendants. I am with you, and I will guard you wherever you go. I will return you to this land."*

Chapter 29

2. **Jacob awakens and makes a vow to G-d:**
   - Jacob awakened from his sleep and he said, indeed, G-d is found in this place and I did not know. Jacob became frightened and said "How awe-striking is this place. This is non other than a house of G-d and it is the gate of Heaven."
   - <u>The Matzeiva</u>: Jacob awoke in the morning and took the stone that he placed around his head and erected it as a pillar, and poured oil on top of it. He called the place "Beth Ail," however Luz was its original name.
   - <u>The vow</u>: Jacob then made a vow, stating *"If G-d will be with me, and guard me on my journey, and provide me with food to eat and clothing to wear, and return me to my father's home in peace, and become for me a G-d, then this stone which I have set up will become a house of G-d, and all that I will earn will be tithed for You."*

Second Aliyah

3. **Jacob arrives to Haran:**
   - <u>The rock sitting on the well</u>: Jacob lifted his feet and traveled towards the land of the east [to Haran]. He arrived [at Haran] and saw three flocks of sheep lying around the drinking well. There was a very large stone sitting on the opening of the well. Customarily, the shepherds would wait until all the flocks of sheep had arrived and they would then together roll the rock off the well and water the sheep.

---

[1] So is followed by Chabad communities. However, Sepharadic communities conclude at 13:5. Ashkenazi communities read from 12:13-14:10.

- Jacob converses with the shepherds: Jacob asked the shepherds "My brothers, where are you from," to which they replied, "we are from Haran." Jacob then asked the shepherds if they knew Laban the son of Nahor and they replied in the affirmative. They said that Laban is doing well, and behold here comes his daughter Rachel with the sheep. Jacob chastised the shepherds, telling them it is not yet time to settle the sheep, as the day is still long, and they should water them and then go back to grazing. They replied that they cannot do so until all the shepherds have gathered and are then able to roll the stone off the well.

- Jacob meets Rachel and removes the stone: While they were talking, Rachel arrived with her father's sheep, as she was a shepherd. When Jacob saw his cousin Rachel, he stepped forward and rolled the rock off the well opening and gave the sheep of Laban to drink. Jacob kissed Rachel and cried with a raised voice. He told her that he is her cousin, the son of Rebecca. Rachel ran to tell her father of the news of his arrival.

- Jacob meets Laban: When Laban heard of his nephew's arrival he ran to greet him. He kissed him and hugged him and brought him into his house. Jacob told Laban all that had transpired [with Esau]. Laban responded to Jacob "Do not worry, you are my bone and my flesh." Jacob lodged by Laban for thirty days.

4. Jacob works to marry Rachel:
- [Jacob began working for Laban for free, and thus] Laban told Jacob that just because they are family does not mean that he has to work for him for free, and that Jacob should ask for a salary.
- Laban's daughters: Laban had two daughters, the older one was Leah and the younger was Rachel. The eyes of Leah were tender while Rachel was beautiful in both figure and appearance.

Third Aliyah
- Jacob works for Rachel: Jacob loved Rachel and he offered Laban to work for him for seven years in exchange for his daughter Rachel's hand in marriage. Laban agreed to the proposal, stating that it is better he gives his daughter to Jacob than to another man. So, Jacob worked in exchange for Rachel for seven years. Due to his great love for her, it appeared in his eyes like only a few days.

5. The wedding scandal:
- The wedding: After completing the years of work, Jacob asked Laban to give him his wife. Laban gathered all the people in the community and they made a wedding feast. At night, Laban took his daughter Leah and gave her to Jacob for a wife, and he consummated the marriage with her. Laban also gave Leah his maidservant called Zilpa, to be a maidservant for her.
- The morning after-The confrontation: In the morning, Jacob noticed that he had been tricked, and was given Leah as a wife. Jacob confronted Laban saying "What have you done to me? I worked for you in exchange for Rachel. Why have you deceived me?" Laban replied, "It is not the custom of our town to marry the younger daughter before the older." Laban then gave Jacob a second offer "Work for me another seven years, and in exchange I will give you also this daughter [Rachel] after the week is up.

- Jacob marries Rachel: Jacob agreed to the proposal and married Rachel at the end of the week. Jacob consummated the marriage with Rachel and loved her more than Leah. He worked for Laban for another seven years.

6. **Jacob has children:**
   - Leah gives birth to Reuben, Simeon, Levi and Judah: G-d saw that Leah was hated and he thus opened her womb, although Rachel was barren. Leah became pregnant and gave birth to a son whom she named **Reuben**, in commemoration of the fact that "G-d has **seen** my suffering, as now my husband will love me." She again became pregnant and had a son whom she named **Simeon**, in commemoration of the fact that "G-d has **heard** that I am hated, and thus gave me another son." She again became pregnant and had a son whom she named **Levi**, in commemoration of the fact that "Now my husband will **attach** to me as I have borne him three sons." She again became pregnant and had a son whom she named **Judah**, as sign of **thanks** to G-d. She then stopped having children.

Chapter 30

- Rachel confronts Jacob: Rachel saw that she had not borne Jacob any children and she was jealous of her sister. She demanded from Jacob to give her children as otherwise "I am like dead." Jacob became angered and chastised her saying "Am I in place of G-d who has withheld children from you?"
- Rachel gives Bilhah to Jacob in marriage: In response, Rachel told Jacob to take her maidservant Bilhah in marriage, so she can have a child through her and raise him. Jacob took Bilhah as a wife and he consummated the marriage with her.
- Bilhah gives birth to Dan and Naftali: Bilhah became pregnant and had a son for Jacob who Rachel named **Dan**, in commemoration of the fact that "G-d has **judged** me [favorably] and heard my voice to give me a son." Bilhah again became pregnant and had a second son for Jacob who Rachel named **Naftali**, in commemoration of the fact that "I have stubbornly offered my prayers to G-d to **bond** with my sister and become an equal."
- Leah gives Zilpah to Jacob in marriage: Leah saw that she stopped giving birth, so she gave her maidservant Zilpah to Jacob in marriage.
- Zilpah gives birth to Gad and Asher: Zilpah gave birth to a son for Jacob who Leah named **Gad**, from the word Bagad, which means a **good fortune** has come. Zilpah again gave birth to a second son for Jacob who Leah named **Asher**, from the word Ashruni, as now "I am **praised/fortunate** because now women will praise me, and deem me fortunate."

Fourth Aliyah

- Rachel trades her night with Jacob in exchange for Reuben's flowers: Reuben went out in the days of the wheat harvest and found Dudaim [jasmine] in the field. He gave them to his mother Leah. Rachel asked Leah to give her some of the flowers of her son. Leah replied, "Is it not enough that you have taken my husband that now you want to take my sons flowers!" In response, Rachel told Leah that in exchange for the flowers, Leah could sleep with Jacob that night. That night upon Jacob's arrival from the field, Leah came to greet him, telling him that she bought off Rachel with the Dudaim flowers of her son. Jacob slept with her that night.

- Leah gives birth to Issachar, Zebulun, and Dina: G-d hearkened to Leah and she became pregnant and gave birth to a fifth son who she named **Issachar**, in commemoration of the fact that "G-d has **rewarded** me for having given my maidservant to my husband." She again became pregnant and had a sixth son for Jacob who she named **Zebulun**, in commemoration of the fact that "G-d has merited me with a **good endowment**, as I have borne my husband six sons and now he will make his permanent home with me." Afterwards Leah had a daughter who she named Dina.
- Rachel gives birth to Joseph: G-d remembered Rachel and hearkened to her and opened her womb. She became pregnant and had a son who she called Joseph in commemoration of the fact that "G-d has **gathered** [and concealed] my disgrace" and as a future prayer that "G-d should **add** on for me another son."

7. **Jacob asks to leave:**
   - After Rachel gave birth to Joseph, Jacob asked Laban to let him go back to his home and take his wives and children with him, as he worked for them in exchange. Laban replied that he does not want Jacob to leave as he has the belief that he was blessed by G-d due to his presence.

Fifth Aliyah

8. **Jacob makes new business arrangement with Laban and becomes wealthy:**
   - The business negotiations: Laban [in attempt to convince Jacob to remain] asked Jacob to specify a wage he would like to receive in exchange for his work in shepherding the flock. Jacob replied that he has been a faithful and successful shepherd, causing Laban's flock to expand tremendously, and now he desires to prosper for his own home. Laban once again asked Jacob what he can offer him as payment, and Jacob replied as follows: "Do not give me anything. If you agree to the following, then I agree to continue working as a shepherd for your sheep."
   - The business agreement: Jacob offered the following business arrangement which was readily accepted by Laban. Jacob would examine all the flocks of sheep and goats and remove from them all speckled, dappled, and brownish lamb, and speckled or dappled goats. My wage will then be all future sheep that are brown, and all future goats that are speckled or dappled. This method would allow Jacob's integrity to remain unshakeable, as it would be blatantly obvious that he stole if he takes any sheep or goats that are not colored as stated above.
   - Separating the brown and speckled sheep/goats: That very day, Laban removed the dappled goats and all the brown sheep, and gave them to his sons. These sheep and goats were moved to a distance of three days from Jacob and his flocks. Jacob then resumed caring for the remaining flock of Laban.
   - Jacob's business schemes to achieve brown and speckled sheep/goats: Jacob took a rod of poplar, hazel and chestnut and peeled stripes into them, in a way that revealed their underlying white skin. Jacob positioned the striped white colored rods into the watering pools where the flock would come to drink. The flock would face these rods when they came to drink and became heated in a way that they conceived and gave birth to ringed, speckled and dappled sheep. Jacob then took these speckled and brown sheep and placed them at the head of the flock, thus causing the animals to face them. Jacob made separate herds for his and Lavin's sheep. During the mating season of the early bearing flocks,

Jacob would place the rods in view of the flock, by the water streams in order to stimulate them. The late bearing flock, however, he did not place in front of the rods, and so it was that the early bearing flocks went to Jacob and the late bearing one's went to Laban.

Chapter 31

- <u>Jacob's wealth and the ensuing jealousy</u>: Jacob became very wealthy, and he amassed much flock, servants, camels and donkeys. Laban's sons became jealous and exclaimed that Jacob had usurped all their father's wealth. When Jacob became aware of this, he noticed that Laban was not happy with him as in previous times.

9. **G-d tells Jacob to leave:**
   - G-d appeared to Jacob and told him to return to his father's land. Jacob summoned Rachel and Leah to meet him in the field. Jacob explained to them the situation with Laban and how he was now no longer on good terms with him.
   - <u>Jacob describes how he managed to amass his wealth despite Laban's schemes</u>: Jacob told his wives the following: Laban had changed my wages tens of times, changing the terms of agreement from me receiving the ringed sheep to me receiving the spotted sheep, although G-d stood by my side and made the flock give birth to whatever was agreed that I would receive, and thus I managed to amass wealth from your fathers flock. Behold, I even saw in a dream that during the mating season [an angel came and brought] the speckled, spotted, and striped male goats to mate. In the dream, the angel told me to see how all the male goats mating are speckled, spotted and striped, as I have seen all that Laban has done to you. The angel then instructed me to return home.
   - <u>Rachel and Leah agree to leave</u>: Rachel and Leah both responded that they no longer have a portion in the father's household, and he treated them like strangers, selling them, and consuming their money. "Now do all that G-d tells you."

Sixth Aliyah

10. **Jacob and family flee:**
    - Jacob arose and lifted his sons and wives onto the camels, and took all his livestock and possessions and traveled to Padan Aram.
    - <u>Rachel steals the Terafim</u>: When this happened, Laban was away shearing his sheep, and Rachel took the opportunity and stole the Terafim [idols] of her father.
    - Jacob deceived Laban by running away without informing him. He crossed the river and set towards Mount Gilead.

11. **Laban discovers Jacob's escape and sets chase for him:**
    - On the third day of Jacob's escape, Laban was informed that he had run away. He took his brethren with him and chased after Jacob for a seven day's journey, and met up with him by Mount Gilead.
    - <u>G-d warns Laban</u>: G-d appeared to Laban in a dream at night and warned him not to speak with Jacob neither good or bad.

12. **Laban confronts Jacob:**
    - Laban arrived to Jacob's location and confronted him saying *"What have you done, that you have deceived me and taken my daughters like captives of war. Why did you flee so*

deceptively and not inform me, so I could send you off with a band and parade? You withheld me from kissing my sons and daughters. You have acted foolishly, as my deities have ability to harm you, but your G-d forewarned me yesterday not to do so. Now, I understand if you are longing for your father's house, but why did you steal my Terafim."

- Jacob responds: Jacob replied that Laban is free to search for his gods and that whoever they are found with will not live. Jacob was not aware that Rachel stole them.

- Laban searches for his idols: Laban went into the tents of Rachel, Leah and the two maidservants, and back to the tent of Rachel, but he did not find them. In truth, Rachel took the Terafim and hid them under the saddle of the camel which she was sitting on. Laban searched through the whole tent but could not find them. Rachel told her father that he should excuse her for not standing up in his honor, as she is menstruating.

- Jacob confronts Laban: Jacob became angered and scolded Laban saying *"What is it that you want? What have I sinned against you that you pursue me? You searched all my belongings, and did you find anything that is yours? I worked for you for twenty years honestly and hard, taking all the loses that occurred to the flock. I worked in the heat of day and snow of night, with little sleep. I worked in exchange of your two daughters for 14 years, and 6 years I worked for your flock, and you changed by wages tens of times. If not for G-d watching me I would have left empty handed."*

Seventh Aliyah

13. Jacob and Laban make a pact:

- Laban replied to Jacob "Everything that you see is mine, the daughters are mine, the sons are mine, the flocks are mine. How could I harm them! Now, let us make a pact with each other."

- The mound and monument: Jacob took a stone and raised it as a monument. Jacob had his sons gather stones and they made a mound, on which they ate. Laban called the area Yegar Sahadusa, while Jacob called it Gal-Aid. Laban stated that the mound is a witness of the pact made and that G-d will watch to see if Jacob oppresses his daughters. The mound is a witness that I may not cross over to do evil to you and you may not cross over it to do evil to me. Jacob swore to the pact in the Dread of his father Isaac. Jacob slaughtered animals and they sat down for a meal, sleeping on the mountain.

Chapter 32

- Laban leaves: In the morning Laban rose and kissed his sons and daughters and blessed them. Laban left the place and returned home.

- Jacob continues his travels: Jacob continued on his journey and met angels of G-d. Jacob exclaimed that this is a G-dly camp, and he thus named it Machanayim.

Parashat Vayishlach
Verses: 154 [Siman: קְלִיטָה]
Haftorah: Ovadia 1:1-21

Number of Mitzvot:
There is a total of **One** Mitzvah in Parashat Vayishlach; **Zero** positive command and **One** negative command. The following are the commands in the order listed by the Sefer Hachinuch.

Negative:
1. **Mitzvah 3/Negative 1:** Not to eat the Gid Hanashe, the Sciatic nerve.

First Aliyah

1. **Jacob prepares to meet Esau:**
   - <u>Messengers sent to Esau</u>: Jacob sends messengers to his brother Esau to the land of Seir, fields of Edom. Jacob instructs them to go and tell Esau that he was with Laban until this time, and thus delayed meeting him. "Tell him that I have a lot of cattle and am coming to my master to find favor in his eyes." The messengers returned from their meeting with Esau and told Jacob that Esau is coming to greet him with 400 men.
   - <u>Jacob splits the camp and prays</u>: Jacob became very fearful, and split his camp of people and cattle into two groups, so if Esau smites one camp, the other camp can survive. Jacob Davened to G-d that in the merit of Abraham and Isaac that he should be saved. "Save me from the hands of my brother Esau. You said you will do good to me, and make my offspring like the sand of the sea that are too numerous to count."

Second Aliyah

2. **Jacob sends presents to Esau:**
   - <u>The content of the present</u>: Jacob slept there that night and prepared to send Esau a present of animals; 200 female goats and 20 male goats, 200 female sheep, and 20 rams, 30 male and female camels, 40 female cows and 10 bulls, 20 female donkeys and 10 male donkeys.
   - <u>The instructions given to the messengers sending the present</u>: Jacob placed the animals in different groups of herds, and instructed the messengers taking the herds to make space between each herd. Jacob instructed them: Upon meeting Esau, you are to tell him that the animals belong to your servant Jacob and he is sending them as a present to his master Esau. Tell him that Jacob too is on his way to greet him. Each group was instructed to tell Esau the above.
   - Jacob slept that night in the camp, after the present was sent.

3. **Jacob battles the angel of Esau:**
   - <u>Crossing his family</u>: Jacob awoke in middle of the night and crossed his two wives and 11 children across the river of Yabok. He also moved all of his belongings. Jacob remained on the other side and fought with a man until day break.

- The battle: The man saw that he was unable to overcome Jacob, so he injured his joint in his thigh. Jacob was holding him when morning arrived and refused to let go of him until he promised to bless him. The man promised Jacob that his name will no longer be Jacob but rather Israel, which means that he has battled and won against men [who are angels]. Jacob asked for his name, and the man did not answer.

Third Aliyah

- Jacob called that place Peniyail, as he saw the face of an angel and was saved.
- Jacob's injury: Jacob was limping after the above encounter.
- The sciatic nerve: We do not eat from the sciatic nerve of an animal until this day due to this injury that Jacob sustained in the battle.

Chapter 33

4. **Jacob meets Esau:**
   - Jacob raised his eyes and saw Esau and his 400 men coming to greet him.
   - The setup of Jacob's family: Jacob separated the children with Rochel and Leah. The maids and their children were placed first, and Rachel and Joseph last.
   - Hugging, kissing and crying: Jacob bowed seven times until he reached his brother. Esau ran towards him, and hugged him and kissed him. He fell on his neck and they both cried. Esau lifted his eyes and saw Jacob's family and asked who they are. Jacob replied that they are the children which G-d has granted "your servant."

Fourth Aliyah

- The maid servants and their children came forward and bowed to Esau. Leah and her children came forth and bowed to Esau and then came Joseph and Rachel.
- Jacob asks Esau to accept the present as seeing him is like seeing the face of G-d. Jacob persists that Esau accept the present and he does so.
- Jacob and Esau part ways: Esau offered to escort Jacob on his journey. Jacob refused the offer under the pretext that his camp travels very slowly. Esau then returned to Seir and Jacob encamped in Sukkot.

5. **Jacob moves to Shechem:**
   - Jacob then moved to Shechem and purchased a field there for 100 Kesita.
   - The altar: He built an altar there and called it the G-d of Israel.

Chapter 34
Fifth Aliyah

6. **Dina is kidnapped and raped:**
   - Dina, the daughter of Leah, came out to see the daughters of Shechem. Shechem, the son of Hamor, the president of the land, saw her. He took her, lay with her, violated her and oppressed her. His soul became attached to Dina. He loved her and spoke to her heart. Shechem requested from his father that he arrange that Dina be given to him as a wife.
   - Jacob and his sons hear the news: Jacob heard that Dina was defiled. He did not say anything until his sons returned from the field. Hamor, the father of Shechem, met with Jacob. The brothers were very angry when they heard what happened.

- The negotiations and agreements with Hamor: Hamor offered that if they give Dina to his son Shechem as a wife, he will let them take their daughters for them as wives and they would be able to live freely on the land. Shechem also pleaded with Jacob and his sons to be given Dina as a wife, and in exchange he will give whatever dowry he is asked. The children of Jacob connivingly answered Shechem and Hamor that they can only agree to the marriage if all the males of the land circumcise themselves. Hamor, and Shechem agreed to the terms, and the circumcision took place right away.

- The circumcision of Shechem: Hamor and Shechem convinced the city inhabitants to circumcise themselves, under the argument that doing so will allow them to unify with Jacob and do commerce with them.

- The city is annihilated and ransacked: On the third day after the circumcision, when the inhabitants were in great pain, Simeon and Levi came and killed all the male inhabitants of the city. They killed Hamor and Shechem with the sword and took Dina from the house of Shechem. They took spoils from the city. They took the cattle, all their wives and children, and all that was in their homes.

- Jacob's reaction: Jacob confronted Simeon and Levi for murdering the city inhabitants, arguing that it will cause the surrounding nations to attack them, and wipe them out. The brothers replied, "Can we allow our sister to be like a harlot."

Chapter 35

7. **Jacob returns to Beth-El:**
   - Building an altar: G-d came to Jacob and told him to return to Beth-El and build an altar in commemoration of running away from Esau his brother.
   - Idol cleansing: Jacob commanded his family to get rid of all the idols that are amongst them, and to change their clothing. Jacob took all the idols, and earrings and buried them under the tree, near Shechem.
   - They traveled, and all the cities feared them and did not begin a war with them.
   - Jacob arrived in Luz, which is Beth El, and built the altar.
   - Devora dies: Devorah, the nurse of Rebecca, passed away, and was buried beneath the mountain of Beth El which Jacob named Alon Bachus.
   - Jacob is blessed: G-d appeared again to Jacob and blessed him. G-d told Jacob that his name will no longer be Jacob, but Israel. Jacob was promised that a great nation would come forth from him.

Sixth Aliyah

- G-d promised Jacob that the land which was promised to Abraham and Isaac, will be given to him. G-d then left him.
- The monument: Jacob established a monument of stone in that area, and poured oil over it. Jacob named the place Beth El.

8. **Rachel's dies during childbirth:**
   - They traveled from Beth El towards Efrat, and Rachel was having a very difficult labor in giving birth. As she gave birth, the midwife told her that it is a son, as Rachel was dying as a result of the birth. His father, Jacob, called his son Benjamin. Rachel died and was buried on the way to Efrat, which is Beth Lachem. Jacob placed a monument on her grave which remains there until this very day.

- Israel traveled and settled his camp near Migdal Eider.

9. Reuben's sin:
- While Israel was living in that land, Reuben went and slept with Bilhah, the concubine of his father. Israel discovered what occurred.

10. The sons of Jacob:
- Jacob had 12 sons.
- <u>The sons of Leah</u>: Reuben the firstborn, Simeon, Levi, Judah, Issachar, Zebulun.
- <u>The sons of Rachel</u>: Joseph and Benjamin.
- <u>The sons of Bilhah</u>, the maidservant of Rachel: Dan and Naftali.
- <u>The sons of Zilpah</u>, the maidservant of Leah: Gad and Asher.

11. Jacob returns to his father:
- Jacob returned to Isaac his father, in Kiryat Arba, Hebron.

12. Isaac passes away:
- Isaac lived for 180 years, passing away at a ripe old age. He was buried by Jacob and Esau.

Chapter 36

13. The descendants of Esau, Edom:
Esau was married to Adah, the daughter of Eilon, and to Ahalivamah, the daughter of Anah and Tzivon, and Basmas the daughter of Ishmael. The following were their children:

1. **Ada's offspring**:
   - Elifaz
2. **Basmas offspring**:
   - Reuel
3. **Ahalivama's offspring**:
   - Yeush
   - Yalom
   - Korach

The above children were born in Eretz Canaan, and Esau then moved from Canaan to Seir, as the land did not contain enough food for the animals to graze for the flocks of both Jacob his brother, and Esau.

The following are the children of Esau, the father of Edom, on the mountain of Seir:

1. **Elifaz's offspring**:
   - Taiman
   - Omar
   - Tzefo
   - Gatam
   - Kenaz
   - Amalek, which was born to Timna, the concubine of Elifaz.
2. **Reuel's offspring**:
   - Nachas
   - Zerach

- Shamah
- Mizah

Seventh Aliyah

14. The descendants of Seir:

The following are the descendants of Seir the Chori:

1. **Lotan**
   - Chori
   - Heimam
2. **Shoval**
   - Alvan
   - Manachas
   - Aival
   - Shefo
   - Onam
3. **Tzivon**
   - Aiyah
   - Anah who discovered the mules.
4. **Anah**
   - Dishon
   - Ahalivamah
5. **Dishon**
   - Chemdan
   - Eshban
   - Yisran
   - Cheran
6. **Aitzer**
   - Bilhan
   - Zaavan
   - Akan
7. **Dishan**
8. **Timna** was the sister of Lotan.

15. The kings who reigned before there was a king for the Jewish people:

The following are the kings who reigned before the Jewish people:

1. Bela Ben Beor, from Dinhavah
2. Yovav the son of Zerach from Batzrah
3. Chusham from Yemen.
4. Hadad Ben Bedad who defeated Midian in the field of Moab.
5. Samlah from Masraikah
6. Shaul from Rechovos Hanahar.
7. Baal Chanan the son of Achbor
8. Hadar from the city of Pau. His wife was Mehaytavail the daughter of Matraid, the daughter of May Zahav.
9. Esau is the father of all the Edomites.

Parashat Vayeishev
Verses: 112[Siman: יבק]
Haftorah: Amos 2:6-3:8

> **Number of Mitzvot:**
> There are no Positive or Negative commands mentioned in Parashat Vayeishev.

Chapter 37
First Aliyah

1. Joseph's relationship with his father and brothers:
- Jacob dwelled in the land of his fathers, in the land of Canaan.
- The slander: Joseph was a lad of 17 years of age. He was a shepherd with his brothers and spent time with the children of the maids. Joseph gave bad reports of his brothers to his father Jacob.
- Favoritism showed to Joseph: Jacob loved Joseph more than any of his other sons, as he was born in his old age. Jacob made for him a beautiful garment. The brothers saw that their father loved Joseph, and could not speak to him in peace.

2. Joseph's dreams:
- Joseph had a dream, and he told his brothers, which led to them hating him even more.
- The first dream: The following was his dream: We were all gathering stalks in the field and my stalk got up and all your stalks turned towards my stalk and bowed to it. The brothers responded to the dream "Will you reign and rule over us," and they continued to hate him.
- The second dream: Joseph had a second dream and he told it to his brothers. "I saw the sun, moon and eleven stars bowing to me." Joseph told the story to his father and brothers, and his father rebuked him saying "Do you really believe that I, your mother and your brothers will bow to you."
- The brothers were envious of Joseph, however, his father preserved the matter in his memory.

Second Aliyah

3. Joseph travels to visit his brothers in Shechem
- Joseph is sent to Shechem: The brothers of Joseph went to graze the sheep in Shechem. Jacob asked Joseph to visit his brothers in Shechem, and see as to their wellbeing, and the wellbeing of the sheep, and report back to him. Joseph was sent from the valley of Hebron and arrived in Shechem.
- Joseph searches for his brothers: A man found Joseph wondering in the field and asked him as to what he is looking for. Joseph replied that he is looking for his brothers "Please tell me where they are grazing the flock." The man replied: They traveled from here as I heard them say "Let us go to Doson." Joseph went searching for his brothers, and found them in Doson.

4. **The plot to kill Joseph:**
   - The brothers saw Joseph from a distance, and prior to his arrival, plotted to kill him. They told each other "Look, the dreamer is coming. Let us kill him and throw him in one of the pits. We will tell [our father] that a wild animal ate him." We will then see what will be with his dreams.
   - Reuben's plan to save the lad: Reuben heard of the plot and disguised a plan to save Joseph, and return him to their father. He told them "Let us not smite his soul and murder him. Instead, place him in the pit that is in the desert, and we will not raise a hand on him."

Third Aliyah

5. **Joseph is placed in the pit and then sold and brought to Egypt:**
   - When Joseph arrived to his brothers, they removed his garments, as well as the Ketonet Hapatim, and they took him and threw him in the pit. The pit did not have water, it was empty.
   - The sale to the Ishmaelites: The brothers sat to eat, and they saw a caravan of Ishmaelites coming from Gilad. The camels were carrying cloves and other good spices, and they were traveling towards Egypt. Judah told his brothers "What gain do we have from killing our brother and covering his blood? Lets sell him to the Ishmaelites, and let our hands not harm him, as he is our brother, part of our flesh." The brothers consented.
   - The sale to the Midianites: A caravan of Midianites passed, and they took Joseph out from the pit and sold him to the Ishmaelites for 20 silver coins. Joseph was brought to Egypt.
   - Reuben returns to the pit: Reuben returned to the pit and saw that it was empty. He tore his clothing and exclaimed to his brothers "The child is not there, and how can I face [my father Jacob]."

6. **Jacob is told of Joseph's death:**
   - The brothers took Joseph's garment and dipped it in the blood of a goat. The garment was then sent to their father Jacob, asking him to identify the garment of his son. Jacob recognized the garment and said that a wild animal must have eaten him. Joseph has been devoured. Jacob tore his clothing and placed on sackcloth. He mourned for his son many days.
   - Comforting Jacob: All his sons and daughters tried to comfort him, but Jacob refused to be comforted. He said, "I will descend to my grave while still mourning my son." Jacob cried over this a lot.

7. **Joseph is sold to Potiphar:**
   - The Midianites sold Joseph to the Egyptians, to Potiphar the head butcher of Pharaoh.

Chapter 38
Fourth Aliyah

8. **Judah moves away, gets married and has children:**
   - At that time, Judah descended from amongst his brothers, and arrived to an Adulami man, whose name was Hira.
   - The marriage: Judah saw there the daughter of a Canaanite man called Shua. He took the daughter and married her.

- The children: She became pregnant and had a son, who was named Er. She again conceived and had a son who was named Onan. She again conceived and had a son who was named Shailah. She was in Keziv when she had him.

9. **The marriage of Judah's sons to Tamar, and their eventual death:**
   - Er marries Tamar and dies: Judah took a wife for Er, his firstborn, and her name was Tamar. Er performed evil in the eyes of G-d, and G-d therefore put him to death.
   - Onan marries Tamar and dies: Judah told Onan to be intimate with the wife of his brother, and enter into levirate marriage with her, and establish offspring for his brother. Onan knew that the child would not be considered his. Therefore, each time he was intimate with his brother's wife, he would destroy [his seed by spilling it] onto the earth, in order not to give offspring to his brother. What he did was evil in the eyes of G-d, and He put also him to death.
   - Tamar returns home: Judah told Tamar, his daughter in-law, to stay in the home of her father until Shailah is old enough [to marry her]. Judah said this because he feared for the life of Shailah. Tamar did as she was told.

10. **Judah is intimate with Tamar:**
    - After the passing of many days, the wife of Judah, the daughter of Shua, passed away. Judah was comforted, and traveled with his friend Hirah to graze the flock in Timna.
    - Tamar dresses like a harlot: Tamar was informed that her father in-law is traveling to Timna to graze the sheep. She removed her widow garments and covered herself with a veil. She sat at the crossroads leading to Timna, being that she saw that Shailah had already grown up and she was still not given to him as a wife. Judah saw her and mistook her for a harlot, being that her face was covered.
    - The negotiations and agreements: Judah came towards her and asked if he could be intimate with her, as he did not know that she was his daughter in-law. She asked him "What will you give me," and he replied that he will send her a young goat from amongst his sheep. She replied that she will only accept his offer if he gives her something as collateral until he brings her the goat. He asked what collateral she wanted, and she asked to be given his signet ring, jacket, and staff. He gave it to her and was intimate with her and she became pregnant from him.
    - Tamar returned home, removed her veil, and put back on her widow garments
    - Judah tries to find the harlot: Judah sent the young goat with his friend to bring to the harlot and receive his collateral back, although she could not be found. They asked the townspeople as to the whereabouts of the harlot who sat by the crossroads and they replied that they know nothing of a harlot in that location. The friend told Judah that she could not be found, and Judah replied that she should keep what she was given, as they tried to find her and if they continue searching, the matter will become publicized and humiliate them.

11. **A pregnant Tamar is almost burnt at the stake:**
    - Three months later Judah is informed that his daughter in-law Tamar is pregnant due to a promiscuous relationship. Judah ordered that she be burned to death.
    - Judah confesses and saves her from death: As she was being brought to be burnt she sent her father in-law the items which he gave her, and told him "I am pregnant from the man

whom these items belong to, please recognize them." Judah recognized the items and responded that she be vindicated of any wrong doing being that he refused to give her to Shailah as a wife, and she is pregnant from him.

- Judah discontinued being intimate with her.

12. Tamar gives birth to twins:

- Tamar gave birth to twins.
- When she gave birth, one of the children stuck out his hand. The midwife took it and tied a red string onto it, as a sign that he came out first.
- After he returned his hand, his brother came out. The [midwife] exclaimed "Why have you burst forth" and he was named Peretz.
- Afterwards, his brother, which had the red string on his hand, was born and he was named Zarah.

Chapter 39
Fifth Aliyah

13. Joseph in Egypt;

- Potiphar, the head butcher of Pharaoh, had purchased Joseph from the Ishmaelites who brought him there.
- G-d blesses the home of Potiphar: G-d was with Joseph, and Joseph was successful while at the home of his master the Egyptian. His master noticed his success and that G-d is with him. As a result, Joseph found favor in his eyes, and was placed in charge of everything in the home. After Joseph was appointed in charge of the estate, and all of his assets, G-d blessed the house of the Egyptian due to Joseph, and blessing was found in everything in the home and field. Joseph was placed in charge of everything, aside for the bread which he eats. Joseph had a beautiful figure and appearance.

Sixth Aliyah

14. Potiphar's wife attempts to lie with Joseph:

- After the above events, the wife of Potiphar placed her eyes on Joseph and asked him to lay with her. He refused, stating that his master has trusted him with everything in the home, and has given him everything except for her. How then can he do such a great evil and sin towards G-d. She tried daily to convince Joseph to be with her, although he refused.
- One day, Joseph came home and there was no one home. The wife grabbed Joseph by his coat, commanding him to lie with her. Joseph slipped out of his coat, leaving it with her, and fled outside. When she saw that Joseph left his coat with her, she screamed for help of her household, saying that the Jewish boy attempted to lie with her. "When I screamed, he left his coat with me and ran away." She remained with the coat until his master returned home. She told him that Joseph attempted to lie with her, and when she screamed he ran away, and left his coat.

15. Joseph is imprisoned:

- Joseph's master imprisoned him. G-d was with Joseph in the prison and he found favor in the eyes of the warden.
- The warden appointed Joseph in charge of all the other prisoners, and he would direct their activities. The warden trusted him as G-d was with him.

Chapter 40
Seventh Aliyah

16. The chamberlain of the cupbearers [i.e. butler] and the chamberlain of the bakers:

- The imprisonment: After the above events, the head butler and baker sinned to their master, the king of Egypt. An angry Pharaoh had them imprisoned, in the same prison that Joseph was located.

- The head butcher placed Joseph in charge of attending to them. They remained in prison for many days.

- The dreams: One evening, the two ministers, the butler and baker, had a dream. Each person dreamt the interpretation of the dream. In the morning, Joseph saw that the two men were very perplexed. He asked them as to what is the matter? They told him of their dreams. Joseph said that the interpretations of dreams belongs to G-d, "Please tell me your dreams."

- The dream of the chamberlain of the cupbearers: The chamberlain of the cupbearers told Joseph his dream. He said that he dreamt of seeing a vine in front of him, and the vine contained three clusters of freshly ripe grapes. I saw myself squeezing the grapes into the cup of Pharaoh and placing the cup into the hand of Pharaoh. Joseph replied that the interpretations of the dream is as follows: The three clusters represent three days, as in three days Pharaoh will reinstate you to your position as the chief butler, and you will once again serve him wine as you did in the past.

- Joseph then asked the butler to mention him before Pharaoh, to have him removed from the prison, as he has done nothing wrong.

- The dream of the baker: The baker saw that the interpretation was good, and he too told Joseph of his dream. He told Joseph that he dreamt of seeing three baskets on his head. In the top basket there was all the baked goods eaten by Pharaoh, and the birds were eating from it. Joseph replied that the three baskets represent three days, as in another three days Pharaoh will have you hung, and the birds will eat your flesh.

- Pharaoh's birthday party: So, it was that on the third day it was the birthday of Pharaoh and he made a great feast for all his servants. He remembers the ministers, the butler and baker. The butler was reinstated to his position and he placed the cup in Pharaohs hand, while the baker was hung, as Joseph interpreted.

- The butler forgot to mention Joseph before Pharaoh.

Parashat Mikeitz
Verses: 146 [Siman: יחזקיהו]
Haftorah: Kings 1 3:15-4:1

Number of Mitzvot:
There are no Positive or Negative commands mentioned in Parashat Mikeitz.

Chapter 41
First Aliyah

1. **Pharaohs dreams:**
   - The first dream: After two years [of Joseph's imprisonment], Pharaoh had a dream in which he saw himself standing by the Nile. He saw seven beautiful and healthy-looking cows, which were grazing in the land. Seven other cows came out after them, from the Nile. These cows looked very bad, and were thin. They stood next to the [other] seven cows, by the bank of the river. The seven bad and thin looking cows then proceeded to consume the seven good looking and fat cows. Pharaoh then awakened.
   - The second dream: Pharaoh fell back asleep and dreamt another dream. He saw seven healthy and good-looking ears of grain sprouting out from one stalk. He also saw seven thin and withered looking ears of grain, due to the east wind, grow after them. The seven thin looking ears of grain then proceeded to consume the seven healthy and fat looking ears of grain. Pharaoh then awakened, and the dream was [complete].
   - Pharaoh seeks an interpretation of the dream: In the morning, Pharaoh was disturbed, and he summoned all the sorcerers of Egypt and their sages to interpret the dream, and they were unable to do so for him.
   - The chamberlain of the cupbearers [butler] suggests to Pharaoh to summon Joseph to interpret the dream: The chief butler spoke to Pharaoh and mentioned to him the sin that had once committed against the king and how he was thrown in prison. He told Pharaoh the entire encounter that occurred in the prison with his dreams, and the dreams of the head baker, and how Joseph accurately interpreted them. "There was a Hebrew lad in the prison, who was a slave to the chief butcher. We told him our dreams, and he interpreted our dreams. Just as he interpreted, so took place, as I was reinstated to my position, while the chief baker was hung."
   - Pharaoh summons Joseph: Pharaoh sent messengers to summon Joseph. Joseph was removed from the pit. He received a haircut and changed his clothing, and then came to Pharaoh.

Second Aliyah

2. **Joseph's interpretation:**
   - Pharaoh tells his dreams to Joseph: Pharaoh told Joseph of his dream and how no one could interpret it properly, and he is thus asking him to interpret it, as he heard that Joseph knows to interpret dreams. Joseph replied that it is not he who can interpret dreams, but G-d. Pharaoh then retold the dream to Joseph in all its detail. He added that after seeing the thin unhealthy cows eat the healthy fat cows, their appearance remained the same, thin and unhealthy.

- The interpretation: Joseph told Pharaoh that both dreams are in truth a single [message] from G-d, who is forewarning Pharaoh of the future occurrences. The seven good looking cows and ears of corn represent seven years, and it is all one dream. The seven bad looking cows and ears of corn are seven bad years of starvation and famine. G-d is foretelling Pharaoh that the coming seven years will be years of enormous wealth of produce in all of Egypt. After those years there will be seven years of severe hunger, which will cause the seven years of plenty to be erased from memory. The famine will destroy the land. The reason the dreams were repeated, is because G-d is telling Pharaoh that these years will come speedily.
- Joseph's advice to Pharaoh: After interpreting the dream, Joseph then advised Pharaoh what should be done to deal with the years of famine. "Pharaoh should see to appoint a wise man over the land of Egypt, who will appoint officials over the land and prepare it during these seven years of plenty. All the food of the years of plenty are to be stored and guarded under the hand of Pharaoh, within the various cities. The food will serve as a reserve for the seven years of famine, in order so the earth not be destroyed in hunger."
- Pharaoh's satisfaction with the interpretation and advice: The matter pleased Pharaoh and his servants, and he exclaimed to them "Is there any man as wise as him, who carries the spirit of G-d"

Third Aliyah

3. **Joseph is appointed viceroy:**
   - Pharaoh told Joseph that since G-d revealed to him all this information, there must be no one as wise as you, and therefore he is appointing him the viceroy. Every order will come through your hands, and only the kingship will I hold over you.
   - The inauguration of Joseph: Pharaoh removed his signet ring and placed it on the hand of Joseph. He garbed him in linen clothing and placed a golden chain around his neck. Joseph was taken for a ride in the king's royal wagon and they proclaimed before him "Avreikh, Kings advisor." Pharaoh told Joseph that he is the king and without Joseph's consent, no one can raise a hand and foot. Pharaoh called Joseph the name Tzafnas Paneach.
   - Joseph gets married: Pharaoh gave Joseph as a wife, a woman named Asnas, the daughter of the chief butcher. Joseph was 30 years old at the time that he became ruler. He went out from the audience with Pharaoh and visited the entire land of Egypt.

4. **The years of plenty:**
   - In the seven years of plenty, the earth produced much grain. The excess grain was gathered from the fields and placed in the cities [in storage]. The grain was as plentiful as the sand of the sea and was uncountable.

5. **Joseph has children:**
   - Joseph had two children with Asnas prior to the arrival of the years of famine.
   - The first son was named Manasseh, after the fact that G-d allowed Joseph to forget his suffering and the home of his father.
   - The second son was named Ephraim, over the fact that G-d made him multiply in his land of suffering.

Fourth Aliyah

6. **The years of famine:**
   - After the end of the seven years of plenty began the seven years of famine, as Joseph had said would occur. There was a famine in all the lands, although in Egypt there was plenty of bread.
   - The people of Egypt screamed to Pharaoh for bread and he sent them to Joseph, and instructed them to do as he commands. Joseph opened all his storehouses and sold grain to Egyptians. The famine was in all the lands of the earth and intensified in the land of Egypt.
   - People from all lands came to Egypt to buy food

Chapter 42

7. **The brothers travel to Egypt to buy produce:**
   - <u>Jacob sends his sons to Egypt</u>: Jacob saw that there is food in Egypt and told his children to travel there and buy food, so they live and not die. The brothers of Joseph did as they were instructed, and traveled to Egypt to buy food. Benjamin was not sent with them as he feared a tragedy may fall upon him.
   - <u>The brothers meet Joseph the viceroy and are accused of espionage</u>: The brothers of Joseph arrived in Egypt and came to buy grain amongst the other customers. Joseph was the ruler of the land and he was the one who sold the grain to all the people of the earth. The brothers came to Joseph and prostrated themselves on the ground before him. Joseph saw his brothers and recognized them, although they did not recognize him. He acted to them like a stranger and spoke to them harshly. He asked them "From where have you come?" and they replied from the land of Canaan to buy produce. Joseph then remembered his dreams and said to them "You are spies who have come to survey the land." The brothers denied any such wrongdoing saying that they are all brothers, the son of one father, and are being honest. They are 12 brothers in total and the younger one has remained home, and one is missing. Joseph refused to accept their denial and continued to accuse them of being spies. He gave them an ultimatum to prove their innocence "Either bring me your younger brother, or I swear by Pharaoh's life that you are spies." One of you will go back to the land of Canaan to bring him, and the remainder of you will remain in prison. The brothers were imprisoned for three days. On the third day, he took them out and reinstructed them to go home and bring back their youngest brother.

Fifth Aliyah

   - Joseph said that one brother will remain imprisoned while the remainder can travel home and bring food for their families, and then bring back the youngest brother in order so they can prove their claim and not die. The brothers did as they were told.
   - <u>The brothers bemoan what they did to Joseph</u>: The brothers turned to each other and said "We are guilty over what we did to our brother, when we saw him pleading with us from his suffering, and we ignored him. This is why this suffering has come upon us." Reuben replied saying "Did I not tell you to not sin with the lad and you guys did not listen to me. Now, we are being held accountable for his blood." They did not know that Joseph understood what they were saying, as he had the interpreter present. Joseph walked away from them and cried.

- The brothers are sent off and Simeon is imprisoned: Joseph returned and placed Simeon in prison, in front of them. Joseph commanded that their bags be filled with food and their money should be replaced, each person in his bag. They should also be given food for the journey, and so was done.
- The return journey: The brothers traveled with their bags on their donkeys, and during one of their rest stops, one of the brothers noticed that his money was returned to his bag. After he informed his brothers they were very frightened and exclaimed "What has G-d done to us?"

8. **The brothers return home to get Benjamin:**
   - The brothers report back to Jacob: The brothers arrived home and told their father Jacob all that had occurred, and that the leader of the land spoke with them very harshly and accused them of being spies. "We denied the claims, saying that we are a family of 12 brothers, and the youngest has remained home, and the leader instructed us to prove our innocence by bringing our younger brother back with us."
   - The brothers discover their moneys were returned: As each brother opened his sack they discovered that their bags of money were all returned.
   - Jacob refuses to send Benjamin: Jacob lamented, saying "You have orphaned me. Joseph is no longer, Simeon is no longer and now you want to take Benjamin. Reuben offered to take responsibility of Benjamin, and that his two sons be put to death if he does not return him. Jacob refused the offer, as his brother had a tragedy occur to him, and Benjamin is all he has left.

Chapter 43

- Jacob runs out of food and is forced to send Benjamin: The famine was very severe, and when all the food that was brought from Egypt was consumed, Jacob instructed his sons to return to Egypt and buy food. Judah told his father that the leader forewarned them that they will not receive an audience unless they bring their brother back with them. Judah gave his father an ultimatum: "If you agree to send our brother with us we will go and buy you food, otherwise we will not go." Israel replied to them "Why did you cause me evil and tell the man that you have a brother." The brothers replied that the man inquired about their family and we answered truthfully. "Could we have known that he would ask us to bring our brother down?" Judah spoke and told his father that he will be responsible for Benjamin's return and if he does not bring him back, he will be held accountable for all his days. "Let us go and live and not die. If we had not delayed until now, we could have returned already twice." Israel their father consented and instructed his sons to take from the products of the land as a gift to the leader. "Take some balsam, honey, wax, birthwort, pistachios, and almonds. Take with you a double sum of money, and bring with you the money's that were returned to your bags. May G-d grant you mercy before the man and he will release your other brother and send him with you, with Benjamin.

9. **The brothers travel with Benjamin to Egypt and meet the viceroy:**
   - The brothers did as they were instructed, and took with them the presents, the moneys, and Benjamin and appeared before Joseph.

Sixth Aliyah

10. The brothers are invited for a meal in the house of Joseph:

- After Joseph saw Benjamin and he told his home manager to invite the men for an afternoon meal. He did as he was told, and the men entered the home of Joseph.

- The brothers fear accusation of robbery: The brothers feared that they are being brought to the home of the leader to be accused of stealing the money that was found in their sack, and be taken as slaves. They approached the manager of the home and spoke to him by the entrance, explaining to him that they had not stolen the money, and they had brought back with them the money found in their sacks, as well as other money's. The manager told them not to worry, as their money was received, and G-d had placed them a treasure in their sacks.

- The hospitality and greeting of Joseph: Simeon was then released to the brothers. The manager entered the men into the home and gave them water to wash their feet, and fodder for their donkeys. The brothers prepared the gift and waited for the return of Joseph in the afternoon. When Joseph returned they gave him the gift and bowed to him on the ground. Joseph asked them as to how their father is doing. They replied that their father is still alive, and bowed. Joseph raised his eyes and saw Benjamin, his brother, and asked them "Is this the younger brother that you told me about?" Joseph then said, "May G-d be gracious to you."

Seventh Aliyah

- Joseph breaks down crying: Joseph was overcome with emotion of mercy for his brothers and went into a nearby room to cry. He washed his face and came out, restraining himself.

- The meal: Joseph instructed for the meal to be served. Joseph and the Egyptians was served separately from his brothers, as they could not eat together with them, as doing so is viewed as an abomination in Egypt. Joseph had each brother seated in accordance to their age, and the brothers looked at each other with surprise. Joseph had a portion given to each one, although to Benjamin he gave a portion that was five times the size of the others. They all ate and drank together and became drunk.

Chapter 44

- The goblet of Joseph is planted in the sack of Benjamin: Joseph instructed his home manager to fill their sacks with food and return their money to their sacks. "My silver goblet should be planted in the sack of the youngest brother." The man did as he was told. In the morning, the brothers were sent off. As soon as they exited the city, Joseph instructed his manager to give chase to them and accuse them of being ungrateful for having stolen his goblet. The manager did as he was told and accused them of stealing. The brothers vehemently denied the accusations, saying that they even returned the money that they found in their sacks, and hence why would they steal anything from the home of the leader. They concluded: "If you shall find the goblet in any of our sacks, that individual will be killed, and we will become slaves to your master." The man however replied that only the individual whose sack contains the goblet will be held as a slave, while the remainder will be held free of accountability.

- The goblet is found in the sack of Benjamin and the brothers return to Joseph: The brothers took down their sacks and opened them. The man searched the sacks, beginning with the eldest brother, and concluding with the youngest, and the goblet was found in the sack of Benjamin. They tore their clothing and replaced the sacks on their donkeys to return to the city. Judah and his brothers returned to the home of Joseph and fell to their faces. Joseph asked them how they could do such a thing and Judah replied that they have nothing to answer, as G-d has found sin with them. Judah offered that they all become slaves to Joseph. Joseph replied that it is beneath him to enslave everyone, and rather only the guilty brother will be held as a slave, while everyone else may return home to their father.

Parashat Vayigash

Verses: 106 [Siman: יהללאל]
Haftorah: Ezekiel 37:15-28

Number of Mitzvot:
There are no Positive or Negative commands mentioned in Parashat Vayigash.

First Aliyah

1. Judah contends with Joseph to release Benjamin:

- Judah confronted Joseph and asked to speak, saying that he is like Pharaoh. Judah recounted before Joseph the chain of events, of how he was asked to provide information about his family.
- He stated that their youngest brother was home, and Joseph then requested that he be brought before him. They implored before Joseph not to do so, as it could cause the premature death of Jacob. "You replied that we will not be able to see you again until we do so."
- "When we came to our rather and recounted what you asked, our father refused to send our youngest brother, due to fear that tragedy may befall him on the way. If we now return without Benjamin [this could have tragic consequences on Jacob's health as] his soul is interconnected with his [i.e. Benjamin's] soul."

Second Aliyah

- When Jacob will see that Benjamin did not return, he will die."
- "I have become a personal guarantor for the return of my brother, let me then sit as a slave in place of my brother, and let the lad return back home with his brothers. How can I return without my brother and witness the evil that will befall my father?"

Chapter 45

2. Joseph reveals himself to the brothers:

- Joseph could no longer hold himself back and he asked everyone [except for his brothers] to leave his presence, so he could reveal himself to his brothers.
- Joseph cried and the news was heard in the Egypt and in the house of Pharaoh.
- Joseph told his brothers "I am Joseph, is my father still alive?" The brothers could not answer him, due to shock. Joseph requested the brothers come forward and repeated and said "I am Joseph your brother who you sold to the Egyptians. Now, do not be saddened or angry that you sold me here, as G-d sent me here to provide food. There has thus far been two years of famine, and another five years remain. G-d sent me here to support you and give you food."

Third Aliyah

- "It is not you who sent me here, but G-d, in order to become ruler of Egypt."

3. **Joseph instructs his brothers and asks them to bring their father to Egypt:**
   - The proposition: Joseph told his brothers to hurry and go back to father and tell him that his son Joseph has become ruler of all Egypt, and that he should come to him. "You will be given the settlement of Goshen to live. You will be close to me, as well as your children and grandchildren, and cattle. I will support you for the remaining five years of famine, lest you all starve." Joseph then turned to his brothers and said "Your eyes see, and the eyes of my brother Benjamin, that it is I who speaks to you. Go tell father of all the honor I have in Egypt, and go and hurry to bring father down here."
   - The embracing of Joseph and his brothers: Joseph fell on the neck of Benjamin, and he cried, and Benjamin cried on his shoulder. Joseph kissed each one of his brothers and cried on them, and then the brothers spoke to him.
   - Pharaoh instructs Joseph to instruct the brothers/father: The house of Pharaoh heard of the arrival of Joseph's brothers, and it found favor in his eyes and the eyes of his servants. Pharaoh instructed Joseph to tell his brothers to take back their loaded donkeys and return to the land of Canaan. "Go bring your father, and household, and I will provide you the best of Egypt, and you will eat the fat of the land."

Fourth Aliyah (according to most Chumashim)

- "Take from Egypt wagons for your children and wives, and carry back your father. Don't worry of leaving your items, as the best of the land of Egypt is yours."
- The brothers listened to the instructions.
- The presents: Joseph gave the brothers wagons as Pharaoh instructed, and he gave them food for the journey. Everyone received clothing. Benjamin received five pairs of clothing and 300 silver coins. To his father, Joseph sent ten donkeys carrying the best of Egypt. Ten mules carrying bread and food for his father for the journey.
- The message: The brothers went off on their journey, with a parting message from Joseph, telling them not to quarrel on the journey.

4. **Jacob is informed that Joseph is alive:**
   - The brothers left Egypt and arrived by Jacob their father.
   - They told him that Joseph is alive, and he is ruler of Egypt. Jacob did not believe them. They told him all the words of Joseph, and Jacob saw the wagons that Joseph sent from Egypt to carry him, and Jacob's spirit was revived.

Fourth Aliyah (according to Torah Temima/Chabad) Fifth Aliyah (according to most Chumashim)

- Israel said, "My son Joseph is still alive, I will go see him before I die."

Chapter 46

5. **Jacob and family travel to Egypt:**
   - Arrival to Beer Sheva: Israel and all his family traveled and arrived to Beer Sheva.
   - Sacrifices: In Beer Sheva, Jacob offered sacrifices to the G-d of his father Isaac.
   - G-dly revelation: G-d appeared to Israel at night and said "Jacob, Jacob" and Jacob replied, "Here I am." G-d said "I am the G-d of your father. Do not fear to enter Egypt, as

I will make you into a great nation there. I will descend with you to Egypt, and I will take you out. Joseph will place his hands on your eyes."

- Jacob traveled from Beer Sheva with all his family, his sons and daughters, and grandchildren, and was brought in the wagons, by his sons, to Egypt.
- They traveled with all their cattle and belongings.

Fifth Aliyah *(according to Torah Temima/Chabad)*

6. **Jacobs family who arrived in Egypt:**
   - The following are the children and grandchildren who traveled with Jacob to Egypt:
   1. The firstborn is **Reuben**. The following are his sons:
      - Hanoch
      - Palu
      - Hetzron
      - Carmi
   2. **Simeon** had the following sons:
      - Yemuail
      - Yamin
      - Ohad
      - Yahin
      - Tzohar
      - Shaul the son of the Canaanite Woman (Dinah).
   3. **Levi** had the following sons:
      - Gershon
      - Kehas
      - Merari
   4. **Judah** had the following sons:
      - Er, who deceased in the land of Canaan.
      - Onan, who deceased in the land of Canaan.
      - Shailah
      - Peretz and his children
         - Hetzron
         - Hamul
      - Zarah
   5. **Issachar** had the following sons:
      - Tola
      - Puvah
      - Yov
      - Shimron
   6. **Zebulun** had the following sons:
      - Sered
      - Ailon
      - Yahle'ail
   - The above were the sons of Leah, in addition to Dina his daughter, for a total of 33 people.

7. **Gad** had the following sons:
   - Tzifyon
   - Chagi
   - Shuni
   - Etzbon
   - Airi
   - Arodi
   - Areli

8. **Asher** had the following sons:
   - Yimnah
   - Yishvah
   - Yishvi
   - Briyah and his children
     - Hever
     - Malkiel
   - Serach their sister

- The above were the sons of Zilpa, who Laban gave to Leah his daughter, for a total of 16 people.
- Rachel, the wife of Jacob, had Joseph and Benjamin.

9. **Joseph** had the following sons in Egypt with his wife, Asnas Bas Poti Fera:
   - Manasseh
   - Ephraim

10. **Benjamin** had the following sons:
    - Bela
    - Becher
    - Ashbail
    - Gaira
    - Naaman
    - Aichi
    - Rosh
    - Mupim
    - Hupim
    - Ard

o The above were the sons of Rachel, for a total of 14 people.

11. **Dan** had the following sons:
    - Hushim

12. **Naftalai** had the following sons:
    - Yachtzeail
    - Guniy
    - Yaitzer
    - Shilaim

- The above were the sons of Bilah, who Laban gave to Rachel his daughter, for a total of 7 people.

- The total number of descendants: The total amount of descendants who came with Jacob to Egypt, aside for the wives of his sons, is 66. Joseph had two sons in Egypt, making it a total of 70.

Sixth Aliyah

7. **Jacob's arrival to Egypt:**
   - Sending Judah to Goshen: Jacob sent Judah ahead of him to direct him to Goshen.
   - Joseph meets his father: Joseph harnessed his wagon and went to meet his father in Goshen. He met with him and fell on his neck and wept. Jacob said to Joseph "I can die now, after seeing your face, as you are still alive."

Chapter 47

- The brothers meet Pharaoh and settle in Goshen: Joseph told his brothers and father that he will inform Pharaoh of their arrival from the land of Canaan. "The people are shepherds, and they brought with them all their cattle." Joseph told his brothers "When Pharaoh summons you, and asks of your occupation, tell him that you have always been shepherds, in order so you will be settled in Goshen, as shepherds are an abomination in Egypt." Joseph came and told Pharaoh of his father's and brother's arrival, and settled in Goshen. Joseph took with him five of his brothers and presented them to Pharaoh. Pharaoh asked the brothers as to what they do, and they replied that they have always been shepherds. They asked Pharaoh permission to settle in the land of Goshen, as they have come with a lot of cattle and require grazing land. Pharaoh replied to Joseph that they could settle wherever they desire, and they could settle in Goshen, and if they are capable, you [i.e. Joseph] should appoint them managers of my livestock.
- Jacob meets Pharaoh: Joseph presented Jacob to Pharaoh and Jacob blessed Pharaoh. Pharaoh asked Jacob as to his age, and he replied that he is 130 years old. They have been few and filled with suffering.

Seventh Aliyah

8. **Jacob and his family settle in Egypt:**
   - Joseph gave his father and brothers land in Rameses, as Pharaoh instructed, and he supported them with food.

9. **Joseph provides food for the nation:**
   - There was no food in the world, and Egypt and Canaan became weary due to hunger.
   - Money is used to purchase food: Joseph gathered all the money in Egypt and Canaan, as a result of their food purchases. The money was brought to the house of Joseph.
   - Cattle is used to purchase food: After the money ran out in Egypt and Canaan, all the people of Egypt approached Joseph and asked him for food, lest they die. Joseph then told them to trade their cattle in exchange for food. So, the Egyptians gave Joseph their horses, sheep, cows, and donkeys in exchange for food.
   - Land and people are traded in for food: After the first year of famine, the Egyptians implored Joseph to buy them as slaves, and buy their lands, in exchange for food. Joseph thus proceeded to purchase the entire land of Egypt for Pharaoh. The only land that was not purchased is the land of the priests, who were provided food by Pharaoh.
   - The people are moved around Egypt: Joseph moved the people from their native towns to the ends of Egypt.

- <u>Joseph distributes seeds for planting</u>: Joseph distributed seeds to the people for them to plant and grow food in the lands. The people were instructed to give 20% to Pharaoh, and the remaining 80% they could keep for themselves.
- Israel settled in the land of Egypt, in Goshen and multiplied.

Parashat Vayechi
Verses: 85 [Siman: פה אל פה]
Haftorah: Kings 1 2:1-12

Number of Mitzvot:
There are no Positive or Negative commands mentioned in Parashat Vayechi.

First Aliyah

1. **Jacob summons Joseph and requests to be buried in Israel:**
   - The length of Jacob's years: Jacob lived in Egypt for 17 years, and he lived for a total of 147 years.
   - As his days of passing were approaching, Jacob summoned his son Joseph and asked him to place his hand under his thigh and "Perform for me kindness and truth, and do not bury me in Egypt. Please carry me out of Egypt and bury me by my forefathers." Joseph replied that he will do as requested.

Chapter 48

2. **Joseph brings his sons to his father, and is blessed:**
   - After the above occurrence, Joseph was told that his father is sick, and he brought to him his sons, Ephraim and Manasseh. Jacob was informed that his son Joseph was arriving, and he strengthened himself to sit on the bed.
   - Ephraim and Manasseh are recognized as tribes: Jacob told his son Joseph that G-d appeared to him in Luz and blessed him that he will have many offspring. "Now, you should know, your two sons, Ephraim and Manasseh, are to me considered like Reuben and Simeon. However, any children born after them will be part of their tribal name."
   - Jacob retells the story of Rachel's death: "When I traveled from Padan Aram, Rachel died on the journey, on the way to Efrat. I buried her there on the road to Efrat, which is Bethlehem."

3. **Jacob blesses Ephraim and Manasseh:**
   - Jacob then looked at the sons of Joseph and asked, "Who are they?" Joseph replied to his father that they are his sons whom G-d has blessed him with. Jacob asked for the sons to be brought to him, to be blessed.

Second Aliyah

   - Jacob's eyes were getting old and as a result he could not see. The sons of Joseph were brought to Jacob, and he kissed them and hugged them. Jacob remarked "I had not even dreamed of seeing you and now I see your children." Joseph removed the children from Jacob's knees and prostrated to the ground.
   - Jacob switches his hands: Joseph brought both sons, and positioned Ephraim to his right, to the left of Israel, and Manasseh to his left, to the right of Israel. Israel placed his right hand on the head of Ephraim and his right hand on the head of Manasseh. He moved his hand with intelligence, as Manasseh was the firstborn.

- <u>The blessing</u>: Jacob blessed Joseph and said "The G-d who has been with me and my forefathers, the angel who has redeemed me from all evil, he should bless the children and they should be called by my name and the name of my forefathers, Abraham and Isaac. They shall multiply on earth like fish."

Third Aliyah

- <u>Joseph attempts to realign the hands of his father</u>: When Joseph saw that his father placed right hand on the head of Ephraim, it displeased him, and he went forward to remove his father's right hand from the head of Ephraim and place it on the head of Manasseh. Joseph said to his father that it is incorrect, as Manasseh is the firstborn, and he deserves the right hand on his head. Jacob refused, and told his son "I know my son that he too will become a nation, however his younger brother will be greater than him, and will multiply amongst the nations."

- <u>The blessing</u>: Jacob blessed the children that day, saying that the Jewish people will bless [their children] by saying "Let G-d place you like Ephraim and like Manasseh" and he said Ephraim before Manasseh.

- Israel told Joseph "I will die, and G-d will be with you, and return you the land of your forefathers. I am giving you Shechem, one portion more than your brothers, of which I took from the hand of the Amorites."

Chapter 49
Fourth Aliyah

4. **Jacob's final message to his children:**
   - <u>What will occur in the end of days</u>: Jacob summoned his sons and asked them to assemble so they can be told what will occur in the end of days.
   - <u>Reuven's final message from his father</u>: "Reuben, you are my first born. You are the first of my strength and vigor, and fit to be greater than all [your other brothers]. However, you were haste like water and caused your father's bed to be defiled by interfering with your father's bed. You will not be privileged to take more [than your other brothers]."
   - <u>Simeon and Levi's final message from their father</u>: "Simeon and Levi, brothers, who use stolen tools as weapons. Do not let my name be mentioned with their schemes, and in their congregation my honor will not take part. With their wrath they killed man, and in their wishes, they uprooted an ox. Let their wrath be cursed, as it is mighty. I will scatter them amongst Israel."
   - <u>Judah's final message from his father</u>: "Judah, your brothers will acknowledge you. Your hand will be at the neck of your enemies, and your fathers' sons will prostate themselves to you. Judah, you are a lion's cub who ascended from prey. You crouch like a lion and who can lift you. The rod shall not depart from Judah, nor legislators from between his feet, until the arrival of Shilo. To him the nations will assemble. He ties the male donkey to the vine and the female donkey to the branch. He launders his clothing in wine and his robe in the blood of grapes. His eyes become red from the wine, and his teeth white from milk."
   - <u>Zebulun's final message from his father</u>: "Zebulun, you shall dwell by the shores of the sea, and at the harbor of ships, until Tzidon."

- Issachar's final message from his father: "Issachar, you are a strong donkey resting between the city borders. He sees that his portion is good, and a land that is fertile. He will bend his shoulder to bear and will pay his dues by serving."
- Dan's final message from his father: "Dan will seek justice for his nation and the tribes of Israel will be as one. Dan will be a serpent on the road and a viper on the path that bites the heels of a horse and causes its rider to fall. For your salvation I await, G-d."

Fifth Aliyah

- Gad's final message from his father: "A battalion will sprout from Gad and he will troop backwards."
- Asher's final message from his father: "From Asher will come rich food and he will provide royal delicacies of a king."
- Naftali's final message from his father: "Naftali is a gazelle who runs quickly, for whom people give thanks and blessing."
- Joseph's final message from his father: "Joseph is a charming son, a charm to the eye. Girls stepped up to see him. They embittered him, fought with him, and the archers hated him. Nonetheless, he remained steadfast and became a shepherd, providing for Israel. G-d will help you and bless you with the blessing of heavens and blessings of the depths below. Let the blessings of my father be upon your head."

Sixth Aliyah

- Benjamin's final message from his father: "Benjamin is a wolf who kills his prey. In the morning he eats his spoils, and in the evening he distributes it."
- All these are the tribes of Israel, 12 in number, and he blessed them, each according to his blessing.

5. Jacob's instructs to be buried in Cave of Machpelah:
- Jacob instructed his sons that after he passes away, he is to be buried in the Cave of Machpeila. This refers to the cave found in the field of Ephron the Hittite, which was bought by Abraham from Ephron. "My ancestors are buried there. Abraham and his wife Sarah were buried there. Isaac and his wife Rebecca were buried there, and there I buried Leah."

6. Jacob passes away:
- After Jacob completed instructing his sons he placed his feet together on the bed and passed away.

Chapter 50

- Joseph fell on his father's face and cried on him and kissed him.
- The embalming: Joseph commanded his servants, the doctors, to embalm his father, and they did so.
- The mourning: After forty days of the embalming, the Egyptians mourned his passing for [a total of] seventy days.

7. **Jacob is buried in Israel:**
   - <u>Asking permission</u>: After the mourning period, Joseph asked the house of Pharaoh for permission to fulfill his oath to his father, to bury him in the land of Canaan. Pharaoh agreed.
   - <u>The funeral procession</u>: Joseph went to bury his father, and all the servants of Pharaoh came with him, and the elders of Egypt. All his and his father's households, his brothers, came with him, and only the children and cattle remained in Goshen. It was a very large procession of people who came.
   - <u>The eulogy and mourning</u>: When they arrived to Goren Haatad a great and heavy eulogy took place and they mourned Jacob for seven days. The Canaanite nations took notice of the great funeral procession, and the mourning, and therefore name this place, Avel Egypt.
   - <u>The burial</u>: The children of Jacob did as they were instructed and buried him in the Cave of Machpelah.

8. **Joseph and his brothers make peace with what they did to him:**
   - After the burial, Joseph, his brothers, and the entire funeral procession returned to Egypt.
   - The brothers feared that now that their father has passed on, Joseph will hate them and take revenge against them for what they did. They thus connivingly told Joseph that prior to Jacob's death he told them to tell Joseph to forgive his brothers. When Joseph heard this, he began to cry. His brothers also cried, and they threw themselves before him offering themselves as slaves. Joseph assured them saying that he is not in the place of G-d, and that G-d set up his kidnapping for the sake of him rising to his position to provide food for the people.

Seventh Aliyah
   - Joseph then promised the brothers not to fear, as he will provide them and their families with food. Joseph comforted them.

9. **Joseph passes away:**
   - <u>His years</u>: Joseph lived a total of 110 years. He saw three generations from his son Ephraim. The sons of Machir, the son of Manasseh, were raised on Joseph's knees.
   - <u>Joseph's final message to his brothers</u>: Joseph told his brothers that he will die, and that G-d will remember them and take them out of Egypt to the land that was promised to Abraham, Isaac and Jacob. Joseph made the brothers swear that when they leave Egypt they will take his bones with them.
   - Joseph passed away at the age of 110. He was embalmed and placed in a coffin in Egypt.

Shemot/Exodus

Parashat Shemot
Verses:124 [Siman: יוקה]
Haftorah:[1] Isaiah 27:6-28:13; 29:22-23

Number of Mitzvot:
There are no Positive or Negative commands mentioned in Parashat Shemot.

Chapter 1
First Aliyah

1. **The family of Jacob who arrived in Egypt:**
   - These are the names of the children of Israel who came to Egypt. Reuben, Simeon, Levi, Judah, Issachar, Zebulun, Benjamin, Don, Naftali, Gad, Asher. A total of seventy souls who descended from Jacob were in Egypt.
   - Joseph and all his brothers and all that generation passed away.
   - The Jewish people reproduced and multiplied to great numbers, and the earth became filled with them.

2. **The slavery begins:**
   - The plan: A new king was appointed over Egypt who did not know Joseph. He told his nation that the Jewish people have multiplied more than us, and therefore we should conspire a plan to deal with them, lest they multiply even more and drive us out of our land.
   - The slavery: Pharaoh appointed tax collectors to make the Jewish people work in hard labor, and had them build cities of storage for Pharaoh, the cities of Pithom and Raamses. The more the Jews were oppressed, the more they multiplied. The Egyptians became disgusted by the Jewish people.
   - The Egyptians enslaved the Jews with crushing labor. They were worked with hard labor involving mortar and bricks and every labor of the field. All the labors they performed were crushing and back breaking work.

3. **The midwives Shifrah and Puah, and the decree to kill the boys:**
   - Pharaoh instructed the Jewish midwives, Shifrah and Puah, to kill all the male children born to the Jewish people. The girls were to be spared. The midwives feared G-d and did not listen to his instructions and allowed the male children to live.

Second Aliyah
   - Pharaoh confronted the midwives and they replied that the Jewish people are akin to wild animals who give birth on their own. The Jewish people thus continued to multiply. G-d gave the midwives homes in reward of them fearing Him.
   - The decree to kill all the male born children in Egypt: Pharaoh then commanded his entire nation to kill their male born children, while sparing the females.

---

[1] So is followed by Ashkenazi and Chabad communities. However, Sefaradi communities read from Yermiyahu 1:1-2:3

Chapter 2

4. **Moses is born and placed in the river:**
   - A Levite man took a Levite daughter for a wife and the woman became pregnant and had a son. The mother saw that he was good and so she hid him for three months.
   - <u>Moses is placed in the river</u>: After this time expired, his mother placed him in a reed basket, smeared it with clay and tar, and entered him into the reeds of the banks of the Nile river. His sister stood from a distance to see what would happen to him.

5. **Baby Moses is rescued:**
   - <u>Bithiah rescues Moses</u>: The daughter of Pharaoh [i.e. Bithiah] was strolling with her maidservants by the river and when she saw the basket, she stretched her hand and took it. She opened it and saw a lad crying and had mercy on him. She exclaimed that the child is from the Jewish people.
   - <u>Jochebed nurses Moses</u>: The sister of Moses [i.e. Miriam] offered Bithiah to bring a Jewish wet nurse to nurse the boy. After her acceptance, she summoned the boy's mother who nursed her son in exchange for payment from Bithiah.
   - <u>Moses grows up</u>: The child grew up and became adopted by the daughter of Pharaoh as a son. She named him Moses, as he was drawn from the river.

Third Aliyah

6. **Moses kills the Egyptian and flees:**
   - Moses grew up and visited his brethren, witnessing their slavery. He saw an Egyptian man hitting one of his Jewish brothers. Moses turned both ways, seeing no one around, he struck the Egyptian, killing him and buried him in the ground.
   - <u>Moses flees</u>: The second day he came out he saw two Jews fighting, and admonished the wicked man for hitting his friend. The wicked man replied, "Who placed you as a ruler over us, will you kill me like you did to the Egyptian?" Moses feared that word of the murder would spread, and eventually the news reached Pharaoh who desired to kill him. Moses fled to Midian to escape death.

7. **Moses in Midian, his marriage and children:**
   - Moses fled to Midian and settled there.
   - <u>Moses gives the sheep of Jethro to drink</u>: Moses sat by the well and saw the seven daughters of Jethro, who was the priest of Midian, coming towards the well in order to give water to their father's flock. The shepherds came and drove them away and Moses got up and saved them and gave their flock to drink.
   - <u>Moses marries Tzipporah and has children</u>: The daughters came home to Reuel their father [i.e. Jethro] who was surprised at their early return home, and asked them as to the reason. They replied that a certain Egyptian man saved them from the shepherds and gave the flock to drink. Jethro replied that they should not have left the man there, and they should go call him to eat bread with us. Moses accepted the request and lived in Jethro's home. Jethro gave his daughter Tzipporah to Moses as a wife. They had a son whom Moses named Gershom, in name of the fact that he was a stranger in a foreign land.

8. **G-d hears the screams of the children of Israel:**
   - After many days, the king of Egypt died [i.e. was afflicted with leprosy] and the Jewish

people groaned and cried due to the labor. Their scream ascended to G-d and He remembered the covenant he made with Abraham and Isaac and Jacob. G-d saw the Jewish people and G-d knew [their suffering].

Chapter 3
Fourth Aliyah

9. The burning bush:

- Moses was grazing the sheep of Jethro his father in-law and he guided the sheep far into the desert. He arrived to the mountain of G-d [i.e. Mount Sinai], towards Horeb. An angel of G-d appeared to him within the bush and Moses saw that the bush was burning but was not getting consumed. Moses said, *"Let me turn to the bush to see this great phenomenon. Why is the bush not getting burnt?"*

- <u>G-d asks Moses to redeem the Jewish people</u>: G-d saw that Moses turned around to see the bush and He called to him from within the bush saying *"Moses, Moses."* *"Here I am,"* replied Moses. G-d replied *"Do not come any closer. Remove your shoes from your feet, as this ground that you are standing on is Holy. I am the G-d of your forefathers; Abraham, Isaac and Jacob."* Moses hid his face as he feared to gaze towards G-d. G-d told Moses *"I have seen the suffering of my people and I have heard their scream and know their pain. I will descend to save them from the hands of the Egyptians and bring them out from Egypt to the good and spacious land which flows with milk and honey. I will bring them to the land of the Canaanite, Hittite, Amorite, Perizi, Hivvite and Jebusite nations. Now, I will send you to Pharaoh to take my nation out of Egypt."*

10. The ensuing conversation of G-d and Moses:

- Moses replied to G-d "Who am I that I should go to Pharaoh and take the Jewish people out of Egypt." G-d responded by saying "I will be with you, and this is the sign [i.e. reason] that I have sent you, as when the nation leaves Egypt they will then serve G-d on this mountain."

- <u>G-d's name</u>: Moses requested G-d for his name, just in case he is question by the Jewish people as to who sent him. G-d replied "Ehyeh Asher Ehyeh, and so you shall tell the Jewish people that Eheyeh sent you to them. Also tell them that the G-d of Abraham, Isaac and Jacob sent you to them." This is my name forever and my remembrance for all generations.

Fifth Aliyah

- <u>Gather the elders of the Jewish people</u>: G-d instructed Moses to gather the elders of Israel and tell them that the G-d of your fathers have appeared to me and He told me "I have remembered that which is being done to you in Egypt, and I shall take you out of the affliction of Egypt to the land of Canaan, a land of milk and honey." G-d told Moses that the elders will listen to his voice.

- <u>The message to Pharaoh</u>: G-d instructed Moses that he and the elders should come all together to the king of Egypt and tell him that G-d the G-d of the Hebrews has come to you, and you request to leave Egypt for a three-day journey to the desert to bring sacrifices to Him. Now, says G-d, I know that he will not adhere to your request to allow you to go, without a mighty hand [striking him].

- <u>G-d promises miracles and wealth</u>: G-d told Moses: I will strike and smite Egypt with all of My wonders, and only afterwards will he send you. I will grant favor of the nation in eyes of the Egyptians and they will not leave empty handed. Each woman will request from her neighbor silver and gold vessels, and clothing, and you will place them on your children and leave Egypt.

Chapter 4

11. Moses argues that the Jewish people will not believe him:
- Moses replied to G-d saying that the Jewish people will not believe him, and not listen to him, as they will claim that G-d did not appear to him.
- <u>Moses's staff turns into a snake</u>: G-d then asked Moses "What is that which you are holding in your hand?" Moses replied, "It is a staff" G-d told Moses to throw it on the ground, and so he did, and it turned into a snake. Moses fled from the snake [out of fright]. G-d told Moses to grab it by the tail, and it turned back into a staff. G-d stated that this was done in order so the Jewish people believe that G-d appeared to you.
- <u>Moses's hand turns white</u>: G-d further told Moses to place his hand in his bosom and he did so. When he took it out, he saw that his hand was white like snow. G-d told Moses to reinsert his hand, and he did so, and when he removed it again it returned back to normal. G-d concluded that if the Jewish people will not believe the first sign then they will believe the second sign.
- <u>A third sign-Turning water into blood</u>: G-d further stated, if they will not listen to the first two signs then you shall take water from the river and pour it on the ground and behold it will turn into blood.

12. Moses argues against being appointed as messenger:
- <u>Moses argues that he can't speak</u>: Moses replied to G-d that he cannot do the job as he has speech disorders and thus cannot articulate his words properly. G-d responded that He is the one who grants the ability to speak, or to be mute, or deaf, or smart, or blind.
- <u>G-d appoints Aaron to join Moses in the mission</u>: Moses again asked G-d to send a different person, and not him. G-d became angry with Moses and told him that his brother Aaron knows to speak, and he has come out to meet him, and he will rejoice in seeing you. G-d told Moses that he should speak to Aaron and tell him what to say and I will be with both of your mouths, and teach you both what to do. Aaron will do the speaking to the nation for you and you will be to him a master. G-d then told Moses to take the staff with him with which the miracles will be performed.

Sixth Aliyah

13. Moses journeys back to Egypt:
- Moses returned to Yeser his father in-law and asked him to allow him to go back to Egypt and visit his brethren. Jethro replied that he can go in peace. G-d appeared to Moses and told him to return to Egypt as all the men who seek to kill him have died.
- Moses took his wife and sons and mounted them on the donkey and returned to Egypt. Moses took the staff with him.
- <u>Moses's job in Egypt and his message to Pharaoh</u>: G-d told Moses that when he returns to Egypt he should perform the miracles before Pharaoh, although I will strengthen his heart and he will not let the nation go. You are to tell Pharaoh: So says G-d, my firstborn son is the Jewish people, send my son out so he can serve Me, and if you refuse to send him I will kill your first-born son.

14. Moses's son is circumcised:

- During the journey, while in the inn, G-d met Moses and desired to kill him [through an angel]. Tziporah took a sharp stone and circumcised the foreskin of her son. She threw it at Moses's feet and exclaimed "You are to me a murderer of my husband." The [angel] then loosened his grip on Moses.

15. Moses meets Aaron in the desert:

- G-d appeared to Aaron and told him to go greet Moses in the desert and he went and met Moses by the mountain of G-d and kissed him there. Moses told Aaron all that G-d spoke to him, and that he had sent him on a mission, and of all the miracles he had commanded him to perform.

16. Moses and Aaron gather the elders and show the signs to the Jewish people:

- Moses and Aaron [arrived and] gathered all the elders of the Jewish people. Aaron spoke all the words that Moses was told, and he performed the miracles in front of the nation. The nation believed them, that G-d had remembered the Jewish people and saw their affliction. The nation bowed their heads and prostrated.

Chapter 5
Seventh Aliyah

17. Moses and Aaron approach Pharaoh and request that he frees the Jewish people:

- Moses and Aaron then approached Pharaoh and told him "So has said the G-d of the Jews, let My people go so they can celebrate for Me in the desert." Pharaoh replied "Who is this G-d that I shall listen to His voice to send the Jewish people? I do not know this G-d and I will not send them." They again persisted "The G-d of the Hebrews came to us, so let us please go for a three-day journey to the desert to offer him sacrifices there, lest He strike us with plague or the sword." Pharaoh replied to them "Why is Moses and Aaron disturbing the people from their work. Go mind your own business. The people of the land are many and you want to have them cease working!"

18. Pharaoh increases the conditions of slavery:

- No more straw but same work quota: After Moses's failed request Pharaoh instructed the taskmasters and police to stop giving the people straw to make bricks and rather they will go themselves and gather the straw. "However, the quota of bricks that must be made daily will remain the same. They are being lazy and lax and that is why they are screaming to leave and slaughter for their G-d. Make them work harder and do not pay attention to words of falsity."
- The Jewish people are told the news: The taskmasters and police told the Jewish people of Pharaoh's new work conditions and that they would need to gather their own straw, although the work quota would remain the same.
- The Jewish police are beaten: The Jewish people scattered throughout Egypt to gather straw and the taskmasters would press them to finish the daily quota, as before. The police officers who were appointed by the taskmasters to supervise the work were beaten, as the Jewish people had not met the quota.
- The Jewish police confront Pharaoh: The Jewish police cried before Pharaoh asking why he is doing this to his servants. "You are not giving us straw and you demand we still

follow the daily quota and as a result we are being beaten. This is a sin upon your people. Pharaoh replied "You are being lazy, that is why you are requesting to leave to sacrifice to your G-d. Now, go back to work and straw will not be given to you, although the work quota will remain the same." The Jewish police had to unfortunately relay the news back to the Jewish people that the quota will remain the same, and they had to see them in their suffering.

19. The Jewish police confront Moses and Aaron:

- The Jewish police met Moses and Aaron who were coming towards them as they left their audience with Pharaoh and they said to them "Let G-d look upon you and judge what you caused, as you have destroyed our standing in the face of Pharaoh and his servants, and you have now given them the sword to kill us."

20. Moses confronts G-d:

- Moses returned to G-d saying "My master, why have you caused evil to befall this nation, why did you send me. Since I have come to Pharaoh to speak in Your name, not only have You not saved them, but he has harmed the people. G-d replied to Moses "Now you will see what I will do to Pharaoh, as with a mighty hand I will send them out of his land."

Parashat Vaeira

Verses: 121 [Siman: גִּיבְעוּל]
Haftorah: Ezekiel 28:25-29:21

Number of Mitzvot:
There are no Positive or Negative commands mentioned in Parashat Vaeira.

Chapter 6
First Aliyah

1. **G-d responds to Moses's accusations:**
   - G-d told Moses that He had appeared to his forefathers, Abraham, Isaac, and Jacob with his name Shakaiy and did not make His name Havaya known to them. He had established His covenant with them to give them the land of Canaan. Now, "I have also heard the cry of the Jewish people who are enslaved in Egypt, and I have remembered my covenant."

2. **The Torah recounts Moses's appointment to approach Pharaoh:**
   - G-d instructed Moses "Now, go tell the Jewish people that I will take them out from the Egyptian slavery, with an outstretched arm and great wonders. I will take you for me as a nation, and I will be your G-d. You will know that I am G-d your G-d who takes you out of the burdens of Egypt. I will bring you to the land that I promised your forefathers and give it to you as an inheritance."
   - Moses spoke these words to the Jewish people, but was ignored due to the enormous work and labor.
   - G-d spoke to Moses saying, "Go speak to Pharaoh the king of Egypt and tell him to send the Jewish people from his land." Moses replied back to G-d, "If even the Jewish people would not listen to me, how can I expect Pharaoh to listen, and I have a speech impairment." G-d spoke to Moses and Aaron, commanding them regarding the children of Israel and Pharaoh, to take the Jewish people out of Egypt.

Second Aliyah

3. **Moses and Aaron's lineage:**
   - The following are the heads of the families of the Jewish people:
   - The firstborn is **Reuben**. The following are his sons:
     i. Hanoch
     ii. Pallu
     iii. Chetzron
     iv. Carmi
   - **Simeon** had the following sons:
     i. Yemuel
     ii. Yamin
     iii. Ohad
     iv. Yachin
     v. Tzochar
     vi. Saul the son of a Canaanite.

- **Levi** had the following sons:
    i. Gershon
    ii. Kehot
    iii. Merari
- Levi lived for a total of 137 years.
- **Gershom** had the following sons:
    i. Libni
    ii. Shimei
- **Kehot** had the following sons:
    i. Amram
    ii. Yitzhar
    iii. Hebron
    iv. Uzziel
- Kehot lived for 133 years.
- **Merori** had the following sons:
    i. Machli
    ii. Mushi
- Amram married his aunt Jochebed, and had Aaron and Moses.
- Amram lived for 137 years.
- **Yitzhar** had the following sons:
    i. Korach
    ii. Nefeg
    iii. Zichri
- **Uzziel** had the following sons:
    i. Mishael
    ii. Eltzafan
    iii. Sisri
- Aaron's family: Aaron married Elisheba the daughter of Aminadov, and their children were: Nadab, Abihu, Elazar, and Ithamar
- Korach's family: The children of Korach were Assir, Elkanah, and Aviasaf.
- Elazara's family: Elazar the son of Aaron married one of the daughters of Putiel, and they had Pinchas.
- These were the leaders of the family of Levites.

Chapter 7
Third Aliyah

4. G-d instructs Moses:
- G-d told Moses to go and tell Pharaoh all that I commanded you, and Moses replied that he has a speech impairment and hence cannot talk. G-d replied to Moses that He has appointed him as a ruler to Pharaoh, and Aaron will be his speaker. "You will speak all that I have commanded you, and Aaron will speak to Pharaoh, and he will send the Jewish people from his land. I will harden Pharaoh's heart and increase my miracles and wonders in Egypt. Pharaoh will not listen to you, and I will smite Egypt and take out my nation from Egypt with great plagues. Egypt will then know that I am G-d." Moses and Aaron did as they were told.

- Moses was 80 years old while Aaron was 83 years old at the time they spoke to Pharaoh.

Fourth Aliyah

5. The staff turns into a snake:
   - G-d instructs Moses and Aaron to throw the staff: G-d told Moses and Aaron that when Pharaoh asks them to show him a wonder, then you Moses should tell Aaron to throw the staff in front of Pharaoh and it will miraculously turn into a snake.
   - Moses and Aaron did as they were instructed, and they appeared before Pharaoh. Aaron threw the staff in front of Pharaoh and his servants, and it turned into a snake. Pharaoh summoned his sages and sorcerers, and they too did the above using witchcraft. They threw their staff and it turned into a serpent. Aaron's staff then went ahead and swallowed their staff. Pharaoh hardened his heart and did not agree to let the people go, as G-d predicted.
   - Moses returned to G-d and G-d said to him that Pharaoh has refused to grant permission for the people to go. G-d then instructed Moses to perform the first plague, the plague of blood.

6. The plague of blood:
   - G-d's instructions to Moses to warn Pharaoh and perform the plague: G-d told Moses: Go to Pharaoh in the morning while he is going down to the river and meet him at the river banks. Bring your staff that was turned into a snake, with you. Tell him that G-d, the G-d of the Hebrews has sent me to you to demand that you let his people go serve him in the desert, and since you have thus far refused, He will now prove to you that He is G-d. "I will smite the river using my staff and it will turn into blood. The fish contained in the river will die and pollute the river. Egypt will not be able to drink water from the river." G-d then told Moses to tell Aaron to take the staff and stretch it over the waters of Egypt, over their rivers, wells, lakes and ponds, and it will turn into blood. All of Egypt will be filled with blood including wood and rocks.
   - Moses and Aaron turn the water into blood: Moses and Aaron did as G-d instructed them and he lifted the staff and struck the water in front of Pharaoh and his servants, and all the water in the river turned into blood. The fish in the river died and the river became polluted. The Egyptians could not drink from the river. There was blood in the entire land of Egypt.
   - Egyptian sorcerers do the same and Pharaoh remains stubborn: Egyptian sorcerers used witchcraft to do the same, and likewise turn water into blood. [As a result] Pharaoh hardened his heart and did not adhere their request, as predicted by Moses. Pharaoh went home and ignored the plague.
   - The effect on Egypt: All the Egyptians dug around the river in search for water, as they could not drink from the river. The river remained in its state of blood for seven days.

Chapter 8

7. The plague of frogs:
   - G-d's instructions to Moses to warn Pharaoh and perform the plague: G-d told Moses to go to Pharaoh and tell him that G-d has commanded him to free His nation, so they can serve Him, and if you refuse to send them, your entire country will be struck by a plague of frogs. The river will become infested with frogs and they will enter your home, your

bedrooms, your bed, the homes of your servants and people, your ovens and your dough. G-d told Moses to tell Aaron to stretch the staff over the rivers, ponds and lakes and bring the frogs over the land of Egypt.

- Moses and Aaron infest Egypt with frogs: Aaron stretched his hand over the waters of Egypt and the frog emerged from the river, and they covered the land

- Egyptian sorcerers do the same: The Egyptian sorcerers used witchcraft to do the same, and likewise brought frogs onto the land of Egypt.

- Pharaoh capitulates to the demands: Pharaoh hardened his heart and did not adhere their request as predicted by Moses. Pharaoh summoned Moses and Aaron and asked them to Daven to G-d to remove the frogs from him and his nation, and I will agree to let the people go to serve G-d. Moses asked Pharaoh as to when he wants him to pray to G-d to remove the frogs from amongst his nation, and Pharaoh replied [that he should pray for them to be removed] the [very] next day. Moses agreed.

Fifth Aliyah

- Moses prays: Moses and Aaron left the presence of Pharaoh and prayed to G-d regarding the frogs. G-d did as Moses requested, and the frogs died within the houses and courtyards and fields. The dead frogs were heaped up into piles and they polluted the land.

- Pharaoh refuses to let them go: Pharaoh saw that his country was relieved of the plague and he hardened his heart to not adhere to G-d's command to let the people go.

8. **The plague of lice:**
   - G-d's instructions to Moses to perform the plague: G-d told Moses to tell Aaron to take the staff and hit the dust of the earth, and it will turn into lice. All of Egypt will be filled with lice.

   - Moses and Aaron turn the dust of the land to lice: Moses and Aaron did as G-d instructed them and he lifted the staff and struck the dust of the earth and there were lice all over the people and animals. All of the dust of Egypt turned to lice.

   - Egyptian sorcerers fail to replicate the miracle, but Pharaoh remains stubborn: The Egyptian sorcerers tried using witchcraft to do the same and were unsuccessful. They came to Pharaoh and told him that this plague is the hand of G-d. Pharaoh, however, hardened his heart and refused to adhere to G-d's demands.

9. **The plague of wild animals [Arov]:**
   - G-d's instructions to Moses to warn Pharaoh and perform the plague: G-d told Moses: awaken early in the morning and greet Pharaoh by the river and tell him that G-d demands that he let His people go so they can serve Him, and if you refuse to send them, I will send against you and your servants wild animals. The wild animals will fill the houses of Egypt and its grounds. I will distinguish on that day between the land of Goshen, on which my nation stands, by not having any wild animals there. You then shall know that I am G-d of the land.

Sixth Aliyah

- The plague: G-d did as he warned, and He brought a heavy mixture of wild animals to Pharaoh's home and the home of his servants, and they caused destruction throughout the entire land

- Pharaoh reaction and the ensuing negotiations: Pharaoh summoned Moses and Aaron and told them that they may make sacrifices to their G-d in Egypt. Moses replied that they cannot do so, as it is an abomination in Egypt to slaughter to G-d, and the Egyptians will stone us for doing so. We need to travel a three-day journey, so we can slaughter for our G-d as He will instruct us. Pharaoh replied that he will agree to send them so they could sacrifice to their Lord in the desert, so long as Moses does not go far and he prays for him. Moses replied that as soon as he leaves, he will pray to G-d on his behalf to remove the wild animals tomorrow, although Pharaoh may no longer retract his word and refuse to let the people go to sacrifice to G-d.

- Moses prays: Moses left his audience with Pharaoh and Davened to G-d. G-d did as Moses asked for and he removed the wild animals from Pharaoh and his nation, not one remained.

- Pharaoh refuses to let them go: Pharaoh hardened his heart this time as well and refused to let the people go.

Chapter 9

10. The animal plague [Dever]:

- G-d's instructions to Moses to warn Pharaoh and perform the plague: G-d told Moses to go to Pharaoh and tell him that G-d the G-d of the Hebrews demands that he let His people go so they can serve Him, and if you refuse to send them, He will send a heavy disease against your animals that are in the field. This includes the horses, donkeys, camels, cattle, and flock. It will be a very severe epidemic. G-d will distinguish between the livestock of the Jewish people and that of the Egyptians, and not one Jewish owned animal will die. G-d set an appointed time, saying that the plague will come the next day.

- The plague: The next day G-d did as he warned, and all the animals of the Egyptians died while amongst the Jewish people not even one died.

- Pharaoh refuses to let them go: Pharaoh sent messengers to confirm that indeed no animals died amongst the Jewish people, although nevertheless his heart became hardened and he refused to let the people go.

11. The plague of boils [Shechin]:

- G-d's instructions to Moses to perform the plague: G-d told Moses and Aaron to take a handful of soot, and Moses should throw it upwards towards the heavens, in the presence of Pharaoh. The soot will spread over all of Egypt and turn into boils and blisters on the people and animals.

- The plague: They took the soot, and in the presence of Pharaoh, Moses threw it towards the heavens and sure enough it turned into boils and blisters on the skin of man and animals.

- Egyptian sorcerers: The sorcerers could not stand in front of Moses due to the boils.

- Pharaoh refuses to let them go: G-d hardened the heart of Pharaoh and he refused to let the people go, as G-d predicted.

12. The plague of hail [Barad]:

- <u>G-d's instructions to Moses to warn Pharaoh</u>: G-d told Moses to awaken early in the morning and stand before Pharaoh and tell him that G-d the G-d of the Hebrews demands that he let His people go so they can serve Him, and if you refuse to send them, this time He will send against you all of his plagues so you know that there is none like Me in Egypt. If I wanted, I could have already wiped you and your nation off the face of the earth. However, I spared you, so you can witness my powers and so My name be declared throughout the world.

Seventh Aliyah

- If you still oppress My people and refuse to release them, tomorrow I will rain upon you a very heavy hail of which there has never been before in Egypt.

- <u>G-d warns the Egyptians to bring in their livestock</u>: Now, send your cattle and everything you have in the field into your homes, as anything that remains outside will be destroyed through the hail. The G-d fearing Egyptians adhered to G-d's warning, and brought their slaves and livestock inside. However, those who did not heed His call, left them outside in the field.

- <u>G-d's instructions to Moses to perform the plague</u>: G-d said to Moses: Stretch your hand towards the heavens and hail will fall in all the land of Egypt, on the people and the animals, and on all the vegetation of the earth of Egypt.

- <u>The plague</u>: Moses did as he was told and stretched his hand towards the heavens and G-d sent thunder and hail and fire struck the ground. The hail contained fire blazing within it. It was very heavy, nothing like Egypt has every seen as a nation. The hail struck everything in the field, from man to animal to vegetation. It broke all the trees. Only in the land of Goshen where the Jewish people lived was there no hail.

- <u>Pharaoh summons Moses</u>: Pharaoh summoned Moses and Aaron and told them that he has truly sinned this time, and that G-d is the righteous and he and his nation are the sinners. Pharaoh asked that Moses pray to G-d for the thunder and hail to end and he will send them out without refusing any longer. Moses replied that he will leave the city and stretch his hands to G-d in prayer so that the thunder and hail should end so that they know that the earth belongs to G-d, although he knows that Pharaoh and his people have yet to fear G-d.

- <u>The damage</u>: The flax and the barley were destroyed although the wheat and spelt survived the hail as they had yet to ripen.

- <u>Moses prays</u>: Moses left his audience with Pharaoh and left the city. He stretched his arms to G-d in prayer, and the thunder and hail ceased, and the rain stopped falling.

- <u>Pharaoh refuses to let them go</u>: Pharaoh saw that the rain and hail ceased, and he hardened his heart

Parashat Bo
Verses: 105 [Siman: ימנה]
Haftorah: Jerimiah 46:13-28

Number of Mitzvot:
There are a total of **Twenty** Mitzvot in Parashat Bo. **Nine** positive commands and **eleven** negative commands.

A. Positive commands:
1. **Mitzvah 4/Positive 3:** To sanctify the new moon.
2. **Mitzvah 5/Positive 4:** To slaughter the Pesach offering on the 14th of Nissan.
3. **Mitzvah 6/Positive 5:** To eat the meat of the Pesach offering on the night of the 15th.
4. **Mitzvah 9/Positive 6:** To destroy Chametz on the 14th day of Nissan.
5. **Mitzvah 10/Positive 7:** To eat Matzah the night of the 15th.
6. **Mitzvah 18/Positive 8:** To sanctify the firstborn son and animal towards G-d.
7. **Mitzvah 21/Positive 9:** To tell over the story of the exodus on the night of the 15th.
8. **Mitzvah 22/Positive 10:** To redeem the firstborn male donkey.
9. **Mitzvah 23/Positive 11:** To break the neck of the first-born donkey if it is not redeemed.

B. Negative commands:
1. **Mitzvah 7/Negative 2:** Not to eat the Pesach lamb raw or cooked, but only roasted.
2. **Mitzvah 8/Negative 3:** Not to leave leftovers of the Pesach lamb.
3. **Mitzvah 11/Negative 4:** To not have Chametz found [i.e. own] throughout all seven days of Pesach.
4. **Mitzvah 12/Negative 5:** Not to eat a food that contains Chametz [i.e. Taaruvos Chametz].[1]
5. **Mitzvah 13/Negative 6:** Not to feed the meat of the Pesach sacrifice to a heretic Jew.
6. **Mitzvah 14/Negative 7:** Not to feed the Pesach lamb to a gentile [even] if he is a Toshev Vesachir.
7. **Mitzvah 15/Negative 8:** Not to remove the meat of the Pesach offering from the Chaburah [i.e. group of people that it is being eaten with].
8. **Mitzvah 16/Negative 9:** Not to break a bone from the Pesach sacrifice.
9. **Mitzvah 17/Negative 10:** That an Aral [i.e. uncircumcised Jew] not eat from the meat of the Pesach offering.
10. **Mitzvah 19/Negative 11:** Not to eat Chametz on Pesach.
11. **Mitzvah 20/Negative 12:** Not to see [i.e. own] Chametz all the seven days of Pesach.

---

[1] Listed by Rambam, Chinuch, Admur, however not by Ramban. See Chinuch ibid

Chapter 10
First Aliyah

1. **Plague of locust:**

- <u>G-d commands Moses to approach Pharaoh</u>: G-d commanded Moses to approach Pharaoh, as He has made his heart, and the heart of his servants, stubborn, in order to publicize His miracles amongst them. "In order for the Jewish people to tell over to their children about the plagues that occurred in Egypt, and the miracles that I performed, and so you will know that I am G-d."

- <u>Moses warns Pharaoh of the upcoming plague</u>: Moses and Aaron approached Pharaoh and related to him "So said G-d, the G-d of the Jewish people: Until when will you refuse to answer my requests? Let my people go free so they can serve me. If you continue refusing to send my people, tomorrow I will bring locust into your country." The locust will cover the earth until the point that the earth will not be seen. They will eat all the leftover produce that remained after the plague of hail. They will fill your homes and the homes of all Egyptians, as you have never seen before. Moses and Aaron then left Pharaoh's presence.

- <u>Pharaoh agrees to send out the Jewish people</u>: The servants of Pharaoh said to him "Until when will this matter be a source of suffering for us. Send the people so they can serve G-d, as do you not know that Egypt is in ruins?" Pharaoh summoned Moses and Aaron to return and said to them "Go serve your G-d. Who will be going?" Moses replied, "We will leave with our lads, and elders, our sons and daughters, our sheep and cattle, as it is a festival for G-d." Pharaoh replied to them "Let G-d be with you if I were to send you and your children, as I see evil coming towards you. This is not how it should be. The men shall go and serve G-d, as that is your request." Pharaoh then had Moses and Aaron banished from his presence.

Second Aliyah

- <u>The locust come attack Egypt</u>: G-d told Moses to stretch his hand over the land of Egypt and He will bring a storm of locust over the land. They will consume all the vegetation of the land that was left over from the plague of hail. Moses did as he was instructed, and G-d brought an eastern wind over Egypt which blew throughout that day and night. In the morning, the eastern wind carried the locust into Egypt and they swarmed the entire country like Egypt has never seen before and will never see again. They covered the land and the sky to the point that they darkened the land [preventing sunlight from passing]. They ate all the vegetation of the earth and all the fruits of the trees, to the point that no fruit or vegetation was left in the entire land of Egypt.

- <u>Pharaoh shows remorse</u>: Pharaoh hurried to call Moses and Aaron and told them that he has sinned against G-d their G-d and against them. "Please forgive me for my sins one more time, and pray for me to your G-d, so that He should remove this death."

- <u>Moses prays, and G-d ends the plague</u>: Moses left Pharaoh's presence and prayed to G-d. G-d sent a very strong western wind that carried the locust swarm and dumped them into the river. Not one locust remained in Egypt.

- <u>Pharaoh refuses to let them go</u>: G-d hardened the heart of Pharaoh and he refused to let the people go.

2. Plague of darkness:

- <u>G-d tells Moses to perform the plague</u>: G-d told Moses to stretch his hand towards the heavens, and there will be darkness in the land of Egypt.

- <u>The plague</u>: Moses did so, and the entire land of Egypt fell under complete darkness for three days. No man saw his friend, and no one could move from his place during the duration of those three days. However, the Jewish people had light in all their settlements.

Third Aliyah

- <u>Pharaoh summons Moses</u>: Pharaoh called Moses and told him that the nation, including the children, could leave to serve G-d, on condition that they leave their cattle and flock in Egypt. Moses replied "Also you will give us animals as sacrifices, so we can offer them to G-d. Our cattle will leave with us to serve G-d, and we will not leave even one hoof in Egypt, as we do not know how we will need to serve Him until our arrival." G-d hardened the heart of Pharaoh and he did not agree to send them. Pharaoh said to Moses "leave me, and you are warned not to ever step back here to see me lest you will be put to death." Moses replied, "You speak words of truth, I shall never come to see you again."

Chapter 11

3. G-d instructs Moses of the Plague of the Firstborns and the ensuing imminent exodus:

- G-d told Moses that He will bring one last plague to Pharaoh and Egypt, and Pharaoh will then capitulate completely and let you go and even force you out of Egypt.

- <u>Leaving with wealth</u>: G-d told Moses that he should speak to the Jewish people and inform them [of the imminent exodus and] that each person should request from their [Egyptian] neighbor gold and silver vessels.

- G-d granted the nation favor in the eyes of the Egyptians, and so too Moses became very great in the eyes of Pharaoh and his servants.

Fourth Aliyah

4. Moses warns Pharaoh of Plague of the Firstborns:

- [During the last meeting of Moses with Pharaoh] Moses told Pharaoh that G-d said that at approximately midnight He will go amidst Egypt and smite every first born in the land of Egypt to death, from the firstborn of Pharaoh who is the prince until the firstborn of the slave woman, as well as all firstborn animals. There will be a great outcry in the entire land of Egypt, of which the liking there never was and will never be seen again. However, the Jewish people will remain safe and a dog will not bark against man or animal, so that you see that I have distinguished between the Jewish people and Egypt. Your servants will then all come down and bow to me asking us to leave, and afterwards we shall leave. Moses left Pharaoh's presence in burning anger.

- G-d told Moses that Pharaoh would not listen to him in order so He can increase His wonders in the land of Egypt. Moses and Aaron performed all these miracles before Pharaoh, and G-d strengthened his heart and he did not let them go.

Chapter 12

5. The Jewish people are commanded their first set of Mitzvot:

- <u>Sanctifying the New Moon</u>: G-d told Moses and Aaron to tell the Jewish people that this month is to be for them the first of the months of the year.
- <u>The Pesach lamb</u>: Tell all the Jewish people, that on the 10th of the month they are to take for themselves a lamb/kid, having one lamb/kid per household. If the family is too small to consume an entire lamb/kid, then they should join with another family, counting each person in proportion to the amount he eats. The lamb/kid must be male, within its first year, and unblemished, and it may be taken either from the sheep or goats. The lamb/kid is to be guarded by you until the 14th day, and on the 14th day it is then to be slaughtered in the afternoon by all of the Jewish people.
- <u>Placing the blood by the doorposts</u>: They shall take from the blood [of the sacrifice] and place it by both doorposts, and on the lintel of the doorposts, of the door of the house that they will be eating the sacrifice in.
- <u>Roasting and eating the lamb</u>: The Pesach lamb/kid is to be eaten that night. It is to be roasted and eaten with Matzot and bitter herbs. It may not be eaten raw, or cooked in water, but rather must be roasted over fire. It is to be roasted in full, its head with its legs and its innards. Its meat may not remain past morning, and whatever does remain must be burnt in the fire. It shall be eaten in a haste, with your loins girded and your shoes on your feet.
- <u>G-d will see the blood and Passover the houses</u>: G-d said: I will pass through Egypt that night and smite all the firstborn Egyptians, from man to animal, including the deities of Egypt. The blood on the doorpost shall serve as a sign that you are there, and when I see the blood I will pass over you, and you shall not be smitten while I strike Egypt.
- <u>Celebrating Pesach</u>: This day shall be for you as a remembrance, and you shall celebrate it as a festival for G-d for all generations.
- <u>Chametz and Matzah</u>: You shall eat Matzah for seven days, although on the first day you shall eliminate Chametz from your homes. Whoever eats Chametz between the first and seventh day, his soul will be cut off from the Jewish people. The Matzot must be guarded, and the Matzot are to be eaten from the evening after the 14th day until the 21st day of the month. For seven days, Chametz may not be found in your homes.
- <u>Labor</u>: On the first and seventh day it shall be a calling of holiness, and you shall therefore not do any labor on that day with exception to food related matters.

Fifth Aliyah

6. Moses instructs the Jewish people regarding the Pesach lamb and the upcoming plague:

- Moses summoned all the elders of Israel and instructed them: Each family should take for themselves one of the flock, and slaughter it as a Pesach offering. You shall take a bundle of hyssop and dip it into the blood that is in the basin, and touch with it the lintel and the two doorposts.
- <u>Not to leave home</u>: No man may leave his house until the morning. G-d will pass through Egypt and smite it, and when he sees the blood on your doorposts, the blood will prevent the plague from entering your home.
- You shall guard the above [Pesach sacrifice] as a statute for all generations. When you arrive to the promised land and you follow these laws, your children will ask you why it

[i.e. the Pesach sacrifice] is done, and you shall inform them that it is in commemoration of the fact that G-d smit the Egyptians and passed over the Jewish houses.

- The Jewish nation bowed and prostrated and they went to do that which G-d commanded through Moses and Aaron.

Sixth Aliyah

7. **The plague of Plague of the Firstborns:**
   - At midnight G-d smote every first born in the land of Egypt to death, from the firstborn of Pharaoh who is the prince until the firstborn of the imprisoned captive, as well as all firstborn animals.
   - Pharaoh asks the children of Israel to leave Egypt: Pharaoh and all his servants arose that night, as there was a great cry in Egypt. There was no house without a corpse. Pharaoh summoned Moses and Aaron that night and told them to rise and leave his people. Everyone shall leave and go serve your G-d as you requested. Take your flock and cattle as you asked, and leave, but bless me as well [that I not die].

8. **The children of Israel leave Egypt:**
   - The dough did not have time to rise: The Egyptian nation urged the Jewish people to leave right away, as they said that they were all dying. The nation took its dough prior to it being able to rise and placed it on a sack on their shoulders. They later baked it, after leaving Egypt, into Matzot and not Chametz, as they were driven out of Egypt in a hurry. They did not bring with them other food.
   - Egypt is emptied of its wealth: The Jewish people did as Moses told them, and asked their neighbors for silver and gold vessels, as well as garments. G-d granted the nation favor in the eyes of the Egyptians and they lent them the above. So it was that the Jewish people emptied Egypt [of money].
   - The first journey: The Jewish people traveled from Rameses to Sukkot.
   - Who left: They were 600,000 men, aside for the children. They went with a great multitude [of Egyptian converts]. They left with a very heavy amount of flock and cattle.
   - Amount of years in Egypt: The Jewish people dwelled in Egypt [and their previous areas of foreign land] for 430 years, and at the end of 430 years, on the essence of this day all the legions of G-d left Egypt.
   - Night of gaurding: This night is a night of guarding for all the Jewish people for all generations.

9. **Laws of the Pesach offering:**
   - The following are the laws of the Pesach sacrifice: No gentile may eat it. A slave must be circumcised prior to eating it. It shall be eaten in one's home. One may not remove its meat from the home, and one may not break any of its bones. A convert must be circumcised prior to eating from it. Anyone who is not circumcised may not eat from it.

Chapter 13
Seventh Aliyah

10. Sanctifying the first born:

- G-d spoke to Moses asking him to command the Jewish people: Every male firstborn of the womb of a person or animal is to be sanctified to me. The firstborn male is to be redeemed.
- Firstborn donkey: Every firstborn donkey is to be redeemed with a lamb or kid, and if not then one is to break its neck.
- If your children ask what this [Mitzvah] is [about], then you shall tell him that G-d took us out from slavery with a strong hand, and he killed the Egyptian firstborns, and therefore I sacrifice to G-d my firstborn male animals, and redeem my firstborn sons.

11. Moses instructs the Jewish people the Pesach laws and commands:

- Chametz and Matzah: Moses spoke to the Jewish people telling them of G-d's commands not to eat Chametz during the seven days of Pesach and to celebrate the seventh day. To eat Matzot during the seven days, and not to see Chametz in one's possession.
- Mitzvah of telling over the story of the Exodus: You shall tell your children on this day that it is on account of this that G-d took you out of Egypt.
- Mitzvah of Tefillin/Phylactery: The above is to be made a sign on your hand and a remembrance between your eyes, in order so the Torah of G-d remain on your mouths.

Parashat Beshalach

Verses: 116 [Siman: יד אמונה]
Haftorah: Judges 4:4[1]-5:31

Number of Mitzvot:
There is a total of **One** Mitzvah in Parashat Beshalach. **One** positive command and **Zero** negative commands.

Positive commands:
1. **Mitzvah 24/Negative 13:** Not to leave the Techum/border on Shabbat.[2]

First Aliyah

1. **The children of Israel journey after leaving Egypt:**
   - The route: After Pharaoh sent the nation, G-d, rather than taking them through the land of the Philistines which was a shorter route, he took them the roundabout route through the desert of the Sea of Reeds. This is because G-d feared perhaps the people would turn back if taken by the short route.
   - Arms: The Jewish people were armed when they left Egypt.
   - Joseph's bones: Moses took with him Joseph's bones out of Egypt, as Joseph made the Jewish people swear to take them when they left.
   - Journeying to Eisam: They traveled from Sukkot to Eisam, which was at the end of the desert.
   - The clouds of glory: G-d went before the Jewish people in a pillar of cloud in order to guide them. At night He went before them in a pillar of fire, to shine for them the night, so they could travel by day and by night.

Chapter 14
   - Turning back to Pi Hachiros: G-d instructed Moses to turn back and encamp by Pi Hachiros which is between Migdal and the sea, opposite Baal Tzefon. "Pharaoh will then exclaim regarding the children of Israel that they have trapped themselves in the desert and I will harden his heart so he gives chase, and then Egypt will know that I am G-d."
   - The Jewish people did as they were instructed.

2. **Pharaoh chases after the children of Israel:**
   - Pharaoh was told that the Jewish people had fled, and he and his servants regretted having sent them out. He thus harnessed his chariot and took his people with him. He took six hundred select chariots, together with all of Egypt's chariots to chase after the Jewish people.
   - G-d hardened the heart of Pharaoh to chase after the children of Israel and meanwhile the Jewish people were going out with a raised hand.

---

[1] So is followed by Ashkenazi and Chabad communities. However, Sefaradi communities begin reading from 5:1
[2] Listed by Rambam, Chinuch, however is not considered a Biblical prohibition according to Ramban. See Chinuch ibid; Admur 396:1 for both opinions.

Second Aliyah

3. **The children of Israel realize they are under attack by the Egyptian army:**
   - The Egyptians gave chase after the Jewish people and caught up with them by Pi Hachiros near the sea.
   - <u>The reaction of the Jewish people</u>: The Jewish people looked up in fright seeing Pharaoh and his army coming in on them. The Jewish people cried out to G-d. They said to Moses "Were there not enough graves in Egypt for you to take us out to die in the desert? Why did you take us out of Egypt? Did we not already tell you that we would rather continue in slavery than to die in the desert?
   - <u>Moses's response</u>: Moses said to the nation: "Do not fear, stand fast and you will see the salvation of G-d that he will do for you today. You will never see Egypt again. G-d will fight for you and you shall remain silent."

Third Aliyah

4. **The sea splits:**
   - <u>G-d instructs Moses</u>: G-d told Moses to stop crying at him, and that the Jewish people are to travel. Raise your staff over the sea and split it, and the Jewish people will enter the sea, on dry land. I will harden the heart of Egypt, so they continue to give you chase, and I will be glorified through their army, and Egypt will know that I am G-d.
   - <u>The clouds protect</u>: The pillar of G-d which usually stood before the camp, then moved behind them between the nation and Egypt. The cloud caused darkness for Egypt but gave light to the Jewish people. The two camps did not meet the entire night.
   - <u>The sea splits</u>: Moses raised his staff over the sea and G-d sent a strong east wind the entire night and He turned the sea to dry land, and the sea split. The Jewish people entered the sea and it became for them a wall on the right and left. The entire Egyptian army followed them into the sea in a chase.
   - <u>G-d causes the Egyptian army to enter into disarray</u>: Towards morning, G-d looked down upon the Egyptian camp with a pillar of fire and cloud and He entered them into disarray. He caused the wheels of the wagons to fall off. The Egyptians exclaimed "We shall flee before the Jewish people, as their G-d is fighting for them."

Fourth Aliyah

5. **The sea returns to normal course, annihilating the Egyptian army:**
   - G-d told Moses to stretch his staff over the sea, and its waters shall return, and drown the Egyptian army. Moses did as he was told, and sure enough towards morning the sea returned to its normal course, with the Egyptians fleeing towards it. G-d shook the Egyptians within the water. The water drowned the entire army, leaving not even one survivor.
   - The Jewish people walked through the dry land within the sea and G-d saved them from the Egyptians. They saw the corpses of the Egyptian army on the sea shore. They saw the great hand of G-d over Egypt, and they feared G-d and believed in G-d and Moses His servant.

Chapter 15

6. The song of Az Yashir:

- Moses and the Jewish people then sang the song of Az Yashir to G-d, praising G-d for all that He has done. They said: *"I will sing to G-d, for He is exalted. The horse and rider he plunged into the sea. G-d's strength and power has been to me a salvation. This is my G-d and I will beautify Him, the G-d of my fathers and I will exalt Him. G-d is the master of war, G-d is His name. He cast Pharaoh's chariots and army into the sea, and his best officers were drowned. The depths of the waters covered them, and they descended like stone. Your right-hand G-d is majestically powerful and crushes the enemy. You devastate your opponents, consuming them like straw with Your wrath. With the breath of Your nostrils you caused the water to pile up, and to stand like a wall. You froze water in the depths of the sea. The enemy stated that he will chase and overtake us and then distribute the plunder. You blew Your wind and the sea covered them. They sank like led. Who is like You G-d, among the powerful and holy. You are too awesome to praise, Doer of wonders. You stretch Your right hand and the earth would swallow them. With kindness you led this people to Your holy abode. People heard, and they trembled, the people of Philistia were struck with terror. The heads of the Edomites and Moabites were shocked and shivered. The inhabitants of Canaan melted. May they remain in fear until this nation passes through. You will bring the nation to Your dwelling place, to Your sanctuary. G-d will reign forever."*

7. Miriam sings:

- Miriam the prophetess, the sister of Aaron, took the tambourine, and all the women followed her with tambourines and dancing. Miriam and the women also sang a song to G-d.

8. The children of Israel travel to Marah and find no water to drink:

- <u>Bitter water</u>: Moses led the Jewish people in travel towards the desert of Shur. They traveled for three days and could find no water. They arrived at Marah, and could still not drink water, for the water that was there was bitter, thus lending it its name.
- <u>Moses sweetens the water</u>: The nation complained to Moses asking what they are to drink. Moses cried to G-d and G-d provided him with a stick which he threw into the water, and sure enough, the water became sweet.
- <u>Laws are given</u>: In that area Moses taught the Jewish people a number of laws. He told them that if they obey the commands of G-d, the illnesses of Egypt will never befall them.

Fifth Aliyah

9. The travels of the children of Israel:

- <u>Elim-Water and dates</u>: They traveled to Elim and found there 12 springs of water and seventy date palm trees, and they encamped there.
- They left Elim and traveled to the desert of Sin. This occurred on the 15th of the second month of leaving Egypt [i.e. Iyar].

Chapter 16

10. The Heavenly bread-The Mun:

- The children of Israel complain in hunger: The entire Jewish people complained against Moses and Aaron, saying if only they would have died in the hands of G-d in Egypt, while enjoying pots of meat, and bread to satiation, then to die in the desert in starvation. They accused Moses of taking them out of Egypt to make everyone die of hunger.

- G-d promises Mun: G-d responded to Moses saying that he will rain bread from heaven, and the nation will gather bread each day for that day, and I will test them to see if they follow my laws. On Friday they will receive a double portion.

- Moses informs the nation: Moses and Aaron responded to the Jewish people that in the evening they will be given meat and see that G-d took them out of Egypt, and in the morning they will be given bread and see the glory of G-d who has heard their complaint. "What are we that you complain against us, it is against G-d you should complain."

Sixth Aliyah

- The falling of the Mun: G-d spoke to Moses saying that He had heard the complaint of the Jewish people, and in the afternoon they will eat meat, while in the morning they will eat bread. So it was towards evening that the Slav pheasant bird ascended and covered the camp, and in the morning there was a layer of dew around the camp. The layer of dew then ascended and behold they saw on the face of the desert a thin item looking like frost on earth. The Jewish people looked at each other and exclaimed "It is Mun" as they did not know what to call it. Moses then told them that this is the food that G-d has provided them to eat.

- How much Mun each should take: G-d commanded that each person is take in accordance to what he eats, which is one Omer per person, in accordance to the number of members of one's family. An Omer is 1/10th of an Eipha [2.49 liter]. The Jewish people did so, and some took too much, and some took too little. [Miraculously] whoever took more than necessary or less than necessary, found the exact amount in their possession.

- Not to leave leftover Mun: Moses instructed them not to leave any leftover Mun [that was taken] until morning. Some people did not listen to Moses and left over the Mun past morning, and it became infested with worms and stunk. Moses became angry with them. All the leftover Mun in the field which was not taken would melt in the sun.

- The Friday double Mun portion: On Friday they gathered a double portion, two Omers per head, and the community leaders came to Moses and informed him [of this anomaly]. Moses told them that this was done because the next day is Shabbat, and they must bake and cook today for today, and all the leftovers are to be eaten the next day. So they did, and indeed the next day the leftover Mun remained without spoiling.

- Keeping Shabbat: Moses informed them on Shabbat that the Mun will not fall that day, and they are to only collect it six days a week. Nonetheless, some individuals went to the field on Shabbat to take the Mun and they did not find it. G-d chastised Moses saying "Until when will you refuse my commands? I have given you the resting day of Shabbat and therefore provided you with a double portion on Friday. No man shall leave his area on the seventh day." So the Jewish people rested on the seventh day

- Its taste and texture: The Jewish people called the food Mun, and it was like a coriander seed and had the taste of a wafer fried in honey.

- <u>Safekeeping some of the Mun as a reminder:</u> Moses stated that G-d commanded that an Omer of the Mun is to be kept for safekeeping for all generations, so they see the bread that G-d fed them in the desert when they left Egypt. Moses told Aaron to take a jar and place in it one Omer of Mun, and it was placed before G-d (before the Aron) for safekeeping for all generations.
- <u>How long the Mun lasted:</u> The Jewish people ate the Mun for 40 years, until they arrived at the border of the land of Canaan.

Chapter 17
Seventh Aliyah

11. No water:

- The nation traveled from the desert of Sin to Refidim, and they had no water to drink. They complained at Moses, demanding him to give them water and accusing him of taking them out of Egypt so they and their families and cattle can die of thirst in the desert. Moses replied back to the nation "What do you want from me? Why do you fight with G-d?" Moses then asked G-d what he can do with this nation, as they may stone him.
- <u>Moses hits the rock:</u> G-d instructed Moses to take with him some of the elders of Israel, and to take his staff, and hit the rock that He will be standing near. Once the rock is hit, water will stream out and the nation can drink. Moses did so in front of the elders of Israel. The area was named Maaseh U'Merivah due to the contention that took place and the challenge against G-d.

12. War with Amalek:

- Amalek came and waged a war against the Jewish people in Refidim. Moses told Joshua to conscript an army and wage war with Amalek. Moses would stand on top of a hill with his staff in his hand.
- <u>Moses raises his hands:</u> Joshua did as told, and Moses, Aaron and Chur ascended the hill. Whenever Moses would raise his hands the Jewish people would gain the upper hand of the battle, and when his hands were lowered Amalek would gain the upper hand. Moses's hands became heavy, and they thus took a stone and placed it under him and he sat on it. Aaron and Chur supported his hand, one on each side. His hands remained up until the sun set.
- <u>The result of the war:</u> Joshua weakened Amalek with the sword.
- <u>Obliterating Amalek:</u> G-d told Moses to write this event in a book and tell it to Joshua. G-d promised to obliterate the memory of Amalek from under the heavens. Moses built an altar and called it G-d Nisi. Moses said that "There is a hand on the throne of G-d, G-d is at war with Amalek for all generations."

Parashat Yitro
Verses: 72 [Siman:יונדב]
Haftorah: Isaiah 6:1-13[1]

Number of Mitzvot:

There are a total of **Seventeen** Mitzvot in Parashat Jethro. **Three** positive commands and **Fourteen** negative commands.

A. Positive commands:

1. **Mitzvah 25/Positive 12:** To believe that the world has one G-d who created all the creations, and that He lived and will live forever, and that He took us out of Egypt and gave us the Torah.
2. **Mitzvah 31/Positive 13:** To sanctify the Shabbat in words by its entrance and exit.
3. **Mitzvah 33/Positive 14:** To honor one's father and mother.

B. Negative commands:

1. **Mitzvah 26/Negative 14:** Not to believe in any deity other than G-d.
2. **Mitzvah 27/Negative 15:** Not to make or manufacture idols.
3. **Mitzvah 28/Negative 16:** Not to bow/prostrate to an idol.
4. **Mitzvah 29/Negative 17:** Not to worship an idol in any of the ways that it is worshiped.
5. **Mitzvah 30/Negative 18:** Not to swear in vain using G-d's name.
6. **Mitzvah 32/Negative 19:** Not to do labor on Shabbat, not us, our children, slaves or animals.
7. **Mitzvah 34/Negative 20:** Not to murder.
8. **Mitzvah 35/Negative 21:** Not to commit adultery with a married woman.
9. **Mitzvah 36/Negative 22:** Not to kidnap a Jew.
10. **Mitzvah 37/Negative 23:** Not to testify falsely.
11. **Mitzvah 38/Negative 24:** Not to covet another's item, such as his house, and contemplate doing actions to take it into his possession.
12. **Mitzvah 39/Negative 25:** Not to make sculptures of humans.
13. **Mitzvah 40/Negative 26:** Not to build the altar using stones that have touched iron, such as if they have been hewed using iron.
14. **Mitzvah 41/Negative 27:** Not to use steps to walk onto the altar.

---

[1] So is followed by Sepharadi communities and Chabad. However, Ashkenazi communities read until verse 7:6 and also add 9:5-6

Chapter 18
First Aliyah

1. **Jethro and family arrive:**
   - Jethro, and Moses's wife/kids travel to him: Jethro the priest of Midian, the father-in-law of Moses, heard all that G-d did for Moses and the Jewish people in taking them out of Egypt. Jethro took with him Tzipporah, Moses's wife, and her two sons Gershom and Eliezer.
   - The names of Moses's sons: Gershom was named after the fact that Moses lived in a foreign land, and Eliezer was named after the fact that G-d helped Moses and saved him from the sword of Pharaoh.
   - The meeting and subsequent meal: Jethro and family arrived at the desert, by Mount Sinai. Moses went out to greet them after Jethro informed him of their arrival. They exchanged greetings and Moses told Jethro all that occurred in Egypt and after their escape. Jethro rejoiced from hearing all the things G-d did for the Jewish people, having saved them from the hands of Egypt. Jethro blessed G-d, thanking Him for what He did, and exclaiming that now he knows that G-d is greater than all deities. Jethro then brought offerings to G-d, and Aaron and all the elders of the Jewish people sat for a meal with Jethro.

Second Aliyah

2. **Jethro advises Moses how to smoothly run the court system:**
   - Jethro witnesses a burdensome judicial system: The next day, Moses sat to judge the nation, from morning until evening. Jethro witnessed all that Moses was doing to the nation and chastised him for doing so, for sitting alone to judge while all the Jewish people await from morning until evening. Moses responded that he is judging the nation and teaching them the laws of G-d. Jethro responded that this is not good, as it is too burdensome for one man to carry this alone, and it is thus also too burdensome on the people.
   - Jethro's advice: "Now" says Jethro "let me advice you that you be for the people the direct speaker to G-d to covey to Him your queries, and to teach the nation of His commands. Find men of valor who are G-d fearing, men of truth who hate bribery, and appoint them as leaders of thousands, leaders of hundreds, leaders of fifties, and leaders of tens. Whatever matter is too difficult for them to arbitrate will be brought to you, but everything else will be judged by them, and so the burden will be lessened off [your shoulders]. If you do so, and G-d agrees with this, then you will be able to be successful, you and the nation."

Third Aliyah

   - Moses listens to the advice: Moses adhered to Jethro's advice in all that he said. Moses appointed men of valor from amongst the nation, and made them leaders upon the people. They judged the nation at all times, only brining Moses those cases that are too difficult for them to arbitrate.
   - Jethro leaves: Moses sent off his father-in-law and he returned to his land.

Chapter 19
Fourth Aliyah

3. The children of Israel arrive on Mount Sinai:
- In the third month after the children of Israel left Egypt, they arrived to the Sinai desert on that day. They traveled from Refidim and reached the desert of Sinai, and they encamped in the desert opposite the mountain. Moses ascended to G-d, and G-d told him to relay the following message to the Jewish people:
- G-d's message: "You have seen all that I have done to Egypt. I have carried you on an eagle's wing and brought you to Me. Now, if you adhere my call and guard my covenant, you will be to Me a treasured nation amongst all the people of the earth. You will be to Me a kingdom of priests, and a holy nation."

Fifth Aliyah

4. Moses tells the nation of the covenant offered by G-d and the nation responds:
- Moses summoned the elders of the nation and explained to them all that G-d commanded him.
- The reply of the nation: The entire nation answered in unison and said "That which G-d spoke we shall do." Moses reported their answer back to G-d.
- Moses relates the response to G-d: G-d told Moses that He will appear to him in the thickness of the cloud, so the nation hear Me speak to you, and they will believe in you forever. Moses then told G-d the nation's response.

5. G-d's instructs Moses to instruct the Jewish people in preparation for the event:
- G-d told Moses to tell the Jewish people to sanctify themselves today and tomorrow, and they should wash their clothing. They should be prepared for the 3rd day, as on the 3rd day G-d will descend on Mount Sinai and appear to the eyes of the entire nation.
- Setting boundaries: G-d told Moses to set boundaries around the mountain, as whoever touches the mountain will die. They will be stoned or cast down. This applies to both man and animal. After the Shofar is sounded, they may ascend.
- Moses descended from the mountain and the nation was sanctified and they washed their clothing. Moses instructed them to be ready for the 3rd day and not to be with a woman until then.

6. The Third Day-G-d appears on Mount Sinai:
- The thunder, lightning, smoke, and Shofar: On the morning of the third day there was thunder and lightning, and a heavy cloud on the mountain. A very loud sound of the Shofar was heard. The nation became petrified. Moses escorted the nation to greet G-d, and they stood under the mountain. The mountain was filled with smoke, as G-d descended upon it with fire. The entire mountain trembled, and the sound of the Shofar grew continuously louder. Moses spoke and G-d would respond to him in a voice.

Sixth Aliyah
- Moses warns the Jewish people and ascends the mountain: G-d descended onto the top of the mountain of Mount Sinai and called onto Moses to ascend, and Moses ascended. G-d told Moses to descend back below and warn the nation [not to come close to the mountain] lest they die. Then Moses and Aaron are to ascend back onto the mountain

although the priests and the people are to remain below, lest they die. Moses descended to the nation and told them.

Chapter 20

7. The Ten Commandments:

G-d spoke all these words saying:

1) I am G-d your God who took you out of Egypt.
2) Do not have other deities. Do not make for yourselves an image or picture that is found in the heavens or earth, or underwater. Do not bow down or worship them, as I am a G-d of retribution who gives judgment for the third and fourth generation for those who hate Me, although I do kindness for a thousand generations for those who love me and fulfill my Mitzvot.
3) Do not recite G-d's name in vain.
4) Remember the Shabbat and sanctify it. Six days a week you shall work and on the seventh day it shall be a day of rest for G-d. You shall not do any work, neither you or your son or daughter, or slave or animal. As in six days G-d created the heaven and earth, the sea and all that is in it, and on the seventh day he rested. Therefore, He blessed the Shabbat and sanctified it.
5) Honor your father and mother so that you live a long life.
6) Do not murder.
7) Do not commit adultery.
8) Do not steal.
9) Do not testify falsely regarding a friend.
10) Do not covet the house of a friend, nor his wife, slave, ox, donkey or any of his assets.

Seventh Aliyah

8. The nations reaction:

- The entire nation saw the sounds and flames, and the sound of the Shofar, and the smoke coming out of the mountain. The nation saw and distanced themselves from the mountain. They asked Moses to speak to them instead of G-d, lest they die. Moses assured them not to worry, and that this was done simply to intimidate them against sinning. Moses then approached the fog, where G-d was staying.

9. More instructions of Mitzvot:

- Idols: G-d instructed Moses to tell the Jewish people that they have readily seen that G-d spoke to them from heaven and they shall not make for themselves deities of gold and silver.
- Altar: "They shall build for me an altar of earth, to offer on it the sacrifices of Olah and Shelamim, from your flock and cattle. In every place where I will mention my name I will come and bless you."
- No metal on stone: If a stone altar is built, it shall not be built from hewed stone, as you have placed your sword on it and defiled it.
- No steps: Do not walk up steps towards my altar

Parashat Mishpatim
Verses: 118 [Siman: עזיאל]
Haftorah: Jerimiah 34:8-22, 33:25-26

Number of Mitzvot:
There are a total of **fifty-three** Mitzvot in Parashat Mishpatim. **Twenty-three** positive commands and **Thirty** negative commands.

A. Positive commands:

1. **Mitzvah 42/Positive 15:** To adjudicate the law of a Jewish slave [i.e. Eved Ivri] in accordance to the Torah regulations and laws.
2. **Mitzvah 43/Positive 16:** For the master to marry his Jewish maidservant [i.e. Ama Ivriya].
3. **Mitzvah 44/Positive 17:** For the master to help the Jewish maidservant [i.e. Ama Ivriya] redeem herself.
4. **Mitzvah 47/Positive 18:** To adjudicate capital punishment by strangulation [i.e. Chenek] to those liable.
5. **Mitzvah 49/Positive 19:** To punish one who injures his friend in accordance to Torah law.
6. **Mitzvah 50/Positive 20:** To adjudicate capital punishment by decapitation [i.e. Sayif/Cherev] to those liable.
7. **Mitzvah 51/Positive 21:** To adjudicate cases of damage or injury caused by the ox of an individual in accordance to Torah law.
8. **Mitzvah 53/Positive 22:** To adjudicate cases of damage or injury caused by a pit of an individual in accordance to Torah law.
9. **Mitzvah 54/Positive 23:** To adjudicate cases of stealing in accordance to Torah law.
10. **Mitzvah 55/Positive 24:** To adjudicate in accordance to Torah law cases of damage caused by an ox of an individual who ate one's produce or destroyed it through walking.
11. **Mitzvah 56/Positive 25:** To adjudicate cases of damage caused by the fire of an individual in accordance to Torah law.
12. **Mitzvah 57/Positive 26:** To adjudicate cases of damage or loss caused to an item while stored by a custodian who was not paid for his services [i.e. Shomer Chinam] in accordance to Torah law.
13. **Mitzvah 58/Positive 27:** To adjudicate cases of civil claims [i.e. Toein Venitaan] in accordance to Torah law.
14. **Mitzvah 59/Positive 28:** To adjudicate cases of damage or loss caused to an item while stored by a paid custodian [i.e. Shomer Sachar], or by a renter, in accordance to Torah law.
15. **Mitzvah 60/Positive 29:** To adjudicate cases of damage or loss caused to an item while borrowed [i.e. Shoel], or by a renter, in accordance to Torah law.
16. **Mitzvah 61/Positive 30:** To adjudicate cases of seduction/statutory rape of a virgin [i.e. Betula] in accordance to Torah law.
17. **Mitzvah 66/Positive 31:** To lend money to a pauper in need.
18. **Mitzvah 78/Positive 32:** To follow the majority opinion in cases of disputes regarding

all Torah matters.

19. **Mitzvah 80/Positive 33:** To remove a heavy burden from on top of an animal.
20. **Mitzvah 84/Positive 34:** To disown all the land produce grown in the sabbatical year [i.e. Shmita].
21. **Mitzvah 85/Positive 35:** To rest from work on Shabbat.
22. **Mitzvah 88/Positive 36:** To visit the Temple during the festivals three times a year.
23. **Mitzvah 91/Positive 37:** To bring the first fruits [i.e. Bikurim] to the Temple.

B. Negative commands:

1. **Mitzvah 45/Negative 28:** Not to sell the Jewish maidservant [i.e. Ama Ivriya] to others.
2. **Mitzvah 46/Negative 29:** Not to infringe on the rights of the Jewish maidservant [i.e. Ama Ivriya] towards food, clothing, and conjugal rights.
3. **Mitzvah 48/Negative 30:** Not to hit one's father or mother.
4. **Mitzvah 52/Negative 31:** Not to eat the meat of an ox which was found liable for capital punishment.
5. **Mitzvah 62/Negative 32:** Not to allow a witch to live, and to judge her with death.
6. **Mitzvah 63/Negative 33:** Not to verbally oppress a convert of the gentile nations.
7. **Mitzvah 64/Negative 34:** Not to monetarily cheat a convert of the gentile nations.
8. **Mitzvah 65/Negative 35:** Not to oppress orphans or widows neither in speech or action.
9. **Mitzvah 67/Negative 36:** Not to demand payment of a loan if one knows he cannot pay it.
10. **Mitzvah 68/Negative 37:** Not to collect or give interest on/to a loan.
11. **Mitzvah 69/Negative 38:** Not to curse judges.
12. **Mitzvah 70/Negative 39:** Not to curse G-d.
13. **Mitzvah 71/Negative 40:** Not to curse the President, which is the king and head of the Sanhedrin.
14. **Mitzvah 72/Negative 41:** Not to tithe the produce in the wrong order.
15. **Mitzvah 73/Negative 42:** Not to eat meat of a Treifa animal.
16. **Mitzvah 74/Negative 43:** Not to listen to the claims of one side not in the presence of the other.
17. **Mitzvah 75/Negative 44:** Not to accept testimony of a sinner.
18. **Mitzvah 76/Negative 45:** Not to follow a simple majority in cases of capital punishment.
19. **Mitzvah 77/Negative 46:** For a judge not to base his ruling on the opinion of other judges unless he comprehends it.
20. **Mitzvah 79/Negative 47:** For a judge not to show compassion in judgment on the weak and poor.
21. **Mitzvah 81/Negative 48:** Not to tilt the judgment of a case against the side of a sinner.
22. **Mitzvah 82/Negative 49:** Not to give capital punishment for a sin unless valid witnesses testify.
23. **Mitzvah 83/Negative 50:** For a judge not to take a bribe even if he plans to judge truthfully.
24. **Mitzvah 86/Negative 51:** Not to swear, or cause others to swear, in the names of idolatry.

25. **Mitzvah 87/Negative 52:** Not to influence others to serve idolatry.
26. **Mitzvah 89/Negative 53:** Not to slaughter the Pesach offering on the 14th of Nissan while still owning Chametz in one's possessions.
27. **Mitzvah 90/Negative 54:** Not to leave the parts of the Pesach offering, and other offerings, that need to be offered to the altar, until morning. [i.e. Nosar]
28. **Mitzvah 92/Negative 55:** Not to cook meat and milk together.
29. **Mitzvah 93/Negative 56:** Not to make a covenant with the seven Canaanite nations.
30. **Mitzvah 94/Negative 57:** Not to allow idolaters to live in our land.

Chapter 21
First Aliyah

1. **The laws of an Eved Ivri/Male Jewish slave:**
   - His terms of service and release: These are the laws that you shall place before them: When you purchase a Jewish slave [Eved Ivri], he shall work for six years and in the seventh year he is to be freed. If he came alone he is to leave alone, while if he came with a wife he is to leave with a wife. If the slave is given a wife by his master, then she and the children are to remain with the master, while he is to go free.
   - If the slave does not want to leave: If the slave states that he enjoys working for his master and does not want to go free, then the master is to take him to the judges and bring him to the doorpost and make a hole through his ear using a peg, and he shall work for him forever.

2. **The laws of an Ama Ivria/Female maidservant:**
   - If one sells his daughter as a Jewish maidservant [Ama Ivriya] her conditions of release are not like that of other slaves. She cannot be sold. He is encouraged to marry her, or to have his son marry her, and give her the regular marital rights maintained by a wife. He must provide her with food, clothing, and conjugal rights. If the above is not performed, she shall go free.

3. **Cases involving injury and homicide:**
   - Murder: One who hits a man and murders him is to be put to death. If it was unintentional, he is to flee to an area of refuge.
   - Hitting one's parents: One who hits his parents is to be put to death.
   - Kidnapping: One who kidnaps a person and sells him is to be put to death.
   - Cursing one's parents: One who curses his parents is to be put to death.
   - Injury: One who injures a person is to pay restitution for damages caused.

Second Aliyah
- Killing a slave: One who kills his slave will be avenged.
- Killing a fetus: One who kills a fetus, shall be penalized.
- If there will be a fatality, then he shall give a life in place of a life. An eye for an eye, a hand for a hand, a foot for a foot, a burn for a burn, a wound for a wound.
- Injuring a slave: One who injures the eyes or teeth of a slave is required to set the slave free.

- <u>One's animal killed</u>: If one's ox kills a man or woman, the ox is to be stoned and not have its meat eaten, while the owner is to be set free. If, however, the owner knew of the ox's murderous nature and was warned, then also the owner is to die. If the ox killed a slave, he is to pay 30 Shekalim to the master of the slave, and the ox is to be stoned.

4. Cases involving monetary damage:
- <u>Pit damages</u>: If one digs a pit, and leaves it uncovered, he must pay for damages if an animal falls in and dies.
- <u>Animal damages</u>: If one's ox gores and injures another ox, he is to pay half the damages. If, however, this ox had a history of goring which was known to the owner, the owner must pay for the full damages.
- <u>Stealing animals</u>: If a man steals an ox or sheep and slaughters or sells it, he is to pay restitution of five times the amount of the ox and four times the amount of the sheep.

Chapter 22
- <u>Robbing a home</u>: If one catches a burglar in the act of stealing in one's home, one may kill him.
- A robber who does not have ability to pay restitution, is to be sold as a slave.
- One who steals must pay double the amount of the item he stole.

Third Aliyah
- <u>Property damage caused by animals</u>: If one's animal ate the food in another person's yard, the owner must pay.
- <u>Fire damage</u>: If one's fire spreads and causes property damage to another, the person who lit the fire must pay.
- <u>Caretaker who lost an object</u>: If a caretaker of an item claims the item was lost or stolen from him, he is to take an oath that he did not take the item. [This applies by a Shomer Chinam-one who was guarding for free, however if he was a Shomer Sechar-guarding for payment, then even] if the item was stolen he must pay for it, although if something happened beyond his control, he is exempt.
- <u>Borrower lost object</u>: If a borrowed item became damaged, the borrower must pay, unless the owner was with him.

5. Miscellaneous laws:
- <u>Statutory rape</u>: If one seduces an unmarried virgin, he is to marry her as a wife, and if her father refuses he must pay her father.
- <u>Witches</u>: Do not allow a witch to live.
- <u>Bestiality</u>: One who lies with an animal is to be put to death.
- <u>Idolatry</u>: One who slaughters to other G-ds shall be destroyed.
- <u>Verbal abuse against converts, widows and orphans</u>: Do not oppress a convert, widow or orphan as if you do G-d will hear their cry and take His wrath out on you, turning your wives to widows and sons to orphans.
- <u>Loans</u>: If you lend money to a Jew you may not collect interest on the loan. You may also not press them to pay. If you collect clothing as collateral of a debt, you shall return it by sundown.

Fourth Aliyah

- You may not curse a judge or curse a leader amongst your people.
- You shall not delay the tithe produce or the Terumah.
- You are to give G-d your firstborn. The newborn animal is to be given to G-d on the 8th day.
- <u>Treifa meat</u>: You may not eat meat of a Treifa animal. Rather, throw it to the dogs.

Chapter 23

6. **Laws involving the judicial system:**
   - Don't listen to meritless reports.
   - Don't join a false witness in testimony.
   - Don't follow the majority to do evil.
   - Do not show compassion in judgment to the weak and poor.

7. **Miscellaneous laws:**
   - <u>Returning lost object</u>: Return a lost animal to its owner even if it belongs to your enemy.
   - <u>Helping load animal</u>: Help your enemy's animal unload if it has a heavy burden.

Fifth Aliyah

- Do not tilt the judgment of a case against a destitute person.
- <u>Lying</u>: Distance yourself from lying.
- Do not kill the innocent.
- <u>Bribery</u>: Do not take a bribe.
- Do not oppress a convert.
- <u>Shemita/Sabbatical year</u>: Plant your field for six years and in the seventh year, leave your field for the destitute and animals to eat from.
- <u>Shabbat</u>: One shall work for six days and rest on Shabbat, you and your household.
- Do not mention other deities on your lips.
- <u>Aliya Leregel</u>: Celebrate with me three times a year. Guard the festival of Matzot for seven days, eat Matzot, and do not come to see me empty handed. By the festival of harvest and of the gathering [you are also to visit me]. Three times a year, all your males are to come see the face of G-d.
- Do not slaughter my sacrifice over Chametz and do not let the fat of my festive offering remain overnight.
- <u>Bikurim</u>: The first fruits of your lands you shall bring to me.
- <u>Meat and Milk/Basar Bechalav</u>: Do not cook a young animal in its mother's milk.

Sixth Aliyah

8. **G-d warns the children of Israel to heed the commands of his angel:**
   - I will send my angel before you, to guide you and guard you on the way to the promised land. Beware not to transgress his words for he will not forgive you. If you obey him, then I will destroy all your enemies. My angel will be sent before you and destroy all the seven nations of Canaan.
   - Do not bow to their gods and do not serve them. Destroy their gods and their statues.

9. **Blessings to be received:**
   - Serve G-d your G-d and He will bless your bread and water and remove illnesses from amongst you.

Seventh Aliyah

- No women will have a miscarriage or be infertile in your land. I will fill the number of your days.
- I will send fear before you, and send the wasp, to drive out all your enemies in the land of Canaan. I will not destroy them all in one year, lest the land become desolate and filled with wild animals, rather I will expel them little by little.
- I will give you borders from the Reed Sea until the Mediterranean.
- Do not make a peace treaty with those nations, lest they remain in your land and bring you to sin, to serve their gods.

Chapter 24

10. **Details of Matan Torah:**
   - G-d told Moses that he, Aaron, Nadab and Abihu, and the seventy elders of Israel are to prostrate themselves from a distance. Moses alone is to ascend to G-d, and not anyone else.
   - We will do and listen: Moses told all the words of G-d to the nation and they said "We shall do."
   - Building an altar, bringing sacrifices and sprinkling blood: Moses awoke in the morning and built an altar under the mountain and twelve monuments, corresponding to the 12 tribes. The youth were sent to offer sacrifices on the altar for G-d. Moses took half the blood and placed it in a bowl, and the other half he threw onto the altar. Moses then took the Torah and read it to the congregation, and they replied, "Everything that G-d has asked we will do and listen." Moses then took the blood and sprinkled it on the nation, as part of the covenant.
   - Ascending the mountain and looking at G-d: Moses, Aaron and the seventy leaders ascended the mountain and they saw G-d, and that under His feet was a sapphire brick, like the purity of the sky. G-d did not take vengeance against these nobles [even though] they gazed at G-d and ate and drank.
   - Moses ascends to receive the Tablets of Stone: G-d told Moses to ascend the mountain and receive the stone Tablets of Stone with the commandments written on them. Moses rose together with Joshua, and Moses ascended the mountain of G-d. He instructed the leaders to remain put until they return, and that in the interim Aaron and Chur would act as the leaders to deal with any issues that occur. Moses ascended the mountain and it was covered by a cloud. Moses remained in the cloud for six days and on the seventh day G-d called him from within the cloud. G-d appeared like a consuming fire on the top of the mountain, before the Jewish people. Moses remained there for 40 days and 40 nights.

Parashat Terumah
Verses: 96 [Siman: יציר]
Haftorah: Kings 1 5:26-6:13

Number of Mitzvot:

There are **Three** Mitzvot in Parashat Terumah. **Two** positive commands and **One** negative command.

A. Positive commands:
  1. **Mitzvah 95/Positive 38:** To build a Temple for G-d.
  2. **Mitzvah 97/Positive 39:** To constantly have bread placed in the Temple. [i.e. Showbread]

B. Negative commands:
  1. **Mitzvah 96/Negative 58:** Not to remove the poles from the Aron.

Chapter 25
First Aliyah

1. **Donating to the Temple:**
   - G-d spoke to Moses saying: Take donations from the people of Israel, from whoever is of generous heart to give. I need the following donations:
     1) Gold,
     2) Silver,
     3) Copper,
     4) Techeiles Turquoise wool,
     5) Argamon purple wool,
     6) Scarlet wool,
     7) Linen,
     8) Goat hair,
     9) Red dyed ram skins,
     10) Techashim skins,
     11) Shittim Acacia wood.
     12) Oil for lighting
     13) Spices for the anointing oil and Ketores incense.
     14) Shoham stones
     15) Filling stones for the apron and breastplate.
   - Make for me a Temple and I will dwell within you. Make it the same exact way that I show you, it and all its vessels.

2. **The Aron:**
   - Material: Make the Aron of acacia shittim wood.
   - Dimensions: It is to be 2.5 cubits in length and 1.5 cubits in width, and 1.5 cubits in height.

- Its particulars: It is to be covered with pure gold both in its interior and exterior. It is to contain a gold crown surrounding it. It is to contain four welded gold rings, two on each side, and have two poles made of acacia shittim wood, and coated with gold, inserted into it for it to be carried with.
- The poles may never be removed from the rings.
- What it contains: The Tablets of the law that I [i.e. G-d] will give you are to be inserted into the Aron.

Second Aliyah

- Kapores (Lid) and Cherubim: You shall make a lid [i.e. Kapores] of pure cold for the Aron. Its dimensions are to be 2.5 cubits in length and 1.5 cubits in width. You are to make two Cherubim of gold on the opposite ends of the Kapores lid. The Cherubim are to be made from the gold of the Kapores lid. The Cherubim are to have wings spread upwards, and are to face each other, and face towards the lid. The Kapores is to be placed on top of the Aron.
- I will speak with you from above the Kapores, from between the Cherubim.

3. **The Shulchan/Table:**
   - Material: Make the Shulchan/Table from acacia-shittim wood.
   - Dimensions: It is to be 2 cubits in length and 1 cubits in width, and 1.5 cubits in height.
   - Its particulars: It is to be coated in gold and contain a gold crown around its rim. It should have a one handbreadth frame around its entire circumference, and the frame should have a gold crown around it. It is to contain four welded gold rings, one by each corner, and have two poles made of acacia-shittim wood, and coated with gold, inserted into it for it to be carried with.
   - Its accessories: You are to make pure gold dishes, spoons, tubes and supports.
   - The Lechem Hapanim-Showbread: You are to always place on the table before G-d the Showbread.

Third Aliyah

4. **The Menorah:**
   - Material: Make the Menorah from pure gold. It is to be made from one Kikar of gold.
   - Dimensions: It is to be 2 cubits in length and 1 cubits in width, and 1.5 cubits in height.
   - Its particulars: It is to contain a base, branches, goblets, knobs and flowers made from the original piece of gold. It is to have six branches, three from each side. Each branch is to contain three goblets, decorated with a knob and flower. The base of the Menorah is to contain four goblets decorated with knobs and flowers. Under each set of branches a button is to be formed. Everything is to be formed from the same piece of gold. It is to have seven candles, and the candles are to light towards its interior.

Chapter 26

5. **The Tabernacle Tapestries of wool and flax:**
   - The Tabernacle is to be made of ten tapestries.
   - Material: The tapestries are to be made of twisted flax, Techeiles Turquoise wool, Argamon Purple wool, and scarlet wool- the work of an artist.
   - Dimensions: Each tapestry is to be 28 cubits long and 4 cubits wide.

- Its particulars: One is to attach the tapestries to each other in two groups of five. The ends of the two groups of tapestries are to contain 50 loops, corresponding to each other. You shall make 50 gold hooks to attach the two groupings together and hence have one Tabernacle.

6. **The Tabernacle Tapestries of goat hair:**
   - Over the Tabernacle [i.e. wool tapestries] you are to make 11 tent panels
   - Material: These panels are to be made of goat hair.
   - Dimensions: Each panel is to be 30 cubits long and 4 cubits wide.
   - Its particulars: One is to attach the tapestries to each other into two groups, one containing five and the second containing six. The ends of the two groups of tapestries are to contain 50 loops, corresponding to each other. You shall make 50 copper hooks to attach the two groupings together and hence have one Tabernacle. The excess tapestry is to be hung half over the front of the Tabernacle and half by the back of the Tabernacle. The excess cubit on each side of the Tabernacle will spread over the sides.
   - The covering of the Ohel tent: You are to make a covering for the tent panels of red dyed ram skin and a covering of Tachash skin above it.

Fourth Aliyah

7. **The Kerashim/beams:**
   - You shall make beams for the Tabernacle. Make 20 beams for the southern side and 20 beams for the northern side. The west side is to have 6 beams, plus two corner beams, for a total of 8 beams.
   - Material: The beams are to be made from acacia-shittim wood. They are to be coated with gold.
   - Dimensions: Each beam is to be 10 cubits in length and 1.5 cubits in width.
   - Its particulars: The beams are to be erected in a standing position. Each beam is to contain two projecting pieces of wood [i.e. tenons] which are perfectly aligned across each other. You are to make silver sockets for the beams, two sockets per beam, for each of its tenons. Thus, the 20 beams of the southern side are to have 40 silver sockets and the 20 beams of the northern side are to have 40 silver sockets. The 8 beams of the southern side are to have 16 silver sockets. Every beam is to contain a groove on each of its sides which will allow for rings to be placed on every pair of beams, thus attaching all the beams together. The rings are to be made of gold.
   - The poles: You are to make five poles of acacia-shittim wood for three sides of the Tabernacle, five for the northern side, five for the southern side, and five for the western side, for a total of 15 poles. The poles are to be inserted into the beams and extend from one end to the next. The poles are to be coated with gold.

Fifth Aliyah

8. **The Parochet curtain:**
   - The material: You shall make a Parochet curtain of Ticheiles wool, Argamon wool, scarlet wool, and twisted linen. It is to be the work of an artist.
   - The beams which hold the Parochet curtain: The Parochet curtain is to be placed on four pillars of acacia-shittim wood which are covered with gold. The pillars are to contain

golden hooks and contain four **silver** sockets. The Parochet curtain is to be hung on those hooks.

- Its location: The Parochet curtain and its beams are to be placed between the Holies and the Holy of Holies, where the Aron and its Kapores covering is kept. The Shulchan/Table and Menorah are to be placed outside the Parochet curtain, the Shulchan/Table being positioned in the northern side and the Menorah on the southern side.

9. **The Masach screen in front of the Holies:**
   - You shall make a screen for the entrance to the Ohel tent.
   - The material: It is to be made of Ticheiles Turquoise wool, Argamon Purple wool, scarlet wool, and twisted linen. It is to be the work of an embroiderer.
   - The beams which hold the Masach screen: You shall make for the screen five pillars of acacia shittim wood which are covered with gold. The pillars are to contain golden hooks and contain five **copper** sockets.

Chapter 27
Sixth Aliyah

10. **The altar:**
    - Material: The altar is to be made of acacia shittim wood.
    - Dimensions: It is to be made into a square, its length being five cubits, and its width also being five cubits. It is to be three cubits high. It is to be hollow.
    - Its particulars: It is to contain horns on each of its four corners, and [the horns and the entire altar] are to be covered with copper.
    - Its accessories: You shall make for it: Pots to remove its ashes, shovels, sprinkling basins, prongs, and fire-pans. It is all to be made of copper.
    - Its netting: A copper netting shall be made which encompasses the altar, and it is to have four copper rings placed on each of its four corners. The netting is to be placed under the band of the altar and is to reach half the height of the altar.
    - Its poles: You shall make poles of acacia shittim wood which are covered with copper. They are to be inserted into the rings and used to carry the altar.

Seventh Aliyah

11. **The courtyard:**
    - You shall make a courtyard for the Tabernacle. It is to be made of curtains which are held up by pillars.
    - Material of the curtains: The curtains are to be made of twisted linen.
    - Dimensions: The length of the courtyard [i.e. the northern and southern side] is to be 100 cubits long. The width of the courtyard is to be 50 cubits wide. Its height is to be ten cubits. The curtain is to be 100 cubits in both the northern and southern side, and 50 cubits on the western side, however, on the eastern side it is to be only 15 cubits from each end.
    - The pillars: There are to be 20 pillars and 20 sockets for each side of the courtyard, for the northern and southern side. There are to be ten pillars and ten sockets for the western side. There are to be three pillars and sockets for each end of the eastern side, for a total of six. All the pillars are to contain silver hooks and belts. The sockets are to be made of copper.

- <u>The entrance to the courtyard</u>: The gate of the courtyard is to contain a screen of twenty cubits. It is to be made of Ticheiles Turquoise wool, Argamon Purple wool, scarlet wool, and twisted linen. It is to be the work of an embroiderer. It is to contain four pillars and four sockets.
- <u>Its accessories</u>: The vessels needed to erect the courtyard, as well as its pegs, are to be made of copper.

Parashat Tetzaveh
Verses: 101 [Siman: מיכאל]
Haftorah: Ezekiel 43:10-27

Number of Mitzvot:
There are **Seven** Mitzvot in Parashat Tetzaveh. **Four** positive commands and **three** negative command.

A. Positive commands:
1. **Mitzvah 98/Positive 40:** To have candles constantly lit before G-d, in the Temple.
2. **Mitzvah 99/Positive 41:** For the Kohanim to wear their special garments while serving in the Temple.
3. **Mitzvah 102/Positive 42:** For the Kohanim to eat the Sacrifices.
4. **Mitzvah 103/Positive 43:** For the Kohanim to offer incense onto the altar twice daily.

B. Negative commands:
1. **Mitzvah 100/Negative 59:** Not to remove the breastplate from the apron.
2. **Mitzvah 101/Negative 60:** Not to tear the rim of the Meil.
3. **Mitzvah 104/Negative 61:** Not to offer onto the gold altar any offering other than the daily incense.

First Aliyah

1. **The Menorah oil and lighting:**
   * Moses is told to command the Jewish people to bring him clear crushed olive oil for illuminating the Ner Tamid [i.e. the Menorah]. The Menorah is to be placed in the Tent of Meeting, outside the Parochet curtain. Aaron and his sons are to make sure it is lit from evening until morning for all generations.

Chapter 28

2. **Appointing Kohanim:**
   * Moses is to bring near Aaron, and his sons, to become priests for G-d. Aaron, Nadab, Abihu, Elazar and Isamar shall be priests.

3. **The Bigdei Kehuna-Preistly garments:**
   * Make for Aaron, your brother, holy garments for glory. Speak with the wise, and they shall make the garments.
   * The following are the garments:
     1) Choshen/Breastplate
     2) Eiphid/Apron
     3) Meil/robe
     4) Kutones of checkered texture. [shirt]
     5) Mitznefet/Turban
     6) Avneit/belt

- The material: The garments are to be made from gold, Ticheiles-Turquoise wool, Argamon-Purple wool, scarlet wool, and twisted linen.

4. **The apron:**
   - The material: The apron is to be made from gold, Ticheiles-Turquoise wool, Argamon-Purple wool, scarlet wool, and twisted linen. It is to be the work of an artist.
   - The shoulder straps: It is to contain two shoulder straps, one by each end. It is to have a belt which is likewise made of the same materials stated above.
   - The Shoham stones: You are to take two Shoham stones and engrave on them the name of the tribes, six on each stone, following their order of birth. The stones are to be inserted into gold settings. They are to be placed on the shoulder straps of the apron, one per strap, and Aaron is to wear them on his shoulders as a remembrance.

Second Aliyah
   - The gold chain: You shall make gold settings and two gold chains, and connect the chains to the settings.

5. **The Choshen Mishpat [breastplate]:**
   - The material: The breastplate is to be made from gold, Ticheiles-Turquoise wool, Argamon- Purple wool, scarlet wool, and twisted linen.
   - Dimensions: The breastplate is to be square, folded, a Zeres its length and width.
   - Its stones: It is to be filled with four rows of stones. The first row is to contain the following stones: Odem, Pitdah, and Barekes. The second row: Nofech, Sapir, and Yahalom. The third row: Leshem, Shevo, and Achlamah. The fourth row: Tarshish, Shoham, and Yashfeh. The stones are to be placed within gold settings. They are to have the names of the tribes inscribed on them, one tribe per stone for a total of 12 tribes and stones.
   - The chains and rings that attach the breastplate to the apron: You shall make two gold chains on the breastplate. Make two gold rings, one for each edge of the [upper part of the] breastplate. The gold chains are to be inserted into these rings and are then to be attached to the gold settings of the apron [thus having the breastplate hang on the straps of the apron]. Make another two gold rings for the bottom corners of the breastplate, place them in the interior of the breastplate. Make two rings on the bottom end of the shoulder straps of the apron, symmetric to the bottom rings of the breastplate. Place a Techeiles-Turquoise woolen string through the two sets of rings, hence attaching the breastplate to the apron belt.
   - The breastplate is not to be moved from the apron, and in the Tabernacle, Aaron is to carry the names of the tribes over his chest as a remembrance before G-d
   - The Urim Vetumim: The Urim and Tumim [G-d's Divine name] is to be inserted into the breastplate, and Aaron is to carry the judgment of the children of Israel constantly.

Third Aliyah
6. **The Meil robe:**
   - The material: The Meil is to be made entirely from Ticheiles-Turquoise wool.
   - Its collar: The Meil is to contain a folded collar and it may not be torn.

- Its bells: Its hem is to be surrounded with pomegranates made of Ticheiles-Turquoise wool, Argamon-Purple wool, and scarlet wool. It is also to contain gold bells all around it. When Aaron walks with it, the bells will make noise, announcing when he enters and exits the Holies so that he not die.

7. **The Tzitz/Golden band:**
   - The Tzitz is to be made of pure gold and have engraved on it the words "Kodesh LaHashem." It shall be placed on a Ticheiles-Turquoise wool string, and on the turban, by its front side. It shall be on Aaron's forehead and he shall bring appeasement for all the sins involving Sacrifices of the Jewish people.

8. **The Kutoness shirt, Avneit belt, turban, and pants:**
   - The material: The Kutones and turbans are to be made of checkered linen for both Aaron and his sons. The Avneit belt is to be made of embroidery.
   - The inauguration of the Kohanim: Aaron and his sons are to be inaugurated for the priesthood through dressing them in the above clothing and pouring on them the anointing oil.
   - The pants: You shall make linen pants for the Kohanim to cover their private area, from the hips to the thighs.
   - The Kohanim are to wear the priestly clothing when they serve in the Temple lest they die.

Chapter 29
Fourth Aliyah

9. **The inauguration procedure:**
   - The following is to be done in order to sanctify the Kohanim to become priests for G-d:
   - The sacrifices and flour offerings: Take one bull, and two rams that are unblemished. Take Matzah bread and loaves that are smeared with oil and Matzah wafers smeared with oil. They are to be made of fine flour. They are all to be placed in one basket and brought together with the bull and two rams.
   - Bathing, dressing and anointing the Kohanim: You shall take Aaron and his sons to the opening of the Tent of Meeting, bathe them with water, and dress them. Aaron is to wear the Kutoness shirt, robe, apron, breastplate, turban, and Tzitz. You are to pour the anointing oil over them. The sons are to be dressed in the Kutoness shirt, the Avneit belt and turbans.
   - Sacrificing the Chatas bull offering: You shall bring the bull in front of the Tent of Meeting, and have Aaron and his sons lean on its head. It is to be slaughtered there. Take from its blood and place it on the corners of the altar using your fingers, and then pour the remaining blood on the base of the altar. You shall take all the fat that covers the intestine, and the diaphragm which is on the liver, and the two kidneys and their fat, and offer it onto the altar. The meat of the bull and its waste is to be burnt in a fire outside of the camp. This offering is a Chatas
   - Sacrificing and offering the first ram Olah offering: You shall bring one ram and have Aaron and his sons lean on its head. It is then to be slaughtered. Take from its blood throw it around the altar. The ram is to be dismembered, and have its innards and feet washed, and then have it joined with its head. The entire ram is to be offered on the altar, as it is an Olah offering to G-d.

Fifth Aliyah

- Sacrificing the second ram Shelamim offering: You shall bring the second ram and have Aaron and his sons lean on its head. It is then to be slaughtered. Take from its blood and place it on the edge of the right ear and right thumb of the hand and toe of Aaron and his sons. The remainder of the blood is to be poured around the altar.
- Anointing the Kohanim with the oil and blood: You are to take the blood that was on the altar, and the anointing oil [Shemen Hamishcha], and sprinkle it on Aaron and his sons and their clothing, and they are to be sanctified.
- Offering the parts of the second ram: You are to take the fat, and the tail and all the fat that covers the intestines and the diaphragm of the liver and the two kidneys, and the right thigh. Also, take one of each of the breads from the basket. Place it all together on the palm of Aaron and his sons and waive them before G-d. Then take the foods off the palm of their hands and offer them before G-d. Moses is to take the breast of the ram and waive it before G-d and it will remain a present to Moses from G-d.
- The portion of the Kohanim in the Sacrifices: The breast and right thigh of the ram, as well as of all Sacrifices, are to be given to the Kohanim for all generations.
- Wearing the priestly garments for inauguration: The Kohen is to wear the priestly garments for seven days as part of his inauguration [as the high priest].
- Cooking and eating the meat of the 2nd ram: The meat of the ram is to be cooked in a holy place. The meat, as well as the bread in the basket, is to be eaten by Aaron and his sons and through doing so they will become inaugurated. A non-Kohen may not eat from it. Any meat and bread that is leftover past the morning, is to be burnt in a fire.
- The number of times to perform the above procedure: The above procedure is to be done daily for seven days.
- Cleansing the altar: The altar is to be cleansed and atoned by having the Chatas bull offering [described earlier] sacrificed on it for seven days. Doing so will make the altar holy, and anything that touches it will contract holiness.

Sixth Aliyah

10. The Tamid offering:

- The following offerings are to be brought daily onto the altar: Everyday two sheep within their first year are to be offered, one in the morning and the second in the evening. It is to be accompanied with a Mincha offering consisting of 1/10th of fine flour, mixed with a ¼ of a Hin of crushed oil. Its libation is to be a ¼ of a Hin, per sheep. This is to be done for all generations.

11. The dwelling of the Shekhinah on the Tabernacle:

- "I will meet with the Jewish people by the Tent of Meeting and be sanctified there through my honor. I will dwell amongst the Jewish people and be for them a G-d, and they will know that I am the G-d who took them out of Egypt in order to dwell with them."

Chapter 30
Seventh Aliyah

12. The gold altar for incense:

- You shall make an altar for the incense offering.
- <u>The material</u>: It is to be made of acacia-shittim wood.
- <u>Dimensions</u>**:** It is to be made into a square, its length being one cubit, and its width also one cubit. It is to be two cubits high.
- <u>Its particulars</u>: It is to contain horns on each of its four corners, and the horns, as well as the entire altar, is to be covered in gold. It is to have a gold crown surrounding it. Make for it two gold rings beneath its crown, one on each corner. These rings will serve to hold the poles with which the altar will be carried.
- <u>Its poles</u>: You shall make poles of acacia-shittim wood which are covered with gold.
- <u>Location</u>: The altar is to be placed in front of the Parochet curtain that is by the Aron.
- <u>Its use</u>: Aaron is to offer incense on it daily each morning when the lamps are cleaned, and every afternoon when the lamps are kindled. One may not offer on it a foreign incense or an Olah or flour offering or wine libation. Aaron will atone on it once a year from the blood of the Chatas offering. The altar is a holy of holies to G-d.

Parashat Ki Tisa
Verses: 139 [Siman: חנגאל]
Haftorah: Kings 1 18:20[1]-39

Number of Mitzvot:
There are **Nine** Mitzvot in Parashat Ki Tisa. **Four** positive commands and **five** negative command.

A. Positive commands:
1. **Mitzvah 105/Positive 44:** For every Jew above age twenty to donate a half Shekel.
2. **Mitzvah 106/Positive 45:** For the Kohanim to wash their hands and feet upon entering the Temple and serving G-d there.
3. **Mitzvah 107/Positive 46:** To make the anointing oil in the prescription given by the Torah.
4. **Mitzvah 112/Positive 47:** To stop working the land during Shemita/Sabbatical year.

B. Negative commands:
1. **Mitzvah 108/Negative 62:** Not to anoint with the anointing oil anyone other than a Kohen.
2. **Mitzvah 109/Negative 63:** Not to make a replica of the anointing oil.
3. **Mitzvah 110/Negative 64:** Not to make a replica of the incense.
4. **Mitzvah 111/Negative 65:** Not to eat from offerings given to idols.
5. **Mitzvah 113/Negative 66:** Not to eat meat and milk that were cooked together.

First Aliyah

1. **The census taking and Half Shekel donation:**
   - G-d spoke to Moses saying: "When you take a census of the Jewish people, each man is to give G-d an atonement of his soul, in order so there should not be a plague amongst them when they are counted."
   - <u>What to give</u>: All those who are counted are to give a half shekel of the holy shekel which is worth twenty Geira. It is a donation to G-d.
   - <u>From what age</u>: Everyone from twenty years and up is to give the donation to G-d to atone for their souls.
   - <u>Its use</u>: The money is to be used for the Temple service and be a remembrance for the Jewish people to atone for their souls.

2. **The Kiyor sink:**
   - G-d spoke to Moses saying: You shall make a Kiyor sink and pedestal for washing. You are to fill it with water.
   - <u>Material</u>: The Kiyor and its pedestal is to be made of copper.
   - <u>Location</u>: It is to be placed between the Tent of Meeting and altar.

---

[1] So is followed by Sepharadi communities and Chabad. However, Ashkenazi communities begin reading from verse 18:1.

- <u>Its use to wash the hands and feet</u>: The Kohanim are to use the Kiyor to wash their hands and feet upon entering the Tent of Meeting, or upon doing service on the altar. This needs to be done so they don't die in their service.

3. **The Shemen Hamishcha/anointing oil:**
   - <u>The ingredients</u>: G-d spoke to Moses saying: Take the following prime spices and make the anointing oil:
     - i. Pure **myrrh**, 500 Shekel's weight.
     - ii. Aromatic **cinnamon**, 250 shekel's weight, brought twice [for a total of 500].
     - iii. Cane of aromatic spice, 250 shekels weight
     - iv. The Kiddah root, 500 Shekel's weight.
     - v. A Hin of olive oil.
   - The above ingredients are to be mixed by a spice blender and be turned into a sacred anointing oil.
   - <u>Its use-What is anointed with it</u>: The Tent of Meeting and the Aron is to be anointed using this oil. Likewise, the Shulchan/Table, Menorah, gold and copper Altar, and all their accessory vessels are to be anointed with this oil. The Kiyor sink and its pedestal is to be anointed with this oil. Through doing so, the vessels will become holy and anything that touches them will become consecrated. Likewise, Aaron and his sons are to be anointed with this oil and they will thus become consecrated to serve me as Kohanim.
   - <u>Not to use it or make a replica</u>: Tell the Jewish people that no man may anoint himself with the above oil and no man may make a replica of the above oil. Anyone who makes a replica of it or who uses it on a non-Kohen, will be cut off from his nation [i.e. Kareis].

4. **The Ketores incense:**
   - <u>The ingredients</u>: G-d spoke to Moses saying: "Take the following prime spices and make the Ketores:"
     - i. Nataf/Stacte.
     - ii. Shecheiles/onycha.
     - iii. Chelbana/galbanum
     - iv. Spices and pure frankincense.
   - All the above ingredients are to be of equal weight. The above ingredients are to be mixed by a spice blender and be turned into the Ketores incense. Some of it is to be finely ground, and some of it is to be placed before the Tent of Meeting. It shall be to you a holy of holies.
   - <u>Not to make a replica</u>: One may not create a replica of the Ketores incense for the sake of smelling it, under the penalty of excision.

Chapter 31
5. **Appointment of Betzalel to build the Tabernacle.**
   - G-d spoke to Moses saying: "I have appointed Betzalel the son of Uri of the tribe of Judah to perform all the work of building the Tabernacle and its accessories. I have filled him with wisdom and understanding to perform all the work. I have appointed to work with him Ohaliav the son of Achisamach from the tribe of Dan. They are to make the Tent of Meeting, the Aron, the Kapores lid, the vessels of the Ohel, the Shulchan/Table,

the Menorah, the Ketores altar, the Olah altar, the Kiyor sink, and all their accessories. They are to make the priestly garments, the anointing oil and Ketores, as I commanded."

6. **Guard the Shabbat:**
   - A covenant between us and G-d: G-d spoke to Moses saying: "Tell the Jewish people that they are to guard the Shabbat as it is a sign and covenant between Me and them for all generations so that they know that I am G-d who sanctifies you."
   - Punishment for desecration: One who desecrates the Shabbat is liable for death and is liable for Kareis, to be cut off from the nation.
   - In commemoration of creation: One is to work six days and on the seventh day it is to be a complete rest, as in six days the world was created and on the seventh day I rested.

Second Aliyah

7. **The Tablets of Stone:**
   - After G-d finished speaking with Moses on Mount Sinai He handed him the two stone Tablets which were written by the finger of G-d.

Chapter 32

8. **The sin of the Golden Calf:**
   - Moses's delayed return and the building of the golden calf: The nation saw that Moses delayed descending from the mountain and they gathered around Aaron telling him that they need to make a new G-d as a leader, as Moses's whereabouts are unknown. Aaron told the nation to gather the gold jewelry worn on the ears of their wives and daughters and have it brought to him. The entire nation removed the golden jewelry that was on their ears and brought it to Aaron. Aaron took the gold from them and bound it in a scarf and made it into a molten calf.
   - The golden calf is worshipped: They saw the calf and proclaimed "Israel, these are your G-ds who took you out of Egypt. Aaron saw what was occurring and built an altar in front of the calf. Aaron then proclaimed that the next day would a be a festival for G-d. They arose early the next day and brought offerings on the altar. They sat to eat and drink and got up to sport.
   - Moses is informed by G-d of the sin: G-d spoke to Moses saying: Go descend from here as your nation who you took out of Egypt has sinned. They have quickly strayed from the path which I commanded them and have made a molten calf and prostrated themselves to it and sacrificed to it and said that it is the G-d who has taken them out of Egypt.
   - Moses pleads to G-d: G-d then told Moses that he has seen that the nation is a stubborn nation, and He desires to be left alone to destroy them, and then make a new nation from Moses. Moses pleaded to G-d not to do such a thing and cause the world to say that He took the Jewish people out of Egypt to destroy them. "Please relent from your anger and reconsider doing evil to the nation. Remember the promises you made to the forefathers Abraham, Isaac and Jacob." As a result of Moses's pleas, G-d retracted from the evil He said He would do to the nation.
   - Moses descends with the Tablets of Stone: Moses descended from the mountain with the two Tablets of Stone in his hand. The Tablets of Stone were inscribed from both sides, from one end to the other, a writing of G-d.
   - Moses reaches the camp breaks the tablets and destroys the calf: Joshua heard shouting coming from the people and told Moses that the sound of battle is in the camp. Moses

replied that it is the sound of blasphemy. When Moses came close and saw the golden calf and the dancing around it he became inflamed with anger and threw the Tablets of Stone, causing them to break on the bottom of the mountain. Moses took the calf that they made and burnt it in a fire, grinding it to dust and then scattering it on water. The Jewish people were given this water to drink.

- Moses confronts Aaron: Moses asked Aaron what the nation did to him that brought him to cause such a grave sin. Aaron replied to Moses that he should not get angry with him, and Moses knows that the nation is in a bad state. "They told me to make a G-d, as they do not know the whereabouts of Moses. I simply asked them for gold and they gave it to me and I threw it into the fire and this golden calf rose up." Moses saw that the nation was exposed, as Aaron had caused them to be uncovered in disgrace.

- Moses has the idol worshipers killed: Moses stood at the head of camp and declared "Whoever is for G-d come to me." All the Levites came to Moses. Moses instructed them, that G-d commanded that each person should take a sword to his thigh and pass through the gates and kill all the perpetrators, whether it be a friend or relative. The Levites did as Moses instructed and killed 3000 men. Moses then blessed them for doing so.

- Moses returns to Heaven to achieve atonement: The next day, Moses told the nation that they have sinned a great sin and that he will try to ascend back to heaven to achieve atonement. Moses returned to G-d and told Him that the nation has sinned a very grave sin and made a gold idol. Moses then told G-d "If you would only forgive their sin, but if not, erase me from your book that You have written." G-d replied that only the sinners will be erased from his book. G-d instructed Moses to go back and lead the people, and told him that an angel will go before them, and He will seek retribution for their sin at a future time of reckoning.

- G-d smote the people who made the calf that Aaron made.

Chapter 33

9. G-d informs Moses that He will not escort the Jewish people any longer:

- G-d told Moses to go lead the nation to the promised land and that He will send His angel before them and drive out the Canaanite nations. I will not ascend with you, said G-d, as you are a stubborn nation and I may annihilate you on the way.

- The nation removes their crown: When the nation heard this bad news, they mourned and did not place their crowns on their heads. G-d told Moses to explain to the people that Him going with them can lead to their annihilation due to their stubbornness. G-d instructed them to remove the crowns from their heads. The Jewish people thus lost the crowns they received on Mount Horeb.

10. Moses distances his tent from the camp:

- Moses took his tent and pitched it outside of the camp and called it the Tent of Meeting. Whoever seeks G-d would come to the Tent of Meeting outside of the camp. The nation would stand upon Moses leaving his tent and look at him until he returned. When Moses would arrive a pillar of cloud would descend upon it and speak to Moses. The nation would see the cloud by the entrance of the tent and they would bow down. G-d spoke to Moses face to face like a friend would speak to a friend and he would the return to the camp. Joshua Ben Nun would not leave the tent.

Third Aliyah

11. Moses pleads to G-d and G-d concedes:

- <u>Moses pleads to G-d to escort the people Himself</u>: Moses told G-d that He had instructed him to lead the people but did not tell him who will escort them. "Now, You have said that I have found favor in your eyes. If this is true, then make Your ways known to me."

- <u>G-d retracts from His decision and agrees to escort the Jewish people</u>: G-d replied that He will no longer send His angel but that He Himself will escort them. Moses replied to G-d that if He will not go with them then they should not go onward, as this is the only way that they will know that they have found favor in His eyes, by G-d traveling with them and setting them apart from all the other nations of the world.

Fourth Aliyah

12. G-d shows Moses His glory:

- G-d responded to Moses that he will acquiesce likewise to the second request [of distinguishing the Jewish people from amongst the gentiles], as you have found favor in My eyes. Moses then asked G-d to be shown His glory. G-d replied that He will pass all His good before Him, although he cannot see His face, as no man can see G-d's face and live. G-d told Moses that he [i.e. Moses] will stand by a cleft within a rock and He will place His hand over him, so he is not injured while His glory passes over. "When I remove My hand, you will see My back but not My face."

Chapter 34
Fifth Aliyah

13. Moses ascends with the second Tablets of Stone:

- G-d instructed Moses to carve for himself two tablets, similar to the first ones, and G-d will write on it the words that were on the original Tablets of Stone that were broken. G-d told Moses to be ready in the morning and ascend Mount Sinai without any other person and wait for Him there. No man or animal shall be in the area.

- Moses did as he was instructed and carved two tablets, rose in the morning and ascended the mountain with the two tablets. G-d descended in a cloud and stood with Moses who called His name.

- <u>The thirteen attributes of mercy</u>: G-d then replied with saying the thirteen attributes of mercy, "G-d, G-d, Keil Rachum Vechanun Erech Apayim Verav Chesed Viemes, Notzer Chesed La'alafim, Nosei Avon Vapesha Vechatah Venakei" This means: G-d is a merciful G-d, slow to anger, and abundant in kindness. He preserves kindness for 200 years. Forgiver of sin, One who absolves but does not absolve completely. He remembers the sin of a father upon the children and grandchildren, up until the 4th generation.

- Moses hurried to bow to the ground and prostrated himself, asking G-d that if he finds favor in His eyes, let Him go with them and forgive their sin.

Sixth Aliyah

- G-d agrees to distinguish the Jewish people: G-d replied that He will make a covenant that He will distinguish the Jewish people from the other nations of the land.

14. List of Mitzvot:

- Banishing the Canaanite nations and idolatry: G-d told Moses that He will drive the Canaanite nations from the land, and that Moses should beware not to make a treaty with them. You are to destroy their altars, statues, and trees of idolatry as G-d is a zealous G-d who will not stand for idolatry. If you make a covenant with these nations, you may be led astray and join them in their feasts of idolatry. You may come to intermarry, and it will cause your children to stray after their G-ds.
- Do not make for yourselves molten G-ds.
- Pesach: Guard the festival of Pesach for seven days and eat Matzot in the month of spring. Do not slaughter the Pesach lamb over Chametz, or leave its meat leftover until morning.
- Firstborns: Every firstborn is Mine, the firstborn male of an ox or sheep. The firstborn donkey is to be redeemed with a sheep, or have its neck broken.
- Pilgrimage: The Jewish people shall not come to see Me empty handed. They are to visit G-d three times a year. Their property will remain protected during their visit.
- Shabbat: You are to work for six days and rest on Shabbat from plowing and harvesting.
- Shavuot: You are to celebrate Shavuot during the time of the wheat harvest.
- Bikurim: You are to bring first fruits to G-d.
- Meat and milk: Do not cook a kid in its mother's milk.

Seventh Aliyah

- G-d told Moses to write the above words.

15. Moses returns with the second Tablets of Stone and a shining face:

- Moses was with G-d for 40 days and nights. He did not eat bread or drink water, and he wrote on the Tablets of Stone the ten commandments, the words of the covenant.
- Moses descended the mountain with the two Tablets of Stone in his hand and he did not know that his face radiated due to that G-d spoke to him. The Jewish people saw the radiance on Moses's face and they feared approaching him. Moses called them and they came and Moses commanded them all that he was told by G-d on Mount Sinai.
- When Moses completed speaking with them, he placed a mask on his face. When Moses came to speak with G-d he would remove the mask until his departure, and then go command the Jewish people that which he was told. The Jewish people would see the radiance on Moses's face. Moses would return the mask to his face until his next meeting with G-d.

Parashat Vayakhel
Verses: 122 [Siman: סנואה]
Haftorah:[1] Kings 1 7:13-26

Number of Mitzvot:
There is **One** Mitzvah in Parashat Vayakhel. **Zero** positive commands and **One** negative command.

Negative commands:
1. **Mitzvah 114/Negative 67:** Not to adjudicate capital punishments on Shabbat.

Chapter 35
First Aliyah

1. **Keeping Shabbat:**
   - Moses gathered the entire Jewish people and told them that G-d commanded as follows: For six days a week you shall perform work and on the seventh day it shall be a complete day of rest for G-d. Whoever does labor shall be put to death. You shall not light a fire in all your dwelling places on Shabbat.

2. **Moses commands the children of Israel regarding the Tabernacle:**
   - The materials needed: Moses told the Jewish people saying that G-d commanded them the following: Every person of generous heart is to give a donation. The following donations are needed:
       1) Gold,
       2) Silver,
       3) Copper,
       4) Techeiles Turquoise wool,
       5) Argamon Purple wool,
       6) Scarlet wool,
       7) Linen,
       8) Goat hair,
       9) Red dyed ram skins,
       10) Tachash skins,
       11) Shittim-Acacia wood.
       12) Oil for lighting
       13) Spices for the anointing oil and Ketores incense.
       14) Shoham stones
       15) Filling stones for the apron and breastplate.
   - The items needed to be made: Every skilled individual is to come and make everything that G-d commanded, which includes the following items:
       o The Tabernacle: The Tabernacle, its tent covering, and its accessories which include its hooks, beams, bars, pillars and sockets.

---

[1] So is followed by Sepharadi communities and Chabad. However, Ashkenazi communities read from 7:40-50

- o <u>Aron</u>: The Aron and its accessories which include its poles and covering.
- o <u>The Shulchan/Table</u>: The Shulchan/Table, its poles, and all of its accessories, including the Showbread.
- o <u>The Menorah</u>: The Menorah and its accessories, including its lamps and oil.
- o <u>The incense altar</u>: The Ketores incense altar, its poles, anointing oil, incense, and entrance screen.
- o <u>The Olah altar</u>: The Olah altar, its copper netting, its poles, and all of its accessories.
- o <u>Kiyor sink</u>: The Kiyor sink, and its accessories.
- o <u>The courtyard</u>: The curtains of the courtyard, its pillars, sockets and the entrance screen. The pegs of the Tabernacle and courtyard and their cords.
- o The priestly garments.
- After hearing the above commands, the Jewish people left Moses's presence.

Second Aliyah

3. The donations come in:
- Those of generous heart came and donated towards the Tabernacle. Both men and women donated. They brought gold jewelry such as bracelets, nose rings, rings, Kumaz. Whoever had Techeiles-Turquoise, Argamon-purple, and scarlet wool donated it. Whoever had the ram skins and Techashim skins donated it. People brought silver and copper. Whoever had acacia-shittim wood, brought it. Women spun yarn of the different types of wool mention above, and donated it. The leaders donated the precious stones, the Shoham stones and Miluim stones for the apron and for the breastplate, and the spices and oil for the lighting and for the anointing oil and the Ketores.

Third Aliyah (Second Aliyah when connected to Pekudei)

4. Appointment of Betzalel to build the Tabernacle.
- Moses told the Jewish people: G-d has appointed Betzalel the son of Uri of the tribe of Judah to perform all the work of building the Tabernacle and its accessories. He has filled him with wisdom and understanding to perform all the work with the gold, silver and copper, stone and wood. Ohaliav the son of Achisamach from the tribe of Dan was appointed to work with him. They shall do the work together with all the skilled individuals.

Chapter 36

5. The Jewish people exceed in donating materials:
- Moses called upon Betzalel and Ohaliav, and all those who are skilled, to come do the work. They came and took from Moses the materials donated, but the Jewish people kept coming each morning, bringing more and more donations. The workers told Moses that too much material had been collected. Moses then went ahead and announced in the camp that the people should cease bringing donation material, and so they ceased. They had enough material to build the Tabernacle and have a surplus.

Fourth Aliyah

6. Making the tapestries:
- The craftsmen made the ten tapestries of twisted linen, Techeiles-Teurquoise wool, Argamon-Purple wool, scarlet wool. They made it the work of an artist. Each tapestry was 28 cubits long and 4 cubits wide. They attached the tapestries to each other in two groups of five. The ends of the two groups of tapestries contained 50 loops, corresponding to each other. They made 50 gold hooks to attach the two groupings together and hence have one Tabernacle.

7. Making the panels of goat hair:
- They made 11 tent panels of goat hair to be placed over the Tabernacle [i.e. the wool tapestries]. Each panel was 30 cubits long and 4 cubits wide. They attached the pannels to each other into two groups, one containing five and the second containing six. The ends of the two groups of panels contained 50 loops, corresponding to each other. They made 50 copper hooks to attach the two groupings together and hence have one Tabernacle.
- They made a covering of red dyed ram skin and a covering of Tachash skin to be placed above the goat hair panels.

Fifth Aliyah

8. Making the Kerashim/beams:
- They made beams for the Tabernacle from shittim-acacia wood. Each beam was 10 cubits in length and 1.5 cubits in width. Each beam contained two projecting pieces of wood [i.e. tenons] which were perfectly aligned across each other.
- Amount: They made 20 beams for the southern side and 20 beams for the northern side. They made 6 beams for the west side, plus two corner beams, for a total of 8 beams.
- Sockets: They made silver sockets for the beams, two sockets per beam, for each of its tenons. Thus, they made 40 silver sockets for the 20 beams of the southern side and 40 silver sockets for the 20 beams of the northern side. They made 16 silver sockets for the 8 beams of the western side.
- Poles: They made five poles of acacia-shittim wood for three sides of the Tabernacle, five for the northern side, five for the southern side, and five for the western side, for a total of 15 poles. They made the middle pole that is to be inserted into the beams and extend from one end to the next. They coated the poles with gold. They made rings of gold.
- The beams were coated with gold.

9. Making the Parochet curtain:
- The material: They made the Parochet curtain of Turquoise-Ticheiles wool, Argamon-Purple wool, scarlet wool, and twisted linen. It was made the work of an artist.
- The beams which hold the Parochet curtain: They made four pillars of acacia-shittim wood covered with gold to hold the Parochet curtain. They made golden hooks and four **silver** sockets for the beams.

10. Making the Masach screen in front of the Holies:
- They made a screen of Turquoise-Ticheiles wool, Argamon-Purple wool, scarlet wool, and twisted linen for the entrance to the Ohel tent. It was made the work of an embroiderer.

- They made for the Masach five pillars of acacia-shittim wood of which their tops were covered with gold. They made gold hooks and five **copper** sockets for the pillars.

Chapter 37

11. Making the Aron:

- Betzalel made the Aron of acacia-shittim wood. It was 2.5 cubits in length and 1.5 cubits in width, and 1.5 cubits in height. He covered it with pure gold both in its interior and exterior and made for it a gold crown surrounding it. He welded onto it four gold rings, two on each side. He made two poles of acacia-shittim wood and coated them with gold. He inserted the poles into the rings for it to be carried with.
- Kapores lid and Cherubim: He made a cover of pure gold for the Aron. Its dimensions were 2.5 cubits in length and 1.5 cubits in width. He made two Cherubim of gold on the opposite ends of the Kapores lid. The Cherubim contained wings spread upwards, and faced each other, and faced towards the lid.

12. Making the Shulchan/Table:

- He made the Shulchan/Table from acacia-shittim wood. It was 2 cubits in length and 1 cubits in width, and 1.5 cubits in height. He coated it with gold and made a gold crown around its rim.
- Rings and poles: He made a one handbreadth frame around its entire circumference, and the frame had a gold crown around it. He welded four gold rings onto it, one by each corner, and made two poles from acacia wood and coated them with gold. The poles were made to be inserted into the rings for the Shulchan/Table to be carried with.
- Accessories: He made the vessels that rested on the Shulchan/Table which include pure gold dishes, spoons, tubes and supports.

Sixth Aliyah (Third Aliyah when connected to Pekudei)

13. Making the Menorah:

- He made the Menorah from pure gold with a base, branches, goblets, knobs and flowers all made from the original piece of one Kikar of gold.
- It had six branches, three from each side. Each branch was made with three goblets, and was decorated with a knob and flower. The base of the Menorah was made with four goblets decorated with knobs and flowers. Under each set of branches a button was made. Everything was formed from the same piece of gold. It had seven candles.

14. Making the gold altar for incense:

- He made an altar for the incense offering from acacia-shittim wood. It was made into a square, its length being one cubit, and its width also one cubit. It was two cubits high. It contained horns on each of its four corners, and the horns, as well as the entire altar was covered in gold. He made a gold crown surrounding it. It had two gold rings beneath its crown, one on each corner. These rings served to hold the poles with which the altar was carried with. The poles were made from acacia-shittim wood and were covered with gold.
- He made the anointing oil and their spices, the work of a spice-blender.

Chapter 38
Seventh Aliyah (Fourth Aliyah when connected to Pekudei)

15. Making the Olah altar:

- He made the Olah altar from shittim-acacia wood. It was made into a square, its length being five cubits, and its width also being five cubits. It was three cubits high. It was hollow. He made horns on each of its four corners, and he covered [the entire altar] with copper.

- <u>Its accessories</u>: He made for it pots to remove its ashes, shovels, sprinkling basins, prongs, and fire-pans. It was all made of copper.

- <u>Its netting</u>: He made a copper netting which encompasses the altar and welded four copper rings on each of its four corners. He made poles of acacia-shittim wood and covered them with copper. He inserted them into the rings for the altar to be carried.

16. Making the Kiyor:

- He made a copper Kiyor sink and pedestal using the mirrors of the women who congregated at the entrance of the Tent of Meeting.

17. Making the courtyard/courtyard:

- He made a courtyard for the Tabernacle from twisted linen. The curtains of the northern and southern side of the courtyard were 100 cubits long. The curtains of the western side were 50 cubits long. The curtains of the eastern side were 15 cubits for each end.

- <u>The pillars</u>: There were twenty pillars and twenty sockets for the northern and southern side, and ten pillars and ten sockets for the western side. There were three pillars and sockets for each end of the eastern side, for a total of six. All the pillars were made with silver hooks and belts and their top was coated with silver. The sockets were made of copper.

- <u>The entrance to the courtyard</u>: The screen of the gate of the courtyard was made of Turquoise Ticheiles wool, Argamon-Purple wool, scarlet wool, and twisted linen and was 20 cubits long and 5 cubits in height. It contained four pillars and four copper sockets and had silver hooks and belts, and the pillars were coated with silver.

- <u>Its accessories</u>: The pegs of the Tabernacle were all made of copper.

Parashat Pekudei
Verses: 92 [Siman: בלי כל]
Haftorah:[1] Kings 1 7:51-8:21

Theme of the Portion:
1. Enumerating the donations that came in for the Tabernacle and what they were used towards.
2. Describing how the priestly garments were made.

Number of Mitzvot:
There are no Positive or Negative commands mentioned in Parashat Pekudei

---

First Aliyah
1. **The accounting of the donation materials and their use:**
   - The following is the accounting of the Tabernacle donations. It was counted by Isamar the son of Aaron, and the Levites, as Moses commanded. Betzalel Ben Uri Ben Chur from the tribe of Judah and Oholiav Ben Achisamach did all that they were commanded for building the Tabernacle.
   - Gold: 29 Kikar and 730 Shekel of gold was donated.
   - Silver: 100 Kikar and 1775 Shekel of silver was donated. A Beka weight of silver was donated for every person 20 years and older during the half shekel donation. The total number of donors of the half shekel was 603,550. The 100 Kikar of silver was used to make the silver sockets for the pillars of the Holies and Parochet curtain, one Kikar per socket. The remaining 1775 silver shekel were used to make the hooks and belts of the pillars.
   - Copper: 70 Kikar and 2400 Shekel of copper was donated. The copper was used to make the copper sockets for the pillars of the Tent of Meeting, courtyard and entrance gate. It was also used to make the copper altar and its netting and all of its accessories. It was also used to make all the pegs of the courtyard.
   - Wool: The Techeiles-Turquoise wool, Argamon-Purple wool, and scarlet wool, were used to make the priestly garments.

Chapter 39
Second Aliyah (Fifth Aliyah when connected to Vayakhel)
2. **The apron:**
   - He made the apron from gold, Turquoise-Ticheiles wool, Argamon-Purple wool, scarlet wool, and twisted linen. Gold strings were cut from thin sheets of gold and woven with the Turquoise-Ticheiles wool, Argamon-Purple wool, scarlet wool, and twisted linen. He made two shoulder straps, one by each end, and a belt which was likewise made of the same materials stated above.

---

[1] So is followed by most Ashkenazi communities and Chabad. However, Sepharadic communities read from 7:40-50

- The Avnie Shoham: He placed the two Shoham stones into their gold settings and inscribed on them the name of the tribes of Israel. He placed the stones on the shoulder straps of the apron, one per strap, as a remembrance.

3. **The breastplate:**
   - He made the breastplate from gold, Turquoise-Ticheiles wool, Argamon-Purple wool, scarlet wool, and twisted linen. The breastplate was square, folded over, a Zeres in its length and width. It was filled with four rows of stones. The first row contained the following stones: Odem, Pitdah, and Barekes. The second row contained the following stones: Nofech, Sapir, and Yahalom. The third row contained the following stones: Leshem, Shevo, and Achlamah. The fourth row contained the following stones: Tarshish, Shoham, and Yashfeh. The stones were placed within gold settings. They had the names of the tribes inscribed on them, one tribe per stone for a total of 12 tribes and stones.
   - The chains and rings that attach the breastplate to the apron: They made two gold chains on the breastplate. They made two gold settings and two gold rings and placed the rings on the two [top] corners of the breastplate. They attached the chains to these two rings. The other end of the chains was attached to the gold settings and then attached to the shoulder straps of the apron. They made another two gold rings for the bottom corners of the breastplate, and placed them in the interior of the breastplate. They made two rings on the bottom end of the shoulder straps of the apron, symmetric to the bottom rings of the breastplate. They placed a Techeiles-Turquoise woolen string through the two sets of rings, and attached the breastplate to the apron belt so that it not move.

Third Aliyah (Sixth Aliyah when connected to Vayakhel)

4. **The Meil robe:**
   - They made the Meil entirely from Ticheiles-Turquoise wool. The Meil contained a folded collar which may not be torn. They made its hem surrounded with pomegranates made of Turquoise-Ticheiles wool, Argamon-Purple wool, scarlet wool. They also made gold bells which were inserted into the pomegranates all around the rim.

5. **The Kutoness shirt; turban, pants and belt:**
   - They made the Kutones, turban, and pants from checkered linen for both Aaron and his sons. The belt was made from checkered linen, Turquoise-Ticheiles wool, Argamon-Purple wool, and scarlet wool, the work of an embroiderer.

6. **The Tzitz, Holy Crown:**
   - They made the Tzitz of pure gold and engraved on it the words "Kodesh LaHashem." They placed on it a Ticheiles-Turquoise woolen string to attach to the turban.

7. **The Tabernacle is brought to Moses:**
   - The work of the Temple was complete, and the Jewish people did all that G-d commanded.

Fourth Aliyah

- They brought the Tabernacle to Moses, including all of its vessels. The following items were brought to Moses: The Ohel tent and its implements, such as the hooks, beams, bars, pillars, and sockets; the ram skin covering, the Techashim skin covering, and the

Parochet curtain; the Aron, its poles and the Kapores lid; the Shulchan/Table, all its vessels, and the showbread; the Menorah, its candles, vessels and oil; the gold altar, the anointing oil and Ketores incense; the screen of the Ohel tent; the copper altar with its copper netting, its poles and all of its vessels; the Kiyor and its pedestal; the curtains of the courtyard, its pillars, ropes and pegs; the priestly garments.

- Moses saw that all the work was done as G-d commanded, and he blessed the Jewish people.

Chapter 40
Fifth Aliyah (Seventh Aliyah when connected to Vayakhel)

8. G-d instructs Moses how to put together the Tabernacle:
- G-d told Moses that on the first day of the first month the Tabernacle is to be erected. The Aron is to be placed in the Tent of Meeting and the Parochet curtain is to be placed as a screen before it. You are to bring the Shulchan/Table and arrange it, and bring the Menorah and light it. The gold altar is to be placed in front of the Aron, and place the screen by the entrance of the Tabernacle. The Olah altar is to be placed in front of the entrance of the Tent of Meeting. The Kiyor sink is to be placed between the Tent of Meeting and altar. It is to be filled with water. You are to erect the courtyard around it and set up the screen at the entrance to the courtyard.
- Anointing the Altar: You are to take the anointing oil and anoint the Tabernacle and all of its content and make it holy. Anoint the Olah altar and all its vessels and make it holy. Anoint the Kiyor and its pedestal and make it holy.
- Inaugurating the Kohanim: You are to bring Aaron and his sons to the entrance of the Tent of Meeting and bathe them there. You are to dress Aaron in the priestly garments, anoint him and sanctify him as a Kohen. You are also to dress his sons in the Kutanos shirt and anoint them there and sanctify them as Kohanim forever.

Sixth Aliyah

9. The Tabernacle is completed:
- The date: So it was on the first day of the first month of the second year the Tabernacle was erected.
- Moses assembles the Tabernacle: Moses erected the Tabernacle. He positioned its sockets, beams, polls and pillars. He spread out the tent over the Tabernacle and placed the skin coverings over it.
- Moses assembles the Aron: He placed the Tablets of Stone in the Aron, and inserted the polls to the Aron, and placed the Kapores lid on top. He brought the Aron into the Tabernacle and placed the Parochet curtain in front of it.
- Moses positions the Shulchan/Table: He placed the Shulchan/Table in the Tent of Meeting towards the northern side, outside the Parochet curtain. He arranged the bread on the Shulchan/Table.
- Moses positions and lights the Menorah: He placed the Menorah in the Tent of Meeting opposite the Shulchan/Table towards the southern side. He lit the candles on the Menorah.
- Moses positions the gold altar: He placed the gold altar in the Tent of Meeting in front of the Parochet curtain. He offered incense on it.

Seventh Aliyah

- He placed the screen of the entrance of the Tent of Meeting.
- <u>Moses positions the Olah altar</u>: He positioned the Olah altar in the opening to the Tent of Meeting and offered on it the Olah sacrifice and meal offering, as G-d commanded.
- <u>Moses positions the Kiyor sink</u>: He positioned the Kiyor sink between the Tent of Meeting and the altar and filled it with water. Moses, and Aaron and his sons would wash their hands and feet with the water when they would enter the Tent of Meeting or come to do the service on the altar.
- <u>Moses erects the courtyard</u>: He erected the courtyard around the Tabernacle and altar and placed the screen by the entrance of the courtyard.
- Moses completed the work.

10. A cloud covers the Tent of Meeting and is used as a signal for travel:
- A cloud appeared and covered the Tent of Meeting, and the glory of G-d filled the Tabernacle. Moses could not enter the Tent of Meeting, as the cloud rested upon it and the Tabernacle was filled with G-d's glory.
- Whenever the cloud would ascend from the Tabernacle, the Jewish people would travel on their journeys. If the cloud remained, then they would not travel until it ascended.
- The cloud would remain on Tabernacle by day and the fire would be there by night, as was witnessed by all of the children of Israel.

Vayikra/Leviticus

Parashat Vayikra
Verses: 111[Siman: דעואל]
Haftorah: Isaiah 43:21-44:23

Number of Mitzvot:
There are a total of **Sixteen** Mitzvot in Parashat Vayikra; **Eleven** positive commands and **Five** negative commands. The following are the commands in the chronological order that they are brought in the Portion.

A. Positive:
1. **Mitzvah 115/Positive 48:** To offer the Olah sacrifice according to its detailed laws.
2. **Mitzvah 116/Positive 49:** To offer the Mincha offering according to its detailed laws.
3. **Mitzvah 119/Positive 50**: To salt all the offerings.
4. **Mitzvah 120/Positive 51**: For the Beth Din to bring a Chatas offering in case of a mistaken ruling involving excision.
5. **Mitzvah 121/Positive 52**: For an individual to bring a Chatas offering in case of a mistaken transgression involving excision.
6. **Mitzvah 122/Positive 53**: To testify in court regarding matters one has witnessed that carry criminal or civil liability.
7. **Mitzvah 123/Positive 54**: To bring a Olah Veyoreid offering for certain sins, which include swearing falsely, Shavuot Haeidus, and entering the Temple while impure.
8. **Mitzvah 127/Positive 55**: For one who benefited from consecrated items [i.e. Meilah] to pay for the benefit plus an additional 1/5th, to the Temple.
9. **Mitzvah 128/Positive 56**: To bring an Asham Taluy guilt offering if one performed an act of questionable transgression that involves a negative command that contains the penalty of excision.
10. **Mitzvah 129/Positive 57**: To bring an Asham guilt offering for certain sins [i.e. Asham Vadaiy], including stealing, sinfully swearing, Meila, and other sins.
11. **Mitzvah 130/Positive 58**: To return a stolen object to its rightful owner.

B. Negative:
1. **Mitzvah 117/Negative 68**: Not to offer honey or Chametz onto the altar.
2. **Mitzvah 118/Negative 69:** Not to bring offerings without salt.
3. **Mitzvah 124/Negative 70**: Not to separate [behead[1]] the bird Chatas offering.
4. **Mitzvah 125/Negative 71**: Not to place oil on the flour sin offering.
5. **Mitzvah 126/Negative 72**: Not to place frankincense on the flour sin offering.

---

[1] Rambam Maaseh Hasacrifices 7/6

Chapter 1
First Aliyah

1. **The Mitzvah of Sacrifices:**
   - G-d called to Moses from the Tent of Meeting and commanded him to relate to the Jewish people the laws involving the sacrifices. These laws relate to the following topics:
   - The type of animal to bring as a sacrifice: A man who desires to bring a sacrifice to G-d, is to bring it from the domestic animal, whether from cattle or sheep.

2. **The cow Olah offering:**
   - If one brings an Olah offering from cattle, it is to be a perfect male. It is to be offered at the opening of the Tent of Meeting.
   - Semicha: One is to rest his hand on the head of the Olah, and it will be an appeasement for him, to bring him atonement.
   - Offering the animal: Once slaughtered, the Kohanim are to offer the blood of the animal onto the altar.
   - The Olah must be skinned and dismembered. The Kohanim are to light a fire on the altar and set up the wood. They are to arrange the limbs on the altar. The intestines and feet are washed and offered on the altar. All of the parts of the Olah are offered to G-d.

3. **The sheep and goat Olah offering:**
   - If one brings an Olah offering from flock, it is to be brought from sheep, or goats, it is to be an unblemished male animal.
   - It is to be slaughtered in the northern part of the altar in front of G-d.
   - The Kohanim are to offer the blood around the altar.
   - The Olah must be dismembered.
   - The Kohanim are to light a fire on the altar and set up the wood. They are to arrange the limbs on the altar. The intestines and feet are washed and offered on the altar. All of the parts of the Olah are offered to G-d. It is a pleasant smell for G-d.

Second Aliyah
4. **The bird Olah offering:**
   - If one brings an Olah offering from birds, it is to be from the turtledoves or young doves.
   - The Kohen is to bring the bird to the altar and remove its head, and offer it to the altar, spraying its blood on the wall of the altar.
   - Its innards is to be removed and discarded to the side of the altar, to the area where the ash rests.
   - The bird is to be partially torn and then offered on the altar, on the wood that is one the fire. It is an Olah offering to G-d.

Chapter 2
5. **The Mincha offering:**
   - When a soul brings a Mincha offering to G-d it is to be made of Soles, fine flour. It is to contain oil and frankincense.

- The Kohen is to take his three full fingerfuls of the flour, and oil, together with all of its frankincense, and offer it to the altar. The remainder of the Mincha is to be distributed to the Kohanim.
- The baked Mincha: If an oven baked Mincha [i.e. Maafeh Tanur] offering is brought, it is to be baked into Matzot. If one bakes loaves, it is to be mixed with oil. If one bakes crackers, it is to be smeared with oil.
- The fried Mincha: If a pan fried Mincha is offered, it is to contain fine flour that is mixed with oil, and is baked into Matzot. It is to be broken to small pieces, and then have oil poured over it.

Third Aliyah

- The deep fried Mincha: If a deep pan Mincha offering is brought, it is to be made of fine flour and oil. You shall bring this Mincha to the Kohen and place it close to the Altar. The Kohen is to take a commemorative portion from the Mincha and offer it to the altar. The remainder of the Mincha is to be distributed to Aaron and his sons, it is a Holy of Holies.
- Chametz: Any Mincha offering may not be made into Chametz, as all Chametz and all honey may not be offered to G-d. They are to be offered as the first offering [on Shavuot] and are not to be brought to the Altar.

6. Salting the offerings:
- Every flour offering is to contain salt, and you shall not discontinue using the salt of G-d's covenant from on the Mincha.
- Every offering is to be salted.

7. The Bikurim-Omer offering:
- When you bring a Mincha offering of the first grains to G-d, it should be made from flour that is ground from ripe ears of grain which is parched over fire. Oil is to be poured over it as well as frankincense. The Kohen is to take a commemorative portion from the flour, oil and its frankincense as an offering to G-d.

Chapter 3
Fourth Aliyah

8. The Shlomim sacrifice from cattle:
- If one brings a Shelamim from cattle, it may be either male or female, although must be unblemished.
- Semicha: One is to rest his hand on the head of his offering, and it is to be slaughtered by the opening of the Tent of Meeting.
- Offering the animal: The Kohanim are to offer the blood of the animal onto the altar, all around. The fat that covers the innards is to be offered. The two kidneys and the fat that is on them, and the diaphragm on the liver and kidneys is to be offered. It is to be offered over the Olah, which is on the wood that is on the fire.

9. The Shelamim sacrifice from sheep:
- If one brings a Shelamim from flock, it may be either male or female, although must be unblemished.

- <u>Semicha</u>: If the offering is a sheep, he is to bring it before G-d and rest his hand on the head of the offering, and it is to be slaughtered by the opening of the Tent of Meeting.
- <u>Offering the animal</u>: The Kohanim are to offer the blood of the animal onto the altar, all around. The entire tail, up until the kidneys, is to be offered, and the fat that covers the innards is to be offered. The two kidneys and the fat that is on them, and the diaphragm on the liver and kidneys is to be offered.

10. The Shlomim sacrifice from a goat:
- If one brings a Shelamim from a goat he is to rest his hand on its head, and it is to be slaughtered by the opening of the Tent of Meeting.
- <u>Offering the animal</u>: The Kohanim are to offer the blood of the animal onto the altar, all around. The fat that covers the innards is to be offered. The two kidneys and the fat that is on them, and the diaphragm on the liver and kidneys is to be offered.

11. Prohibition of eating Chelev fat or blood:
- It is an eternal decree for all generations that one may not eat any fat or blood.

Chapter 4
Fifth Aliyah

12. The Chatas sin offering of a Kohen Moshiach:
- G-d spoke to Moses saying that he should tell the Jewish people the following laws relating to a sin offering that is brought if a soul unintentionally sins and transgresses one of the commands that G-d prohibited.
- <u>The sin offering of a Kohen Moshaich</u>: If the anointed Kohen sins, he is to bring a **young bull** which is unblemished as a Chatas offering for G-d. The bull is to be brought to the entrance of the Tent of Meeting and he is to rest his hands on the head of the bull and sacrifice it before G-d.
- <u>Offering the blood</u>: The Kohen is to dip his finger in the blood and sprinkle it seven times before G-d, onto the face of the Parochet curtain. The Kohen is to take from the blood and place it on the corners of the altar used for the incense. The remaining blood is to be spilled on the base of the altar that is outside the Tent of Meeting.
- <u>Offering the animal</u>: All the fat that covers the innards is to be offered. The two kidneys and the fat that is on them, and the diaphragm on the liver and kidneys is to be offered on the Olah altar. The skin of the bull and its meat, head, feet, innards and waste is to be taken outside of the camp to a pure place where the ashes are poured, and is to be burnt there using wood.

13. The Chatas sin offering of the congregation/Sanhedrin:
- If the entire Jewish people accidently sin, then the congregation is to offer a **young bull** as a Chatas offering for G-d. The bull is to be brought to the entrance of the Tent of Meeting. The elders of the congregation are to rest their hands on the head of the bull and slaughter it before G-d.
- <u>Offering the blood</u>: The Kohen Hamoshiach is to bring the blood to the Tent of Meeting and dip his finger in the blood and sprinkle it seven times before G-d, onto the face of the Parochet curtain. The Kohen is to take from the blood and place it on the corners of the

altar used for the incense. The remaining blood is to be spilled on the base of the altar that is outside the Tent of Meeting.

- Offering the animal: All of its fat is to be offered to the altar. Everything that is done to the offering of the Kohen Moshaich is likewise to be done to this offering. Doing so will bring atonement and G-d will forgive them. The bull is to be removed to outside the camp and be burnt just as described by the previous offering.

14. The Chatas sin offering of a President:
- If a leader accidently sins, he is to bring a **male goat** which is unblemished as a Chatas offering for G-d. He is to rest his hands on the head of the goat and sacrifice it before G-d in the same area as the Olah offering.
- Offering the blood: The Kohen is to take from the blood and place it on the corners of the altar used for the incense. The remaining blood is to be spilled on the base of the Ohel altar.
- Offering the animal: All of its fat is to be offered to the altar. Doing so will bring atonement and G-d will forgive him.

Sixth Aliyah
15. The goat Chatas sin offering of an individual:
- If an individual accidently sins, he is to bring a **female goat** which is unblemished as a Chatas offering for G-d. He is to rest his hands on the head of the goat and sacrifice it before G-d in the same area as the Olah offering.
- Offering the blood: The Kohen is to take from the blood and place it on the corners of the altar used for the incense. The remaining blood is to be spilled on the base of the Ohel altar.
- Offering the animal: All of its fat is to be offered to the altar. Doing so will bring atonement and G-d will forgive him.

16. The sheep Chatas sin offering of an individual:
- If an individual accidently sins, and he bring a **female sheep** which is unblemished as a Chatas offering for G-d. He is to rest his hands on the head of the goat and sacrifice it before G-d in the same area as the Olah offering.
- Offering the blood: The Kohen is to take from the blood and place it on the corners of the altar used for the incense. The remaining blood is to be spilled on the base of the Ohel altar.
- Offering the animal: All of its fat is to be offered to the altar. Doing so will bring atonement and G-d will forgive him.

Chapter 5
17. The Olah Veyoreid offering for specified sins:
- Anyone who has transgressed the following sins is responsible to bring a Chatas offering:
  1. Swearing falsely: If an individual sins, by swearing falsely that he does not have testimony of something that he witnessed, then he will bear his sin.
  2. Impurity: Likewise, an individual who touches an impure item or a carcass and he became impure, and he forgot of his impurity and sinned [through entering the Temple or eating offerings].

3.<u>Vow</u>: An individual who made a vow and forgot and transgressed it.

- <u>The animal offering</u>: Anyone who is guilty of the above is to confess his sin and bring his guilt offering before G-d. It is to be a female sheep or goat, and the Kohen is to atone for him.
- <u>If he is poor-the bird offering</u>: If one cannot afford to bring an animal then he is to bring two turtledoves or two young doves to the Kohen. The first is to be offered as a Chatas offering and have Melika performed on its head, by its neck area, although it is not to be beheaded. The blood of the Chatas offering is to be sprayed on the wall of the altar, and the remaining blood is to be poured on the base of the altar. The second bird is to be offered as an Olah.

Seventh Aliyah

- <u>If he is very poor-The Mincha offering</u>: If one cannot afford even birds, then he is to bring a tenth of an Ephah of fine flour as a Chatas offering. It is not to contain oil or frankincense, as it is a sin offering. It is to be brought to the Kohen and he removes three fingerfuls from it and offers it to G-d. The Kohen atones for his sin and it will be forgiven. The Kohen receives the flour offering [for himself to eat].

18. The Asham Vadaiy guilt offering for Meila-Benefiting from consecrated items:

- G-d spoke to Moses saying: An individual who has accidently committed misuse of consecrated items is to bring his Asham guilt offering to G-d. He is to bring an unblemished ram with a value of the silver Shekalim. He is to compensate that which he deprived from the consecrated items, as well as an additional fifth. The ram is to be given to the Kohen and he will atone for him.

19. The Asham Taluiy guilt offering:

- Anyone who possibly transgressed a sin and does not know for certain, is to bring an unblemished ram the value of a guilt offering as an Asham to the Kohen. The Kohen is to atone for his sin and he will be forgiven.

20. The Asham Vadaiy guilt offering for swearing falsely:

- If an individual swears falsely to deny that he possesses the item of another which he truly has in his possession, he must a) return the item, adding an additional fifth to its value and b) bring a guilt offering.
- The offering is to be an unblemished ram. The Kohen is to atone for him and he will be forgiven.

Parashat Tzav
Verses: 97 [Siman: צז]
Haftorah: Jeremiah 7:21-28[1], 9:22-23

Number of Mitzvot:
There are a total of **eighteen** Mitzvot in Parashat Tzav; **Nine** positive commands and **Nine** negative commands. The following are the commands in the chronological order that they are brought in the Portion.

A. Positive:
1. **Mitzvah 131/Positive 59**: To remove the ash from the altar [i.e. Terumas Hadeshen].
2. **Mitzvah 132/Positive 60**: To keep a fire constantly alit on the altar and to daily light a stack of wood on the altar.[2]
3. **Mitzvah 134/Positive 61:** For the Kohanim to eat the leftovers of the flour offering.
4. **Mitzvah 136/Positive 62:** For the Kohen Gadol to offer a daily Mincha offering in the morning and afternoon.
5. **Mitzvah 138/Positive 63:** For the Kohanim to perform the Chatas offering according to the laws mentioned in the Torah.
6. **Mitzvah 140/Positive 64:** For the Kohanim to perform the Asham guilt offering according to the laws mentioned in the Torah.
7. **Mitzvah 141/Positive 65:** For the Kohanim to perform the Shelamim offering according to the laws mentioned in the Torah.
8. **Mitzvah 143/Positive 66:** The Mitzvah to burn any leftovers of the Sacrifices, which remain past their time [i.e. Nosar].
9. **Mitzvah 146/Positive 67:** The Mitzvah to burn Sacrifices which have become impure.

B. Negative:
1. **Mitzvah 133/Negative 73:** The prohibition to extinguish a fire from on the altar.
2. **Mitzvah 135/Negative 74:** The prohibition to bake the leftover flour offering into Chameitz.
3. **Mitzvah 137/Negative 75:** The prohibition for the Mincha of a Kohen to be eaten, and rather it is entirely offered to G-d.
4. **Mitzvah 139/Negative 76:** The prohibition to eat from the Chatas offering which is offered in the Heichal.
5. **Mitzvah 142/Negative 77:** The prohibition to have any leftovers from the Toda offering, or other offerings, left until the morning [i.e. Nosar].
6. **Mitzvah 144/Negative 78:** The prohibition to eat Pigul, which is an offering that was slaughtered or offered with intent to offer or eat past its time.
7. **Mitzvah 145/Negative 79:** The prohibition to eat offerings that are impure.
8. **Mitzvah 147/Negative 80:** The prohibition to eat the Cheilev fat of a Kosher domestic animal.
9. **Mitzvah 148/Negative 81:** The prohibition to eat the blood of an animal or fowl.

---

[1] So is followed by Chabad communities. However, Ashkenazi and Sepahardi communities read until verse 8:3 and then add the verses 9:22-23
[2] See Minchas Chinuch ibid that according to the Rambam the Mitzvah is to make sure that a flame is always alit on the altar, while according to the Chinuch the Mitzvah is light a pile of wood on the altar every morning and evening.

Chapter 6
First Aliyah

1. The constant fire on the altar, the Olah offering & Terumas Hadeshen [ash cleaning of the altar]:

- G-d spoke to Moses and told him to command Aaron and his children the following laws [of Sacrifices]:
- The law of the burning of the Olah offering on the altar, is that it shall remain burning on the altar throughout the night.
- Terumas Hadeshen-Removing the ashes: The Kohen is to wear his linen shirt and pants on his flesh upon removing the ash of the sacrifices. The ash is to be placed next to the altar. He is to change clothing and remove the ash out of the encampment, to a place of purity.
- The constant fire: The fire on the altar is to remain there constantly and is not to be extinguished. The Kohen is to place wood on the altar each morning to fuel the fire. The Kohen is to arrange the Olah offering on it and cause the fats of peace offering to go up in smoke.

2. The laws of the Mincha/flour offering:

- The children of Aaron are to offer the Mincha offering to the altar.
- They are to remove three fingersful of the fine flour of the Mincha, including its oil and all of its frankincense, and offer it on the altar.
- The remainder of the Mincha is to be eaten by the Kohanim in the courtyard of the Tent of Meeting. It is to be eaten as Matzah [unleavened], and not Chameitz [leavened]. It is considered Holy of Holies like the Chatas and Asham offering.
- Every male Kohen is allowed to eat its leftovers. This law applies for all generations.
- Whatever touches the offering becomes Holy.

Second Aliyah

3. The offering of the Kohanim on the day of their inauguration:

- On the day of his inauguration, Aaron and his children are to offer to G-d a 10th of an Eipha [2.49 liter[3]] of flour as a Mincha offering. It is to be fine flour [i.e. Soles]. Half is to be offered in the morning and half in the evening.
- Fried crackers: It is to be fried in oil in a pan and broken to small pieces.
- This offering is to be brought in each generation by the Kohen who inherits the mantle of priesthood from his father.
- Entirely offered: The entire Mincha is to be offered to G-d and no part of it is to be eaten.

4. The laws of the Chatas offering:

- The following are the laws of the Chatas offering: It is to be slaughtered in the same area as the Olah, in front of G-d. This offering is a holy of holies.
- The eating: It is to be eaten by the Kohen who offers it. It is to be eaten in a holy area, in the courtyard of the Tent of Meeting. It is to be eaten by all male Kohanim.
- Its taste: Whatever touches [and absorbs from] its flesh becomes holy.

---

[3] Shiureiy Torah

- The garments: Any garment that gets wet from its blood is to be laundered in the holy place.
- The vessel: The earthenware vessel in which it is cooked is to be destroyed, while if it is cooked in a copper vessel, it is to be cleaned and washed with water.
- Invalidations: Any Chatas which its blood is entered into the Tent of Meeting to atone is not to be eaten. It is rather to be burnt in fire.

Chapter 7

5. **The laws of the Asham offering:**
   - The following are the laws of the Asham offering: This offering is a holy of holies.
   - Where: It is to be slaughtered in the same area as the Olah and its blood is to be sprinkled all around the altar.
   - What is offered: All its fat is to be offered, as well as its tail, and the fat covering the intestines. The two kidneys and their fat which are on them are to be offered. The diaphragm which is on the liver is to be removed. It is to be offered by the Kohen onto the altar.
   - The eating: It is to be eaten by all the male Kohanim in a holy area.

6. **Who keeps the meat and skin of the Sacrifices?**
   - The Chatas and Asham have the same law; it is given to the Kohen who offers it. Likewise, the Kohanim who offer the Olah of an individual gets to keep its skin. Likewise, any baked and fried Mincha which is offered by a Kohen, is to be given to that Kohen. Any Mincha offering that is mixed with oil or is dry, belongs to all of Aaron's sons.

Third Aliyah

7. **The laws of the Shelamim, Toda offering:**
   - The following is the law of the Shelamim offering:
   - The Todah and its breads: If a Todah Shelamim offering is brought, it is to have [four types of breads, three which are] Matzah breads offered with it. The breads are to be mixed with oil [type #1], and contain Matzah crackers which are smeared with oil [type #2], and fine broiled flour which is mixed with oil [type #3]. In addition, Chametz bread is also to be brought with the offering. [type #4]
   - Distributing the breads and eating the meat: One loaf of each of the breads of the Todah offering are to be donated to G-d and given to the Kohen who throws the blood of the Shelamim. The meat of the Toda is to be eaten that day and is not to remain until morning.

8. **The sacrificial laws of leftovers, Pigul, impurity:**
   - Voluntary offering-leftovers: If one donates a Shelamim offering, it may be eaten that day and the next day, however any leftovers may not be eaten. The leftovers [i.e. Nosar] of the third day are to be burnt in a fire.
   - Pigul: If the meat is [intended] to be eaten on the third day, the sacrifice is invalid for the person who brought it, as it is considered Pigul [distanced]. One who eats it is liable [for punishment].
   - Impure meat: If the meat become impure, it may not be eaten and is to be burnt in the fire.

- Impure person: The meat of the offering may only be eaten by a person who is pure. One who eats the meat while he is in a state of impurity, receives the penalty of excision. A person who touches anything that is impure due to man [i.e. Tumas Meis] or animal [i.e. Carcass] is considered impure.

9. The laws of Cheilev/forbidden fats:
- The forbidden fats of an ox, sheep or goat may not be eaten. The forbidden fats of a carcass of Treifa may be used for all ones needs, although may not be eaten. Whoever eats the forbidden fats of a an offering [or other animal] receives the penalty of excision.

10. The law of blood:
- One may not eat any blood of a bird or animal in any of the encampments. One who eats any of the blood receives the penalty of excision.

11. The Shelamim offering:
- The Shelamim is to have its fat rest on its breast and be waved before G-d.
- The Kohen is to offer the fat on the altar and the breast is distributed to the Kohanim [to eat].
- The right leg is to be given as a present to the Kohen. It is given to the Kohen who offers the blood and fats of the sacrifice. This is an eternal gift to the priests from G-d.
- The above is the laws of all the Sacrifices of the Olah, Mincha, Chatas, Asham, and Shelamim which G-d commanded Moses on Mount Sinai, and the Jewish people were told to offer in the desert of Sinai.

Chapter 8
Fourth Aliyah
12. The inauguration of Aaron and his sons:
- G-d told Moses to take Aaron and his sons and perform the inauguration. He is to take the clothing, the anointing oil, the sacrifices which include the Chatas cow, the two rams and the basket of Matzot.
- The entire congregation is to be gathered to the opening of the Tent of Meeting.
- Dressing Aaron: Moses did as instructed, and bathed Aaron and his sons in water and dressed them. He placed on Aaron the Kutones shirts, and wound the belt around him, the Meil robe, the apron, and the belt of the apron, the breastplate and the Urim Vetumim. He placed the turban on his head, and on the turban, towards his face, he placed the Tzitz [golden band].
- Anointing with oil: Moses took the anointing oil and anointed the Tabernacle and all of its vessels, and sanctified it. He sprinkled the oil onto the altar seven times, and anointed the altar and all its vessels with the oil, as well as the Kiyor sink. He poured the anointing oil on the head of Aaron to sanctify him.
- Dressing the sons of Aaron: Moses clothed also the sons of Aaron in their four priestly garments

Fifth Aliyah
13. Offering the Sacrifices by the inauguration

- <u>The Chatas bull</u>: Aaron and his sons performed Semicha to the head of the Chatas bull offering. It was slaughtered, and its blood was taken by Moses and placed on the corners of the Altar with his fingers. The remainder of the blood was poured on the foundation of the altar and it was sanctified to atone. Moses offered onto the altar the fat that covers the intestines and the diaphragm of the liver and the two kidneys. The bull itself, its skin, meat and waste he burnt in a fire outside of the camp, as G-d commanded Moses.
- <u>The Olah ram</u>: Aaron and his sons performed Semicha to the head of the Olah ram offering. It was slaughtered, and its blood was thrown by Moses around the Altar. The ram was dismembered, and Moses offered its head and other limbs onto the altar. Its innards were washed in water. Moses offered the entire ram to the altar as it is an Olah offering to G-d.

Sixth Aliyah
14. The second inauguration ram:

- Aaron and his sons performed Semicha to the head of the second Olah ram offering.
- <u>Placing the blood on the ears and thumbs</u>: It was slaughtered, and its blood was taken by Moses and placed on the edges of the right ear and right thumb of the hand and toe of Aaron and his sons. The remainder of the blood was poured around the altar.
- <u>Waving the offering and the Kohanim</u>: Moses took the fat, and the tail and all the fat that covers the intestines and the diaphragm of the liver and the two kidneys, and the right thigh. He also took one bread from each of the baskets and he placed them on the fats and the right leg. He placed them all on the palm of Aaron and his sons and waved them before G-d. Moses removed the foods off the palm of their hands and offered them before G-d.
- Moses took the breast of the ram and waved it before G-d. It was a present to Moses from G-d.

Seventh Aliyah
15. Anointing the Kohanim with the oil and blood:

- Moses took the anointing oil [Shemen Hamishcha] and blood that was on the altar and sprinkled on Aaron and his sons and their clothing, and they were all sanctified.

16. Eating the sacrifices:

- Moses told Aaron and his sons to cook the meat in front of the Tent of Meeting and eat it there. Likewise, the bread is to be eaten there. The leftover meat and bread is to be burnt.
- <u>Not to leave the Tent of Meeting</u>: Aaron and his sons are to remain for the full seven days, day and night, in the opening of the Tent of Meeting, until the end of the inauguration. They are not to leave the area, lest they die.
- Aaron and his sons followed all the instructions they were given.

Parashat Shemini
Verses: 91 [Siman: עבדיה]
Haftorah: Samuel 2 6/1-19[1]

Number of Mitzvot:
There are a total of **seventeen** Mitzvot in Parashat Shemini; **Six** positive commands and **Eleven** negative commands. The following are the commands in the chronological order that they are brought in the Portion.

A. Positive:
1. **Mitzvah 153/Positive 68:** To know and check the Kashrut signs of an animal.[2]
2. **Mitzvah 155/Positive 69**: To know and check the Kashrut signs of fish.[3]
3. **Mitzvah 158/Positive 70:** To know and check the Kashrut signs of locust.
4. **Mitzvah 159/Positive 71:** That the eight rodents listed in the Torah impurify a person.
5. **Mitzvah 160/Positive 72:** To guard the laws of impurity of food and drink, as required by Torah law. Such as that all produce that is detached from the ground, becomes susceptible to impurity upon it becoming wet.
6. **Mitzvah 161/Positive 73:** That the carcass impurifies a person and one act in accordance to its laws.

B. Negative:
1. **Mitzvah 149/Negative 82:** The prohibition for the Kohanim to enter the Temple with long hair.
2. **Mitzvah 150/Negative 83:** The prohibition for the Kohanim to enter the Temple with torn clothing.
3. **Mitzvah 151/Negative 84:** The prohibition for the Kohanim to leave the Temple during their service.
4. **Mitzvah 152/Negative 85:** Not to enter the Temple, or give Torah rulings, while under the influence of wine or alcohol.
5. **Mitzvah 154/Negative 86:** Not to eat impure/non-Kosher animals.
6. **Mitzvah 156/Negative 87:** Not to eat impure/non-Kosher fish.
7. **Mitzvah 157/Negative 88:** Not to eat impure/non-Kosher fowl.
8. **Mitzvah 162/Negative 89:** Not to eat insects that crawl on the ground.
9. **Mitzvah 163/Negative 90:** Not to eat insects that grow in fruits and legumes while attached to the ground.
10. **Mitzvah 164/Negative 91:** Not to eat water insects.[4]
11. **Mitzvah 165/Negative 92:** Not to eat insects of spontaneous generation, created from rotting produce.

---
[1] So is followed by Sepharadi and Chabad communities. However, Ashkenazi communities read until verse 7:17
[2] This Mitzvah is listed by the Rambam, although according to the Ramban it is not included as one of the 613. See Chinuch ibid
[3] This Mitzvah is listed by the Rambam, although according to the Ramban it is not included as one of the 613. See Chinuch Mitzvah 153
[4] This Mitzvah is listed by the Rambam, although according to the Ramban it is not included as one of the 613. See Chinuch ibid

Chapter 9
First Aliyah

1. **The order of the eighth day of inauguration:**
   - On the eighth day Moses summoned Aaron, his sons, and the elders of Israel and commanded them the order of sacrifices for the day of inauguration.
   - Aaron's offerings: Aaron is commanded to take a calf for a Chatas, and a ram for an Olah and to offer it to G-d.
   - The offering of the people: The Jewish people are commanded to take a he-goat for a Chatas, and a calf and sheep in their first year for an Olah, and a bull and ram for a Shelamim, and a Mincha mixed with oil. The Jewish people brought all the offerings and came to the front of the Tent of Meeting.
   - Moses tells the Jewish people that through doing the above service the Shekhinah will be seen.
   - The meat offerings: Aaron is told to offer the Chatas and Olah and atone for himself and for the nation. He is then to offer the Sacrifices of the nation. Aaron did as he was told and slaughtered his calf Chatas sacrifice and he dipped his finger in the blood and placed it on the Altar. The fat, kidneys, and diaphragm of the liver of the Chatas was offered to the Altar. The meat and skin were burnt outside the camp. The Olah was then slaughtered and its blood was sprinkled around the Altar. The limbs and its head were offered to the Altar. The innards and legs were offered. The Chatas of the nation was slaughtered similar to the first Chatas. The Olah of the nation is offered.

Calves	2 calves [One for **Chatas** for Aaron, and one for an **Olah** of the Jewish people]
Rams	2 rams [One for **Olah** for Aaron, and one for **Shelamim** of Jewish people]
Goat	1 Goat [For **Chatas** for Jewish people]
Sheep	1 Sheep [For an **Olah** of the Jewish people]
Ox	1 Ox [For a **Shelamim** of the Jewish people]
Mincha	1 Mincha

Second Aliyah

- The Mincha: The Mincha of the nation was offered. He filled his hand from it and offered it onto the altar.
- The Shelamim: The Shelamim bull and ram of the nation was slaughtered and offered. The sons brought Aaron the blood and he threw it upon the Altar, all around. The fats of the bull and the ram, and the tail and the kidneys and the diaphragm of the liver were brought. The fats were placed on the breasts and were then offered on the altar. The breast and the right thigh were waved by Aaron before G-d.
- Birchas Kohanim: Aaron raised his hands towards the nation and blessed the Jewish people, and then descended from [the altar after] having performed the offerings.
- G-d appears: Moses and Aaron finished blessing the Jewish people and the Shekhinah appeared before the nation.

Third Aliyah

- A fire came from before G-d and consumed the offerings, the Olah and the fats. The entire nation witnessed this and praised G-d and fell on their faces.

Chapter 10

2. The passing of Nadab and Abihu:

- Nadab and Abihu took a pan with coals and incense and offered a foreign fire to G-d, of which they were not commanded. A fire came out from G-d and consumed them, and they died before G-d.
- Moses comforted Aaron saying that G-d had told him that his sons merited to be chosen by G-d to have the Temple sanctified through them. Aaron was silent.
- Moses summoned Mishael and Eltzafan, the second cousins of Nadab and Abihu, to remove the bodies of their brothers from the Holy and remove them from the camp. They approached and removed Nadab and Abihu through their clothing to outside the camp.
- Mourning customs: Moses instructed Aaron and his sons Elazar and Ithamar not to let their hair grow long or tear their clothing, or leave the Tent of Meeting, lest they die, and G-d become wrathful with all the Jewish people. The Jewish people will mourn the burning that G-d made.

3. Not to work while intoxicated:

- G-d commanded Aaron that the Kohanim may not perform service in the Temple under intoxication of alcohol, lest they die. This applies for all generations. This is necessary in order to distinguish between the holy and profane, and pure and impure and for them to instruct the Jewish people the laws of G-d.

Fourth Aliyah

4. The eating of the Sacrifices:

- Moses instructed Aaron and his surviving sons Elazar and Isamar to eat the leftovers of the Mincha offering as Matzah, as it is a Holy of Holies. It is to be eaten in a holy area because it is your portion from the Sacrifices of G-d.
- Eating the Shelamim: The breast and thigh [of all Shelamim sacrifices] are to be eaten in a pure area by the sons and daughters of the Kohanim. The breast and thigh are to be waved with the fats before G-d.

Fifth Aliyah

5. The goat sin offering is burnt and not eaten.

- Moses discovers the goat offering was not eaten: Moses questioned why the male goat offering was completely burnt and not eaten. He became angry with Elazar and Isamar, the remaining children of Aaron, asking them why they did not eat the Chatas which was given to atone for the congregation, in a holy area. "Its blood was not entered into the Holies, and hence you should have eaten it in the holies as I instructed."
- Aaron's explanation: Aaron replied to Moses that it is not befitting in the eyes of G-d to eat the offering on a day like this when these tragedies occurred to me [i.e. the death of Nadab and Abihu]. Moses approved of this response.

Chapter 11
Sixth Aliyah

6. The Kashrut laws:

- G-d spoke to Moses saying, tell the Jewish people the following laws of Kashrut:

- Signs of Kosher animals: You may eat the following animals from amongst all the animals on earth: Any animal that has completely split hooves and chews their cud [regurgitates their food], may be eaten.

- The non-Kosher animals: The following you may not eat amongst those who chew their cud or have split hooves: The camel, hyrax and rabbit, as although they chew their cud they do not have split hooves. Likewise, the pig may not be eaten as it has split hooves but does not chew its cud. You may not eat their flesh, and if their corpse is touched one becomes impure.

- Kosher fish: All fish that have fins and scales may be eaten. All fish that do not have fins and scales are not Kosher and are considered an abomination for you.

- Non-Kosher birds: The following [20] birds are not Kosher and are considered an abomination to eat [the identification of these birds from the original Hebrew is mostly unknown]: 1) Eagle; 2) Peres; 3) Ozniah; 4) Daah; 5) Ayah; 6) Raven; 7) Bas Hayaanah; 8) Tachmos; 9) Shachaf; 10) Netz [i.e. sparrow hawk]; 11) Kos; 12) Shalach [i.e. seagull] 13) Yanshuf [i.e. owl] 14) Tinshemes; 15) Kaas; 16) Racham; 17) Chasidah [i.e. stork]; 18) Anafah; 19) Duchifas [i.e. wild rooster]; 20) Atalef [bat].

- Insects: All flying creatures that walk on all four legs is an abomination to you.

- Locusts: The following insects may be eaten: Those locusts who walk on four legs and have an additional two jumping legs which they use to jump upon the earth, of these the following may species be eaten: Arbeh; Salam; Chargol; Chagav.

7. Laws of impurity:

- The following carcasses cause one to contract impurity if they are touched or carried. If one touches them he becomes impure until evening and if he carries them he and his clothing become impure, and he is to wash his clothing.

- Animal carcasses who give off impurity: The carcasses of all animals that do not have completely split hooves and do not chew their cud are impure, and whoever touches them becomes impure. All animals that walk on their paws are impure to you and whoever touches their carcass is impure until evening.

- Creeping animal carcasses which give off impurity: The following creeping creatures give off impurity: 1) Choled [i.e. weasel]; 2) Achbar [i.e. rat]; 3) Tzav [i.e. turtle]; 4) Hanaka [i.e. porcupine] 5) Koach; 6) Letaah [i.e. lizard]; 7) Chomet [i.e. snail]; 8) Tinshemes [i.e. mole]. One who touches their dead bodies is impure until evening.

- Vessels becoming impure: If the above carcasses fell on a garment of leather, or sackcloth, or on a vessel, it must be immersed and remains impure until evening.

Seventh Aliyah

- <u>Earthenware vessels</u>: An earthenware vessel that becomes impure due to a carcass falling in it must be broken.
- <u>Food</u>: All food that contacts liquid [after being detached from the ground] can become impure. Likewise, liquids can become impure.
- <u>A Mikveh</u>: A spring or well is pure.
- <u>Carcasses of Kosher animals</u>: The carcasses of Kosher animals likewise give off impurity if one touches them.

8. **Prohibition to eat insects:**
   - All creeping creatures on the ground are forbidden to be eaten. Whatever walks on its belly, on four legs, or with many legs is an abomination for you and may not be eaten
   - Do not abominate your souls by eating these creatures, as I am G-d your G-d and you shall be holy, for I am holy.

Parashat Tazria
Verses:67 [Siman: בניה]
Haftorah: Kings 2 4:42-5:19

Number of Mitzvot:

There are a total of **Seven** Mitzvot in Parashat Tazria; **Five** positive commands and **Two** negative commands. The following are the commands in the chronological order that they are brought in the Portion.

A. Positive:

1. **Mitzvah 166/Positive 74:** That a woman who gives birth is to be impure for her husband and Taharos, and follow the related Torah regulations.
2. **Mitzvah 168/Positive 75:** That a woman who gives birth is to bring Sacrifices at the end of her pure days.
3. **Mitzvah 169/Positive 76:** To follow the laws of one afflicted with Tzara'at and have him brought to the Kohen and purified or be deemed impure.
4. **Mitzvah 171/Positive 77:** That one afflicted with Tzara'at follow the laws relating to him, such as to have torn garments and long hair.
5. **Mitzvah 172/Positive 78:** To follow the laws instructed regarding clothing that grows Tzara'at.

B. Negative:

1. **Mitzvah 167/Negative 93:** For an impure person not to eat offerings until he is purified.
2. **Mitzvah 170/Negative 94:** Not to shave the hair of the Temple.

Chapter 12
First Aliyah

1. **The laws of a woman who gives birth:**
   - A male child: If a woman gives birth to a male child, she is impure for seven days. On the eighth day the child is to be circumcised. She remains with Demei Tohar [blood of Purity] for 33 day. She may not enter the Temple or touch offerings during this time.
   - A female child: If a woman gives birth to a girl she is to remain a Niddah for 14 days. She remains with Demei Tohar for 66 days.
   - The Sacrifices: At the completion of her pure days for a male and female she is to bring to the Kohen a year-old sheep as a Chatas offering and a bird for an Olah offering. The Kohen offers the sacrifice on her behalf and purifies her. If she cannot afford a sheep, she is to bring two birds, one for an Olah offering and the second for a Chatas offering.

Chapter 13

2. **The laws of Tzara'at:**
   - Showing it to the Kohen: One who has a lesion of Tzara'at on his skin is to be brought to the Kohen for examination. The Kohen is to view the ailment and if its hair is white and deeper than the skin, it is Tzara'at, and he is declared impure by the Kohen.

- <u>Confinement</u>: If its hair is not white and it is not deeper than the skin, the Kohen is to confine him for seven days. The Kohen is to re-examine the Tzara'at on the 7th day, and if it has not changed, and has not spread, he is to re-confine him for a further seven days.

Second Aliya

- The Kohen is to again examine the Tzara'at on the 7th day [of the second week], and if it has lightened in color, and has not spread, he is to purify it. The Metzora is to clean his clothing and he is then purified.
- <u>Respreads</u>: If the Tzara'at re-spreads after the purification, it is to be reshown to the Kohen and he is to be deemed impure.

3. **Tzara'at that has healthy skin:**
   - If the white lesion has a white hair but contains an area of healthy skin, it is in truth an old Tzara'at. The Kohen is to deem him impure. He is not to be secluded, as he is impure.

4. **Tzara'at that covers the entire body:**
   - If the Tzara'at covers the entire body from head to toe, he is to be deemed pure by the Kohen. If fresh skin ever appears on the body, he is to be deemed impure.

Third Aliyah

5. **Tzara'at on a blister:**
   - If a skin lesion appears on a blister and resembles the signs of Tzara'at, it is to be shown to the Kohen. If it appears lower than the skin and has white hair it is Tzara'at that has grown on the blister. He is to be declared impure by the Kohen. If it does not have these signs, the Kohen is to segregate him for seven days. If the lesion spreads, then he is impure. If the lesion does not spread, it is not Tzara'at but rather a skin ailment on the blister and he is pure.

Fourth Aliyah (Second Aliyah when connected to Metzora)

6. **Tzara'at on a burn:**
   - If a skin lesion of reddish and whitish color appears on a burn, it is to be shown to the Kohen. If it appears lower than the skin and has white hair, it is Tzara'at that has grown on the burn. He is to be declared impure by the Kohen. If it does not have these signs, the Kohen is to segregate him for seven days. The Kohen is to view him on the seventh day and if the lesion spreads then he is impure. If the lesion does not spread, it is not Tzara'at but rather a skin ailment on the burn and he is pure.

Fifth Aliyah

7. **Tzara'at on the head or beard:**
   - If a skin lesion appears on the head or beard, it is to be shown to the Kohen. If it appears lower than the skin and has yellow hair it is a Nesek Tzara'at that has grown on the head or beard. He is to be declared impure by the Kohen.
   - <u>No yellow hair</u>: If it does not have these signs but also does not have black hair, the Kohen is to segregate him for seven days. The Kohen is to view him on the seventh day and if the lesion does not appear lower than the skin and has not spread and the hair is not

yellow then the surrounding area of the Nesek is to be shaven and he is to be segregated for a further period of seven days. The Kohen is to view him on the seventh day and if the lesion does not spread and it does not appear lower than the skin, the Kohen is to deem him pure. He is to launder his clothing and he is pure. If the lesion spreads after his purity, he is deemed impure even if it does not have a yellow hair. If it grows a black hair, he is to be deemed pure.

8. White spots:
- If a man or woman has white spots on their skin, it is to be shown to the Kohen and he or she is to be deemed pure.

Sixth Aliyah (Third Aliyah when connected to Metzora)
9. Tzara'at on a bald or beardless person:
- One who does not have hair on his head, or one who does not have a beard, is pure. [He is to be judged with the laws of Tzara'at and not Nesakim.] If it grows a reddish, whitish, skin ailment, it is considered Tazraas. The Kohen is to see it and deem him impure.

10. The laws of one afflicted with Tzara'at:
- The one afflicted with Tzara'at must follow the following laws:
  - He is to wear torn clothing.
  - He is to have long hair and a long mustache.
  - He is to announce to others that he is impure.
  - He is to sit in seclusion outside of the Jewish camp.

11. Tzara'at on clothing:
- When a clothing of wool or linen or leather, or a vessel of leather has Tzara'at that is red or green it is to be shown to the Kohen. The clothing is to be secluded for seven days. On the seventh day the Kohen is to view the item and if the lesion spread the item is to be deemed impure. The garment or vessel is to be burnt.
- If the lesion did not spread on the clothing, then it is to be washed and secluded for a second set of seven days.

Seventh Aliyah (Fourth Aliyah when connected to Metzora)
- If the lesion on the clothing did not change color, it is impure and is to be burnt in the fire. If the lesion lightened in color, the area of the lesion is to be torn off the garment. If the lesion ever returns to the garment or vessel, it is to be burned. If the lesion disappeared after being laundered, it is to be laundered a second time and then purified.

Parashat Metzora
Verses: 90 [Siman: עידו]
Haftorah: Kings 2 7:3-20

Number of Mitzvot:

There are a total of **Eleven** Mitzvot in Parashat Metzora; **Eleven** positive commands and **Zero** negative commands. The following are the commands in the chronological order that they are brought in the Portion.

A. Positive:

1. **Mitzvah 173/Positive 79:** To follow the process instructed for purifying Tzara'at, such as to take two birds, the cedar wood, hyssop, crimson wool, fresh water and do as instructed for the purification.
2. **Mitzvah 174/Positive 80:** To shave off all the hair of the body of one afflicted with Tzara'at.
3. **Mitzvah 175/Positive 81:** To immerse in a Mikveh when one desires to purify oneself from impurity.
4. **Mitzvah 176/Positive 82:** For the one afflicted with Tzara'at to bring an offering when he is cured.
5. **Mitzvah 177/Positive 83:** To follow the laws instructed regarding a house which has grown Tzara'at.
6. **Mitzvah 178/Positive 84:** To attribute laws of impurity to a Zav.
7. **Mitzvah 179/Positive 85:** For a Zav to bring a offering after he is healed.
8. **Mitzvah 180/Positive 86:** To attribute laws of impurity to one who expels or touches Shichvas Zera/semen.
9. **Mitzvah 181/Positive 87:** To attribute laws of impurity to a Niddah.
10. **Mitzvah 182/Positive 88:** To attribute laws of impurity to a Zava.
11. **Mitzvah 183/Positive 89:** For a Zava to bring an offering after she is healed.

Chapter 14
First Aliyah

1. **The laws of the purification of a Metzora [i.e. one afflicted with Tzara'at]:**
   - The following are the laws of a Metzora on the day of his purification when he is brought to a Kohen. The Kohen is to come visit the Metzora outside of the camp. If the Metzora is seen to be healed of his Tzara'at, the Kohen is to begin his purification process.
   - The first stage of purification: The Metzora is to take two birds, cedar wood, a wool string, and hyssop. One bird is to be slaughtered and have its blood poured into an earthenware vessel that is filled with water. The cedar wood, a wool string, and hyssop are to be bound and dipped into the water and blood. The live bird is to also be dipped into the vessel. The above items are then to be sprinkled seven times onto the Metzora. The bird is then to be let free. The Metzora is to wash his clothing and shave all his hair and immerse in a Mikveh. He is then able to enter the camp. He must however remain outside his tent for another seven days.

- The second stage of purification after seven days: On the seventh day, he is to have all his hair shaved a second time. He is to wash his clothing and immerse in a Mikveh.
- The Sacrifices on eighth day: On the eighth day, he is to take two unblemished male lambs and a female lamb in its first year, and three tenth-ephahs of flour and one Lug of oil. The Kohen is to place the Metzora in front of the opening of the Heichal, before G-d. One lamb is to be offered as an Asham with the oil and then they are both taken and waved before G-d.

Second Aliyah

- The Asham blood: The Asham is to be slaughtered in the same area that the Chatas and Olah is slaughtered. The blood of the Asham is to be placed on the Metzoras right ear lobe and right thumb of his hand and foot.
- The oil: The oil is to be poured into the left palm of the Kohen and the Kohen is to dip his right finger into the oil and sprinkle the oil seven times in front of G-d. The remaining oil is to be placed on the Metzora's right ear lobe and right thumb of his hand and foot, on top of the blood. The remaining oil is then to be poured on the head of the Metzora.
- The Kohen is then to offer the Chatas and then offer the Olah and then the Mincha. The Metzora is now pure.

Third Aliyah (Fifth Aliyah when connected to Metzora)

2. **The Sacrifices of a pauper Metzora:**
   - A Metzora who cannot afford to take three animals, is to take a single male lamb for an Asham, and flour mixed with oil for a Mincha, and a Lug of oil, and two birds, one for a Chatas and one for an Olah. The same purification process is to be repeated. [The Torah goes on to repeat every single step mentioned above, without change.]

Fourth Aliyah (Sixth Aliyah when connected to Metzora)

3. **The laws of Tzara'at on a house:**
   - G-d spoke to Moses and Aaron saying that when they come to Eretz Canaan, G-d will place Tzara'at in houses. One who has Tzara'at in his house is to approach the Kohen and tell him that there is a Tzara'at like lesion in his house. The Kohen is to have the entire house cleared of all its belongings prior to him coming to examine the lesion. This is done to prevent the belongings from becoming impure.
   - The examination: If the lesion on the wall is green or red and it is lower than the rest of the wall then the following is done: The Kohen leaves the house and seals it for seven days. The Kohen is to return on the seventh day and see if the lesion has spread.
   - The Tzara'at spread-The purification process-stage 1: If the lesion spread, the Kohen is to have the stones of the wall that have the lesion, removed and taken outside the camp, to an impure place. The area around the lesion is to have a layer of its material removed and have that material thrown outside of the camp, to an impure place. New stones are to be placed into the wall, and the peeled area of the wall is to be filled in.
   - If the Tzara'at returns: If the Tzara'at returns after this, then the house is impure. The entire house is to be destroyed and all of its material is to be removed outside of the camp. [The examination to check whether the Tzara'at returned takes place seven days after the purification process.] Whoever enters the house during this time becomes impure.

- If the Tzara'at does not return-Purification process-stage 2: If the Tzara'at does not return, then the house is to be purified. Two birds, cedar wood and crimson wool string are taken. One bird is to be slaughtered and have its blood poured into an earthenware vessel that is filled with water. The cedar wood, a wool string, and hyssop are to be bound and dipped into the water and blood. The bird is also to be dipped into the vessel. The above items are then to be sprinkled seven times onto the house. The bird is then to be let free to outside of the city.

Fifth Aliyah:
- This concludes the laws of all the types of Tzara'at.

Chapter 15
4. The Zav impurity:
- G-d spoke to Moses and Aaron telling them to speak to the children of Israel regarding the laws of Zav. A man who has a flow of semen like fluid is to be declared impure.
- Contact with the Zav: Whatever bed he lies on and whatever seat he sits on becomes impure. One who touches his bed becomes impure until the night. Whoever sits on his seat becomes impure until the night. Whoever touches the skin of the Zav is impure until the night. If the Zav spits on a person, he is impure until the night. Whatever ride the Zav rides on becomes impure and whoever touches it is impure. Whoever the Zav touches becomes impure. An earthenware vessel that is touched by the Zav becomes impure and is to be destroyed. A wood vessel is to be immersed in water.
- Purification process of Zav: The Zav is to count seven days and immerse his clothing and body in water. On the eighth day he is to take two birds and bring them to the Tent of Meeting to the Kohen. The Kohen is to offer one as a Chatas and one as an Olah.

Sixth Aliyah (Seventh Aliyah when connected to Metzora)
5. The impurity of Shichvas Zera/Discharge of semen:
- A man who releases semen is to immerse in water and he is impure until the evening.
- Any garment or leather that touches the semen is impure and is to be immersed in water.
- A woman who lies with a man and he released semen into her, they are both impure until the evening and are to immerse in water.

6. The impurity of a Niddah:
- When a woman sees blood, she is to be in the state of Niddah for seven days.
- Contact with her: Whoever touches her is impure until the evening. Whatever bed she lies on and whatever seat she sits on becomes impure until the evening. One who touches her bed becomes impure until the night. Whoever sits on her seat becomes impure until the night. If a man lies with her, he is impure for seven days just like her.

7. The impurity of a Zava:
- When a woman sees blood for many days outside of her menstruation period, she is to be in the state of impurity for the amount of days that she bled.
- Contact with her: Whatever bed she lies on and whatever seat she sits on becomes impure until the evening. Whoever touches it is impure until the evening.

- <u>Purification process of Zava</u>: When she stops seeing the blood she is to count seven days and is to become pure.

Seventh Aliyah

- On the eighth day she is to take two birds and bring them to the Tent of Meeting to the Kohen. The Kohen is to offer one as a Chatas and one as an Olah. She then becomes purified of her impurity.
- The children of Israel are to be warned of all the above impurities. This concludes the laws of all these impurities.

Parashat Acharei Mot
Verses: 80 *[Siman: כי כל]*
Haftorah:[1] Amos 9:7-15

Number of Mitzvot:
There are a total of **28** Mitzvot in Parashat Acharei Mot; **2** positive commands and **26** negative commands. The following are the commands in the chronological order that they are brought in the Portion.

A. Positive:
1. **Mitzvah 185; Positive 90**: For the Kohen Gadol to perform all the duties of Yom Kippur regarding the Sacrifices and service.
2. **Mitzvah 187; Positive 91**: To cover the blood of a slaughtered wild animal and bird.

B. Negative:
1. **Mitzvah 184; Negative 95:** The prohibition for a Kohen to enter the Holies, with exception to the times of service.
2. **Mitzvah 186; Negative 96:** Not to slaughter offerings outside the Temple courtyard.
3. **Mitzvah 188; Negative 97:** Not to perform sexually stimulating activities with an Erva, such as hugging and kissing, staring, flirting etc.
4. **Mitzvah 189; Negative 98:** Not to reveal the Erva of one's father [i.e. have intercourse].
5. **Mitzvah 190; Negative 99:** Not to reveal the Erva of one's mother [i.e. have intercourse].
6. **Mitzvah 191; Negative 100:** Not to reveal the Erva of one's father's wife [i.e. have intercourse].
7. **Mitzvah 192; Negative 101:** Not to reveal the Erva of one's sister, even if not from father's wife [i.e. have intercourse].
8. **Mitzvah 193; Negative 102:** Not to reveal the Erva [i.e. have intercourse] of one's granddaughter, one's son's daughter.
9. **Mitzvah 194; Negative 103:** Not to reveal the Erva [i.e. have intercourse] of one's granddaughter, one's daughter's daughter.
10. **Mitzvah 195; Negative 104:** Not to reveal the Erva of one's daughter [i.e. have intercourse].
11. **Mitzvah 196; Negative 105:** Not to reveal the Erva of one's sister if she is one's father's wife's daughter.
12. **Mitzvah 197; Negative 106:** Not to reveal the Erva of one's aunt, one's father's sister [i.e. have intercourse].
13. **Mitzvah 198; Negative 107:** Not to reveal the Erva of one's aunt, one's mother's sister [i.e. have intercourse].
14. **Mitzvah 199; Negative 108:** Not to reveal the Erva of one's uncle, one's father's brother [i.e. have intercourse].
15. **Mitzvah 200; Negative 109:** Not to reveal the Erva of one's aunt, one's father's

---

[1] So is followed by Ashkenazi and Chabad communities. However, Sepharadi communities read from Yechzkal 22:1-16. [See Rama 428:8 and Poskim ibid]

brother's wife [i.e. have intercourse].

16. **Mitzvah 201; Negative 110:** Not to reveal the Erva of one's daughter in-law, one's son's wife [i.e. have intercourse].

17. **Mitzvah 202; Negative 111:** Not to reveal the Erva of one's sister in-law, one's brother's wife [i.e. have intercourse].

18. **Mitzvah 203; Negative 112:** Not to reveal the Erva of a mother and daughter if married to one of them [i.e. have intercourse].

19. **Mitzvah 204; Negative 113:** Not to reveal the Erva of a mother and her granddaughter, the daughter of her son, if married to one of them [i.e. have intercourse].

20. **Mitzvah 205; Negative 114:** Not to reveal the Erva of a mother and her granddaughter, the daughter of her daughter, if married to one of them [i.e. have intercourse].

21. **Mitzvah 206; Negative 115:** Not to reveal the Erva of one's sister in-law, one's wife's sister [i.e. have intercourse].

22. **Mitzvah 207; Negative 116:** Not to reveal the Erva of a Nida [i.e. have intercourse].

23. **Mitzvah 208; Negative 117:** Not to give one's offspring to the Moleich idolatry.

24. **Mitzvah 209; Negative 118:** For a man not to have homosexual intercourse with a man.

25. **Mitzvah 210; Negative 119:** For a man not to have sexual relations with an animal.

26. **Mitzvah 211; Negative 120:** For a woman not to have sexual relations with an animal.

Chapter 16
First Aliyah

1. **Death of Aaron's sons:**
   - The Torah recounts the death of Aaron's sons and the commands G-d told Moses as a result.

2. **The service of Yom Kippur:**
   - Aaron may only enter the Holies when the cloud is on the Kapores lid.
   - The offerings: Aaron is to bring a **bull** as a Chatas offering and a **ram** as an Oleh offering when he enters the Holies. He is to wear four linen garments during the service and is to immerse in a Mikveh prior to doing so. The nation is to bring to Aaron two **goat** offerings as a Chatas and a single **ram** as an Oleh.
   - Aaron is to offer his bull as a Chatas and atone for himself and family.
   - The service done with the two Chatas goats: The two goats are to be placed before the Tent of Meeting. A raffle is to be made and one of the goats is to go to G-d and the second is to go to Azazel. The goat which came out to G-d is to be offered as a Chatas. The Azazel goat is to be sent to the desert.
   - The bull of Aaron is to be offered.
   - The Ketores: Coals and Ketores are to be brought to the Parochet curtain. The Ketores incense is to be placed on the coals before G-d.
   - Sprinkling the blood in the Holies: The blood of the bull is to be sprinkled with his finger seven times onto the Parochet curtain. The goat which came out to G-d is to be offered as a Chatas and its blood sprinkled seven times by the Parochet curtain. This procedure is followed in order to purify the children of Israel and atone for their sins. No person is to be in the Tent of Meeting when the Kohen enters into the Holies.

Second Aliyah
   - Sprinkling the blood on the altar: The blood of the goat and bull is to be placed on the corners of the Altar. The blood is to be sprinkled seven times on the Altar.
   - The live goat: The live goat is to be brought to Aaron. He is to lean on it and confess. The goat is then sent with an escort to the desert. The goat carries all the sins of the Jewish people.
   - The Olah: Aaron is to change his clothing and offer his Olah offering, and the Olah offering of the nation.

Third Aliyah (Second Aliyahi when connected to Kedoshim)
   - The fat of the Chatas is to be offered onto the altar.
   - The escort of the Azazal goat is to wash his clothing and immerse, prior to entering the camp.
   - The bull and goat Chatas are to be taken outside of the camp and burnt. The one who burns the bull/goat is to wash his clothing and immerse, prior to entering the camp.
   - Yom Kippur laws: The above service is to be done in the 7th month, on the 10th day of the month. On this day everyone is to oppress himself. On this day no labor may be performed by anyone. On this day G-d grants us atonement for our sins. It is a Shabbat of complete rest [i.e. Shabbat Shabbason], a day of oppression, forever. The Kohen Gadol is to perform the above service each year.

Chapter 17
Fourth Aliyah

3. **Not to offer a sacrifice outside of the Temple:**
   - One who does not bring the offering to the Temple, and rather slaughters it in the camp, or outside the camp, is liable for excision. Since he did not bring the sacrifice before G-d, in the Tabernacle, it is considered like blood for that man. He has spilled blood and he shall be cut off from his people. The Jewish people are to bring the offering to the Tabernacle before G-d, to the Kohen, and have it slaughtered there. The Kohen will sprinkle its blood and offer its fat as a satisfying aroma for G-d. They shall no longer slaughter their sacrifices to the demons who they stray after. This is an eternal law for all generations.

Fifth Aliyah (Third Aliyah when connected to Kedoshim)
   - Tell the Jewish people and their converts that if they bring an Olah or Shelamim offering outside the Temple, that man will be cut off from his people.

4. **Prohibition against eating blood:**
   - Any man of Israel who eats any blood is liable for excision, and I will cut him off from the Jewish people. The soul of all flesh is found in its blood, and it has been designated to be offered to the altar, to atone for your souls. Therefore, no man or convert shall eat blood.

5. **The Mitzvah to cover blood:**
   - Any Jew or convert who traps a wild animal [i.e. Chayah] or bird that may be eaten, is to have its blood covered with earth, as the soul of all flesh is found in its blood. Tell the Jewish people not to eat the blood of any flesh, as its soul is its blood, and one who consumes it will be cut off.

6. **Impurity received through eating carcass/Treifa bird:**
   - One who eats a carcass or Treifa [of a bird] becomes impure, and requires purification. He is to wash his garments and immerse in water and remains impure until evening. If he does not wash his clothing and does not immerse his flesh [and eats an offering or enters the Holies], he shall carry his sin.

Chapter 18

7. **Not to follow the ways of the gentiles:**
   - G-d spoke to Moses saying, tell the Jewish people: Do not follow the ways of the land of Egypt where you lived, or the ways of the land of the Canaanites where I will bring you. Do not follow their statutes. Follow my laws and decrees as I am G-d your G-d. Follow them and you shall live.

Sixth Aliyah:

8. **The forbidden relations/Arayos:**
   - One is not to come close to any [of the following] relatives, to reveal their nakedness [and engage in marital relations].
   - Do not reveal the Erva/nakedness of your **father or mother** [i.e. have intercourse].

- Do not reveal the Erva of your **father's wife**.
- Do not reveal the Erva of your **sister,** including a half sister.
- Do not reveal the Erva of your **granddaughter**.
- Do not reveal the Erva of your sister if she is your **father's wife's daughter** (half sister).
- Do not reveal the Erva of your **father's sister**.
- Do not reveal the Erva of your **mother's sister**.
- Do not reveal the Erva of your **father's brother or his wife**.
- Do not reveal the Erva of your **daughter in-law**.
- Do not reveal the Erva of your **brother's wife**.
- Do not reveal the Erva of your **mother and daughter or granddaughter**.
- Do not reveal the Erva of your **wife's sister**.
- Do not reveal the Erva of a **Nida**.
- Do not sleep with **another man's wife**.
- Do not give your offspring to the Moleich idolatry, do not desecrate the name of G-d.

Seventh Aliyah (Fourth Aliyah when connected to Kedoshim)

- Do not lie with **a man** as one lies with a woman. It is an abomination.
- A man may not lie with an **animal**.
- A woman may not lie with an animal.

9. **A warning to keep the land pure and not be expelled:**
   - Do not impurify your souls with all the above, as the gentiles who I am expelling became impure with them. They defiled the land and it vomited its inhabitants. You, however, shall guard yourselves from all of this, and not perform any of these abominations. Don't cause the land to vomit you out due to your defilement as it did to the nations before you.
   - Punishment of excision: Anyone who performs any of the above abominations shall be cut off from the Jewish people.

Parashat Kedoshim

Verses: 64 *[Siman: מִי זָהָב]*
Haftorah:[1] Ezekiel 20:2-20

Number of Mitzvot:
There are a total of **51** Mitzvot in Parashat Kedoshim; **13** positive commands and **38** negative commands. The following are the commands in the chronological order that they are brought in the Portion.

A. Positive:
1. **Mitzvah 212; Positive 92**: To fear one's mother and father.
2. **Mitzvah 216; Positive 93**: To leave the corner of one's field to the poor [i.e. Peiah]
3. **Mitzvah 218; Positive 94**: To leave Leket, which are the bundles that fall to the ground during harvest, to the poor.
4. **Mitzvah 220; Positive 95:** To leave a corner or Olalaos [i.e. small grapes not in clusters] of the vineyard to the poor.[2]
5. **Mitzvah 222; Positive 96:** To leave the Peret of the vineyard to the poor. This refers to the grapes that fall during harvest.
6. **Mitzvah 235; Positive 97:** To judge justifiably and not honor one side of the case more than the other.
7. **Mitzvah 239; Positive 98:** To rebuke a sinner
8. **Mitzvah 243; Positive 99:** To love a fellow Jew.
9. **Mitzvah 247; Positive 100:** To eat the fruit of the fourth year of the tree in Jerusalem [i.e. Neta Rivaiy]
10. **Mitzvah 254; Positive 101:** To fear the Temple.
11. **Mitzvah 257; Positive 102:** To honor the Sages and elders and stand for them.
12. **Mitzvah 259; Positive 103:** To have honest weights and measurements.
13. **Mitzvah 261; Positive 104:** To burn one who is liable for the capital punishment of burning.

B. Negative:
1. **Mitzvah 213; Negative 121:** Not to pursue idolatry in neither thought, speech, or even sight.
2. **Mitzvah 214; Negative 122:** Not to make idols for oneself or for other people.[3]
3. **Mitzvah 215; Negative 123:** Not to eat Nosar, the leftover meat of offerings that has passed its Halachic expiration date.
4. **Mitzvah 217; Negative 124:** Not to harvest the entire field and rather leave the corner of the field for the poor.
5. **Negative 219; Negative 125:** Not to take the bundles that fall to the field during harvest, but rather to leave them to the poor.
6. **Negative 221; Negative 126:** Not to take all the grapes off the vine and rather to leave

---

[1] So is followed by Sefaradi and Chabad communities. However, Ashkenazi communities read from Yechzkal 22:1-16.
[2] The Rambam learns this Mitzvah is to leave grapes on the tree for the poor, while the Ramban learns the Mitzvah to leave the small grapes is in addition to the Mitzvah of leaving the corner. See Chinuch Mitzvah 221
[3] See Minchas Chinuch Mitzvah 214 in name of Rambam that one who makes idols for himself transgresses this command while one who makes idols for others transgresses command 27.

the corner/Olalos to the poor.[4]

7. **Negative 223; Negative 127:** Not to take the Peret of the vineyard, but rather to leave it for the poor.

8. **Negative 224; Negative 128:** Not to steal any money or item.

9. **Negative 225; Negative 129:** Not to deny having another's money in one's possession.

10. **Negative 226; Negative 130:** Not to swear falsely regarding money that one owes.

11. **Negative 227; Negative 131:** Not to swear falsely.

12. **Mitzvah 228; Negative 132:** Not to withhold money that belongs to another.

13. **Mitzvah 229; Negative 133:** Not to rob a person.

14. **Mitzvah 230; Negative 134:** Not to delay the payment of a worker.

15. **Mitzvah 231; Negative 135:** Not to curse any Jew.

16. **Mitzvah 232; Negative 136:** Not to place a stumbling block [i.e. bad advice] in front of a person.

17. **Mitzvah 233; Negative 137:** Not to judge unjustifiably, contrary to Torah law.

18. **Mitzvah 234; Negative 138:** For a judge not to honor one of the sides during the judgment.

19. **Mitzvah 236; Negative 139:** Not to slander [i.e. Rechilus/Lashon Hara].

20. **Mitzvah 237; Negative 140:** Not to standby when Jewish blood is spilled but rather to help save him.

21. **Mitzvah 238; Negative 141:** Not to hate a fellow Jew in one's heart.

22. **Mitzvah 240; Negative 142:** Not to embarrass a fellow Jew.

23. **Mitzvah 241; Negative 143:** Not to take revenge from a Jew.

24. **Mitzvah 242; Negative 144:** Not to hold a grudge against a Jew.

25. **Mitzvah 244; Negative 145:** Not to mate two different species of animals.

26. **Mitzvah 245; Negative 146:** Not to plant two different species of seeds together in Israel.

27. **Mitzvah 246; Negative 147:** Not to eat Arla fruits, which are fruits within three years of planting.

28. **Mitzvah 248; Negative 148:** Not to eat and drink like a glutton

29. **Mitzvah 253; Negative 149:** Not to do Nechisha, which is to follow superstitious signs.

30. **Mitzvah 250; Negative 150:** Not to do Onen, which is to follow superstitious times or to do magic tricks.

31. **Mitzvah 251; Negative 151:** Not to shave the corners of the head [i.e. Peios].

32. **Mitzvah 252; Negative 152:** Not to shave the corners of the beard.

33. **Mitzvah 253; Negative 153:** Not to make a tattoo on one's skin.

34. **Mitzvah 255; Negative 154:** Not to do the sorcery of Ov or pursue them.

35. **Mitzvah 256; Negative 155:** Not to do the sorcery of Yidoni.

36. **Mitzvah 258; Negative 156:** Not to use dishonest measurements and weights in your sales

37. **Mitzvah 260; Negative 157:** Not to curse one's father or mother.

38. **Mitzvah 262; Negative 158:** Not to go in the paths of the gentiles.

---

[4] The Rambam learns this prohibition is against removing all the grapes from the tree, while the Ramban learns the prohibition is against taking the small grapes [i.e. Olalos] from the tree. See Chinuch Mitzvah 221

Chapter 19
First Aliyah

1. List of Mitzvot:

G-d spoke to Moses saying, tell the Jewish people the following commands:

- Be Holy, as I am holy.
- Fear your father and mother.
- Guard Shabbat.
- Don't go after idolatry and don't make idols.
- Sacrifices: When you sacrifice a Shelamim offering to G-d, do so with proper thoughts to appease G-d. Eat the meat of the sacrifice that day and the next day, and any leftover on the 3rd day is to be burnt. Don't eat any leftover [i.e. Nosar]. One who eats the meat on the 3rd day [i.e. Nosar] receives excision as he has defiled the sacred to G-d, and his soul shall therefore be cut off from its people.
- Harvest: When you harvest your field do not to take the corner of the field. Do not take the Leket, the fallen stalks, of the field. Do not take the Olalos [young grapes] of your vineyard. Do not to take the Peret [fallen grapes] of the vineyard. Rather, it is to be left to the poor and converts.
- Stealing: Do not steal [discreetly]. Do not deny money that you owe to your friend. Do not swear falsely on money that you owe. Do not to swear falsely using My name. One who does so has desecrated the name of G-d. Do not cheat your friend [by withholding his wages]. Do not rob a person. Do not delay the payment of a worker past morning.
- Do not curse the deaf.
- Do not place a stumbling block in front of the blind.
- Fear G-d.

Second Aliyah (Fifth Aliyah when connected to Acharei Mot)

- Justice: Do not do injustice. Do not favor a poor man and do not honor a great man in judgment. Judge your fellow righteously.
- Between man and friend: Do not speak Lashon Hara. Do not standby when Jewish blood is being spilled. Do not hate a fellow Jew in your heart. Reproof a sinner, although do not carry sin in the process [by embarrassing a fellow Jew]. Do not take revenge and do not hold a grudge against a member of your people. Love your friend as yourself.
- Mix breeds: Do not mate two different species of animals. Do not plant two different species of seeds together. Do not wear a garment of wool and linen [i.e. Shatnez].
- Relations with a half freed maidservant [Shifcha Charufa]: One who sleeps with a Shifcha Charufa, who is a female slave who has not been [fully] redeemed who belongs to another man, is not to be killed. He is to bring a ram as an Asham offering to G-d, to the Temple. The Kohen is to atone for him with the Asham ram for his sin, and he is to be forgiven.

Third Aliyah

- Mitzvah of Orlah and Neta Rivai fruits: When the Jewish people come to Israel and you plant fruit trees, the fruits of the first three years are Orlah and are forbidden to be eaten. In the fourth year the fruits are to be Kodesh Hilulim, fruits of praise for G-d. In the fifth year you may eat the fruit. The above Mitzvah was given to increase your crop.
- Don't eat over the blood [of a sacrifice, meaning before its blood is sprinkled].

- Avoiding the ways of idolaters: Do not practice Nechisha/divination. Do not believe in superstitious times. Do not shave the corners of the head. Do not shave the corners of the beard. Do not cut your skin in mourning. Do not make a tattoo on your skin.
- Don't give your daughter over to prostitution lest the earth be filled with promiscuity.
- Observe the Shabbat.
- Revere the Temple (by not entering with his staff, shoes, or belt).
- Do not turn to the actions of the Ovos and Yidonim [i.e. necromancy]. Do not seek to become impure through them. I am G-d your G-d.
- Stand up for an old person and honor the Sages.
- Fear your G-d. I am G-d.

Fourth Aliyah (Sixth Aliyah when connected to Acharei Mot)

- Converts: Do not oppress the converts. The convert is to be like any other Jew. You shall love the convert as you love yourself as you were also converts in the land of Egypt
- Honesty in business: Do not be dishonest in business. You are to have honest weight stones and scales. I am G-d who took you out of Egypt.
- You are to guard all my commands and judgments. I am G-d.

Chapter 20
Fifth Aliyah

2. Punishment of Molech idolatry:
- G-d spoke to Moses saying: Tell the Jewish people that if anyone gives their child to Molech they will die. They will be stoned to death by the people. The man will be cut off from his nation as he gave his child to Molech in order to defile my Temple and desecrate my name. If the people will ignore the man and ignore giving him his due punishment, I myself will cut off him and his family, as well as all the other followers of Molech.

3. List of punishments for sins:
- One who turns to the necromancy of the Ov or Yidoni and follows them, will be cut off from his nation. You are to be holy as I am G-d your G-d.

Sixth Aliyah (Seventh Aliyah when connected to Acharei Mot)
- You are to guard my commands and perform them, I am G-d your G-d.
- One who curses his father and mother is to be put to death.
- Punishments for adultery and incest: One who sleeps with a **married woman**, both are to be put to death.
- One who sleeps with his **father's wife** has revealed his father's Erva [i.e. intercourse], both are to be put to death.
- One who sleeps with his **daughter in-law** has done Tevel/perversion and both are to be put to death.
- One who sleeps with a **male** has done an abomination, both are to be put to death.
- One who sleeps with his **mother in-law** has done Zima/depravity, they are to be put to death.
- A man who sleeps with an **animal** both are to be put to death.
- A woman who sleeps with an animal, both are to be put to death.

- One who sleeps with his **sister** has done a disgrace. Both will be cut off from their nation, as he has revealed his sisters Erva.
- One who sleeps with a **Niddah**, if he has performed Hearah [penetration], both will be cut off from their nation.
- One may not sleep with his **aunt**, and if they do so they will carry their sin. If one sleeps with his aunt, they will both die without children.
- One who sleeps with his **brother's wife** has committed Niddah, an offense, and both will die childless.
- One is to guard all of My commandments and perform them and in this way the land of Israel will not repel you.

Seventh Aliyah

4. **Final Mitzvot and tidings:**
   - <u>Not to follow the ways of the gentiles</u>: Do not walk in the statutes of the gentiles, as I have despised them. I have inherited their lands to you, a land of milk and honey. I am G-d your G-d who has separated you from the nations.
   - <u>Kashrut dietary laws</u>: You shall distinguish between the pure and impure animals and birds. You shall not defile your souls with eating these forbidden animals and birds and the creeping creatures. You are to be holy to me as I am holy and I have separated you from the nations so you be mine.
   - <u>Ov and Yidoni</u>: A man or woman who is an Ov or Yidoni sorcerer will be killed through stoning.

Parashat Emor
Verses: 124 [Siman: עוזיאל]
Haftorah Ezekiel 44:15-31

Number of Mitzvot:
There are a total of **63** Mitzvot in Parashat Emor; **23** positive commands and **40** negative commands. The following are the commands in the chronological order that they are brought in the Portion.

A. Positive:
1. **Mitzvah 264; Positive 105**: For a Kohen to impurify himself to specific relatives.
2. **Mitzvah 269; Positive 106**: To sanctify the descendants of Aaron the Kohanim and treat them with the stature of priesthood.
3. **Mitzvah 272; Positive 107:** For a Kohen Gadol to marry a virgin.
4. **Mitzvah 293; Positive 109:** For the animal used as a sacrifice to be at least eight days old.
5. **Mitzvah 296; Positive 110:** To sanctify G-d's name and give up one's life for his name.
6. **Mitzvah 297; Positive 111:** To rest from labor on the first day of Pesach.
7. **Mitzvah 299; Positive 112:** To bring a Musaf offering on each of the seven days of Pesach.
8. **Mitzvah 300; Positive 113:** To rest from labor on the seventh day of Pesach.
9. **Mitzvah 302; Positive 114:** To bring the Omer offering on the 2nd day of Pesach.
10. **Mitzvah 306; Positive 115:** To count 49 days from when the Omer if offered.
11. **Mitzvah 307; Positive 116:** To bring on Shavuot the two loaf Chametz offering from new wheat.
12. **Mitzvah 308; Positive 117:** To rest from work on Shavuot.
13. **Mitzvah 310; Positive 118:** To rest from non-food related work on the 1st of Tishreiy [i.e. Rosh Hashanah].
14. **Mitzvah 312; Positive 119:** To bring a Musaf offering on Rosh Hashanah.
15. **Mitzvah 313; Positive 120:** To fast on Yom Kippur.
16. **Mitzvah 314; Positive 121:** To bring a Musaf offering on Yom Kippur.
17. **Mitzvah 317; Positive 122:** To rest from all work on Yom Kippur.
18. **Mitzvah 318; Positive 123:** To rest from non-food related work on the first days of Sukkot.
19. **Mitzvah 320; Positive 124:** To bring a Musaf offering each day of Sukkot.
20. **Mitzvah 321; Positive 125:** To rest from non-food related work on the 8th day of Sukkot.
21. **Mitzvah 322; Positive 126:** To bring a Musaf offering on the 8th day of Sukkot.
22. **Mitzvah 324; Positive 127:** To shake Lulav and 4 Minim on the first day of Sukkot.
23. **Mitzvah 325; Positive 128:** To dwell in a Sukkah for seven days.

B. Negative:
1. **Mitzvah 263; Negative 159:** For a Kohen not to impurify himself with a corpse.
2. **Mitzvah 265; Negative 160:** The prohibition for a Kohen Tevul Yom to serve in the Temple.
3. **Mitzvah 266; Negative 161:** For a Kohen not to marry a Zonah.
4. **Mitzvah 267; Negative 162:** For a Kohen not to marry a Challalah.

5. **Mitzvah 268; Negative 163:** For a Kohen not to marry a divorcee.

6. **Mitzvah 270; Negative 164:** For a Kohen not to enter into a house that contains a corpse.

7. **Mitzvah 271; Negative 165:** For a Kohen Gadol not to impurify himself to any corpse, even a relative.

8. **Mitzvah 273; Negative 166:** For a Kohen Gadol not to marry a widow.

9. **Mitzvah 274; Negative 167:** For a Kohen Gadol not to have relations with a widow.

10. **Mitzvah 275; Negative 168:** For a Kohen with a blemish not to serve in the Temple.

11. **Mitzvah 276; Negative 169:** For a Kohen with a passing blemish not to serve in the Temple.

12. **Mitzvah 277; Negative 170:** For a Kohen with a blemish not to enter the Heichal.

13. **Mitzvah 278; Negative 171:** For an impure Kohen not to serve in the Temple.

14. **Mitzvah 279; Negative 172:** For an impure Kohen not to eat Teruma.

15. **Mitzvah 280; Negative 173:** For a non-Kohen not to eat Teruma.

16. **Mitzvah 281; Negative 174:** For a gentile who is the Toshev and Sachir [i.e. worker] of a Kohen not to eat offerings.

17. **Mitzvah 282; Negative 175:** For a Kohen who is an Aral not to eat Teruma

18. **Mitzvah 283; Negative 176:** For a Challal not to eat offerings.

19. **Mitzvah 284; Negative 177:** Not to eat Tevel [untithed produce].

20. **Mitzvah 285; Negative 178:** Not to sanctify a blemished animal to the altar.

21. **Mitzvah 287; Negative 179:** Not to blemish an offering.

22. **Mitzvah 288; Negative 180:** Not to throw the blood of a blemished offering onto the altar.

23. **Mitzvah 289; Negative 181:** Not to slaughter an animal with a blemish as a offering.

24. **Mitzvah 290; Negative 182:** Not to offer the limbs of a offering which is blemished.

25. **Mitzvah 291; Negative 183:** Not to castrate an animal, or human, or fowl.

26. **Mitzvah 292; Negative 184:** Not to offer a blemished offering that belongs to a gentile.

27. **Mitzvah 294; Negative 185:** Not to slaughter an animal and her offspring on the same day.

28. **Mitzvah 295; Negative 186:** Not to desecrate G-d's name.

29. **Mitzvah 298; Negative 187:** Not to do labor on first day of Pesach.

30. **Mitzvah 301; Negative 188:** Not to do labor on seventh day of Pesach.

31. **Mitzvah 303; Negative 189:** Not to eat Chadash grains before the 16th of Nissan.

32. **Mitzvah 304; Negative 190:** Not to eat Chadash roasted kernels before the 16th of Nissan.

33. **Mitzvah 305; Negative 191:** Not to eat Chadash Karmel, which are stalks of roasted grains, before the 16th of Nissan.

34. **Mitzvah 309; Negative 192:** Not to do labor on Shavuot.

35. **Mitzvah 310; Positive 118:** To rest from non-food related work on the 1st of Tishreiy [i.e. Rosh Hashanah].

36. **Mitzvah 311; Negative 193:** Not to do non-food related labor on first day of Tishreiy [i.e. Rosh Hashanah].

37. **Mitzvah 315; Negative 194:** Not to do any labor on Yom Kippur.

38. **Mitzvah 316; Negative 195:** Not to eat or drink on Yom Kippur.

39. **Mitzvah 319; Negative 196:** Not to do non-food related labor on first day of Sukkot.

40. **Mitzvah 323; Negative 197:** Not to do labor on eighth day of Sukkot.

Chapter 21
First Aliyah

1. Mitzvot of Kohanim:

- G-d told Moses to tell the Kohanim, the sons of Aaron the following laws relating to the Kehuna:
- Impurity to corpse: The Kohanim may not become impure to a corpse, with exception to a relative. A Kohen may become impure to his mother, father, son, daughter, brother, and his virgin sister who was never yet married. A husband may not become impure to his [forbidden] wife.
- Cutting skin/beard: They may not cut their skin, or heads, or shave their beards.
- The Kohanim must adhere to extra standards of Holiness, being that they serve G-d in the Temple.
- Marriage: Kohanim may not marry a divorcee, Chalalah, or Zona because they are holy.
- If the daughter of a Kohen commits adultery, she is to be burnt.
- Kohen Gadol: The Kohen Gadol may not grow out his hair or tear his clothing [in mourning]. He may not become impure even to relatives. He may not leave the Temple. The Kohen Gadol must marry a virgin.

Second Aliyah

2. Kohen with a blemish:

- A Kohen with a blemish is invalid to serve in the Temple. He may however eat from the offerings.
- The following matters are defined as a blemish:
    o One who is blind
    o One who is lame
    o One who is disfigured
    o One who has an enlarged limb
    o One who has a broken leg
    o One who has a broken arm
    o Eye dysfunctions or disfigurations, such as unusual eyebrows, or a cataract, or a mixing in his eye
    o One who has a Garav or Yalefes (different types of boils)
    o One who has crushed testicles.
- The Kohanim are warned not to desecrate the offerings of the Jewish people.

Chapter 22

3. Impure Kohen:

- A Kohen who offers an offering in a state of impurity receives excision.
- If a Kohen is impure due to Tzara'at or Zav, he may not eat offerings until he becomes pure.
- One who touches one who is impure due to a corpse, or impure due to semen, or due to touching a creeping animal [i.e. a Sheretz], or an impure person, is considered impure and may not eat offerings until he immerses his flesh in a Mikveh. Only after the sun sets may he eat the offerings.
- He may not eat a carcass or Treifa to become impure.

4. Non-Kohen eating offerings:

- A non-Kohen may not eat the offerings, including the worker of a Kohen. However, the slave and the members of the household of a Kohen may eat offerings.
- <u>Kohenes</u>: The daughter of a Kohen may not eat offerings if she marries a non-Kohen. If she gets divorced or widowed, and does not have children from him, she may eat offerings.
- <u>If a non-Kohen ate offerings</u>: If a non-Kohen accidently ate offerings, he must pay a fine of 120% its value to the Kohen.

Third Aliyah

5. Laws of Sacrifices:

- <u>An Olah voluntary offering</u>: Any Jew may volunteer to bring a voluntary Olah offering to G-d. It is to be an unblemished male, either a male cow, sheep or goat. The offering may not have a blemish.
- <u>Blemishes</u>: The following matters are defined as a blemish:
  - The animal is blind
  - The animal is broken
  - The animal has a cut eyelid
  - The animal has a wart.
  - The animal has a limp
  - The animal has an enlarged limb.
  - The animal has crushed or destroyed reproduction organs.
- It is forbidden to castrate any animal.
- You shall not take an offering from a stranger, it will likely have a blemish.
- <u>Slaughtering after 8 days</u>: When an ox, sheep, or goat, gives birth, the baby is to be with its mother for seven days. The animal may be offered from the 8th day and onwards.
- <u>Mother and child</u>: One may not slaughter a mother and child of an ox or sheep on the same day.
- <u>Leftovers</u>: One may not leave the meat of the offering over until morning.

6. Mitzvah of Kiddush G-d:

- Do not desecrate G-d's name, and you are to sanctify G-d amongst the Jewish people.

Chapter 23
Fourth Aliyah

7. The Moadim-Jewish Holidays:

- G-d spoke to Moses saying, tell the Jewish people that these are my festivals which are to be a calling of holiness:
- <u>Shabbat</u>: One is to work for six days and on the seventh day it is a complete day of rest. It is a calling of Holiness; one is not to do any work in all your settled places.
- <u>Pesach</u>: On the 14th of Nissan, it is a Pesach for G-d [and a offering is to be brought]. On the 15th of the month, it is festival of Matzot for G-d. Matzot are to be eaten for seven days. One may not do any laborous work on the first day and seventh day. Sacrifices are to be brought throughout the seven days.
- <u>Omer offering</u>: After entering Israel and harvesting the land, the Omer, which is the first of the harvest season, is to be brought to the Kohen. The Omer is to be waved before G-d

on the 16th of Nissan. On that day of the waving, an unblemished sheep is to be offered to G-d as an Olah. Its Mincha of two tenth-ephahs of fine flour mixed with oil and its Nesachim [i.e. poured-offering] of ¼ of a Hin of wine is to accompany the offering.

- Chadash: One may not eat the new bread, parched grain, and plumped grain, until the Omer offering is brought.
- Sefirat Haomer: Count for yourselves seven weeks starting from when the Omer is offered. Count for 50 days.
- Shavuot Sacrifices: On the 50th day of count, a new Mincha is to be offered. From your settlements you are to bring two breads of elevation, made from Chametz, each bread is made of two tenth-ephahs of flour. It is a Bikurim to G-d. It is to be accompanied by seven unblemished lambs in their first year, one young male calf, and two rams as an Olah. A single goat is to be brought as a Chatas, as well as two lambs of a year old as a Shelamim. The Kohen is to waive the two sheep upon the bread Bikurim, a waving before G-d. That day is to be a day of Holiness. No laborious work may be done as a law for all generations.
- Mitzvah of leaving produce for the pour [Leket, Shichicha, Peia]: Upon harvesting the field, one is not to completely remove the corner of the field and the Leket of your harvest is not to be gathered. It is to be left to the poor and the converts.

Fifth Aliyah

- Rosh Hashanah: On the first of the seventh month [i.e. Tishreiy] one is to rest, it is to be a day of remembrance of the Shofar, a calling of holiness. One is not to perform any laborious activity, and Sacrifices are to be brought before G-d.
- Yom Kippur: The 10th day of the month is a day of atonement. It is a day of holiness for you and you shall oppress your soul and bring an offering to G-d. You shall not perform any work on this day, as it is a day of atonement for G-d to atone for you. Any soul who does not fast on this very day will be cut off from his people. Any soul who performs labor on this day, I will destroy him from amongst his people. One may not do any work for all generations, in all your settlements. It is a day of complete rest, and you shall afflict your souls. On the ninth of the month, from evening to evening, you shall rest on that day.

Sixth Aliyah

- Sukkot-Sacrifices and labor: On the 15th day of the seventh month is the seven-day Sukkot Holiday. One may not perform laborious work on the 1st or 8th day. You are to bring an offering for seven days. On the eighth day, it is to be a call of Holiness for you and you shall bring an offering to G-d. It is an Atzeres, all laborious activity may not be performed. These are the Holidays of G-d which are to be called a calling of holiness to bring sacrifices to G-d, Mincha, and Nesachim, each day's requirement on its day. This is aside for the Shabbasos of G-d, and one's voluntary offerings which are given to G-d. On the 15th day, which is when you gather the grain, you are to celebrate the festival for seven days, on the first day you shall rest and on the eight day you shall rest.
- Daled Minim: You shall take for yourselves on the first day [of Sukkot] a beautiful fruit [i.e. Etrog], the date palm branch [i.e. Lulav], branches of a cordlike tree [i.e. Hadas] and willows of a river [i.e. Aravot] and rejoice before G-d your G-d for seven days. You are

to celebrate the festival for G-d seven days a year for all generation, during the seventh month.

- <u>Sukkah dwelling</u>: One is to dwell in the Sukkah for seven days. Every native of Israel is to dwell in the Sukkah so that all your generations will know that I caused the Jewish people to dwell in Sukkot when I took them out of Egypt.
- Moses told the Jewish people of all the Holidays of G-d.

Chapter 24
Seventh Aliyah

8. **Lighting the Menorah:**
   - G-d told Moses to command the Jewish people to bring to him clear crushed olive oil for the sake of illumination, to light the eternal candle [i.e. the Menorah]. It is to be lit outside the Parochet curtain in the Tent of Meeting. Aaron is to light it from evening to morning before G-d continuously for all generations. The candles are to be set up on the pure Menorah, before G-d constantly.

9. **The Showbread:**
   - You are to take fine flour and bake twelve breads from it, each Challah being two tenth-ephahs. They are to be organized in two stacks, six in each stack, on the pure table that is before G-d. Pure frankincense is to be placed on the stack and it shall be a bread of remembrance for G-d. The Showbread is to be organized weekly from Shabbat to Shabbat before G-d continuously, as an everlasting covenant. The bread is to be distributed to Aaron and his sons and eaten in a holy place, as it is a Holy offering.

10. **Ish Hamikalel-The man who cursed G-d:**
    - <u>The curse</u>: A Jewish man, the son of an Egyptian father, but Jewish mother, was involved in an argument with another Jew. His mother's name was Shlomit Bat Dibri from the tribe of Dan. The Jewish man cursed and blasphemed the name of G-d and was brought before Moses. The man was imprisoned for his actions until further instructions would be received from G-d.
    - <u>The punishment</u>: G-d instructed Moses to have the man taken out of the camp, and to have all those who heard the curse lean their hands on his head, and the entire assembly shall stone him. Tell the children of Israel that any man who blasphemes G-d will carry his sin. One who pronounces the name of G-d in a blasphemous way shall be put to death. The entire nation is to stone him.
    - The nation did as they were instructed and stoned the man to death outside of the camp.

11. **Murder and injury:**
    - <u>Punishment for murder</u>: One who murders another person is to be killed.
    - <u>Restitution for killing animal</u>: One who kills an animal is to pay, a life for a life.
    - <u>Injuring a friend</u>: One who injures his friend is to have the same done upon him. A break for a break, an eye for an eye, and a tooth for a tooth, as he did to his friend so shall be done to him [that he should pay the value to the injured friend].

Parashat Behar
Verses: 57 [Siman: חטיל]
Haftorah: Jerimiah 32:6-22[1]

Number of Mitzvot:

There are a total of **24** Mitzvot in Parashat Behar; **7** positive commands and **17** negative commands. The following are the commands in the chronological order found in the Portion.

A. Positive:

1. **Mitzvah 330; Positive 129:** To count the years leading up to the Jubilee year.
2. **Mitzvah 331; Positive 130:** To blow the Shofar on Yom Kippur of the Jubilee year.
3. **Mitzvah 332; Positive 131:** To sanctify the Jubilee year and treat it like a year of Shemita/Sabbatical year.
4. **Mitzvah 336; Positive 132:** To follow the laws of business acquisitions, as instructed by the Torah.
5. **Mitzvah 340; Positive 133:** For buyers to give up all land and homes to the original owners during the Jubilee year.
6. **Mitzvah 341; Positive 134:** For buyers to allow homes in a walled city to be purchased back until the end of the first year from the sale.
7. **Mitzvah 347; Positive 135:** For a slave to work for his master forever, and not be freed by his master.

B. Negative:

1. **Mitzvah 326; Negative 198:** Not to perform work to the land during Shemita/Sabbatical year.
2. **Mitzvah 327; Negative 199:** Not to perform work to the trees during Shemita/Sabbatical year.
3. **Mitzvah 328; Negative 200:** Not to harvest the Sefichim [products] during Shemita/Sabbatical year as normally done in other years, and rather it is to be treated like unowned.
4. **Mitzvah 329; Negative 201:** Not to harvest the fruits of the tree as normally done in other years, and rather it is to be treated like unowned.
5. **Mitzvah 333; Negative 202:** Not to work the land during the Jubilee year.
6. **Mitzvah 334; Negative 203:** Not to harvest the Sefichim [products] during the Jubilee year, as normally done in other years, and rather it is to be treated like unowned.
7. **Mitzvah 335; Negative 204:** Not to harvest the fruits of one's orchard during the Jubilee year as normally done in other years, and rather it is to be treated like unowned.
8. **Mitzvah 337; Negative 205:** Not to cheat someone in business.
9. **Mitzvah 338; Negative 206:** Not to offend another in words.
10. **Mitzvah 339; Negative 207:** Not to permanently sell a field in Israel.
11. **Mitzvah 342; Negative 208:** Not to change the zones and allotments of the outskirts of the Levite cities and fields.
12. **Mitzvah 343; Negative 209:** Not to lend money with interest.
13. **Mitzvah 344; Negative 210:** Not to make a Hebrew slave perform a belittling task.

---

[1] So is followed by Chabad communities. However, the other communities read until 32:26

14. **Mitzvah 345; Negative 211:** Not to sell a Hebrew slave as a regular slave is sold.
15. **Mitzvah 346; Negative 212:** Not to give a Hebrew slave laborious activity.
16. **Mitzvah 348; Negative 213:** Not to allow a gentile to give his Hebrew slave laborious activity.
17. **Mitzvah 349; Negative 214:** Not to prostrate on a stone surface even for the sake of G-d.

Chapter 25
First Aliyah

1. **The Mitzvah of Shemita/Sabbatical year:**
   - Resting the land from planting: G-d told Moses on Mount Sinai to tell the Jewish people that when they arrive to the promised land, they are to sow the land for six years and are to rest the land on the seventh year. One may not sow the land on the seventh year, as it is a year of rest for G-d.
   - Not to harvest for personal use: In the seventh year one may not harvest the field. The produce of the field shall be food for you, your slaves, and for all who reside with you. It shall also be available for all the animals in your land. [The produce of the fields is to be considered ownerless and allowed to be taken by all people during this year.]

2. **Mitzvah of the Jubilee year:**
   - Counting the years: One is to count seven sets of seven years for a total of 49 years. On the 50th year, on Yom Kippur, the Shofar is to be blown throughout all your lands.
   - Freeing the slaves: The 50th year is to be sanctified and is to be proclaimed a year of freedom. All lands are to return to their original owner and all slaves are to be set free during this year to return to their homes.
   - This 50th year is called the Jubilee year.
   - Not to sow or harvest: In the fiftieth year one may not sow or harvest the field. The produce of the field shall be food for you.

Second Aliyah

3. **Business ethics:**
   - Overcharge: One may not overcharge or underpay another person in a sale without their knowledge.
   - Selling land: The price that the land is to be sold for is to be based on the amount of years remaining until the next Jubilee year. If many years remain until the Jubilee year then it is to be sold for a larger sum, if only a few years remain until the Jubilee year it is to be sold for a smaller sum, as one is not selling the land itself but is leasing it for a certain sum of years.

4. **Not to offend another Jew:**
   - One may not verbally harass or offend another Jew using words.

Third Aliyah (Second Aliyah when connected to Bechukotai)

5. **Sustenance during years of Shemita/Sabbatical year:**
   - The land will give plentiful of produce and you will eat to satisfaction and dwell securely on it. Now, if you ask "What shall we eat in the 7th year if we cannot sow the land or harvest our grain" I promise you my blessing to support the Jewish people during Shemita/Sabbatical year by making the 6th year grow plenty of produce. You will sow in the 8th year and still eat from the 7th years produce until the new crop arrives in the 9th year.

6. **Selling and redeeming ancestral fields:**
   - A property of ancestral heritage may not be sold eternally, for it belongs to G-d. It is rather to be redeemed.

Fourth Aliyah

   - <u>Redeeming</u>: If one becomes poor and sells his plot of ancestral heritage then his relative is to come to his aid and redeem it. If a relative cannot redeem it, and the original owner comes to redeem it, then he is to pay the buyer in accordance to the amount of years remaining towards his lease.
   - <u>Returns by the Jubilee year</u>: If he is unable to redeem it, then the property is to remain in the hands of the buyer until the Jubilee year, and in the Jubilee year it is to be returned to its owner.

Fifth Aliyah (Third Aliyah when connected to Bechukotai)

7. **Selling and redeeming a house:**
   - <u>Walled city</u>: If a man sells a house that is within a walled city, then it can be redeemed only within the first year of the sale. If it was not redeemed within the first year, it becomes the property of the buyer and remains with him forever, even after the Jubilee year.
   - <u>Unwalled city</u>: If, however, the city is unwalled, it may be redeemed until the Jubilee year. If it was not redeemed before the Jubilee year, then when the Jubilee year arrives it is to be returned to its owner.

8. **Selling and redeeming Levite property:**
   - <u>Houses of Levites</u>: The houses of Levites found within their cities retain eternal redemption rights by the Levites and they hence may be redeemed at any time. If they are not redeemed they are to be returned to their original Levite owner by the Jubilee year.
   - <u>Levite fields</u>: The open fields of the city of the Levites may never be sold, as it is an eternal heritage for them.

9. **The Mitzvah of Charity and lending money without interest:**
   - If your brother becomes impoverished, you shall support him so that he can live with you.
   - <u>Interest</u>: One is not to collect interest from the loan to the pauper and you shall fear G-d and allow your brother to live with you. Do not lend him money with interest. I am G-d your G-d who took you out of Egypt, to give you the land of Canaan.

Sixth Aliyah (Fourth Aliyah when connected to Bechukotai)

10. Slave laws:

- <u>Jewish slave</u>: When your brother is sold to you as a slave do not work him with slave labor. He shall be like a hired laborer or a resident and shall stay with you until the Jubilee year and he is then to return to his family with his sons and to his ancestral heritage. The Jewish people are my slaves who I took out of Egypt. Do not sell them like a slave and do not work them hard. I am G-d your G-d.
- <u>Gentile slave</u>: You shall buy slaves from the surrounding nations, and they shall become for you an ancestral heritage. You shall inherit them to your sons after you. They shall serve you forever.

Seventh Aliyah

11. Jewish slave sold to gentile:

- <u>Redeeming the slave</u>: If a Jew becomes impoverished and is sold as a slave to a gentile, he is to be redeemed. It is a Mitzvah upon his relatives, such as his uncle or cousin or other family relative, to redeem him. If the slave himself has the means to do so, then he is to redeem himself. The price for the redemption is to be based on the amount of years remaining until the next Jubilee year. If many years remain until the Jubilee year then he is to be sold for a larger sum, if only a few years remain until the Jubilee year he is to be sold for a smaller sum, as one is not selling the slave himself but is hiring him for a certain sum of years.
- <u>Hard labor</u>: One may not allow the gentile to make the Jewish slave work laborous activity.
- <u>The Jubilee year</u>: If the salve is not redeemed, he is to be set free by the Jubilee year.
- The Jewish people are my slaves who I took out of Egypt.

12. Idolatry, statues, and stone floors:

- One may not form idols for himself or build statues and pillars. One may not make stone floors in the land for the sake of prostration.

13. Guard the Shabbat and fear the Temple:

- Guard my Shabbatot and revere the Temple, I am G-d.

Parashat Bechukotai
Verses: 78 *[Siman:* עדא*]*
Haftorah: Jerimiah 16:19-17:14

Number of Mitzvot:
There are a total of **12** Mitzvot in Parashat Bechukotai; **7** positive commands and **5** negative commands. The following are the commands in the chronological order that they are brought in the Portion.

A. Positive:
1. **Mitzvah 350; Positive 136**: To follow the laws of redemption of a human [i.e. Erechin], that one give the worth of a human to Hekdesh if he made a vow to do so.
2. **Mitzvah 352; Positive 137**: That the exchanged animal be considered holy.
3. **Mitzvah 353; Positive 138:** To follow the laws of Erechin of an animal, that one gives the worth of an animal to Hekdesh.
4. **Mitzvah 354; Positive 139:** To follow the laws of Erechin of a house, that one give the worth of the house to Hekdesh.
5. **Mitzvah 355; Positive 140:** To follow the laws of Erechin of a field, that one gives the worth of the field to Hekdesh.
6. **Mitzvah 357; Positive 141:** To follow the laws of consecration, that the consecrated property be given to the Kohanim.
7. **Mitzvah 360; Positive 142:** To tithe one's animals each year and eat it in Jerusalem.

B. Negative:
1. **Mitzvah 351; Negative 215:** Not to make an exchange of offerings.
2. **Mitzvah 356; Negative 216:** Not to change the status of an offering from one type of offering to another type of offering.
3. **Mitzvah 358; Negative 217:** Not to sell land or objects that was declared as consecration, and rather to give it to the Kohanim.
4. **Mitzvah 359; Negative 218:** Not to redeem a field of consecration and rather to give it to the Kohanim.
5. **Mitzvah 361; Negative 219:** Not to sell the tithed animal.

Chapter 26
First Aliyah

1. The Blessings received for obeying G-d's commands:

- If the Jewish people follow the statutes of G-d and observe His commands, I will bless them with the following blessings:
  - Rain at the appropriate time.
  - The earth will give produce.
  - The trees will grow fruits.
  - There will be so much abundance of produce that it will last until the next year's harvest
  - You will eat your bread to satiation [and become satiated with small amounts of food].
  - You will dwell securely in your land.

Second Aliyah

- I will provide peace in the land, and you will lie without fear.
- I will remove wild animals from the land.
- A sword [of war] will not pass through your land.
- You will chase your enemies and they will fall before you.
- Five men will chase 100 enemy soldiers and 100 men will chase 10,000 enemy soldiers. Your enemies will fall before you to the sword.
- I will cause you to be fruitful and multiply and establish my covenant with you.

Third Aliyah (Fifth Aliyah if connected to Behar)

- You will still be able to eat from the old fruit when the new harvest arrives.
- I will place my Tabernacle amongst you and will not become disgusted of you. I will walk amongst you and will become a G-d for you and you will become for Me a nation. I am G-d who took you out of Egypt from being slaves. I broke the pegs of your yoke and I led you erect.

2. The curses received for disobeying G-d's commands:

- If you do not listen to Me, do not obey all these commands, despise My statutes, and are repulsed by My laws to break My covenant, then I will do the following to you:
  - I will make you panic and make you waste away.
  - You will get fever, causing your eyes to sting.
  - Your sowing of the seed will be in vain as your enemies will eat your produce.
  - You will fall before your enemies and they will rule over you.
  - You will flee even though no one is chasing you.

- If you still do not listen to me, I will increase tormenting you in seven ways for your sins:
  - I will break your pride.
  - I will turn your heavens into iron and your land like copper.
  - You will exert your energy in vain as your land will not give off produce and its trees will not give off fruit.
- If you still do not listen to me, I will increase tormenting you in seven ways for your sins:
  - I will send wild animals to attack you and bereave you.

- o I will exterminate your cattle and diminish you.
- o Your roads will be destroyed.

- If despite these you still do not listen to me, I will increase tormenting you in seven ways for your sins:
  - o I will bring upon you an attack by the sword to avenge my covenant.
  - o You will gather in your cities and have a plague sent against you.
  - o You will be delivered to the hands of the enemies.
  - o I will break for you the staff of your sustenance.
  - o Ten women will bake bread in one oven and bring the bread back by weight.
  - o You will eat but not be satiated.

- If despite this you still do not listen to me, I will increase tormenting you in seven ways for your sins:
  - o You will eat the flesh of your children, the flesh of your sons and daughters.
  - o Your towers and idols will be destroyed.
  - o I will pile your carcasses on the carcasses of your idols, and I will despise you.
  - o I will destroy your cities and Temple.
  - o I will not smell the scent of your offerings.
  - o I will make your land desolate from you and your enemies.
  - o I will disperse you amongst all the nations and empty the sword after you.
  - o Your cities will be put to ruin.
- <u>Appeasing the Shemita/Sabbatical years</u>: Through the above, the land will become appeased from its Shemita/Sabbatical years, from all its years of desolation. All its days of it being desolate it will rest for whatever it did not rest during the years you dwelled on it.
  - o The survivors, I will make them paranoid in the lands of their exile. They will flee from the sound of the rustling of a leaf and they will fall without anyone chasing them.
  - o You will die from the sword of a friend without anyone chasing you.
  - o You will be unable to overcome your enemies. You will become lost amongst the nations and will be consumed by them.
- You will suffer due to the sins of your forefathers. Then you will confess your sins and the sins of your ancestors due to ignoring my commands. I therefore also treated you with ignorance and brought you to the land of your enemies so that the hardness of your heart become humbled and you will then receive appeasement for your sins.

3. The salvation after the suffering:
- I will remember the covenant with Jacob and Isaac and Abraham and remember the land. The land will be bereaved of you and receive appeasement.
- Even when you are amongst the enemies, I will not abhor you or reject you, to destroy you and the covenant I made with you, as I am G-d Your G-d. I will remember that I took you out of Egypt and to be a G-d onto you.
- These are the laws that G-d gave the Jewish people on Mount Sinai through Moses.

Chapter 27
Fourth Aliyah (Sixth Aliyah if connected to Behar)
4. Erechin redemptions-Nedarim/vows:
- G-d spoke to Moses saying tell the Jewish people the following laws. When a man makes a vow to donate the value of a soul the following shall be the value to be donated.
- Ages 20-60: The Erech [i.e. value] of a man between 20-60 years of age will be 50 silver Shekel. The Erech of a woman between 20-60 years of age will be 30 Shekel.
- Ages 5-20: The Erech of a male child between 5-20 years of age will be 20 Shekel. The Erech of a female child between 5-20 years of age will be 10 Shekel.
- Ages 0-5: The Erech of a male child between 0-5 years of age will be 5 Shekel. The Erech of a female child between 0-5 years of age will be 3 Shekel.
- Above 60: The Erech of a man over 60 will be 15 Shekel. The Erech of a woman over 60 will be 10 Shekel.
- If the donor is poor and he cannot pay the value stated above, he is to be evaluated by the Kohen and is to pay whatever he can afford.

5. Temura/Exchanging offerings:
- It is forbidden to exchange an offering for a different animal to have it take its place. This applies whether the second animal is of a better condition or a worse condition. If one went ahead and did so, then it and its substitute shall be holy.

6. Hekdish-Donations of items to the Temple and their redemption status:
- Animals: If one donates an impure [i.e. blemished] animal that cannot be brought as a sacrifice, it shall be brought to the Kohen and be evaluated by him. Whatever value the Kohen gives it is to be its sale price. If the original owner buys it, he is to add 20% to its value.
- Home: One who donates his house, its value shall be based on the evaluation of the Kohen. If the original owner desires to redeem it, he is to add an extra 20% to its value and it shall then be his.

Fifth Aliyah (Seventh Aliyah if connected to Behar)
- Ancestral Field: One who donates his ancestral field to G-d, its value is to be 50 silver Shekel per every area of land that a Chomer of barley can be sowed. Now, if the field was donated by the start of the Jubilee year, then the above is its value. However, if it was donated after the Jubilee year, then the Kohen is to sell it based on the amount of years remaining until the Jubilee year and subtract it from total value. If the original owner desires to redeem it, he is to add an extra 20% to its value and it shall then be his. If the owner does not redeem his field and it is sold to another, it may no longer be redeemed. It becomes the property of the Kohen when the Jubilee year arrives.

Sixth Aliyah
- Purchased Field: One who donates his purchased field to G-d, its value [of redemption] is to be based on the amount of years remaining until the Jubilee year. That sum is to be given as a donation to G-d. In the Jubilee year that field is to return to its original owner.
- Firstborn animal: A firstborn from one's livestock, ox or sheep is not to be sanctified as it belongs to G-d. One is not to sanctify a firstborn to the Temple. If the animal is impure, it

is to be redeemed according to its value, and if the owner desires to redeem it, he is to add 20% to its price.

- Cherem/consecration: All property that will be declared segregated to G-d, whether from an animal or field, is not to be sold or redeemed. It is a Holy offering for G-d.

Seventh Aliyah

- Person in excommunication: Any person that was put in excommunication (by the court for punishment) may not be redeemed, he is put to death.

7. The first tithe [i.e. Maaser Rishon]:

- All tithes from produce of the land and fruits of the tree are holy to G-d. If one redeems it, he must add 20% to its value.

8. Tithe of animals [i.e. Maaser Behemo]s:

- The 10th animal of cattle or flock which passes under the staff is to be consecrated to G-d.
- It is forbidden to switch an offering to a different animal, whether good to bad or bad to good. If one went ahead and did so, then it and its substitute shall be holy, and shall not be redeemed.
- These are the Mitzvot that G-d commanded Moses to teach the Jewish people on Mount Sinai.

Bamidbar/Numbers

Parashat Bamidbar
Verses: 159 [Siman: חלקיהו]
Haftorah: Hosea 2:1-22

Number of Mitzvot:
There are no Mitzvot in Parashat Bamidbar.

The Main Themes:
- The census taking of the Jewish people, per tribe.
- The areas of encampments of each tribe.
- The services of the Levites.

Chapter 1
First Aliyah

1. **G-d commands Moses to take a census of the Jewish people:**
   - <u>When</u>: G-d spoke to Moses in the Sinai desert in the Tent of Meeting on the first day of the second month [i.e. 1st of Iyar] in the second year of leaving Egypt.
   - <u>Who is counted</u>: He commanded him to count the Jewish people according to their families, counting every male who is twenty years of age and above.
   - <u>Choosing tribal leaders</u>: One leader and representative of each tribe shall count with you. The following are the names of these leaders:
       1) **Reuben:** Elitzur Ben Shedeur
       2) **Simeon:** Shelumiel Ben Tzurishadai
       3) **Judah:** Nachshon Ben Amminadav
       4) **Issachar:** Nisanel Ben Tzuar
       5) **Zebulun:** Eliav Ben Cheilon
       6) **Ephraim:** Elishama Ben Ammihud
       7) **Minasheh:** Gamliel Ben Pedahtzur
       8) **Benjamin:** Avidan Ben Gideoni.
       9) **Dan:** Achiezer Ben Amishaddai
       10) **Asher:** Pagiel Ben Ochran
       11) **Gad:** Eliasaf Ben Deuel
       12) **Naftali:** Ahira Ben Einan
   - Moses took all the above-mentioned individuals and he gathered the entire congregation on the first of the second month and the genealogy of each family was established. All men above 20 years of age were counted as G-d commanded Moses.

Second Aliyah

2. **The census of men in the Twelve tribes above age 20:**
   1) **Reuben:** The census of the tribe of Reuben, the firstborn of Jacob, showed a population of **46,500** men above the age of 20.
   2) **Simeon**: The census of the tribe of Simeon showed a population of **59,300** men above the age of 20.

3) **Gad:** The census of the tribe Gad showed a population of **45,650** men above the age of 20.

4) **Judah:** The census of the tribe of Judah showed a population of **74,600** men above the age of 20.

5) **Issachar:** The census of the tribe of Issachar showed a population of **54,400** men above the age of 20.

6) **Zebulun:** The census of the tribe of Zebulun showed a population of **57,400** men above the age of 20.

7) **Ephraim:** The census of the tribe of Ephraim showed a population of **40,500** men above the age of 20.

8) **Manasseh:** The census of the tribe of Manasseh showed a population of **32,200** men above the age of 20.

9) **Benjamin:** The census of the tribe of Benjamin showed a population of **35,400** men above the age of 20.

10) **Dan:** The census of the tribe of Dan showed a population of **62,700** men above the age of 20.

11) **Asher:** The census of the tribe of Asher showed a population of **41,500** men above the age of 20.

12) **Naftali:** The census of the tribe of Naftali showed a population of **53,400** men above the age of 20.

- This concludes the census taking of the Jewish people, which was performed by Moses Aaron and the 12 tribal representatives
- The total count of men above age 20 within the 12 tribes was **603,550**.

3. **The tribe of Levi:**
   - <u>No census</u>: G-d commanded Moses that the tribe of Levi is not to be counted.
   - <u>Carrying the Tabernacle, dismantling and assembling it</u>: You should appoint the Levites to oversee the Tabernacle and its vessels. They are to carry it during travel, minister to the vessels, and encamp around the Tabernacle. When it's time to travel the Levites are to dismantle the Tabernacle, and when it's time to encamp they are to erect the Tabernacle. A non-Levite who does this service shall die.

Chapter 2
4. **The position of encampment and travel of the tribes:**
   - The Jewish people are to encamp, each man in the area of their tribe.
   - The Levites are to encamp around the Tabernacle. They will guard the Tabernacle and prevent wrath from falling upon the Jewish people.
   - The Jewish people did all that Moses was commanded by G-d.

Third Aliyah
- G-d told Moses that the following is the order that the Jewish people are to encamp around the Tabernacle:
  1) **In the East:** In the east is to encamp the tribes of **Judah, Issachar and Zebulun**. This camp is led by the tribe of Judah. The census of the tribe of Judah showed a population of 74,600 [men above the age of 20]. Its leader was Nachshon Ben Aminadav. The census of the tribe of Issachar showed a population of 54,400 [men

above the age of 20]. Its leader was Nethanel Ben Tzuar. The census of the tribe of Zebulun showed a population of 57,400 [men above the age of 20]. Its leader was Eliav Ben Cheilon. The total population for the camp of Judah was **186,400** [men above age 20]. They were the first to journey.

2) **In the South:** At the south is to encamp the tribes of **Reuben, Simeon, and Gad**. This camp is led by the tribe of Reuben. The census of the tribe of Reuben, showed a population of 46,500 [men above the age of 20]. Its leader was Elitzur Ben Shedeur. The census of the tribe of Simeon showed a population of 59,300 [men above the age of 20]. Its leader was Shelumiel Ben Tzurishaddai. The census of the tribe Gad showed a population of 45,650 [men above the age of 20]. Its leader was Eliasaf Ben Reuel. The total population for the camp of Reuben was **151,450** [men above age 20]. They were the second to journey.

3) **In the West:** At the west is to encamp the tribes of **Ephraim, Manasseh, and Benjamin**. This camp is led by the tribe of Ephraim. The census of the tribe of Ephraim showed a population of 40,500 [men above the age of 20]. The leader of Ephraim was Elishama Ben Amihud. The census of the tribe of Manasseh showed a population of 32,200 [men above the age of 20]. The leader of the tribe of Manasseh was Gamliel Ben Pedahtzur. The census of the tribe of Benjamin showed a population of 35,400 [men above the age of 20]. The leader of the tribe of Benjamin was Avidan Ben Gideoni. The total population for the camp of Ephraim was **108,100** [men above age 20]. They were the third to journey.

4) **In the North:** At the north is to encamp the tribes of **Dan, Asher and Naftali**. This camp is led by the tribe of Dan. The census of the tribe of Dan showed a population of 62,700 men above the age of 20. Its leader was Achiezer Ben Amishaddai. The census of the tribe of Asher showed a population of 41,500 men above the age of 20. Its leader was Pagiel Ben Ochran. The census of the tribe of Naftali showed a population of 53,400 men above the age of 20. Its leader was Ahira Ben Einan. The total population for the camp of Dan was **157,600** [men above age 20]. They were the last to journey.

- Traveling order: The Tent of Meeting and the Levite camp are to travel in the middle of the camps. All the camps are to travel the same direction and group that they are positioned.

- The total count [of men above age 20] within the 12 tribes was **603,550**. The Levites were not included in this count, as G-d commanded Moses.

Chapter 3
Fourth Aliyah

5. **The descendants of Aaron:**
   - The following are the offspring of Aaron and Moses: Nadab the firstborn, Abihu, Elazar and Itamar. All were anointed as Kohanim. Nadab and Abihu died before G-d when they offered foreign incense. They did not have children.

6. **The job of the Levites to guard the Tabernacle:**
   - G-d spoke to Moses saying he should appoint the tribe of Levi to be of assistance to Aaron and serve him. They are to guard the Tabernacle and its utensils.

- <u>In exchange for the firstborns</u>: The Levites were taken from amongst the Jewish people in exchange for the firstborns. "The firstborns became Mine on the day I smote the firstborn Egyptians, and I sanctified the firstborn humans and animals to be Mine. The Levites are thus Mine in place of the firstborns."

Fifth Aliyah

7. **The Levite census, their jobs, leaders, and area of encampment:**
   - G-d spoke to Moses saying he should take a census of the Levites, counting them per family. Every male above the age of one month is to be counted. The following is the census of the families:
   - <u>Gershon</u>: His sons were Libni and Shimi. Their total number of males above the age of one month was **7,500**. They encamped behind the Tabernacle, to the west. Their family leader was Eliasaf Ben Lael. They were entrusted with the job of [dismantling, carrying, and mantling] the Tabernacle and Ohel tapestry coverings, the courtyard curtains, entrance screen, and its rope.
   - <u>Kehot</u>: His sons were Amram, Yitzhar, Hebron and Uzziel. Their total number of males above the age of one month was **8,600**. They encamped on the side of the Tabernacle, to the south. Their family leader was Elitzaphan Ben Uzziel. They were entrusted with the job of [dismantling, carrying, and mantling] the Aron, Shulchan/Table, Menorah, Altar, holy vessels and the screen.
   - <u>The tribal leader of Levi</u>: Elazar the son of Aaron was the tribal leader of the tribe of Levi.
   - <u>Merari</u>: His sons were Machli and Mushi. Their total number of males above the age of one month was **6,200**. Their family leader was Tzuriel Ben Avichayil. They encamped north of the Tabernacle. They were entrusted with the job of [dismantling, carrying, and mantling] the beams of the Tabernacle, its poles, pillars and sockets, and all its accessories. The pillars of the courtyard, their sockets, pegs and ropes.
   - <u>Moses and Aaron</u>: Moses, Aaron and their sons encamped in front of the Tabernacle, to the east. They guarded it from the Jewish people so no alien enter and die.
   - <u>Total Levite population</u>: The total Levite population was **22,000** males above the age of one month [not including 300 Levites who were themselves firstborns].

Sixth Aliyah

8. **Counting of firstborns:**
   - G-d spoke to Moses saying he should take a census of the firstborn of the Jewish people, counting all males one month old and above. You shall designate the Levites and their animals for Me in exchange for the firstborns of the Jewish people and their firstborn animals.
   - Moses counted the firstborns of the Jewish people as G-d commanded and there was a total of 22,273 firstborn males above the age of one month.

9. **Redeeming the firstborns with the Levites:**
   - G-d commanded Moses to exchange the Levites and their animals for the firstborns of the Jewish people and their firstborn animals, and they shall be for Me.

- For the redemption of the 273 Israelite firstborns who are in surplus to the Levite count, you shall take five Shekalim per head, each Shekel being the worth of 20 Geira. Give the money to Aaron and his sons.
- Moses took the money from the surplus firstborns and gave it to Aaron and his sons as G-d commanded. It was a total sum of 1,365 Shekel.

Seventh Aliyah

10. The census and services of the Levite family of Kehot:

- G-d commanded Moses to count all the male members of the Kehot family who are between the ages of 30-50. They were appointed with the following tasks to be done after the Kohanim performed their tasks. The task of the Kehot family serviceman is considered holy of holies.

11. The tasks of the Kohanim in preparing the Tabernacle for travel:

- <u>Preparing the Aron for travel</u>: When the camp travels, Aaron and his sons are to take down the Parochet curtain and cover the Aron with it. A Tachash leather cover is to be placed on top of it, and a turquoise [i.e. Techeiles] wool cover on top of that.
- <u>Preparing the Shulchan/Table for travel</u>: The Shulchan/Table is to be covered with a turquoise wool cover and have its vessels placed on top of it. This includes the dishes, spoons, supports, tubes, and bread. On top of them they shall spread a scarlet wool covering, and a Tachash leather cover is to be placed on top of that.
- <u>Preparing the Menorah for travel</u>: The Menorah and all its vessels are to be covered with a turquoise wool cover. This includes the lamps, tongs, and scoops, and all the vessels of its oil. All this is then to be placed into a Tachash hide cover and place it on the pole.
- <u>Preparing the gold Altar for travel</u>: The gold altar is to be covered with a turquoise wool cover, which is then to be covered by a Tachash hide cover.
- <u>Preparing the service vessels of the Tabernacle for travel</u>: All the service vessels which are used in the Tabernacle [for Ketores] are to be placed into a turquoise cloth, which is then to be covered by a Tachash hide cover and placed on the pole.
- <u>Preparing the copper Altar for travel</u>: The [copper] altar is to be cleaned of ash and then have an Argamon [i.e. purple] wool cloth placed over it. All its vessels are to be placed on it, which include the firepans, forks, shovels and basins. They are to then cover it with a Tachash hide cover.
- <u>The Kehot family's job of carrying the vessels</u>: After Aaron and his sons complete the wrapping of the vessels of the Tabernacle, the Kehot family servicemen are to come and carry it. [They are not to carry it before it is properly covered] lest they touch the holy and die.
- <u>Elazar's position</u>: Elazar the son of Aaron was appointed the task of carrying the illuminating oil, the incense spices, the Mincha, and anointing oil. He was also appointed to oversee the work of the Kehot family.
- G-d told Moses and Aaron not to cause the Kehot family to become extinct upon them coming to do the service with the Holy of Holies. To prevent this, they are to oversee everyone's job [and make sure the vessels are properly covered before they come].

Parashat Naso

Verses: 176 *[Siman:* עמינדב*]*
Haftorah: Judges 13:2-25

The Mitzvot:

There are **eighteen** Mitzvot in Parashat Naso. **Eight** positive commands and **ten** negative commands

A. Positive:

1. **Mitzvah 362; Positive 143:** To send the impure people outside of the camp called Shekhinah.
2. **Mitzvah 363; Positive 144:** To prevent any impure people from entering the Temple.
3. **Mitzvah 364; Positive 145:** To confess one's sins to G-d.
4. **Mitzvah 365; Positive 146:** To bring a suspected adulteress wife to the Kohen to have done to her as instructed in the Torah.
5. **Mitzvah 374; Positive 147:** For the Nazirite to grow his hair.
6. **Mitzvah 377; Positive 148:** For the Nazirite to shave his hair and bring Sacrifices at the end of his Nazarite period.
7. **Mitzvah 378; Positive 149:** For the Kohanim to bless the Jewish people.
8. **Mitzvah 379; Positive 150:** For the Kohanim to carry the Aron on their shoulders during travel.

B. Negative:

1. **Mitzvah 366; Negative 220:** Not to place oil on the offering of the suspected adulteress wife.
2. **Mitzvah 367; Negative 221:** Not to place frankincense on the offering of the suspected adulteress wife.
3. **Mitzvah 368; Negative 222:** The prohibition for the Nazirite to drink wine.
4. **Mitzvah 369; Negative 223:** The prohibition for the Nazirite to eat grapes.
5. **Mitzvah 370; Negative 224:** The prohibition for the Nazirite to eat raisins.
6. **Mitzvah 371; Negative 225:** The prohibition for the Nazirite to eat grape seeds.
7. **Mitzvah 372; Negative 226:** The prohibition for the Nazirite to eat grape peels.
8. **Mitzvah 373; Negative 227:** The prohibition for the Nazirite to shave his head.
9. **Mitzvah 375; Negative 228:** The prohibition for the Nazirite to enter a home which contains corpse.
10. **Mitzvah 376; Negative 229:** The prohibition for the Nazirite to impurify himself to a corpse.

Chapter 4
First Aliyah
1. **The census and services of the Levite family of Gershon:**
   - G-d commanded Moses to count all the male members of the Gershon family who are between the ages of 30-50.
   - <u>The Gershon family's job of carrying the vessels</u>: The Gershon family servicemen are to carry the tapestries of the Tabernacle, the spread of the Tent of Meeting and its Tachash leather cover that is on it and the screen of the entrance to the Tent of Meeting. They are to carry the curtains of the courtyard and its entrance screen, the ropes and all their accessories.
   - <u>Ithamar the supervisor</u>: Ithamar the son of Aaron was appointed to supervise their work.

Second Aliyah (according to Torah Temima/Chabad)
2. **The census and services of the Levite family of Merari:**
   - G-d commanded Moses to count all the male members of the Merari family who are between the ages of 30-50.
   - <u>The Merari family's job of carrying the vessels</u>: The Gershon family servicemen are to carry the beams of the Tabernacle, its poles, pillars and sockets, and all its accessories. The pillars of the courtyard, their sockets, pegs and ropes.
   - <u>Ithamar the supervisor</u>: Ithamar the son of Aaron was appointed to supervise their work.

3. **The census of working men in the three families:**
   - <u>Kehot</u>: The family of Kehot had 2,750 working men between the age of 30-50.

Second Aliyah (according to most Chumashim)
   - <u>Gershon</u>: The family of Gershon had 2,630 working men between the age of 30-50.
   - <u>Merori</u>: The family of Merari had 3,200 working men between the age of 30-50.
   - <u>Total number of worker</u>: The total number of working Levites between the age of 30-50 was 8,580.

Chapter 5
Third Aliyah
4. **Expelling the impure from the camp:**
   - G-d spoke to Moses saying that he should command the children of Israel to expel from their camp any person, male or female, who is a Metzora, a Zav, or is impure to a corpse so that they do not impurify the camp in which G-d dwells. The children of Israel did as instructed.

5. **Laws relating to one who swears falsely:**
   - G-d spoke to Moses saying that he should tell the children of Israel that any man or woman who has committed sacrilege against G-d [by swearing falsely regarding a stolen object] is to be held accountable. They are to confess their sin before G-d and reimburse the person [who the object was stolen from] plus an additional fifth. If the victim is not alive and does not have any heirs to whom one can return the debt, then it is to be given to the Kohanim, per G-d's instructions. All the above is in addition to bring a sacrificial ram for atonement.

6. **Giving the Kohen his designated presents:**
   - All the donations [of Bikkurim] of the Jewish people is to be given to the Kohen. However, the donor reserves the right to decide which Kohen to give it to. One who gives the Kohen will receive [monetary blessing].

Fourth Aliyah

7. **The suspected adulteress wife [i.e. Sotah]:**
   - G-d spoke to Moses saying that he should tell the Jewish people the Sotah laws.
   - <u>The sin</u>: If a wife strayed from her husband and betrayed him, having sexual relations with another man, unaware to her husband, then if she was warned by her husband [not to seclude herself with another man and she transgressed] and secluded herself, then she must follow the Sotah procedure.
   - <u>Bringing her and her offering to the Kohen</u>: The Sotah woman is to be brought by her husband to the Kohen. He is to bring with him, her Mincha offering, which is 1/10th of an Eipha of unsifted barley flour without oil or frankincense, as it is a sin offering.
   - <u>The procedure</u>: The Kohen is then to stand her before G-d. The Kohen is to take holy water in an earthenware vessel and place onto it earth that was taken from the Tabernacle floor. The Kohen is to uncover the woman's hair and place the Mincha offering on her palm. He is to remain holding the bitter waters.
   - <u>Administering the oath and bitter waters</u>: The Kohen is to administer an oath to the woman saying that if she did not betray her husband then she will be found innocent of the bitter waters. If, however, she is guilty, then a curse will befall her and the bitter water will cause her thigh to fall and her stomach to swell. She is to answer Amen Veamen. The above curse is to be written on a scroll and erased in the water and then given to the woman to drink.
   - <u>The offering</u>: The Kohen is to take the Mincha offering from the woman and waive it before G-d and then offer a portion of it onto the altar. The woman is to be given the water to drink only after the Mincha is offered.
   - <u>The effect of the waters</u>: If the woman is guilty of adultery, her stomach will swell, and her thigh will fall off. If she is innocent, she will have children.

Chapter 6

8. **The Nazirite:**
   - <u>The prohibitions</u>: A man or woman who swears to become a Nazirite to G-d may not drink wine or eat grapes throughout the period of his Nesirus. He may not cut his hair or defile himself by contacting a corpse throughout the entire Nazirite period, even if it is the corpse of a relative. A Nazirite is holy to G-d.
   - <u>If the Nazirite becomes impure</u>: If he does become impure to a corpse he is to shave his head on the 7th day, and on the 8th day he is to bring two doves to the Kohen, one for a Chatas offering and one for an Olah offering. After the Nazirite period is complete he is to bring a sheep in its first year as an Asham offering.
   - <u>The Nazirite procedure</u>: After the Nazirite period is complete he is to come to the entrance of the Tent of Meeting and bring with him a sheep in its first year as an Olah offering and a female sheep within its first year as a Chatas offering, and a ram as a Shelamim offering. He is to bring a basket of Matzot, their flour offering and libations. The Kohen is to offer all the above offerings and shave the head of the Nazirite in the

entrance to the Tent of Meeting. The hair is to be placed on the fire used to cook the Shelamim. Afterwards, the Kohen is to take a cooked foreleg of the ram and two different Matzot and place it on the palm of the Nazirite and waive them before G-d. The Nazirite may then drink wine.

9. Birchas Kohanim:

- G-d spoke to Moses saying that he should tell Aaron and his sons that they should bless the Jewish people with the priestly blessing of *Yivarechicha G-d Veyishmirecha etc.*

Chapter 7
Fifth Aliyah

10. The Sacrifices of the tribal leaders:

- On the day that Moses completed the erecting the Tabernacle and anointing all the vessels the leaders of the tribes brought an offering before G-d. They brought six covered wagons and 12 oxen, intending there to be 2 oxen per wagon and one wagon for every two tribes. G-d instructed Moses to take the wagons and give it to the Levites to use to perform the work of the Tent of Meeting. The Gershon family received 2 wagons and 4 oxen. Merari received 4 wagons and 8 oxen and Kehot did not receive any wagons as they must carry the items of the Tabernacle on their shoulders.
- The tribal leaders came to bring their offering to the Altar to inaugurate it and G-d instructed Moses that each tribe should bring their offering on a separate day.
- The first day: On the first day, **Nachshon Ben Aminadav** of the tribe of **Judah** brought a offering. The offering consisted of: One silver bowl which weighed 130 Shekel. One basin of silver which weighed 70 Shekel. Both were filled with fine flour which was mixed with oil, as a Mincha offering. One ladle of gold which weighed 10 Shekel filled with incense. One young bull, one ram and one sheep within its first year as an Olah offering. One goat as a Chatas offering. For a Shelamim sacrifice was brought 2 cattle, five rams, five male goats, and five sheep within their first year.
- The second day: On the second day, **Nethanel Ben Tzuar** of the tribe of **Issachar** brought an offering. The offering consisted of the same items as that offered on the first day by Nachshon.
- The third day: On the third day, **Eliav Ben Cheilon** of the tribe of **Zebulun** brought an offering. The offering consisted of the same items as that offered on the first day by Nachshon.
- The fourth day: On the fourth day, **Elitzur Ben Shedeur** of the tribe of **Reuben** brought an offering. The offering consisted of the same items as that offered on the first day by Nachshon.
- The fifth day: On the fifth day, **Shelumiel Ben Tzurishaddai** of the tribe of **Simeon** brought an offering. The offering consisted of the same items as that offered on the first day by Nachshon.

Sixth Aliyah

- The sixth day: On the sixth day, **Eliasaf Ben Deuel** of the tribe of **Gad** brought an offering. The offering consisted of the same items as that offered on the first day by Nachshon.

- The seventh day: On the seventh day, **Elishama Ben Amihud** of the tribe of **Ephraim** brought an offering. The offering consisted of the same items as that offered on the first day by Nachshon.
- The eighth day: On the eighth day, **Gamliel Ben Pedahtzur** of the tribe of **Manasseh** brought an offering. The offering consisted of the same items as that offered on the first day by Nachshon.
- The ninth day: On the ninth day, **Avidan Ben Gidoni** of the tribe of **Benjamin** brought an offering. The offering consisted of the same items as that offered on the first day by Nachshon.
- The tenth day: On the tenth day, **Achiezer Ben Amishaddai** of the tribe of **Dan** brought an offering. The offering consisted of the same items as that offered on the first day by Nachshon.

Seventh Aliyah (according to most Chumashim)

- The eleventh day: On the eleventh day, **Pagiel Ben Ochran** of the tribe of **Asher** brought an offering. The offering consisted of the same items as that offered on the first day by Nachshon.
- The twelfth day: On the twelfth day, **Ahira Ben Einan** of the tribe of **Naftali** brought an offering. The offering consisted of the same items as that offered on the first day by Nachshon.

Seventh Aliyah (according to Torah Temima/Chabad)

- The total number: The total number of Sacrifices brought were:
  - 12 silver bowls which weighed 130 Shekel.
  - 12 basins of silver which weighed 70 Shekel for a total of 2400 shekel of silver
  - 12 ladles of gold which weighed 10 Shekel filled with incense for a total of 123 shekel of gold.
  - 12 young bulls, 12 rams and 12 sheep within its first year as an Olah offering.
  - 12 goats as a Chatas offering.
  - For a Shelamim sacrifice was brought 24 cattle, 60 rams, 60 male goats, and 60 sheep within their first year.
- When Moses entered the Tent of Meeting to speak with G-d he would hear G-d speak from between the Cherubim.

Parashat Behalotecha

Verses: 136 *[Siman:* מהללאל*]*
Haftorah: Zechariah 2:14-4:7

The Mitzvot:
There are a total of **five** Mitzvot in Parashat Behaalotecha. **Three** positive commands, and **two** negative commands.

A. The positive commands:
1. **Mitzvah 380; Positive 151:** For anyone who was unable to bring the Pesach offering before Pesach to perform the second Pesach on the 14th of Iyar
2. **Mitzvah 381; Positive 152:** For those obligated in the second Pesach to eat it's meat with Matzah and Maror.
3. **Mitzvah 384; Positive 153:** To blow trumpets daily in the Temple, and during times of suffering.

B. The Negative commands:
1. **Mitzvah 382; Negative 230:** The prohibition to leave any leftovers from the meat of the second Pesach.
2. **Mitzvah 383; Negative 231:** The prohibition to break the bones of the second Pesach sacrifice.

Chapter 8
First Aliyah

1. The Menorah:
- G-d spoke to Moses saying: Tell Aaron that the seven candles of the Menorah are to be lit facing towards the Menorah. Aaron did as Moses instructed. The Menorah was made of a pure block of gold, as G-d showed Moses.

2. The inauguration process for the Levites:
- G-d spoke to Moses saying: Take the Levites for G-d from amongst the Jewish people. Purify them through sprinkling on them purification waters and shaving all their hair off their skin. They are to immerse their garments and then become pure.
- Their offering: They are to take a young bull [as an Olah offering] and its Mincha of flour mixed with oil, and a second young bull as a Chatas offering.
- Semicha to the Levites: All the Levites, together with all the Jewish people, are to be brought before the Tent of Meeting, and the Jewish people will lean their hands on the Levites.
- Waving: Aaron will waive the Levites before G-d and they shall perform their service.
- Semicha to the animals: The Levites shall rest their hands on the heads of the bulls, and one is to be offered as a Chatas while the second as an Olah.

Second Aliyah

- After the above process is complete the Levites shall serve in the Tent of Meeting as the representatives of the children of Israel, having been redeemed in exchange for the firstborns, and given to the Kohanim.
- Moses, Aaron and the Jewish people did to the Levites as they were instructed, and the Levites were purified, had their clothing immersed, and were waved.

3. The years of service of the Levites:

- The Levites are to serve in the service of the Tent of Meeting beginning from 25 years of age until 50 years of age. They are to retire from this service at age 50 but they shall serve as a safeguard in the Tent of Meeting.

Third Aliyah

4. The Pesach offering in the desert:

- G-d spoke to Moses in the Sinai desert, on the first month of the second year after the exodus saying that the Jewish people shall perform the Pesach sacrifice on time, in the afternoon of the 14th day of this month according to all its laws.
- The Jewish people did as they were instructed.

Chapter 9

5. The second Pesach [i.e. Pesach Sheiyni]:

- The complaint: Certain individuals who were impure due to contact with a corpse came to Moses complaining why they could not perform the Pesach sacrifice, and why they should miss out on this opportunity. Moses brought their complaint to G-d, to which G-d replied with the following laws:
- Its laws: G-d spoke to Moses saying: Any man who is impure or a distance away [from the area of slaughter, i.e. Jerusalem, on the 14th of Nissan] is to offer the Pesach sacrifice in the 2nd month on the 14th day. It is to be eaten with Matzah and Maror. It may not be leftover until morning, and its bones may not be broken.
- Transgressed and did not offer: One who is pure, and is not a distance away and still does not bring the Pesach sacrifice, is to be cut off from its nation.

Fourth Aliyah

6. The order of traveling in the desert:

- On the day the Tabernacle was erected the cloud covered it. At night, a fire appeared on the Tabernacle until the morning. The Jewish people would travel upon the cloud ascending from the Ohel tent, and they would encamp in the area where the cloud would settle. At times they remained encamped for many days and at times for only one day. They traveled and encamped according to the word of G-d.

Chapter 10

7. Blowing the trumpets:

- G-d spoke to Moses saying that he should make two trumpets of pure silver to be used to gather the congregation, and to announce the time to travel.

- Signal for gathering: If you blow a Tekia using both of them, this is a sign for the congregation to gather by the entrance of the Tent of Meeting. If you blow [a Tekia using] one trumpet, this is a sign for the tribal leaders to gather.
- Signal for traveling: If you blow a Teruah, short blasts, it is a sign for traveling. By the first Teruah, the eastern camp is to travel. By the second Teruah, the southern camp is to travel. The trumpets are to be blown by the Kohanim.
- Signal for G-d during war: During war against your enemies, a Teruah should be blown from the trumpets and G-d will remember you and save you from your enemies.
- During Holidays: On days of joy and holidays and Rosh Chodesh you shall blow the Shofar during the sacrifices and it will be a remembrance for you before G-d.

Fifth Aliyah

8. The travels of the children of Israel:
- The date: On the 20th day of the second month of the second year the cloud ascended from the Tabernacle and the Jewish people traveled. The cloud rested in the Paran desert.
- The order of the travel: The first to travel was the camp of Judah, which included the tribes of Issachar and Zebulun and their leaders. The Tabernacle was then dismantled and the Gershon and Merari family carried the [tapestries and beams of the] Tabernacle. The next camp to travel was the camp of Reuben, which included the tribes of Simeon and Gad and their leaders. The Kehot family then traveled carrying the [vessels of the] Temple. The Tabernacle was erected prior to their arrival. The next camp to travel was the camp of Ephraim, which included Manasseh and Benjamin and their leaders. The final camp to travel was the camp of Dan, which included Asher and Naftali and their leaders.
- Jethro desires to leave: Moses spoke to Chovav, his father in-law, and told him that they are traveling to the place that G-d has promised them. Moses asked Jethro to come along with them and he will be repaid with good. Jethro refused to go and said that he planned to return to his homeland. Moses implored for him to remain with them and serve as an advisor as he has been until now.
- They traveled from the mountain of G-d a journey of three days and the Aron of G-d traveled with them to find them a resting place. The cloud of G-d accompanied them during the day

Sixth Aliyah
- Traveling of the Ark: When the Aron traveled, Moses would say "Arise G-d and disperse your enemies and let those who hate you flee." When the Aron rested, Moses would say "Reside tranquilly G-d, among the myriads of Jewish people."

Chapter 11
9. Fire breaks out in the Camp:
- The people complained in an evil way before G-d, and G-d heard and became angry. A fire shot forth from G-d and consumed those at the edge of the camp. The nation screamed to Moses and Moses spoke to G-d and the fire subsided. That area was called Taveirah, as the fire of G-d consumed there.

10. The complaint for meat and the Slav birds:

- The lust for meat: The mixed multitude amongst the Jewish people lusted after meat, and they and the Jewish people cried and complained that they do not have meat. They said, "We remember the fish, cucumbers, melons, leeks, onions and garlic that we ate in Egypt for free and now all we have is the Mun before our eyes."

- The Mun: The Mun was like a coriander seed and was the color of the Bedolach. The people would gather it and grind it in the mill, or mortar, and cook it into cakes. It tasted like dough kneaded with oil.

- Moses is angered and confronts G-d for help in the leadership: Moses heard the people crying with their families by the entrances to their tent. G-d became very angry and it was bad in the eyes of Moses. Moses turned to G-d and complained as to why He has caused him evil by placing the entire burden of the nation on him, as if he has born them and must carry them in his bosom to the promised land. "From where do I have meat to give them all that they should complain to me. I can no longer carry the burden of this nation alone, and if this is your decision then please kill me and do not see my suffering." G-d said to Moses that he should gather 70 elders of Israel and bring them to the Tent of Meeting where they will receive from the spirit of Moses and be able to carry the burden of the nation together with him.

- G-d promises meat: G-d instructed Moses to tell the nation to prepare themselves tomorrow to eat meat, as you have cried to the ears of G-d saying it was better off in Egypt where you had meat. You will have meat for thirty days until it comes out of your nostrils and become repulsive to you.

- Moses does not believe G-d: Moses replied to G-d that it is not possible to feed 600,000 souls in the desert for a full month. Even if you slaughter all the flock and cattle and fish it will not suffice them. G-d chastised Moses saying that the hand of G-d is not limited, and that he will see that G-d's word will be fulfilled.

- Moses gathers the 70 elders and makes them leaders: Moses left and informed the Jewish people of G-d's words. He gathered 70 elders and positioned them around the Tent of Meeting. G-d descended with a cloud and spoke to Moses and He set aside from the spirit of Moses onto the seventy elders. When this happened, they began to prophesize. Two people remained in the camp, one called Eldad and the second Meidad, and they prophesied there. A youth ran to inform Moses that Eldad and Meidad were prophesying in the camp. Joshua told Moses that he should finish off with them. Moses, however, replied that there is no need to be zealous for his sake and if only G-d would make them all prophets.

Seventh Aliyah

- The Slav arrive: G-d brought a wind that carried with it the Slav pheasant birds from the sea. They swarmed the camp for the distance of one day's travel from each direction. They were approximately two cubits height from the ground. That entire day and night and next day the nation collected the Slav. The least that a person gathered was ten heaps worth of Slav. The [dead] birds were spread and piled throughout the camp. While the people ate the bird, while the meat was still in between their teeth, the wrath of G-d smote them and many died. That area was named "Kivros Hataavah," as in the area was buried the people who were craving.

- From Kivros Hatava the nation traveled to Chatzeiros.

Chapter 12

11. Miriam and Aaron speak against Moses:

- The slander: Miriam and Aaron spoke regarding the black woman that Moses married saying that it is not only to him that G-d speaks but also to them [and hence why is he celibate]. G-d heard, and Moses was the humblest man on earth.

- G-d punishes Miriam with Tzara'at: G-d suddenly appeared and summoned Moses, Aaron and Miriam to come to the Tent of Meeting. G-d asked for Aaron and Miriam, and explained to them that Moses is unlike anyone else in prophecy as "I speak to Him face to face without any riddles and he sees the image of G-d constantly. Why then did you not fear speaking against My servant Moses." G-d's anger flared up and He left. When the cloud ascended from the Tent of Meeting, Miriam was stricken with Tzara'at as white as snow and Aaron noticed. Aaron asked Moses for forgiveness and to have mercy on their sister. Moses screamed to G-d in supplication that He should heal her. G-d instructed for her to be placed outside the camp for seven days. The camp did not travel during those days until Miriam's return.

- They then traveled from Chatzeiros to the desert of Paran.

Parashat Shelach
Verses: 119 [Siman: פלט]
Haftorah: Joshua 2:1-24

Number of Mitzvot:

There are a total of **Three** Mitzvot in Parashat Shelach; **Two** positive commands and **One** negative command. The following are the commands in the chronological order that they are brought in the Portion.

A. Positive:
  1. **Mitzvah 385; Positive 154:** To separate Challah from dough and give it to a Kohen.
  2. **Mitzvah 386; Positive 155:** To tie Tzitzis fringes to the corner of one's garments.

B. Negative:
  1. **Mitzvah 387; Negative 232:** The prohibition to swerve after the thoughts of the heart and sight of the eyes regarding matters that are contrary to Torah theology.

Chapter 13
First Aliyah

1. **Moses sends spies to Eretz Canaan:**
   * G-d spoke to Moses saying that he should send men to tour the promised land of Canaan. One person is to be chosen from each tribe. Moses did as he was instructed and sent them from the Paran desert to the land of Canaan. All the men in the group were distinguished leaders of Israel.
   * The names of those chosen for the delegation:
     o **Reuben:** Shammua Ben Zaccur
     o **Simeon:** Shafat Ben Chori
     o **Judah:** Kaleb Ben Yefuneh
     o **Issachar:** Yigal Ben Joseph
     o **Ephraim:** Hosheia Ben Nun. Moses called him Joshua.
     o **Benjamin:** Palti Ben Rafu
     o **Zebulun:** Gaddiel Ben Sodi
     o **Manasseh:** Gaddi Ben Susi
     o **Dan:** Ammiel Ben Gemalli
     o **Asher:** Setur Ben Michael
     o **Naftali:** Nachbi Ben Vofsi
     o **Gad:** Geuel Ben Machi.
   * The purpose and instruction of their mission: Moses sent the above delegation to tour the land of Canaan and he told them to travel from the south and ascend the mountain. They should see the quality of the land, if it is good or bad, and if the nations that dwell on it are strong or weak, few or numerous, and if the cities are fortified or open. They should see if the land is fertile or lean, if it has trees or not. Moses asked them to bring back with them from the fruits of the land. That period of the year was the time of the ripening of the grapes.

Second Aliyah

2. **Their journey:**
   - They went and toured the land from the Tzin desert until Chamas.
   - <u>The giants</u>: They went up the south and arrived at Hebron where the giants Achiman, Sheshai and Talmai are found. Hebron was built seven years before the city of Tzoan in Egypt.
   - <u>The fruits</u>: They arrived at the Eshkol region and cut fruits from there. They took a cluster of grapes and two people carried it on a pole. They took pomegranates and figs.

3. **Their return and slanderous report:**
   - They returned to the camp of the Jewish people in the desert of Paran after a forty-day journey and reported what they saw and showed them the fruits of the land. They said that the land flows with milk and honey, contains mighty nations who live in large fortified cities, and contains giants. Amalek lives in the south, and the Hittite, Jebusite and Amorite live on the mountain. The Canaanite lives by the sea and near the Jordan river.
   - <u>Kaleb responds</u>: Kaleb quieted the nation and told them that they would be able to conquer them. However, the other members of the delegation said that it is not possible, as those nations are much more powerful. They said that the land consumes its inhabitants. They described feeling like grasshoppers in the eyes of the giants. They spoke slander against the land.

Chapter 14

4. **The nations reaction:**
   - The nation cried that night and complained against Moses and Aaron saying if only they would have died in Egypt, or in this desert, rather than be brought by G-d to that land to die by the sword and have their wives and children taken captive. It is better that we return to Egypt, and so they decided to appoint a leader to return to Egypt.
   - Moses and Aaron fell on their faces. Joshua Ben Nun and Kaleb Ben Yefuna tore their clothing and they told the Jewish people that the land which they toured is very, very good.

Third Aliyah
   - If G-d desires to bring us, He will bring us there, it is a land of milk and honey. Do not rebel against G-d, and do not fear the other nations as they will be like bread to us. Their protection has departed, and G-d will be with us. Do not fear!
   - The entire nation wanted to pelt them with stones, and the glory of G-d suddenly appeared in the Tent of Meeting to all the Jewish people.

5. **G-d's response:**
   - <u>G-d responds with a threat of annihilation</u>: G-d lamented to Moses of the state of the nation that after all the miracles He has done they still do not believe in Him and anger Him. "I will smite the nation and annihilate them and make a new greater nation from you Moses."
   - <u>Moses's defense</u>: Moses pleaded to G-d not to destroy the nation, as this would cause the Egyptians and other nations to say that You could not conquer the promised land and

therefore you made them die in the desert. Now, strengthen Your power "G-d, a G-d of mercy and compassion, slow to anger and abundant in kindness, Who forgives inquity." Please forgive this nation just as you have forgiven them in Egypt until now. G-d replied that He agrees to forgive them as requested.

- The punishment: Nonetheless, the people will not go unpunished. All those who experienced and saw my miracles in Egypt and in the desert and challenged Me ten times and did not heed My voice, they will not see the promised land. However, My servant Kaleb, being he was not part of the slanderous report, he will enter the land.

- Travel: The Amalekites and Canaanites dwelled in the valley, and G-d instructed the Jewish people to return and journey towards the desert the next day.

Fourth Aliyah

- Moses informs the Jewish people of the punishments: G-d told Moses and Aaron to inform the Jewish people that their request was granted, and they will die in this dessert. Only Kaleb and Joshua, as well as their children whom they said would be taken captive, will enter the promised land. Your corpses will drop in this desert and your children will wander for forty years in it to bear your guilt, one year for each day of your journey.

- The Meraglim die: The spies who spoke slander of the land died in a plague before G-d.

6. Attempt to conquer Amalek:

- Moses informed the children of Israel of all the above and they entered a deep state of mourning. They arose in the morning and ascended the mountain with intent to repent and enter the promised land. However, Moses warned them that they would not be successful as G-d does not allow it anymore. They will be smitten by their enemies if they continue, as G-d is no longer with them. However, they were stubborn and did not listen and ascended the mountain. Moses and the Aron did not move from the camp. The Amaleikites and Canaanites who lived on that mountain annihilated them.

Chapter 15
7. Voluntary Sacrifices of a vow and their Mincha and Nesachim:

- G-d told Moses to tell the Jewish people that when they arrive to the land and bring a voluntary offering from the cattle, or flock, due to a vow, or during the festivals, then it should be accompanied by a Mincha offering and wine libations.

- Sheep: For every sheep you should have a tenth of an Eipha of fine flour for a Mincha, mixed with a quarter of a Hin of oil, and a quarter of a Hin of wine as a libation.

- Ram: For every ram you should have two tenths of an Eipha of fine flour for a Mincha, mixed with a third of a Hin of oil, and a third of a Hin of wine as a libation.

Fifth Aliyah

- Bull: For every bull you should have three tenths of an Eipha of fine flour for a Mincha, mixed with half of a Hin of oil, and half of a Hin of wine as a libation.

- This applies both for you and for the converts who dwell with you. You will all follow the same laws.

Sixth Aliyah

8. The Mitzvah of Hafrashas Challah:

- G-d told Moses to tell the Jewish people that when they enter the land and eat from the bread of the land, they shall set aside a portion for G-d. The first of the kneading is to be tithed as a Challah for G-d, similar to the Teruma separation.

9. Sacrifices for unintentional sins:

- <u>Entire congregation sinned</u>: If the entire congregation performs a sin [relating to idolatry] due to an inaccurate ruling, then they are to bring one bull within its first year as an Olah offering, and its mincha and libation, and one he-goat as a Chatas ofering. G-d will forgive the nation.

Seventh Aliyah

- <u>Individual sinned</u>: If a single individual performs a sin [relating to idolatry] he is to bring one she-goat as a Chatas. G-d will forgive him for his sin.
- <u>A brazen sinner</u>: One who brazenly sins [with idolatry] will be cut off from his nation.

10. The wood gatherer:

- The Jewish people were in the desert and they found a man gathering wood on Shabbat and brought him to Moses and Aaron for further instruction of what shall be done to him. He was placed in custody as they did not know what his punishment should be.
- <u>The punishment</u>: G-d said to Moses that the man shall die through stoning. The entire congregation is to stone him outside of the camp. The nation did as they were instructed, and he was stoned to death outside the camp.

11. Mitzvah of Tzitzis fringes:

- G-d told Moses to tell the Jewish people to make Tzitzis fringes on the corners of their garments, and place a thread of Techeiles turquoise wool on each corner. By seeing the Tzitzis they will remember the Mitzvot of G-d and perform them and not stray after their hearts and eyes.
- I am G-d who took you out of Egypt

Parashat Korach
Verses: 95 [Siman: דניאל]
Haftorah: Samuel 1 11:14-12:22

Number of Mitzvot:
There are a total of **nine** Mitzvot in Parashat Korach; **Five** positive commands and **Four** negative commands. The following are the commands in the order listed by the Sefer Hachinuch.

A. Positive:
1. **Mitzvah 388; Positive 156:** For the Kohanim and Levites to guard the Temple every night, throughout the nights.
2. **Mitzvah 392; Positive 157:** To redeem a firstborn son.
3. **Mitzvah 394; Positive 158:** For the Levites to work in the Temple as guards, and singers.
4. **Mitzvah 395; Positive 159:** To separate 10% of the land produce to the Levites [i.e. Maaser].
5. **Mitzvah 396; Positive 160:** For the Levites to separate a portion [i.e. Teruma] from the tithe that they receive.

B. Negative:
1. **Mitzvah 389; Negative 233:** The prohibition for the Levites to perform services of the Kohanim or vice versa.
2. **Mitzvah 390; Negative 234:** The prohibition for a non-Kohen to perform service in the Temple.
3. **Mitzvah 391; Negative 235:** The prohibition to leave the Temple unguarded anytime throughout the night.
4. **Mitzvah 393; Negative 236:** The prohibition to redeem the firstborn animal.

Chapter 16
First Aliyah

1. **Korach and his men confront Moses and Aaron:**
   - Korach, the son of Yitzhar, the son of Kehot, the son of Levi, took with him Datan, Abiram and On Ben Peles from the tribe of Reuben and confronted Moses. They came with a group of 250 leaders of the Jewish people who joined their fight against Moses. The group confronted Moses and Aaron with the claim that they made themselves the elite of the Jewish people when in truth all the Jewish people are holy.

2. **Moses's response:**
   - Moses heard and fell on his face in reaction of their complaint.
   - The offering of Ketores and G-d choosing the leader: Moses replied to Korach that by morning G-d will relate to everyone who in truth is meant to be the leaders of the Jewish people. This will be accomplished by having all the contenders, who desire to be leaders, offer Ketores incense onto the altar and whoever G-d chooses, he will be the holy one.

Each man is to take a pan filled with fire and Ketores incense and offer it before G-d tomorrow.

- <u>Moses admonishes the Levites</u>: Moses reproached the tribe of Levi telling them that they should be satisfied with the fact that they were chosen by G-d to be the representatives of the Jewish people to serve G-d in the Tabernacle. "It is not right that you now step forward and demand to also become Kohanim. Why do you complain against Aaron, what is he that you should protest against him?"
- <u>Moses summons Datan and Abiram</u>: Moses summoned Datan and Abiram, the accomplices of Korach, to speak with them but they refused to come. They replied, "Moses took them out of a land of milk and honey to die in the dessert and he has no right to rule over us."

Second Aliyah

- Datan and Abiram continued saying against Moses that he has not brought us into the Promised Land, and even if he would have their eyes bulged out they would not approach Moses.
- Moses's wrath boiled at such an insidious reply and he turned to G-d stating "Do not accept their Ketores offering. I have not taken one donkey from these people and I have not done wrong to any of them."

3. **Moses instructs the congregation regarding the Ketores offering:**
- Moses told Korach that he and his entire congregation are to stand before G-d tomorrow together with Aaron. Each man is to take a pan filled with Ketores and offer it before G-d. There would be 250 pans of Ketores being offered [from Korach's group]. Each of the contestants are to offer the Ketores in their pan.
- They placed fire in the pan and then placed the incense on top of the fire and brought it before the Tent of Meeting. Moses and Aaron were present.
- <u>The Shekhinah appears</u>: Korach gathered his entire group around Moses and Aaron, in front of the Tent of Meeting and the Shekhinah then appeared to the entire congregation.

Third Aliyah

4. **G-d instructs Moses:**
- G-d spoke to Moses and Aaron saying that they are to separate themselves from the congregation as they will be destroyed in a moment. Moses and Aaron prostrated themselves before G-d and beseeched for his mercy, and that he should not punish the entire congregation because of the sin of one man.

5. **Moses instructs the Jewish people to disperse from the tent of Korach, Datan and Abiram:**
- G-d instructed Moses to tell the congregation to disperse from the area of the encampments of Korach and Datan and Abiram. Moses, together with the elders of the Jewish people, approached Datan and Abiram's [camp] and told the congregation to disperse from the tents of these evildoers, and not to touch anything that is theirs, lest they will be killed for their sins. The congregation listened and dispersed from the area of Korach's and Datan and Abiram's tent.

6. **Moses confronts Korach and Datan and gives them a severe warning:**
   - Datan and Abiram confronted Moses and came out of their tents with their wives and entire family.
   - Moses warned them that G-d sent him to do all of these actions and the following will be the sign that I did not fabricate it from my heart. If you die like a regular man, then you know that I am a fraudster and G-d did not send me. If, however G-d will create a new creation, and the earth will open its mouth and swallow you, and all that you own, into the depths of purgatory, then that will the sign that you have started a fight with G-d.

7. **The earth swallows Koarch and kills his accomplices:**
   - As Moses finished speaking, the earth that was under them opened its mouth and swallowed their entire families and houses, and all the men who joined Korach, as well as all their property. They all descended alive into the depths of the earth and the earth covered them and they became lost from the congregation.
   - The people surrounding the area began fleeing with fright, having heard the screams of those who were swallowed, as they feared that they too would be consumed.
   - A fire exited from G-d and consumed the 250 men that offered the Ketores incense.

Chapter 17

8. **The pans of the Ketores are used to plate the altar:**
   - G-d instructed Moses to tell Elazar to gather all the Ketores pans, as the pans have become holy. The pans are to be used for covering the Altar, and serve as a sign for the Jewish people. Elazar did as Moses commanded, and he gathered the pans and made it into a coating for the Altar to serve as a sign for the Jewish people that a non-Kohen may not offer Ketores before G-d, and that one is not to be like Korach and his accomplices.

9. **The congregation confronts Moses and Aaron:**
   - The next day, the entire Jewish people confronted Moses and Aaron with the claim that they killed G-d's nation. As they were voicing their complaints the cloud of glory covered the Tent of Meeting and G-d appeared.
   - Moses and Aaron entered the Tent of Meeting.

Fourth Aliyah

10. **G-d sends a plague to Israel:**
   - G-d spoke to Moses saying that he should remove himself from the congregation as He will kill them instantly. Moses [and Aaron] prostrated themselves before G-d.
   - The plague began. Moses instructed Aaron to hurry and offer Ketores in order to atone for the nation and stop the plague. Aaron did as he was instructed and hurried to offer the Ketores, and the plague ended. A total of 14,700 Jews died in the plague, in addition to the deaths of Korach and his congregation

Fifth Aliyah

11. A staff is gathered from each tribe and the staff of Aaron blossoms:

- G-d instructed Moses to take a staff from each one of the tribes of the Jewish people for a total of 12 staffs. Each tribe's name is to be inscribed on their staff. Aaron's name is to be written on the staff of the tribe of Levi. The staffs are to be placed in the Tent of Meeting and whoever is chosen, his staff will blossom, and thus the complaint of the Jewish people will subside.

- Moses spoke to the people of G-d's instructions and the people did as Moses commanded, and the staffs were placed by Moses inside the Ohel tent. The next day, when Moses entered the Ohel tent he found that the staff of Aaron had blossomed and grew almonds. Moses removed all the staffs from before G-d and each person took his staff.

Sixth Aliyah

- G-d instructed Moses to preserve the staff of Aaron, and place it in the Heichal as a sign for the rebels and to end their complaint against Me.

12. The Jewish people are in despair:

- After all the above events, the Jewish people cried to Moses in despair that they will all be doomed, as anyone who breaches the boundaries of the Kohanim is bound to die.

Chapter 18

13. G-d instructs Aaron to guard the Tabernacle:

- G-d told Aaron that he and his children will carry the responsibility of preventing breaches of non-Kohanim entering into the Temple.

- The tribe of Levi was given to Aaron to assist him in his work. The Levites are to guard the borders of the Tabernacle, although are not to serve in the Temple.

14. G-d designates gifts to Aaron and the Kohanim:

- Offerings: G-d spoke to Aaron saying that He has given the Kohanim the rights to eat the meat of all the sacrifices, and flour offerings. Everything set aside from the sacrifcies is given to them. Only males are to eat the sacrifices in a most holy way. Only pure Kohanim may eat it.

- Teruma: The people are to give a Teruma donation to the Kohanim. The best of the grains and best of the wine and oil.

- Bikurim: The first of all their produce that is brought to G-d is given to you. It is to be eaten by those who are pure in your home.

- Cherem: Every Cherem [consecrated property] is to go to the Kohanim.

- Firstborns: The firstborn of a person and animal is to go to the Kohanim. The firstborn human and impure animals [i.e. donkey] are to be redeemed. The firstborn son is to be redeemed with five Shekalim after 30 days. The firstborn of pure animals is not to be redeemed, and is rather to have its blood and fat offered to the altar, as it is holy. You are, however, to eat its meat.

- Inheritance of the land: G-d told Aaron that the Kohanim will not receive an inheritance of the land in Israel, as I am your portion and heritage among the children of Israel.

Seventh Aliyah

15. G-d designates gifts to the Levites:

- Tithe [i.e. Maaser]: The Levites are to receive a tithe of produce [i.e. Maaser] from the Jewish people in exchange for their work in the Temple, so that the Jewish people are to no longer come close to the Tent of Meeting and die.
- Inheritance of the land: The Levites will not receive an inheritance of land in Israel, as they were given the Maaser as their inheritance.
- Tithing the tithe [i.e. Terumas Maaser]: G-d commanded Moses to tell the Levites that they are to give Terumos Maaser [i.e. a tithe] from the Maaser that they receive from the Jewish people. The Teruma is to be given to Aaron the Kohen [and his sons the Kohanim]. Once the Teruma is set aside, they may then partake in the Maaser they received just like all other produce.
- The Maaser tithe may be eaten anywhere, by one's entire family, as it is his wages for working in the Tent of Meeting.

Parashat Chukat
Verses: 87 [Siman: פ, עזי]
Haftorah: Judges 11:1-33

Number of Mitzvot:
There are a total of **three** Mitzvot in Parashat Chukat; **Three** positive commands and **Zero** negative commands. The following are the commands in the order listed by the Sefer Hachinuch.

A. Positive:
1. **Mitzvah 397/Positive 161**: To prepare ash of the red cow for purification purposes.
2. **Mitzvah 398/Positive 162**: To follow the laws dictated by the Torah for one who has become impurified by contacting a corpse [i.e. Tumas Meis].
3. **Mitzvah 399/Positive 163**: To purify the impure using the Mei Niddah [water mixed with red heifer ashes] in accordance to the Torah law.

Chapter 19
First Aliyah

1. The Mitzvah of the red heifer:
- G-d spoke to Moses and Aaron saying that they should tell the Jewish people about the Mitzvah of Parah Adumah. The Mitzvah of the Parah Adumah is the statute of the Torah.
- Criteria of the cow: The Jewish people should bring to you a perfectly red cow that is unblemished and has never worked.
- The service performed with the cow: Elazar Hakohen is to be given the cow and he is to take it outside the camp where it shall be slaughtered in his presence. Elazar is to take from its blood and sprinkle its blood with his finger seven times towards the Tent of Meeting. The entire cow is to be burnt in his presence, including its skin, meat, blood and waste. The Kohen is to take cedar wood, hyssop, and a wool crimson string, and throw it into the fire which is burning the cow.
- The Kohen becomes impure: The Kohen, and the one who burned the cow, are to immerse themselves and their clothing, and they shall be impure until evening, and may then enter the camp.
- The ash: The ash is to be gathered by a pure man and stored in a pure area outside the camp. The ash will be preserved for the Jewish people. The person who gathers the ash is to immerse his clothing, and he is impure until evening. These laws apply for all generations.

2. The laws of impurity to a corpse [i.e. Tumas Meis]:
- Touching corpse: One who touches a corpse of any human is impure for 7 days. He is to be purified [with the Parah ash] on the 3rd and 7th day, otherwise he remains impure. If he enters the Temple prior to being purified with the Mei Niddah, he receives excision.
- Tent of a corpse: Anyone who enters the tent of a corpse is impure for 7 days. Likewise, everything in the tent shall be impure for seven days. An open vessel shall be impure.

- Touching grave: Whoever touches a man killed by a sword, or a corpse or a human bone or a grave is impure for seven days.

3. The process of purification:
- Spring water is to be poured into a vessel, onto the ash of the cow

Second Aliyah
- A pure man is to dip Hyssop into the water and sprinkle it onto the tent, on all the vessels, and on all the people that are impure on the 3rd and 7th day. On the 7th day he is to immerse his clothing and body in water, and he becomes pure at night. If he enters the Temple prior to being purified with the red heifer water [i.e. Mei Niddah], he has defiled the Temple and will be cut off from his nation.
- The impurification of the purifier: One who sprinkles the Niddah water must immerse his garments and one who touches the Niddah water becomes impure until evening.
- Touching the impure person: Anything the impure person touches becomes impure until the evening.

Chapter 20
4. Miriam passes away:
- The nation arrived at the desert of Tzin in the first month and they settled in Kadeish.
- Miriam passed away there in the desert of Tzin and was buried there.

5. The drought-Mei Meriva:
- After Miriam's passing, there was a drought. The nation gathered around Moses and Aaron and fought with them [complaining that they did not have water]. "If only we would have died with our brothers. Why did you bring the congregation of G-d to this desert to die there, us and our animals? Why did you bring us out of Egypt to this evil place which has no seed or figs, grapes or pomegranates, and there is no water to drink?"
- Moses and Aaron left the people and entered the Tent of Meeting, and fell on their faces, and G-d's glory appeared to them.

Third Aliyah (Second Aliyah when combined with Balak)
- Moses hits the rock: G-d instructed Moses to take the staff and gather the people, and Aaron, and speak to the rock in front of them, and it will give water to them and their animals. Moses did as G-d instructed him, and he took the staff from before G-d. Moses and Aaron gathered the nation before the rock and he chastised the Jewish people saying, "Listen rebels, will this rock give forth water for you?" Moses lifted his hand and he hit the rock twice with his staff and a lot of water came out, and the congregation and their animals drank.
- G-d admonishes and punishes Moses and Aaron: G-d told Moses and Aaron that because they did not believe in Him, and sanctify Him before the Jewish people, they will not enter into the Promised Land. This episode is called Mei Meriva as this is the area where the children of Israel fought with G-d and He was sanctified through them.

Fourth Aliyah

6. Moses asks for passage through Edom:

- o The request: Moses sent messengers from Kadeish to the king of Edom asking permission to pass through their land. Moses told him of all the troubles that their brother, the Jewish people have surpassed. He told him of the suffering of the Jewish people in Egypt and how G-d saved them after they screamed to Him. "We are now in the city of Kadeish, which is at the edge of your border, please let us pass through your land. We will not pass through fields or vineyards and will not drink the well water. We shall travel the king's road and not swerve right or left."

- o The response: Edom refused to allow the Jewish people to pass, and threatened to greet them with the sword. The Jewish people replied [with a counter offer] that they will travel through the highway and drink their waters for payment. Still, the Edomites refused and they came to greet the Jewish people with a heavy army. The Jewish people [had no choice] and swerved away to a different direction.

Fifth Aliyah (Third Aliyah when combined with Balak)

7. Aaron passes away:

- The instructions: the children of Israel traveled from Kadeish and arrived to Mount Hahar. G-d told Moses and Aaron on Mount Hahar of Aaron's forthcoming death. "Aaron will pass away as he will not enter the promised land due to having defied Me by Mei Meriva." G-d told Moses to take Aaron and Elazar up to the mountain and remove the clothing of Aaron and dress Elazar his son, and Aaron will die there.

- The passing: Moses did as G-d instructed and brought them up the mountain in front of the entire nation. Moses removed Aaron's priestly clothing and he dressed Elazar in them. Aaron passed away on the summit of the mountain and Moses and Elazar descended from the mountain. The entire congregation saw that Aaron passed away and they cried [and mourned] his passing for thirty days.

Chapter 21

8. Amalek attacks the Jews:

- The Canaanite king of Arad who dwells in the south [and is otherwise known as Amelik] heard that the Jewish people are in the vicinity, and they fought against the Jewish people and captured a captive.

- The vow: the children of Israel made a vow to G-d that if He gives this nation into their hands, and they win the battle, they will consecrate all of the city spoils to the Temple. G-d heard their pleas and handed the Canaanites to their hands.

- The victory: the children of Israel captured the nation and their cities and consecrated it for G-d. That area was called Charmah.

9. Complaint against water and food and the subsequent plague of snakes:

- The complaint: The Jewish people traveled past Mount Hahar and circumvented the land of Edom. The nation became tired of the travel and complained against G-d and Moses asking why he took them out of Egypt to die in the desert. "There is no food or water and we have reached our limit with the insubstantial bread."

- The plague of snakes: G-d smote the nation with burning snakes and they bit the Jewish people, and many people died. The Jewish people remorsefully came to Moses confessing to their sin of speaking against him and G-d. They asked Moses to Daven for them to G-d and remove the snakes. Moses Davened on their behalf.

- The cure: G-d instructed Moses to make a snake and place it around a pole and whoever was bitten is to look at it and live. Moses did as he was instructed and made a copper snake, placing it by the pole. Whoever was bitten by the snake would look at the copper snake and live.

Sixth Aliyah

10. The travels of the children of Israel:
- The children of Israel traveled and camped in Ovos. They traveled from Ovos and camped in Iyei Ha'avarim, which faces Moab at the east. From there they traveled and camped in the Valley of Zered. From there they traveled and encamped on the other side of Arnon, which is on the border between Moab and the Amorites.
- The failed ambush: [The Amorites were killed by G-d as they attempted an ambush. The mountains came together and crushed them in their caves. The well revealed the great miracle to the Jewish people and hence] the Jewish people sang praise to G-d for the well.

Seventh Aliyah

11. War with Sihon and Og:
- The request: The Jewish people sent messengers to Sihon the Amorite king asking permission to pass through his land. "Let us pass through your land. We will not pass through fields or vineyards and will not drink the well water. We shall travel the king's road until we cross your border."
- The battle with Sihon: Sihon refused entry to the Jewish people and he gathered his entire nation to greet the Jewish people in the desert and wage war with them. the children of Israel waged a successful war against Sihon and conquered all of his cities and settled in them.
- The battle of Yaazor: Moses sent spies to Yaazor and they conquered the city and drove out the Amorites from there.
- The battle of Og: They left from there towards Bashan and Og. The king of Bashan came to battle them with all of his nation. G-d told Moses not to fear Og as he, his nation, and his land, will be delivered to his hands, just as was done with Sihon. Og and his entire nation were smitten to the point of no survivors and they took possession of his land.
- The Jewish people traveled and encamped in the plains of Moab, opposite the Jordon, near Jericho.

Parashat Balak
Verses: 104 [Siman: מנוח]
Haftorah: Micah 5:6-6:8

Number of Mitzvot:
There are no Mitzvot in Parashat Balak.

Chapter 22
First Aliyah

1. **Balak requests from Balaam to curse the Jewish people:**
   - The meeting to discuss the threat: Balak the son of Tzippor, the king of Moab at that time, saw all that the Jewish people did to the other nations and Moab became very frightened of the Jewish people. Moab met with the elders of Midian and discussed the threat that "Now they will chew up our entire surroundings like the ox chews the vegetation of the field.
   - Hiring Balaam: He sent emissaries to Balaam the son of Beor to come curse the Jewish people. They told him that a nation has left Egypt and has covered the eye of the land and is now standing opposite me [i.e. Moab]. "Now, please come and curse this nation for me, as they are much more powerful than me, and perhaps I will be successful in driving them out, as I know that whomever you bless is blessed and whom you curse is cursed." The emissaries arrived at the house of Balaam to deliver the request.

2. **The response of G-d to Balaam, and Balaam to Balak:**
   - G-d instructs Balaam not to go: Balaam replied to the messengers that they should stay the night as he must discuss with G-d whether he may fulfill their request. G-d appeared to Balaam and inquired as to who the visitors were. Balaam replied that they are messengers of Balak, the king of Moab, who are asking from him to curse the nation who left Egypt. Upon hearing Balaam's reply, G-d told him not to go with them and not to curse the Jewish people, as the Jewish people are blessed.

Second Aliyah (Fifth Aliyah when combined with Chukas)
   - In the morning Balaam told the messengers that they should return to Balak and tell him that he cannot go with them, as G-d does not allow him to go. The emissaries of Balak returned to him, and informed him that Balaam refuses to go with them.
   - Balak sends a second delegation: Balak sent a second, and more respected and dignified, delegation to try to convince Balaam to come. They told Balaam "So said Balak, do not refuse our request to come with us. I will honor you greatly, and whatever you tell me I shall do. Please just curse this nation." Balaam once again replied to the delegation of Balak that even if they were to offer him Balak's entire house filled with gold and silver he could not go against G-d's instructions, for small or big. Balaam told also the second delegation to stay the night and see what G-d would reply.
   - G-d agrees to allow Balaam to go: G-d appeared to Balaam that night and told him that he may go, although he will only be able to speak the words that He places in his mouth.

Third Aliyah

3. **Balaam's journey:**
   - Balaam awoke in the morning and saddled his female donkey and traveled with the dignitaries of Moab.
   - The angel blocks Balaam's path three times and he smites his donkey: G-d's wrath boiled over the fact that Balaam was traveling to curse the Jews and He therefore positioned an angel with a drawn sword in front of the path that they were traveling. Upon the donkey seeing the angel of G-d with a drawn sword on the road, he circumvented it and went off the road, to the field. Balaam proceeded to hit the donkey to get her back on the road. Again, the angel stood in the path of the donkey by a path in the vineyard. The donkey, upon seeing the angel of G-d, went off to the side of the road which was gated and consequently crushed the foot of Balaam. Balaam once again hit the donkey. Again, the angel stood in the path of the donkey, but this time there was no room for the donkey to circumvent him. The donkey simply stopped and crouched down. Balaam hit the donkey in fury.
   - The donkey speaks: G-d suddenly opened the mouth of the donkey and she began to speak, rebuking Balaam for hitting her. "What have I done to you that you hit me three times?" Balaam replied, "You mocked me; if only I had a sword I would kill you." The donkey replied "Am I not your donkey that you have ridden from your inception until this day. Have I ever done this to you?" And Balaam replied "No."
   - G-d reveals the angel: G-d then opened Blaam's eyes and he saw the angel with the drawn sword standing on the road. Balaam prostrated himself before him. The angel of G-d chastised Balaam for hitting his donkey three times, telling Balaam that he had stood in the donkey's way as an impediment, and the donkey saved his life by swerving away. If the donkey would not have swerved away, I would have killed you and let it live. Balaam replied to the angel that he has sinned, and he did not know that the angle was in the way. "Now, if you do not desire me to go then I will turn back." The angel replied that he may go, although he will only be able to speak the words that he places in his mouth. Balaam continued his travels with the delegation of Balak.

4. **Balaam arrives:**
   - Balak heard of Balaam's imminent arrival and he went to greet him by the border of Arnon. Balak asked Balaam why he had refused to come until now, to which Balaam replied that he is limited and cannot speak anything that G-d does not place in his mouth.

Fourth Aliyah (Sixth Aliyah when combined with Chukas)

   - The tour and meal: Balak takes Balaam [on a tour of Moab to] Kiryat Chutzos. Balak sacrificed cattle and flock and sent it to Balaam and the dignitaries [to eat].

Chapter 23

5. **Balaam's first attempt to curse turns to blessings:**
   - The next morning: In the morning, Balak took Balaam to a cliff and looked at the Jewish encampment from there.
   - The sacrifices: Balaam instructed Balak to build seven altars and bring seven cows and seven rams as sacrifices. Balak did as he was instructed and offered the animals on the altar. Balaam told Balak to stand ground by the altar while Balaam goes to meet with G-d

to see if he can curse the Jewish people. G-d appeared to Balaam and Balaam told Him that he has prepared seven altars and offered bulls and rams. G-d placed words in the mouth of Balaam and instructed him to relate the message to Balak. Balaam returned to Balak and the Moabite dignitaries and told them as follows:

- The blessing: "Balak instructed me to curse the Jewish people, but I cannot curse a people who G-d has not cursed and has not gotten angry with."
- "They are a nation that we see from the hilltops; they dwell alone and are not counted amongst the other nations."
- "Who can count the dust of Jacob and Israel, and may I die a death like theirs."
- Balak's response: Balak admonished Balaam for blessing the Jewish people instead of cursing them. Balaam replied that he already forewarned Balak that he must say what G-d tells him.

Fifth Aliyah

6. **Balaam's second attempt to curse turns into blessings:**
   - Balak took Balaam to a second area from which only part of the Jewish people could be seen, to try to curse the Jewish people from there.
   - The sacrifices: They built seven altars and offered a cow and ram as a sacrifice on the altar. Balaam told Balak to stand guard by the altar while Balaam goes to meet with G-d to see if he can curse the Jewish people. G-d places the following words in the mouth of Balaam and instructed him to relate the message to Balak:
   - The blessing: Balaam returned to Balak and the Moabite dignitaries and was asked by Balak as to what G-d told him. Balaam told Balak to stand while he relays the prophesy:
   - "G-d is not a man who speaks lies and that regrets what He says. If He says something, He will fulfill it. G-d blessed the Jewish people, and He will not retract it"
   - "He does not see sin in Jacob, or iniquity in Israel"
   - "He took them out of Egypt"
   - "There is no sorcery in Jacob or Israel, and He tells them what they need to know"
   - "They are a nation that wake up like a lioness, and do not sleep until they eat their spoils and drink the blood of the slain."
   - Balak's response: Balak admonished Balaam for blessing the Jewish people instead of cursing them and tells him that if he can't curse them then at the very least he should not bless them. Balaam replied that he already forewarned Balak that he must say what G-d tells him.

Sixth Aliyah (Seventh Aliyah when combined with Chukas)

7. **Balaam's third set of blessings:**
   - Balak took Balaam to a third area from which to try to curse the Jewish people from there. Balak took Balaam to the area called Rosh Peor.
   - The sacrifices: Balaam instructed Balak to build seven altars and bring seven cows and rams as sacrifices. Balak did as he was instructed and offered the sacrifices on the altar. Balaam saw that G-d desires to bless the Jewish people and therefore did not go as he did the previous times, and he faced the desert. Balaam saw the Jewish people's encampment in accordance to tribe and he received the spirit of G-d and began his third set of blessings:

- The blessings: "Says the man with the closed eye, the one who hears the words of G-d and sees Him, falling to ground."
- "How good are the tents of Jacob, the dwelling places of Israel. They are like streams and gardens and like cedars by water. Water flows from his buckets and his seed is abundant."
- "His king will be exalted over Agag."
- "G-d, who took them out of Egypt will consume their enemies, and their bones He will break and take His portion from the spoils."
- "They lie like a lion and like a lioness, who can stand them up."
- "Those who bless them are blessed and those who curse them are cursed."
- Balak's response: Balak became enraged with Balaam and clapped his hands and told him "I brought you to curse my enemies and instead you blessed them three times. Now, get out of here and go back to your place. I said I would honor you, but I see G-d has withheld your honor." Balaam replied that he already forewarned Balak and his messengers that he must say what G-d tells him, and that even if he offers him his house filled with gold and silver he cannot transgress the word of G-d for good or for bad.

Chapter 24
Seventh Aliyah

8. Balaam's fourth set of blessings and prophecy:
- Prior to his departure, Balaam advised Balak as to what the Jewish people will do to Moab in the end of days.
- Balaam prophesized and said: "Says the man with the closed eye, the one who hears the words of G-d and knows the knowledge of High falling to ground"
- "I will see it but not now. A star will sprout from Jacob and a staff from Israel who will destroy Moab and the children of Seth."
- "Edom and Seir will conquer and their wealth will be inherited by Israel."
- He saw Amalek and stated, "The first of the nations is Amalek and at the end they will be obliterated."
- He saw the Keni and he said "How strong is your position, and your nest rests on a rock"
- "Ashur will capture you."
- "Woe, who will live from the decrees of G-d."
- "The Kitim/Romans and Ashur will be forever destroyed."
- Balaam goes home: Balaam got up and returned home and also Balak went on his way.

Chapter 25

9. The sin with the daughters of Moab:
- The sin: The Jewish people settled in Shitim and were promiscuous with the daughters of Moab. They participated in sacrifices to idolatry and they ate and prostrated to the idols. They attached to the idolatry of Peor and G-d became very angry with Israel.
- Capital punishment: G-d told Moses to gather the leaders and have the violators hung in front of the sun and then His wrath will be extinguished from the Jewish people. Moses instructed the leaders to kill those who attached to Peor,
- Zimri and Cozbi: There was a certain man who approached Moses and the entire congregation with a Midianite woman while the children of Israel were crying in their

tent. Pinchas the son of Elazar, the son of Aaron Hakohen took a spear in his hand and speared the man and the woman in their private areas and the plague ended.

- <u>Total number of dead in plague</u>: There were 24,000 people who died in that plague.

Parashat Pinchas
Verses: 168 [Siman:לְחַלֵק]
Haftorah: Kings 1 18:46-19:21

Number of Mitzvot:
There are a total of **six** Mitzvot in Parashat Pinchas; **Six** positive commands and **Zero** negative commands. The following are the commands in the order listed by the Sefer Hachinuch.

A. Positive:
1. **Mitzvah 400/Positive 163**: To abide by the laws of inheritance.
2. **Mitzvah 401/Positive 164**: To offer the Tamid offering daily, twice a day.
3. **Mitzvah 402/Positive 165**: To offer a Musaf sacrifice of two lambs every Shabbat.
4. **Mitzvah 403/Positive 166**: To offer a Musaf sacrifice of two cows, one ram, and seven lambs, every Rosh Chodesh.
5. **Mitzvah 404/Positive 167**: To offer a Musaf sacrifice on Shavuot.
6. **Mitzvah 405/Positive 168**: To hear the Shofar on Rosh Hashana.

First Aliyah

1. **Pinchas is blessed with priesthood:**
   - G-d said: The vengeance Pinchas took [against Zimri and Cozbi] has calmed my anger and prevented me from destroying the Jewish people in my vengeance. In reward for the above act, Pinchas is granted a covenant of eternal Kehuna/priesthood for him and all his offspring.
   - The identification of those slain by Pinchas: The name of the slain Israelite who was slain together with the Midianite woman was Zimri the son of Salu, the head of the tribe of Simeon. The name of the woman was Cozbi the daughter of Tzur, who was the head of the people of Midian.

2. **Moses is commanded to take vengeance against the Midianites:**
   - G-d commanded Moses to antagonize the Midianites and destroy them for conspiring against the children of Israel and causing them to stumble with Baal Peor and with Cozbi.

Chapter 26

3. **The Jewish people are counted for the census:**
   - After the plague, G-d asked Moses and Elazar to take a census of the Jewish people. Every [male] person of recruitment age, above age twenty, was counted.

Second Aliyah

o Reuben:
- Family descendants: Hanoch; Pallu; Chetzron; Carmi
- Population: 43,730
- Datan and Abiram-sin of Korach: Palu had a son named Eliav who had three sons named Nemuel, Datan and Abiram. This is the same Datan and Abiram who were part of the rebel group led by Korach and were killed by being miraculously swallowed in the ground together with Korach. The other 250 men were consumed by fire. The children of Korach did not die.

o Simeon:
- Family descendants: Nemuel; Yamin; Yachin; Zerach; Shaul
- Population: 22,200

o Gad:
- Family descendants: Tzefon; Chagi; Shuni; Ozni; Eri; Arod; Areili
- Population: 40,500

o Judah:
- Family descendants-Died: Er; Onen who died
- Family descendants: Sheila; Peretz; Zerach; Chetzron; Chamul
- Population: 76,500

o Issachar:
- Family descendants: Tola; Puvah; Yashuv; Shimron
- Population: 64,300

o Zebulun:
- Family descendants: Sered; Eilon; Yachliel
- Population: 60,500

o Joseph-Manasseh:
- Family descendants: Machir; Gilad; Iezer; Chelek; Asriel; Shechem; Shemida; Chefer; Tzelafchad
- Tzelafchad did not have sons. His daughters were named Machla; Noah; Choglah; Milkah; Tirtzah
- Population: 52,700

o Joseph-Ephraim:
- Family descendants: Shuselach; Becher; Tachan; Eran
- Population: 32,500

o Benjamin:
- Family descendants: Bela; Ashbel; Ahiram; Shefufam; Chufam; Ard; Naaman
- Population: 45,600

- Dan:
  - Family descendants: Shucham
  - Population: 64,400

- Asher:
  - Family descendants: Yimna; Yishvi; Beriah; Chever; Malkiel. The daughter of Asher was Serach.
  - Population: 53,400

- Naftali:
  - Family descendants: Yachtziel; Guni; Yeitzer; Shillem
  - Population: 45,400
- Total population: 601,730 [and 57 families]

Third Aliyah

4. **The fashion in which the land of Israel will be divided:**
   - The land is to be inherited according to the population [of each tribe or family]. Those of larger population are to receive a larger area, and those of smaller population are to receive a smaller area. The land will be divided based on raffle, in accordance to the tribes/families.

5. **The tribe of Levi is counted:**
   - Family descendants: Gershon; Kehot; Merari; Libni; Hebroni; Machli; Mushi; Karchi. Kehot had Amram, who had Moses, Aaron and Miriam. Aaron had Nadab, Abihu, Elazar and Isamar. Nadab and Abihu died before G-d when they brought a foreign fire.
   - Population: 23,000 males from the age of one month
   - The tribe of Levi was not counted together with the rest of the Jewish people, as they do not receive an inheritance.
   - The above population did not include any of the people from the census that was taken in the desert [prior to the sin of the Meraglim], as they all died in the desert, with exception to Kaleb and Joshua.

Chapter 27

6. **The daughters of Tzelafchad**
   - The daughters of Tzelafchad approached Moses, Elazar, the leaders, and the entire congregation by the entrance of the Tent of Meeting and inquired as to why they will not be receiving an inheritance of land on behalf of their father. Their father did not die as a result of the sin of Korach and rather died due to his own sin, and he did not leave any sons. They demanded to receive their father's portion of inheritance in place of a son.
   - Moses brought their claim before G-d.

Fourth Aliyah

- G-d spoke to Moses saying that the daughters of Tzelafchad are correct and that they are to receive the inheritance from their father.

7. **Laws of inheritance:**
   - <u>No son</u>: When a man dies and does not leave a son, the inheritance is to go to the daughter.
   - <u>No daughter</u>: If he does not have a daughter, the inheritance is to go to the deceased's [father, and if his father is not alive then it is to go to his] brothers.
   - <u>No brother</u>: If he does not have a brother, the inheritance is to go to the deceased's [grandfather and if his grandfather is not alive then it is to go to his] uncle from his father.
   - <u>No uncle</u>: If he does not have an uncle from his father, the inheritance is to go to his closest relative.

8. **Moses looks at the land of Israel:**
   - Moses is told by G-d to ascend Mount Havarim and look at the view of Israel. Moses is told that he will pass away as did Aaron his brother and will not enter Israel due to the sin committed by Mei Meriva.

9. **Joshua is appointed leader after Moses:**
   - Moses asks G-d to appoint someone over the Jewish people after his passing, so they are not like sheep without a shepherd. G-d told Moses to take Joshua Ben Nun and lean his hands on him and appoint him as leader in front of Elazar and in front of all the Jewish people. You shall place your splendor onto him, so that all the children of Israel will listen to him. Joshua shall stand before Elazar the Kohen and ask him through the Urim Vetumim, and according to his reply they shall follow.
   - Moses did as he was instructed by G-d and positioned Joshua before Elazar the Kohen, and before the entire congregation, and he leaned his hands on him.

Chapter 28
Fifth Aliyah

10. **The Tamid sacrifice:**
    - G-d told Moses to command the children of Israel and tell them to offer two male lambs, every day as a Tamid sacrifice. One sacrifice is to be offered in the morning and the second in the afternoon.
    - <u>The Mincha and Nesachim</u>: A Mincha offering of 1/10th of an Ephah of flour mixed with ¼ of a Hin of oil is to be brought with the animal. A wine libation of ¼ of a Hin is to be brought per lamb.

11. **The Shabbat sacrifice:**
    - On Shabbat you are to offer two male lambs in their first year of age.
    - <u>The Mincha and Nesachim</u>: A Mincha offering of 2/10ths of an Ephah of flour mixed with oil is to be brought with the animal. A wine libation is to be brought with the animal.
    - This is in addition to the Tamid sacrifice.

12. **The Rosh Chodesh sacrifice:**
    - On Rosh Chodesh you are to offer two young bulls, one ram, and seven unblemished lambs within their first year. One goat is to be offered as a Chatas for G-d. This sacrifice is in addition to the Tamid sacrifice.

- The Mincha and Nesachim: A Mincha offering of 3/10^{ths} of an Ephah of flour mixed with oil is to be brought individually for each bull. A wine libation of 1/2 of a Hin is to be brought for the bull. A Mincha offering of 2/10^{ths} of an Ephah of flour mixed with oil is to be brought individually for the ram. A wine libation of 1/3 of a Hin is to be brought for the ram. A Mincha offering of 1/10th of an Ephah of flour mixed with oil is to be brought individually for each lamb. A wine libation of 1/4 of a Hin is to be brought per lamb.

Sixth Aliyah

13. The festival of Pesach:

- The date: On the 14th day of the 1st month is a Pesach for G-d. On the 15th day of the month is a festival. One is to eat Matzah for seven days.
- Labor: One is not to do labor on the first day and seventh day.
- The Sacrifices: On each of the seven days of Pesach you are to offer as an Olah two young bulls, one ram and seven unblemished male lambs within their first year. One goat is to be offered as a Chatas to atone for you. This sacrifice is in addition to the Tamid sacrifice.
- The Mincha: A Mincha offering of 3/10^{ths} of an Ephah of flour mixed with oil is to be brought individually for each bull. A Mincha offering of 2/10^{ths} of an Ephah of flour mixed with oil is to be brought individually for the ram. A Mincha offering of 1/10th of an Ephah of flour mixed with oil is to be brought individually for each sheep. A wine libation is to be brought individually with the animal.

14. The festival of Shavuot:

- On the day of the Bikurim, First Fruits, when the new Mincha offering is brought, one is not to do labor.
- The offering: On Shavuot you are to offer as an Olah offering two young bulls, one ram and seven male lambs within their first year. One male goat is to be offered as a Chatas to atone for you. This sacrifice is in addition to the Tamid sacrifice.
- The Mincha: A Mincha offering of 3/10^{ths} of an Ephah of flour mixed with oil is to be brought individually for each bull. A Mincha offering of 2/10^{ths} of an Ephah of flour mixed with oil is to be brought individually for the ram. A Mincha offering of 1/10th of an Ephah of flour mixed with oil is to be brought individually for each lamb. A wine libation is to be brought individually with the animal.

Chapter 29

15. Rosh Hashanah

- On the 1st day of the seventh month one is not to do labor. It is a day of Shofar blowing for you.
- The Sacrifices: On Rosh Hashanah you are to offer as an Olah offering one young bull, one ram and seven male lambs within their first year. One male goat is to be offered as a Chatas to atone for you. This sacrifice is in addition to the Rosh Chodesh and Tamid sacrifice.
- The Mincha: A Mincha offering of 3/10^{ths} of an Ephah of flour mixed with oil is to be brought individually for the bull. A Mincha offering of 2/10^{ths} of an Ephah of flour mixed with oil is to be brought individually for the ram. A Mincha offering of 1/10^{ths} of an

Ephah of flour mixed with oil is to be brought individually for each lamb. A wine libation is to be brought individually with the animal.

16. Yom Kippur
- On the 10th day of the seventh month one is to oppress his soul and is not to do labor.
- The Sacrifices: On Yom Kippur you are to offer as an Olah offering one young bull, one ram, and seven male lambs. One goat is to be offered as a Chatas. This is in addition to the Yom Kippur Chatas and Tamid sacrifice.
- The Mincha: A Mincha offering of 3/10[ths] of an Ephah of flour mixed with oil is to be brought individually for the bull. A Mincha offering of 2/10[ths] of an Ephah of flour mixed with oil is to be brought individually for the ram. A Mincha offering of 1/10[ths] of an Ephah of flour mixed with oil is to be brought individually for each lamb. A wine libation is to be brought individually with the animal.

Seventh Aliyah

17. The festival of Sukkot:
- On the 15th day of the seventh month one is not to do labor. One is to celebrate a festival for G-d for seven days.
- The Sacrifices: On Sukkot, on the first day you are to offer as an Olah offering 13 young bulls, 2 rams and 14 male lambs in their first year. On the second day of Sukkot you are to offer as an Olah offering 12 bulls, 2 rams and 14 male lambs in their first year and so on and so forth each day of Sukkot diminishing one cow, until on the seventh day of Sukkot you offer 7 young bulls, 2 rams and 14 male lambs in their first year. On each day one he-goat is to be offered as a Chatas. This is in addition to the daily Tamid sacrifice.
- The Mincha: A Mincha offering of 3/10[ths] of an Ephah of flour mixed with oil is to be brought individually for each of the bulls. A Mincha offering of 2/10[ths] of an Ephah of flour mixed with oil is to be brought individually for each of the two rams. A Mincha offering of 1/10[ths] of an Ephah of flour mixed with oil is to be brought individually for each of the 14 lambs. A wine libation is to be brought individually with the animal.

18. Shemini Atzeres:
- On the 8th day one is not to do labor.
- The offering: On Shemini Atzeres, one is to offer as an Olah offering one cow, one ram and seven unblemished male lambs within their first year.
- The Mincha: A Mincha offering of flour mixed with oil is to be brought individually for each animal. A wine libation is to be brought individually with the animal. One goat is to be offered as a Chatas. This is in addition to the Tamid sacrifice.

Parashat Matot
Verses: 112 [Siman: בקי]
Haftorah: Jerimiah 1:1-2:3

Number of Mitzvot:
There are a total of **two** Mitzvot in Parashat Matot; **One** positive command and **One** negative command. The following are the commands in the order listed by the Sefer Hachinuch.

A. Positive:
1. **Mitzvah 406/Positive 169:** Annulling vows.

B. Negative:
1. **Mitzvah 407/Negative 239:** Not to transgress a vow.

Chapter 30
First Aliyah

1. **The laws of vows:**
   * G-d spoke to Moses to speak to all the heads of tribes saying: A person who made an oath or vow is to keep his word.
   * <u>Daughter in her youth</u>: If a woman, while in her youth [i.e. Na'arah], makes a vow, then her father can either accept it or annul it on the day he hears of the vow. If he remains quiet after hearing of the vow, then the vow shall stand valid. If, however, her father restrained her from the vow, on the day that he heard of her vow, then the vow is abolished, and G-d will forgive her.
   * <u>Naarah who is engaged</u>: If a wife [who is a Naarah and is only engaged, Kiddushin/Eirusin] makes a vow, then her husband [and father] can either accept it or annul it on the day he hears of the vow. If the husband [or father] remains quiet after hearing of the vow, then the vow shall stand valid. If, however, her husband [and father] restrained her from the vow, on the day that he heard of her vow, then the vow is abolished, and G-d will forgive her.
   * <u>A married woman</u>: If a wife who is married makes a vow regarding a matter that causes personal affliction, then her husband can either accept it or annul it on the day he hears of the vow. If he remains quiet after hearing of the vow, then the vow shall stand valid. If, however, her husband restrained her from the vow, on the day that he heard of her vow, then the vow is abolished, and G-d will forgive her.
   * <u>A single woman</u>: The vow of a [single woman such as a] widow or divorcee stands valid.

Chapter 31
Second Aliyah

2. **The children of Israel wage war against Midian:**
   * G-d spoke to Moses saying that he should take vengeance against Midian and he will then pass on. Moses recruited 1000 soldiers from each Tribe. They went to battle together with Pinchas the son of Elazar, and the sacred vessels of the Temple [i.e. Aron], and the trumpets in hand.

- The outcome of the battle: They killed every male, including all the five kings of Midian who were named Evi, Rekem, Tzur, Chur and Reva. Balaam the son of Beor was killed by the sword. They captured all the wives and children of Midian and all their animals and assets. Their cities and houses and buildings were all set on fire. The army brought all the spoils of people, animals and items to Moses and Elazar.

Third Aliyah (Second Aliyah when combined with Maasei)

- Moses is enraged that the females survived: Moses, Elazar and the tribal leaders came to greet the soldiers outside of the camp. Moses became enraged at the officers and generals for allowing the women to live, despite them being the ones who caused the plague to fall upon the children of Israel when they seduced them according to the advice of Balaam.
- Killing the captives: Moses commanded them to kill all male children and all the women who have reached age of marriage. The remaining females were taken as captives.

3. **The laws of impurity to a corpse:**
   - Moses told the soldiers who returned from battle that all those who killed someone or touched a corpse are required to stay outside the camp for seven days and be sprinkled with the red heifer water on the 3rd and 7th day. Likewise, all the vessels that touched the impure must be purified with the Mei Niddah.

4. **Laws of Kashering:**
   - Elazar the son of Aaron told the children of Israel that all the metal vessels of gold, silver, copper, iron, tin and lead, that they took from the Midianites, need Kashering. Those vessels that are used with fire must be purified with fire and Mei Niddah. Those vessels used with water are to be purified with water.
   - On the 7th day, the clothing is to be washed and purified and one can then enter the camp.

Fourth Aliyah

5. **The spoils are distributed:**
   - G-d told Moses to count all of the captives and animals and then divide the spoils amongst the soldiers and the rest of the Jewish people.
   - The taxes: The soldiers are to give a tax to Elazar the Kohen which consists of 1:500 of every human and animal captured. the children of Israel are to give a tax to the Levites which consists of 1:50 of every human and animal captured.
   - Moses and Elazar did as G-d asked.
   - The final amount of distribution of the spoils and taxes: The following was the count of the spoils: 675,000 sheep; 72,000 cattle; 61,000 donkeys; 32,000 women below the age of marriage. The soldiers received 337,500 sheep; 36,000 cattle; 30,500 donkeys; 16,000 women. G-d's tax from the soldier's spoils was: 675 sheep; 72 cattle; 61 donkeys; 32 women.

Fifth Aliyah

- The Jewish people received 337,500 sheep; 36,000 cattle; 30,500 donkeys; 16,000 women.
- Moses gave the tax from the children of Israel's spoils to the Levites.
- <u>The commanders give a donation</u>: The commanders of the soldiers approached Moses and told him that no soldier was killed in the war and they therefore have brought Moses a present of gold vessels for atonement. The present consisted of gold vessels, anklets and bracelets, earrings, and Kumaz. Moses took the vessels and gave them to Elazar Hakohen to place in the Tent of Meeting as a remembrance.

Chapter 32
Sixth Aliyah (Third Aliyah when combined with Maasei)
6. **The sons of Gad and the sons of Reuben receive the land of Og and Sihon:**
   - <u>The request</u>: The sons of Reuben and Gad had a lot of livestock, and they desired to receive the land area of Yazer and Gilead for their animals to graze. They approached Moses, Elazar, and the tribal leaders and asked to receive this land in exchange for the land that is across the Jordon.
   - <u>Moses's reply and the subsequent agreement</u>: Moses replied to the sons of Gad and the sons of Reuben by criticizing them for their request, saying they are discouraging the children of Israel from wanting to enter Israel and are repeating the mistake of the Meraglim. They replied to Moses saying that they will build cities for their families and animals and then wage war with the rest of the children of Israel in Israel. Furthermore, they will be on the front lines of the battle and will not return home until all the children of Israel have inherited their land.

Seventh Aliyah (Fourth Aliyah when combined with Maasei)
- Moses replied that if they fulfill these conditions then he agrees to give them the land. Moses told over the above agreement to Elazar and Joshua and the heads of the tribes.
- <u>The land is given</u>: Moses then gave the sons of Gad, The sons of Reuben and half of Manasseh a portion in the area past the Jordon, the land of Og and Sihon. The sons of Gad and Reuben built cities there.
- The sons of Machir, from the tribe of Manasseh, waged war against the Amorite city of Gilead and captured it. Moses consequently granted the city to Machir.
- Yair the son of Manasseh captured other cities, which he named "villages of Yair." Novach captured Kenas and named it in his name, Novach.

Parashat Maasei
Verses: 132 [Siman: מחלה חולה]
Haftorah: Jerimiah 2:4-28; 4:1-2[1]

Number of Mitzvot:
There are a total of **Six** Mitzvot in Parashat Maasei; **Two** positive commands and **Four** negative commands. The following are the commands in the order listed by the Sefer Hachinuch.

A. Positive:
1. **Mitzvah 408/Positive 171:** To distribute cities to the Levites and that they are to serve as cities of refuge.
2. **Mitzvah 409/Positive 172:** To send to a city of refuge one who killed Beshogeg-by accident.

B. Negative:
1. **Mitzvah 410/Negative 238:** Not to kill one who is liable for death until he is brought to court.
2. **Mitzvah 411/Negative 239:** The prohibition for a witness to also act as a judge in the case.
3. **Mitzvah 412/Negative 240:** Not to take a ransom to exempt a murderer from being killed.
4. **Mitzvah 413/Negative 241:** Not to take a ransom to exempt an accidental murderer from being exiled.

Chapter 33
First Aliyah

1. **The Travels of the children of Israel:**
   - These are the travels of the Jewish people from Egypt, under the leadership of Moses and Aaron. Moses wrote of the travels of the children of Israel.
     1) On the 15th of the 1st month, the children of Israel left Rameses/Egypt in the presence of all the Egyptians. The Egyptians were busy burying their dead while the Jews were leaving. G-d also punished their gods during this time.
     2) Next, they traveled to Sukkot.
     3) Next, they traveled to Eisam in the edge of the desert.
     4) Next, they traveled to Pi Hachiros.
     5) Next, they traveled a journey of three days to Marah.
     6) Next, they traveled to Elim which had 12 fountains of water and 70 date palms.
     7) Next, they traveled to Sea of Reeds.

Second Aliyah (according to most Chumashim)
   8) Next, they traveled to the desert of Sin.

---
[1] So is followed by Sepharadi and Chabad communities. However, Ashkenazi communities do not read these two verses and rather add verse 3:4.

9) Next, they traveled to Dophkah.
10) Next, they traveled to Alush.
11) Next, they traveled to Rephidim, and there was no water to drink.
12) Next, they traveled to the desert of Sinai.
13) Next, they traveled to Kivros Hataavah.
14) Next, they traveled to Chatzeros.
15) Next, they traveled to Rithmah.
16) Next, they traveled to Rimmon Peretz.
17) Next, they traveled to Livnah.
18) Next, they traveled to Rissah.
19) Next, they traveled to Kehelasah.
20) Next, they traveled to Mount Shafer.
21) Next, they traveled to Charadah.
22) Next, they traveled to Makhelos.
23) Next, they traveled to Tachas.
24) Next, they traveled to Terach.
25) Next, they traveled to Mithkah.
26) Next, they traveled to Chashmonah.
27) Next, they traveled to Moseiros.
28) Next, they traveled to Benei Yaakan.
29) Next, they traveled to Chor Hagidgad.
30) Next, they traveled to Yatvasah.
31) Next, they traveled to Avronah.
32) Next, they traveled to Etzion Gaver.
33) Next, they traveled to Kadesh-the desert of Tzin.
34) Next, they traveled to Mount Hahor, which is at the end of the land of Edom.

- <u>The death of Aaron:</u> Aaron ascended Mount Hahor and passed away in the 40th year on the first of the 5th month. Aaron was 123 years old at his death. The king of Arad from Canaan heard of Aarons death.

35) Next, they traveled to Tzalmonah.
36) Next, they traveled to Punon.
37) Next, they traveled to Ovos.
38) Next, they traveled to Iyei Haavarim on the border of Moab.
39) Next, they traveled to Divon Gad.
40) Next, they traveled to Almon Divlasaimah.
41) Next, they traveled to Harei Haavarim.
42) Next, they traveled to Arvos Moab, by the Jordon at Jericho. They encamped by the Jordon from Beit Hayeshimos until Avel Shittim

Second Aliyah (according to Torah Temima/Chabad) Third Aliyah (according to most Chumashim) (Fifth Aliyah when combined with Matos)

2. **Commands associated with the conquer of Israel:**
   - G-d instructed Moses to command the children of Israel that upon entering Israel and conquering the nations they are to destroy all their temples, all their idols and their accessories. All the inhabitant nations are to be driven out of the land.

Third Aliyah (according to Torah Temima/Chabad)

- <u>Inheritance</u>: The portions of inheritance of the land are to be distributed through a raffle system. To the many you shall increase the inheritance while to the few you are to decrease. Wherever the lot shall fall for the individual, that is where he will inherit.
- <u>The dangers of not driving out the nations</u>: If you do not drive out the gentile inhabitants, they will harass you and cause you anguish and suffering, and I will do to you that which I intended to do to them.

Chapter 34

3. The borders of Israel:
- G-d spoke to Moses saying that he is to command the Jewish people of the borders of Israel.
- <u>Southern border</u>: The southeast border is at the edge of the Dead Sea and the desert of Tzin. The border is to stretch to Maaleh Akrabbim and Kadesh Barneia and from Atzmon to Nachalas Egypt, which is the southwest border.
- <u>Western border</u>: The western border is the Mediterranean Sea.
- <u>Northern border</u>: The northwest border is Mount Hahar. The northern border is to stretch to Chamas towards Tzedad. The border is from Zifronto Chatzar Einan.
- <u>Eastern border</u>: The eastern border begins with Shafam to Rivlah, till the Kinneret. The border descends to the Jordan River, till the edge of the Dead Sea.
- Moses commanded the children of Israel that the above borders of land are to be distributed to the 9 1/2 tribes, excluding the tribes of Reuben, Gad and half of Manasseh, who already took their portion on the eastern side of the Jordon.

Fourth Aliyah (Sixth Aliyah when combined with Matos)

4. The people inheriting the land:
- G-d spoke to Moses saying that the following are the names of those who will be inheriting the land to the Jewish people: Elazar Hakohen and Joshua Ben Nun and one leader per tribe is to inherit the land for their tribe. The following are the names of the tribal leaders.
  - o <u>The tribe of Judah</u>: Kaleb Ben Yefuneh
  - o <u>The tribe of Simeon</u>: Samuel Ben Amihud
  - o <u>The tribe of Benjamin</u>: Elidad Ben Kislon
  - o <u>The tribe of Dan</u>: Bukki Ben Yogli
  - o <u>The tribe of Manasseh</u>: Channiel Ben apron
  - o <u>The tribe of Ephraim</u>: Kemual Ben Shiftan
  - o <u>The tribe of Zebulun</u>: Elitzafan Ben Parnach
  - o <u>The tribe of Issachar</u>: Paltiel Ben Azzan
  - o <u>The tribe of Asher</u>: Achihud Ben Shelomi
  - o <u>The tribe of Naftali</u>: Padahel Ben Ammihud

Chapter 35
Fifth Aliyah

5. The cities of the Levites:
- G-d spoke to Moses by the Jordan saying that he is to command the children of Israel to distribute cities to the Levites from amongst their inheritance of land.

- The space surrounding the cities: The Levite cities are to contain an open space of 1000 cubits surrounding their cities to be designated for their animals and property. The city is to have a total of 2000 cubits of open space surrounding it, [the first thousand as a Migrash and the second for their fields and vineyards].
- The cities of refuge: The Levites are to receive six cities of refuge for murderers to seek refuge in, and 42 cities for them to dwell in, for a total of 48 cities.
- From whose property are the Levite cities appropriated: Those tribes who have a larger portion of land are to allocate from within their property more cities to the Levites, while those tribes who have a smaller portion of land are to give them less cities.

Sixth Aliyah (Seventh Aliyah when combined with Matos)
6. **The cities of refuge:**
   - G-d spoke to Moses saying that he is to command the children of Israel that upon then passing the Jordan towards the land of Canaan they are to designate cities of refuge for one guilty of unintentional manslaughter. The cities will be used by the murderer as a refuge from the relative of the victim. The murderer is not to be killed until he has a court case.
   - Amount and locations: There are to be six cities of refuge. Three of the cities are to be in Israel and the other three past the Jordan river. They are to be a city of refuge for all accidental murderers, whether a Jew or a convert.
   - An intentional or unintentional murderer: If the murderer intentionally or premeditatedly killed someone using a metal object, or a stone object, or a wooden object, then he is to be put to death. The Goal Hadam [relative of the victim] is to kill the murderer. If, however, the murderer killed him without intent and he is not his enemy, then the assembly shall judge between him and the relatives and save him from being killed by the relatives. They are to escort him to the city of refuge.
   - The conditions of the cities of refuge: The accidental murderer is to remain in the city of refuge until the anointed Kohen Gadol passes away. If the murderer leaves the city of refuge, he has given up his blood and may be killed by the Goal Hadam (avenger).
   - Laws of a murder trials: A single witness may not be used as testimony to kill a murderer. One may not take a ransom from the murderer to save him from punishment of death or cities of refuge. "Do not corrupt and defile the land that I dwell in by not giving due punishment to the murderers, as the land will not have atonement for the spilled blood. I am G-d who dwells amongst the Jewish people."

Chapter 36
Seventh Aliyah
7. **The marriage of the daughters of Tzelafchad:**
   - The family of Gilead, son of Machir, who is the son of Manasseh, approached Moses complaining that the lands inherited by the daughters of Tzelafchad will be inherited by their husbands and consequently leave our tribe. G-d agreed with their complaint and Moses thus commanded the daughters of Tzelafchad to marry within their tribe. He also commanded all the Jewish people that all female heirs may only marry into their tribe in order to prevent a family heritage from falling into the hands of other tribes.
   - The daughters of Tzelafchad; Machlah, Tirtzah, Chaglah, Milcah, and Noah did as they were instructed and married their cousins from the tribe of Manasseh.

Devarim/Deuteronomy

Parashat Devarim
Verses: 105 [Siman: מלכיה]
Haftorah: Isaiah 1:1-27

Number of Mitzvot:
There are a total of **Two** Mitzvot in Parashat Devarim; **Zero** positive commands and **Two** negative commands. The following are the commands in the order listed by the Sefer Hachinuch.

A. Negative:
1. **Mitzvah 414/Negative 242:** Not to appoint judges who are not knowledgeable in Torah law.
2. **Mitzvah 415/Negative 243:** The prohibition for the judges to fear anyone in their verdict.

Chapter 1
First Aliyah

1. Moses recounts the past occurrences since Matan Torah:

- The date: The following are the words that Moses spoke to all the Jewish people, across the Jordan, an eleven-day journey from Horeb. This was said on the first day of the 11th month [Shevat], in the 40th year, after conquering Sihon and Og. Moses began clarifying the Torah saying:
- Traveling from Sinai: G-d spoke to us, saying that we have sat enough time by the mountain and we should travel to the Amorite mountains, to the land of Canaan. "I have given you the land, go conquer the land that I promised to your forefathers." Moses told the children of Israel at that time that he could not carry their governance alone, being that G-d has made them into a multitude.
- Moses's blessing: Moses blessed the children of Israel "May G-d the G-d of your fathers add to you a thousand-fold and bless you [to be fruitful and multiply].

Second Aliyah[1]

- Appointing judges: Moses stated "How can I carry alone all of your disputes? Bring judges of proper wisdom and quality and appoint them to be your leaders." the children of Israel consented to Moses's request and Moses appointed the tribal leaders as judges to arbitrate the disputes between one man and another. Moses instructed the judges to judge properly and not show favoritism in judgment or fear any man. All cases that are beyond the scope of the judge's ability to arbitrate are to be brought to Moses. The sons of Yisrael were commanded at that time all the laws [of judgment].
- Traveling from Choreiv: the children of Israel traveled from Horeb until Kadeish Barnea and the Amorite mountain and I then told you that G-d has given you the land, go and inherit the land of Israel.

---

[1] Some begin the second Aliyah prior to Moses's blessing. This is done in order to avoid beginning the Aliya with a negative verse of Eicha. [See Sefer Haminhagim p. 61; Luach Kolel Chabad; Hiskashrus]

Third Aliyah

- <u>The incident of the spies</u>: [After telling you to go conquer the land] you then all came to me and asked me to send spies to the land. I agreed and appointed 12 people from amongst you to be part of the delegation, one person per tribe. They returned with the fruits of the land and reported that the land is good, and you, the nation, did not desire to ascend it and you rebelled against G-d. You slandered against G-d saying that He took you out of Egypt in order to have you annihilated by the Amorites. Your hearts were melted after hearing the reports that the land contains a strong nation, giants and fortified cities. I, however, told you not to fear them or worry as G-d will lead you and fight for you just as He did in Egypt, and as He has done for you thus far in the desert. Yet, you did not believe in G-d's ability and He became angry with you and swore that none of you would ever see the land and only Kaleiv Ben Yefuneh would see it. Also with me G-d became angry because of you, and He said I would not enter the land. Joshua Ben nun will now lead you and you shall strengthen him, as he will conquer the land for you.

Fourth Aliyah

- <u>The aftermath of the spy incident and the failed battle</u>: Your children who you said would become spoils of the enemy will inherit the land, and now you should turn around and return to the desert towards the Reed Sea. You then regretted what you did and had a change of heart to gather an army and go fight to conquer the land. However, G-d warned me that it is too late, and He will not assist you, and hence you should desist from going. I tried convincing you, but yet, here too you did not listen to the word of G-d and ascended to wage battle against them. They destroyed you and chased you like bees and you sat and cried before G-d but He refused to listen to you. You therefore sat in Kadeish for many days [for a total of 19 years]. We then traveled to Mount Seir and went around it for many days.

Chapter 2
Fifth Aliyah

- <u>Moses recounts passing the borders of Esau</u>: G-d said to me that we have spent enough time circling the mountain and we should travel towards north. We were warned by G-d that while traveling through the border of Esau we are to take great heed not to instigate them, as we will not inherit even one parcel of their land. We shall buy food and water from them.
- <u>Moses recounts passing the borders of Moab</u>: So, we passed the border of Esau and traveled towards the desert of Moab. G-d warned us not to oppress Moab or instigate them into war, as their land will not be given to us as an inheritance. We were then instructed to travel across Nachal Zared. It took us 38 years to travel from Kadeish until crossing Nachal Zared, by which time the entire generation had already passed away.
- <u>Moses recounts passing the borders of Ammon</u>: G-d told us that we will be passing the border of Moab and arrive by the nation of Ammon. G-d warned us not to oppress or instigate them, as it will not be given to us as an inheritance.
- <u>Moses recounts passing the border of Sihon</u>: G-d told us to go travel past Nachal Arnon and instigate a war with Sihon the Amorite king, as he will be handed into our hands. I sent envoys to Sihon with a peaceful message saying that we request to pass though his land, and we will go through the kings road and not swerve right or left. We will

purchase food and drink from you, just as was done when we passed the land of Seir and Moab. However, Sihon refused our entry due to G-d hardening his heart so he be handed over to us.

Sixth Aliyah

- <u>Moses recounts the conquering of Sihon</u>: G-d told me that He has begun handing over Sihon and his land to us, and so it was that Sihon confronted us in battle and we smote them with G-d's help. We captured all of the cities, women and children and left no survivors. We took only the animals and possessions of the city as booty.

Chapter 3

- <u>Moses recounts conquering Og</u>: We turned and traveled towards the Bashan, and Og the king of Bashan confronted us in battle with his entire nation. G-d told me not to fear him, as He has handed him into our hands just as he did with Sihon. And so it was that G-d handed to us Og and his entire nation, we left no survivors. We captured all of his cities, sixty in total. The cities were fortified with high walls. We destroyed every city and all its inhabitants, men, women, and children. The animals and its possessions we took as spoil. Og was a giant who came from the Refaim. He was nine cubits tall and four cubits wide.
- <u>Moses recounts the distribution of land to the tribes of Reuben, Gad and half of Manasseh</u>: I gave the land of Sihon to Reuben and Gad, while the land of Og was given to half the tribe of Manasseh. Yair the son of Manasseh captured the region of the Refaim.

Seventh Aliyah

- Machir was given the Gilad, while Reuben and Gad were given the entire region of the Jordon river, the Kineret and dead sea.
- <u>The condition for Reuben, Gad and Manasseh to join the battle</u>: I instructed you [the tribes who settled past the Jordon] to join the battle together with the rest of Israel, and to leave your wives, children, and cattle in the cities. Once the Jewish people have crossed the Jordon, and conquered and settled the land, then you may return.
- I commanded Joshua that he should look and see all that G-d has done to these two kings, and that so would be done to all the kings across [the Jordon]. You shall not fear, as G-d will be with you and wage war for you.

Parashat Vaetchanan
Verses: 118 [Siman: עזיאל]
Haftorah: Isaiah 40:1-26

Number of Mitzvot:
There are a total of **Twelve** Mitzvot in Parashat Vaetchanan; **Eight** positive commands and **Four** negative commands. The following are the commands in the order listed by the Sefer Hachinuch.

A. Positive:
1. **Mitzvah 417/Positive 173:** To unify G-d's name in Shema Israel and accept his unity upon us.
2. **Mitzvah 418/Positive 174:** To love G-d and contemplate his greatness until a love is aroused.
3. **Mitzvah 419/Positive 175:** To learn Torah.
4. **Mitzvah 420/Positive 176:** To read the Shema morning and evening.
5. **Mitzvah 421/Positive 177:** To don the hand Tefillin/Phylactery.
6. **Mitzvah 422/Positive 178:** To don the head Tefillin/Phylactery.
7. **Mitzvah 423/Positive 179:** To put Mezuzot on one's doors.
8. **Mitzvah 425/Positive 180:** To destroy the seven Canaanite nations.

B. Negative:
1. **Mitzvah 416/Negative 244:** Not to covet the item of another even in one's heart.
2. **Mitzvah 424/Negative 245:** Not to doubt or question the prophets.
3. **Mitzvah 426/Negative 246:** Not to have mercy on idolaters or find favor with their service.
4. **Mitzvah 427/Negative 247:** Not to marry a gentile.

First Aliyah
1. **Moses pleads to G-d to allow him to enter into Israel:**
   - I [i.e. Moses] implored G-d at that time saying: "G-d, you have begun showing your servant your greatness [in conquering Sihon and Og] let me now cross and see the good land on the other side of the Jordon. "G-d became angry at me due to you (the children of Israel) and replied that I may not enter and should not continue praying for it."
   - G-d shows Moses the land: G-d instructed Moses to ascend a large cliff to see the land [of Israel] as he will not inherit it.
   - Encouraging Joshua as the new leader: G-d instructed Moses to command Joshua and strengthen him as he will lead the Jewish people to conquer the land.
   - The children of Israel stayed in the valley opposite Beth Peor.

Chapter 4
2. **Moses commands the children of Israel to follow the Torah:**
   - Moses tells the Jewish people to listen to the laws that he is teaching today so that they shall live and enter and inherit the promised land.

- <u>Lo Sosif</u>: You shall not add or subtract to the Mitzvot.
- <u>Baal Peor</u>: the children of Israel's own eyes witnessed that which happened to those who worshiped Baal Peor and how they were decimated and those who have attached to G-d remained alive today.

Second Aliyah

- <u>The Torah is our wisdom</u>: The Torah is the wisdom of the Jewish people in the eyes of the nations. The nations will declare how wise the Jewish people are. There is no nation that is closer to G-d than the Jewish people.
- <u>Remembering Matan Torah</u>: We must never forget our witnessing of the giving of the Torah and are to teach it to our children. We stood under the mountain and a fire came out from the mountain until the heavens and G-d's voice came out from the fire. We were commanded 10 commands and they were written on two Tablets of Stone. G-d commanded Moses the remaining commands that he must tell the Jewish people.
- One must guard his soul very much.
- <u>Idolatry</u>: Moses warns the children of Israel against performing idolatry. "One is not to make a replica of a human, male or female, or of an animal or bird or fish. Lest your eyes look at the heavens and you see the sun, moon and stars and worship them.
- G-d has removed you from the iron crucible of Egypt and chosen you as a nation."
- <u>Moses will not enter Israel</u>: G-d became angry with Moses due to the sons of Israel and told him that he will not enter Israel, although the children of Israel will enter.
- <u>Prophecy that the Jewish people will go astray and their punishments</u>: "When you have many descendants and live long in the land, you will go astray and in corrupt ways, performing evil in the eyes of G-d. I forewarn you today that you will perish from the land. G-d will disperse you amongst all the lands and you will serve their gods. You will search for G-d your G-d there and you will find him. G-d is merciful, and He will not destroy you or forget the covenant with your forefathers."
- <u>Moses recounts the miracles G-d has done and that there is nothing but Him</u>: "Inquire and see, has there ever been a time that a nation has heard the voice of G-d and taken one nation out from another with miracles and wonders. You have been shown today that G-d is G-d and there is nothing aside for Him. Internalize this message into your heart."

Third Aliyah

3. **Moses separates three cities of refuge:**
   - Moses then separated three cities of refuge on the eastern side of the Jordon. The cities were built to serve as a refuge for the inadvertent killer, for him to escape to there and live. The names of these three cities are:
     o Betzer, which was in the land of Reuben.
     o Ramos, which was in land of Gad.
     o Golan, which was in Bashan, in the land of Manasseh.
   - The Torah recounts the conquering of the lands of Sihon and Og.

Chapter 5
Fourth Aliyah
4. Moses recounts the giving of the Torah on Mount Sinai:
- Moses called all the Jewish people and told them to hear the commands of G-d. G-d made a covenant with us by Horeb. This covenant was not just made with our forefathers, but also with us. G-d spoke to you on the mountain face to face from within the fire. I stood between G-d and you at that time to relate to you G-d's words, as you feared the fire and did not ascend the mountain.

5. Moses repeats the Ten Commandments:
1) "I am G-d your G-d who took you out of Egypt.
2) Do not have other deities. Do not make for yourselves an image or picture that is found in the heavens or earth, or underwater. Do not serve them, as I am a G-d of retribution who gives judgment against the third and fourth generation for those who hate Me, although I do kindness for a thousand generations for those who love me and fulfill my Mitzvot.
3) Do not recite G-d's name in vain.
4) **Guard** the Shabbat to sanctify it. Six days a week you shall work and on the seventh day it shall be a day of rest for G-d. You shall not do any work, neither you or your son or daughter, or slave or animal. You shall remember that you were a slave in Egypt and G-d took you out with an outstretched arm. Therefore, He commanded you to keep the Shabbat.
5) Honor your father and mother so you live a long life on the land.
6) Do not murder.
7) Do not commit adultery.
8) Do not steal.
9) Do not testify falsely regarding a friend.
10) Do not covet the wife of a friend, nor shall you desire his house, slave, ox, donkey or any of his possessions."

Fifth Aliyah
6. The children of Israel asked Moses to speak instead of G-d:
- G-d spoke the above words before you all, within a fog, and in a loud endless voice. He wrote them on two stone tablets and gave them to me. When you heard the voice of G-d, all your tribal leaders and elders approached me saying that you could no longer handle hearing the voice of G-d, lest you die, as there is no one who can hear G-d and stay alive. You asked me to be the intermediary to tell you of His commands. G-d agreed to your request, saying that if only they would learn from here to fear Me all their days, so I can benefit their children forever. "Go tell them to return to their tents, but you [Moses] shall remain with Me and I will teach you all the laws and commands that they shall perform in the promised land."

Chapter 6
Sixth Aliyah
7. The Portion of Shema and Veahavta:
- The Mitzvot of unity of G-d, Love, Torah learning, Shema, Tefillin, and Mezuzzah: "Hear Israel, G-d is our G-d and G-d is one. You shall love G-d with all your heart and soul and possessions. These words shall be on your heart and you shall teach it to your children and speak of them at home and on the road, when you lie down and when you

rise. You shall bind them to your arm and eyes and write them on the doorposts of your homes and gates."

8. Moses forewarns the children of Israel not to forget G-d after they conquer the land:
- "Upon entering the promised land, you will find great cities that you did not build. The homes will be filled with all good, vineyards and olive orchards and you will eat and be satiated. Do not forget G-d who took you out of Egypt. You shall fear Him and serve Him and swear by His name. You shall not stray after their gods, lest G-d become angry with you and destroy you from the land. Do not test G-d like you did in Massah. Do the fair and proper in the eyes of G-d."

9. The question of the wise son [i.e. Chacham]:
- "When your son asks you tomorrow as to why we keep these laws, you are to answer him that we were slaves in Egypt and G-d took us out with miracles and a mighty hand. He did this in order to bring us to the Promised Land where we can keep His commands."

Chapter 7
Seventh Aliyah

10. Moses commands the children of Israel to destroy all the nations of the land of Canaan:
- "When you enter the promised land, G-d will drive out many nations from before you who are greater and mightier than you. They will be given to your hands and you are to annihilate them completely. You shall not make a covenant with them or have them find favor in your eyes.
- Intermarriage: Do not marry them. Do not give them your daughter in marriage and do not take as a wife for your son from amongst them. They will cause your son to go astray and serve other gods. G-d will then become angry with you and hurriedly destroy you.
- You are to destroy all of their idols and their accessories, such as their altars, statues, trees of idolatry and idols."

11. G-d expresses His love for the Jewish people:
- "You are a holy nation onto G-d who has chosen you as a treasure amongst all people that roam the earth. He did not choose you because you are greater, as in truth you are smaller, but rather because He loved you and due to the covenant that He made with your forefathers. You shall know that G-d is trusted to safeguard the covenant for a thousand generations for those who keep his Mitzvot, and to punish. You shall guard the Mitzvot that I commanded you today."

Parashat Eikev
Verses: 111 [Siman:יעלא]
Haftorah: Isaiah 49:14-51:3

Number of Mitzvot:
There are a total of **Eight** Mitzvot in Parashat Eikev; **Six** positive commands and **Two** negative commands. The following are the commands in the order listed by the Sefer Hachinuch.

A. Positive:
1. **Mitzvah 430/Positive 181:** To bless G-d after eating bread.
2. **Mitzvah 431/Positive 182:** To love the convert.
3. **Mitzvah 432/Positive 183:** To fear G-d.
4. **Mitzvah 433/Positive 184:** To serve G-d and Daven to Him daily.
5. **Mitzvah 434/Positive 185:** To attach to the Sages and Torah scholars.
6. **Mitzvah 435/Positive 186:** To swear using G-d's name.

B. Negative:
1. **Mitzvah 428/Negative 248:** Not to benefit from the ornaments of idolatry.
2. **Mitzvah 429/Negative 249:** Not to benefit from any item of idolatry.

First Aliyah

1. **The blessings received for guarding the Mitzvot:**
   - If you adhere by the commands of G-d, He will guard with you the covenant that he made with your forefathers.
     - He will love you and bless you and multiply you.
     - You will have many offspring, and the land will give off much produce. You will be blessed amongst all the nations.
     - You and your animals will not be infertile.
     - He will remove all illnesses from you and rather place them onto your enemies
     - You will destroy all your enemies.

2. **Moses encourages the children of Israel not to fear the nations of Canaan:**
   - "If you tell yourself that the nations are too mighty and many to be destroyed, do not fear. Remember what G-d did to Egypt, as He will do the same to those nations. He will send the wasp against them until no survivor remains. Do not fear them, as G-d is amongst you. G-d will annihilate them little by little and not quickly, lest the animals of the field increase.
   - Idolatry: Destroy their idols in fire. Don't desire to take any of their ornaments of idolatry as it is an abomination of G-d. You shall loathe it and abominate it."

Chapter 8

3. Recounting the desert experience:

- "Remember the entire 40-year journey in the desert where He challenged you to see if you would follow his word.
- <u>The Mun</u>: G-d gave you the Mun in the desert to test you and teach you that man does not live on bread alone, but on the word of G-d.
- <u>Clothing</u>: Your clothing did not wear out and your foot did not swell."

4. The greatness of the promised land:

- "The land G-d is giving you contains water and springs. It is a land of wheat and barley and grapes, figs, rimon, olives and date-honey. It is a land of abundance of food. A land whose stones are iron and whose mountains contains copper.
- <u>Birchas Hamazon</u>: You shall eat and be satiated and bless G-d for the good land that He gave you."

Second Aliyah

5. Moses warns the children of Israel not to become accustomed to the luxuries and forsake G-d:

- "Be careful that you do not forget G-d by not keeping His commands. Perhaps you will eat and be satiated and have good houses built and settled, and have much gold and silver and you will become haughty and forget G-d who took you out of Egypt. You may tell yourself that your power and strength is what made you accomplish this and not G-d. Remember that G-d is the one who gives you strength to be successful.
- If you do forget G-d and sway after idolatry, I am forewarning you today that you will be destroyed."

Chapter 9

6. Conquering the land:

- "Hear Israel, you are going today to the promised land which contains nations that are mightier than you, and have cities fortified to the heavens. You shall know today that G-d your G-d is the one who will pass before you, and He will destroy them."

Third Aliyah

- "Don't tell yourselves that those nations are being destroyed before you because you are more righteous than them, and they were evil. This is not the case. Rather, it is due to their wickedness that they are being destroyed, and in order to upkeep G-d's promise to your forefathers. It is not due to your righteousness, as you are a stubborn nation."

7. Moses recounts in detail the sin of the golden calf:

- "Remember that you angered G-d in the desert, and G-d desired to destroy you. When I ascended the mountain to carry down the Tablets of Stone, I was there for 40 days and nights without eating or drinking. I was given the Tablets of Stone by G-d and at the conclusion of the 40 days was told to descend back down as the nation has sinned and made an idol. G-d said to me that the nation is stubborn, and He wishes to destroy them and make a new and better nation from me. I descended the mountain with the Tablets of Stone and behold I saw that you sinned to G-d. I took the two Tablets of Stone and threw them, breaking them in front of you. I then fell before G-d another 40 days and nights, not eating or drinking, to plead for forgiveness for your sins. G-d became enraged at Aaron and desired to destroy him, so I also prayed for him. I took the sinful calf and burnt it within fire and turned it into dust. I threw the dust in the valley/river that descended from the mountain."

- <u>Moses recounts other rebelliousness</u>: "Remember the provocation made in Taveira and Kivros Hataava. When G-d sent you from Kadesh to go inherit the land, you replied with disbelief in His ability to do so.
- I prayed for you forty days and nights to rescind the decree of destruction against you. I asked G-d not to destroy His nation which He redeemed from Egypt, lest the nations say You took them out to murder them."

Chapter 10
Fourth Aliyah
8. Moses recounts the giving of the 2nd Tablets of Stone:

- "At that time G-d told me to carve two new sets of stone just like the first ones, and ascend the mountain. I made an Aron of acacia-shittim wood and carved the stones and ascended the mountain. G-d wrote on the Tablets of Stone the same words that were written on the first tablets and He gave them to me. I descended from the mountain and placed the Tablets of Stone in the Aron."

9. Moses recounts the travels:

- "We traveled to Moseirah and Aaron passed away and was buried there. Elazar, his son, became the priest in his place. From there we traveled to Gudgod, and from there to Yatvasah, a land of channels of water.
- At that time, G-d set apart the Levites to carry the Aron and serve before Him, and bless in His name until this day. For this reason, the Levites do not have a portion with their brothers, as G-d is their portion.
- I stood by the mountain for forty days and G-d listened to me not to destroy you. G-d told me to arise and go travel towards the promised land."

Fifth Aliyah
10. Moses commands the children of Israel several Mitzvot:

- "What does G-d ask from you but to fear Him and follow His ways. To love Him and serve Him with all your heart and soul. To guard His commands for your own benefit.
- Everything in the heaven and earth belongs to G-d and yet He chose you. G-d loved our ancestors and hence chose us as His nation.
- You shall remove the foreskin of your hearts and not be stubborn, as G-d is the great and mighty G-d who cannot be bribed and does justice for the widow and orphan.
- One is to love the convert, as you too were converts in Egypt.
- You shall fear and love G-d, attach to Him and swear by Him."

Chapter 11

- <u>The miracles G-d did for us</u>: "He is your G-d who performed for you all the miracles that you witnessed. He brought you to Egypt with 70 souls and now you have become as abundant as the stars. You saw what He did to Egypt and how He smote them by the sea, and what He did for you in the desert. You saw what He did to Datan and Abiram for whom the earth opened, and it swallowed them and their homes and tents."

- Moses encourages the children of Israel to guard the Mitzvot and hence solidify their stay in Israel and merit a long life in the land of milk and honey.

Sixth Aliyah

11. The greatness of Israel:

- "The land of Israel is unlike the land of Egypt from where you exited in which you had to irrigate the fields. This land that you will inherit is a land of mountains and valleys which drinks the waters of the heavens.
- It is a land that G-d seeks, and His eye is constantly watching over it from the beginning of the year to the end of the year."

12. The Portion of Vehaya Im Shamoa:

- "If you adhere by all the commands, to love G-d and serve Him with all your heart and soul, then I will give you rain on time. You will gather your grain, wine, and oil. Your animals will be provided grass, and you will eat and be satiated.
- Beware, lest your hearts be seduced, and you sway after other gods and worship them. G-d will get angry with you, and stop the rain, and growth of produce, from the good land that he gave you. You shall place these words on your heart and soul and you shall bind them to your hands and eyes. Teach them to your children and speak of them in your house, and on the road, and when you lie, and when you rise. Write them on the doorposts of your homes and gates so that I may increase your days in the promised land."

Seventh Aliyah

- "If you listen to G-d, He will guard his covenant with you, and drive out all the mighty nations from the land, and your enemies will fear you."

Parashat Re'eh

Verses: 126 [Siman:פליאה]
Haftorah: Isaiah 54:11-55:5

Number of Mitzvot:

There are a total of **Fifty-five** Mitzvot in Parashat Re'eh; **Seventeen** positive commands and **Thirty-eight** negative commands. The following are the commands in the order listed by the Sefer Hachinuch.

A. Positive:

1. **Mitzvah 436/Positive 187:** To destroy all idolatry, and their houses, and any remnant of them.
2. **Mitzvah 438/Positive 188:** To bring all obligatory offerings, or voluntary sacrifices, by the first holiday.
3. **Mitzvah 440/Positive 189:** To offer all the Sacrifices in the Temple.
4. **Mitzvah 441/Positive 190:** To redeem Sacrifices that have a blemish.
5. **Mitzvah 451/Positive 191:** To slaughter animals and poultry that one desires to eat.
6. **Mitzvah 453/Positive 192:** To bring all Sacrifices in the Diaspora of Chatas, Asham and Olah to the Temple.
7. **Mitzvah 463/Positive 193:** To interrogate witnesses.
8. **Mitzvah 464/Positive 194:** To burn a city of idolatry.
9. **Mitzvah 470/Positive 195:** To check the Kashrut signs of birds
10. **Mitzvah 473/Positive 196:** To separate a second tithe [i.e. Maaser Sheiyni] in the 1-2nd, and 4th-5th years of the Shemita cycle.
11. **Mitzvah 474/Positive 197:** To separate the pauper tithe [i.e. Maaser Ani] in the 3rd and 6th year of the Shemita cycle.
12. **Mitzvah 476/Positive 198:** To demand a gentile who is a debtor to pay his debts.
13. **Mitzvah 477/Positive 199:** To abolish all debts in the Shemita/Sabbatical year.
14. **Mitzvah 479/Positive 200:** To give charity and support to those in need with a happy and glad heart.
15. **Mitzvah 482/Positive 201:** To give severance pay to a slave.
16. **Mitzvah 488/Positive 202:** To rejoice on the Holidays.
17. **Mitzvah 489/Positive 203:** To visit the Temple on each of the three Holidays.

B. Negative:

1. **Mitzvah 437/Negative 250:** Not to destroy holy items, such as the Temple and Sefarim.
2. **Mitzvah 439/Negative 251:** Not to offer Sacrifices outside of the Temple area.
3. **Mitzvah 442/Negative 252:** Not to eat the second tithe [i.e. Maaser Sheiyni] of grain outside of Jerusalem.
4. **Mitzvah 443/Negative 253:** Not to eat the second tithe [i.e. Maaser Sheiyni] of wine outside of Jerusalem.
5. **Mitzvah 444/Negative 254:** Not to eat the second tithe [i.e. Maaser Sheiyni] of oil outside of Jerusalem.
6. **Mitzvah 445/Negative 255:** For the Kohen not to eat a firstborn animal outside of Jerusalem.

7. **Mitzvah 446/Negative 256:** Not to eat the meat of the Chatas and Asham offering outside of the Temple.

8. **Mitzvah 447/Negative 257:** Not to eat from the Olah sacrifice.

9. **Mitzvah 448/Negative 258:** Not to eat from Kodshim Kalim offerings prior to the blood being thrown on the altar.

10. **Mitzvah 449/Negative 259:** The Kohanim may not eat from the Bikkurim prior to it being placed in the Temple courtyard.

11. **Mitzvah 450/Negative 260:** Not to abstain from giving the Levites their presents and rejoicing with them by the Holidays.

12. **Mitzvah 452/Negative 261:** Not to eat a limb from a live animal [i.e. Eiver Min Hachaiy].

13. **Mitzvah 454/Negative 262:** Not to add to the Torah prohibitions.

14. **Mitzvah 455/Negative 263:** Not to subtract from the Torah prohibitions.

15. **Mitzvah 456/Negative 264:** Not to listen to one who prophesizes in name of idolatry.

16. **Mitzvah 457/Negative 265:** Not to listen to, or find favor with, an instigator of idolatry.

17. **Mitzvah 458/Negative 266:** Not to stop hating an instigator of idolatry.

18. **Mitzvah 459/Negative 267:** Not to save the life of an instigator of idolatry from danger.

19. **Mitzvah 460/Negative 268:** The one influenced is not to learn merit on an instigator of idolatry.

20. **Mitzvah 461/Negative 269:** The one influenced is not to refrain from finding fault with the instigator of idolatry.

21. **Mitzvah 462/Negative 270:** Not to lead a Jew astray to follow idolatry.

22. **Mitzvah 465/Negative 271:** Not to build a city of idolatry.

23. **Mitzvah 466/Negative 272:** Not to benefit from a city of idolatry.

24. **Mitzvah 467/Negative 273:** Not to cut our bodies like idolaters.

25. **Mitzvah 468/Negative 274:** Not to shave one's head in mourning.

26. **Mitzvah 469/Negative 275:** Not to eat invalid Sacrifices.

27. **Mitzvah 471/Negative 276:** Not to eat non-Kosher locusts or any flying creature.

28. **Mitzvah 472/Negative 277:** Not to eat meat that was not ritually slaughtered.

29. **Mitzvah 475/Negative 278:** Not to demand payment of a loan during Shemita/Sabbatical year, and rather to forgive it.

30. **Mitzvah 478/Negative 279:** Not to abstain from giving charity, kindness, and mercy.

31. **Mitzvah 480/Negative 280:** Not to abstain from lending money due to fear of Shemita/Sabbatical year.

32. **Mitzvah 481/Negative 281:** Not to send a slave away without severance pay.

33. **Mitzvah 483/Negative 282:** Not to do work with offerings.

34. **Mitzvah 484/Negative 283:** Not to sheer the wool of offerings.

35. **Mitzvah 485/Negative 284:** Not to eat Chametz after midday of Erev Pesach.

36. **Mitzvah 486/Negative 285:** Not to let meat remain from the Chagiga offering into the third morning.

37. **Mitzvah 487/Negative 286:** Not to bring the Pesach sacrifice on a private altar [i.e. Bama].

38. **Mitzvah 490/Negative 287:** Not to visit the Temple on the Holidays without bringing Sacrifices.

First Aliyah

1. **The Blessings and Curses of Mount Gerizim and Mount Ebal:**
   - "See that I am giving you today the blessings and curses. The blessings are received if you fulfill G-d's will, while the curses are received if you transgress G-d's will and you go astray after foreign gods."
   - Mount Gerizim and Mount Ebal: Upon your arrival to the promised land, the blessings will be given on Mount Gerizim while the curses will be given on Mount Ebal.

Chapter 12

2. **Commandments relating to conquering the land:**
   - The following are the laws that you shall follow upon entering the promised land: "You are to destroy all the areas of worship of the gentile nations. You are to destroy their altars, statues, and idols, and burn their trees of idolatry, and all their apparatus.
   - Do not do this to G-d your G-d [to destroy items of Holiness]."

3. **Commandments relating to Sacrifices, meat and tithes:**
   - Bringing the sacrifices to Shilo: "You are to offer all the Sacrifices only in the Temple, in the area that G-d has chosen to reside. You are to eat there before G-d and rejoice there. You will no longer bring sacrifices on Bamos as you are accustomed today."

Second Aliyah

- Bringing the sacrifices to Jerusalem: You are to offer all the Sacrifices only in the Temple, in the area that G-d has chosen to reside. You are to eat there before G-d and rejoice there. You may not bring sacrifices in other areas.
- Shechita: You may slaughter animals as you desire, and you may eat their meat in any area, while pure or impure.
- Blood: You may not eat the blood of the animal.
- The second tithe [i.e. Maaser Sheiyni]: The second tithe [i.e. Maaser Sheiyni] may not be eaten outside of the chosen area [i.e. Jerusalem].
- Firstborn: The firstborn animal may not be eaten outside of the chosen area [i.e. Jerusalem].
- The Levite: Do not abstain from giving the Levites their presents and rejoicing them by the Holidays.
- Voluntary offerings: You shall offer the sacrifices that you vowed to offer onto the altar. Its blood is to be spilled on the altar, while its meat is to be eaten.

Third Aliyah

4. **Commandments relating to the inhabitants of the conquered land:**
   - "When you enter the land that G-d has conquered before you, do not be fooled to seek out their idolatry and worship them. You shall not do this to G-d, as all the abominations which G-d hates they did towards their gods, and they burned their children in fire.
   - You are to guard all the commands and not add or subtract from the commands."

Chapter 13

5. **Laws relating to a prophet of idolatry:**
   - "When a prophet or dreamer rises from amongst you who performs miracles, and he states that he received a prophetic vision from G-d that one is to serve idolatry, you are not to listen to him. G-d is testing you to see if you love Him with all your heart and soul. The above prophet is to be killed, and you should destroy the evil from your midst.
   - You shall go in the path of G-d, fear Him, guard His commands, serve Him, and attach to Him."

6. **Laws relating to a Meisis-Missionaries of idolatry:**
   - "If your brother, or son, or daughter, or wife, or friend tries to persuade you to serve idolatry, telling you "Let us go and worship the gods of other nations" you are not to listen to him. You are to have no mercy on him, or protect him, and cover up for him. Rather, you shall kill him. Your hand should be the first to kill him and the hand of the nation will be the last. You shall stone him until he dies, and all the Jewish people will hear and witness, so they do not do the same."

7. **Laws relating to city of idolatry:**
   - "If you hear that missionaries have persuaded an entire city to serve idolatry, you are to properly inquire the matter, and if found true the city is to be destroyed. All of the city's possessions are to be gathered in the square and burnt. The city is never to be rebuilt. It is forbidden to take any spoils from the city.
   - If you do the above, you will quench G-d's anger and He will have mercy on you."

Chapter 14
Fourth Aliyah

8. **Cutting skin in mourning:**
   - "You are children of G-d and a holy nation. Therefore, you are not to cut your skin or shave your head in mourning of a loved one.

9. **Laws relating to Kashrut:**
   - You are not to eat any abominating item.
   - The Kosher animals: You may only eat the following animals: The ox, sheep, goat, ram, deer, Yachmur, Akko, Dishon, Teo and Zamer. You may eat all animals that have split hooves and chew their cud. The following animals you may not eat amongst those who chew their cud or have split hooves: The Shesuah, camel, rabbit, and hyrax, as although they chew their cud they do not have split hooves. Likewise, the pig may not be eaten, as it has split hooves but does not chew its cud. You may not eat their flesh, and may not touch their corpse [during the festivals].
   - Kosher fish: The following sea creatures may be eaten: All fish that have fins and scales may be eaten. All fish that do not have fins and scales are not Kosher and are considered impure for you.
   - Non-Kosher birds: You may eat all pure birds. The following [20] birds may not be eaten: [the identification of these birds from the original Hebrew is mostly unknown] 1) Eagle; 2) Peres; 3) Ozniah; 4) Raah, Ayah, and Dayah; 6) Raven; 7) Bas Hayaanah; 8) Tachmos; 9) Shachaf; 10) Netz [i.e. sparrow hawk]; 11) Kos; 12) Yanshuf [i.e. owl] 13)

Tinshemes; 14) Kaas; 15) Rachamah; 16) Shalach [i.e. seagull]; 17) Chasidah [i.e. stork]; 18) Anafah; 19) Duchifas [i.e. wild rooster]; 20) Atalef [bat].

- <u>Insects</u>: All flying creatures are impure for you and may not be eaten.
- <u>Fowl</u>: All pure fowl may be eaten.
- <u>Carcass</u>: A carcass may not be eaten, and it is to be given to the strangers who live with you, or sold to the gentiles, as you are a holy nation onto G-d.
- <u>Meat and milk</u>: You shall not eat meat and milk together.

Fifth Aliyah
10. Laws relating to the second tithe [i.e. Maaser Sheiyni]:
- "You shall tithe all the produce of your field annually.
- <u>Where to eat it</u>: This tithe is to be eaten in the chosen place where G-d rests [i.e. Jerusalem] so that you learn to fear G-d all your days. The tithe of your grains, wine, oil, and the firstborn of your cattle and flock. [This tithe is called Maaser Sheiyni.] If you live a distance from the area, and are unable to carry all the produce there, then you shall redeem the produce with money and take the money to the chosen place [i.e. Jerusalem]. That money shall than be used [in Jerusalem] to buy cattle, flock, wine, and everything that you desire.
- You and your family are to rejoice there. You are not to ignore the Levite."

11. The law of Biur Maaser-Ridding one's home of tithes:
- "At the conclusion of the 3rd year you are to remove all of your tithes from your home and place it within your gates. The Levite, and convert, orphan and widow will come and eat it to satiation. Do this so that G-d shall bless you in all your actions."

Chapter 15
Sixth Aliyah
12. The laws of loan abolition/Shemitas Kesafim:
- "At the conclusion of the seventh year you are to perform a Shemita/Sabbatical year release. The following is the release that you are to do: You are to abolish all debts that you are owed. You are to no longer press your friend to pay back the loan. However, a gentile is to be pressed to pay what he owes."

13. Poverty:
- "<u>No poor people if listen to G-d</u>: You will have no poor people amongst you as G-d will bless you if you adhere His words. You will lend to nations and will not need to borrow from them and they will not rule over you.
- <u>Tzedaka to the poor</u>: If there shall be a poor person from amongst you, you are to support him. Do not close your heart and hands from giving to your brother the pauper. You shall open your hands to him and grant him whatever he lacks.
- <u>Not to abstain from lending the poor because of Shemita</u>: Beware, lest you tell yourself not to lend your destitute brother due to the approach of the Shemita/Sabbatical year. He will call out to G-d against you and you will have sinned. You shall grant him a loan and not be of bad heart to abstain, as by doing so G-d will grant you blessing in all that you do.

- There will always be poor people: You will always have poor people amongst your land [if you disobey G-d's will], and therefore I am commanding you to support them."

14. Laws relating to freeing a slave:
- "Seventh year let free: If your brethren, a man or woman, are sold to you, the slave shall serve you for six years and is to be let free in the seventh year.
- Severance pay: When you send him free, you are not to send him emptyhanded. Grant him presents from your flock and grains and wine, and from everything that G-d has blessed you with. Remember, that you were once a slave in Egypt and G-d redeemed you from there, and hence I too am now commanding you to do as stated above.
- A slave who does not wish to leave: If the slave tells you that he does not wish to leave, as he likes his house and his dwelling with you. Then you shall take the awl and pierce his ear by the doorpost, and he is then to become an eternal slave. The same shall be done for a maidservant."

Seventh Aliyah

15. Laws of firstborn:
- "Every firstborn animal that will be born to your cattle and flock is to be sanctified to G-d.
- Work and use: You are not to perform work with the firstborn ox, nor sheer the sheep.
- Where to eat: It is to be eaten [by the Kohen] in the chosen area by G-d [i.e. Jerusalem].
- Blemish: If it has a blemish, such as being lame or blind, it is not to be slaughtered to G-d your G-d, and is rather to be eaten in your cities by the pure and impure.
- Blood: One may not eat its blood and it is rather to be spilled on the earth like water."

Chapter 16

16. Laws relating to Pesach:
- "One is to guard the month of Aviv/spring to celebrate Pesach, as in this month G-d took you out of Egypt at night.
- The sacrifice: The Pesach offering is to be brought to the area that G-d chooses to reside [i.e. Jerusalem]. It is to be offered in the afternoon. You shall cook it and eat it in the area that G-d chooses, and then leave back home the next morning. You may not let the meat remain past the morning.
- Chametz and Matzah: One may not eat Chametz with it, and one is to eat Matzot for seven days, as you left Egypt in a haste. You may not see [i.e. own] Chametz or yeast [i.e. leavened bread] in all your borders for seven days.
- Labor: On the seventh day one may not do labor."

17. Laws relating to Shavuot:
- To count the Omer: "You shall count for yourselves seven weeks from when the harvest of the Omer takes place.
- Shavuot: You are to celebrate the festival of Shavuot for G-d [on the 50th day] in accordance to what you have to offer from that which G-d has bequeathed you.
- Rejoicing: You shall rejoice before G-d, you and your children and slaves, the Levite, orphan, and widow who is in your midst, in the area that G-d has chosen."

18. Laws relating to Sukkot:

- "You shall celebrate the festival of Sukkot for seven days, when you gather from your fruits and from the wine pit.
- <u>Visamachta Bechagecha-To rejoice on Sukkot</u>: You are to rejoice for seven days, you and your children and slaves, and the Levite, orphan and widow who is in your midst, in the area that G-d has chosen. As G-d has blessed you in your harvest and you are to be happy."

19. Laws relating to pilgrimage:

- "Three times a year every male is to see G-d in the area of His choosing [i.e. Jerusalem], during the festival of Matzot, Shavuot and Sukkot.
- <u>Reiya offering</u>: One is not to come see My face empty handed. Each man is to bring in accordance to that which he can afford."

Parashat Shoftim

Verses: 97 [Siman:סלוא]
Haftorah: Isaiah 51:12-52:12

Number of Mitzvot:
There are a total of **Forty-one** Mitzvot in Parashat Judges; **Fourteen** positive commands and **Twenty-seven** negative commands. The following are the commands in the order listed by the Sefer Hachinuch.

A. Positive:
1. **Mitzvah 491/Positive 204:** To appoint judges and police in every Jewish city.
2. **Mitzvah 495/Positive 205:** To adhere to the words of the supreme court.
3. **Mitzvah 497/Positive 206:** To appoint a king.
4. **Mitzvah 503/Positive 207:** For the king to write his own personal Sefer Torah.
5. **Mitzvah 506/Positive 208:** To give the arm, cheek, and stomach, of an animal to the Kohen.
6. **Mitzvah 507/Positive 209:** To separate Teruma Gedola from grain, wine and olive oil.
7. **Mitzvah 508/Positive 210:** To give the first sharing of wool from sheep to the Kohen.
8. **Mitzvah 509/Positive 211:** For the Kohanim and Levites to set up shifts and rotations of service in the Temple.
9. **Mitzvah 516/Positive 212:** To adhere to the voice of a Navi/prophet.
10. **Mitzvah 520/Positive 213:** To separate cities of refuge.
11. **Mitzvah 525/Positive 214:** To punish Eidim Zomimim/false witnesses measure for measure for what they desired to do.
12. **Mitzvah 527/Positive 215:** To anoint a Kohen during times of war to speak to the soldiers.
13. **Mitzvah 528/Positive 216:** To give an option of surrender and peace to an enemy city if the war being waged is optional.
14. **Mitzvah 531/Positive 217:** To break the neck, and follow the process of, the Egla Arufa.

B. Negative:
1. **Mitzvah 492/Negative 288:** Not to plant a tree in the Temple.
2. **Mitzvah 493/Negative 289:** Not to build a Matzeiva, a tall stone structure designated for worship.
3. **Mitzvah 494/Negative 290:** Not to sacrifice an offering that has a blemish.
4. **Mitzvah 496/Negative 291:** Not to argue with the Sages.
5. **Mitzvah 498/Negative 292:** Not to appoint a non-Jew or Ger as a king.
6. **Mitzvah 499/Negative 293:** The prohibition for a king to have many horses.
7. **Mitzvah 500/Negative 294:** Not to return to live in Egypt.
8. **Mitzvah 501/Negative 295:** The prohibition for a king to have too many wives.
9. **Mitzvah 502/Negative 296:** The prohibition for a king to have more gold and silver than necessary.
10. **Mitzvah 504/Negative 297:** The prohibition for the tribe of Levi to receive a portion

in Israel.

11. **Mitzvah 505/Negative 298:** The prohibition for the tribe of Levi to take any spoilage from war.
12. **Mitzvah 510/Negative 299:** The prohibition to perform Kesima-actions to clear one's mind to receive prophetic vision.
13. **Mitzvah 511/Negative 300:** Not to perform magic.
14. **Mitzvah 512/Negative 301:** Not to perform Chaver, which is the saying of charms to mystically cure various maladies.
15. **Mitzvah 513/Negative 302:** Not to seek the service of an Ov.
16. **Mitzvah 514/Negative 303:** Not to seek the service of a Yidoni.
17. **Mitzvah 515/Negative 304:** Not to seek to exhume the spirit of the dead.
18. **Mitzvah 517/Negative 305:** Not to say a false prophesy in name of G-d.
19. **Mitzvah 518/Negative 306:** Not to prophesize in name of idolatry.
20. **Mitzvah 519/Negative 307:** Not to fear a false prophet, and not to fear killing him.
21. **Mitzvah 521/Negative 308:** Not to have mercy on a murderer, or one who injured another.
22. **Mitzvah 522/Negative 309:** Not to steal property by changing the line of the border.
23. **Mitzvah 523/Negative 310:** Not to accept the testimony of a single witness.
24. **Mitzvah 525/Negative 311:** Not to fear the enemy during war.
25. **Mitzvah 528/Negative 312:** Not to allow any soul of the seven Canaanite nations to live.
26. **Mitzvah 529/Negative 313:** Not to destroy trees that surrounds a city under siege.
27. **Mitzvah 531/Negative 314:** Not to cultivate the channel where the Egla Arufa was killed.

First Aliyah

1. **Appointing honest judges and police:**
   - You shall appoint judges and police in all your cities. The judges are to judge righteously and may not take bribes, as bribes blinds the eyes of the wise. You shall pursue justice so that you live and inherit the land.

2. **Miscellaneous commandments:**
   - Tree in Temple: You shall not plant a tree for idol worship or any tree near G-d's altar.
   - Monument: You shall not build a Matzeiva, monument, which G-d despises.

Chapter 17

- Offering with blemish: You shall not sacrifice an offering that has a blemish, as this is an abomination for G-d.
- Death penalty for idol worshipers: If you find a man or woman who is an idol worshiper, then you shall investigate the matter appropriately and if it is found to be true the person is to be killed. He is to be removed from your city and stoned to death.
- Two witnesses: One may only be put to death if there are two witnesses to the crime. One may not accept testimony from one witness to kill a man. The witnesses are to be the first to kill the guilty one, and the remainder of the nation is to be last.

- <u>To listen to the words of the supreme court</u>: If a certain matter of judgment in Torah law is beyond your understanding then you shall go to the area chosen by G-d, and address the issue to the priests and Levites and judges of those times and they will instruct you as to the ruling. You must obey their teachings and directives and not swerve to the right or left. One who does not obey them will be put to death.

Second Aliyah

3. **Mitzvot relating to a king:**
   - When you arrive onto the promised land, you are to appoint a king over you like all the other nations. You are to appoint a king from whom G-d has chosen. One may not appoint a non-Jew, or Ger, as a king.
   - <u>Horses</u>: The king may not have too many horses, so he does not return the nation to Egypt.
   - <u>Wives</u>: The king may not have too many wives so that his heart not go astray.
   - <u>Wealth</u>: The king may not have too much gold and silver.
   - <u>Sefer Torah</u>: When the king sits on his throne he is to write two copies of his own personal Sefer Torah. It is to be with him, and he is to read from it for his entire life in order so that he follows the commands. In order so his heart does not become haughty and so he may merit his children to reign under him.

Chapter 18
Third Aliyah

4. **Mitzvot relating to the Levites and Kohanim:**
   - <u>Inheritance</u>: The tribe of Levi shall not receive a portion in Israel. His portion is the sacrifices of G-d.
   - <u>The arm, jaw, and stomach presents</u>: The Kohen receives the rights towards the arm, jaw (including the tongue) and stomach of a slaughtered animal of the people, whether oxen or sheep. One is to give it to the Kohen.
   - <u>Teruma</u>: The Kohen is to be given the first of your grain, wine, and oil [i.e. Teruma Gedola].
   - <u>Sheering of sheep</u>: One is to give the Kohen the first sharing of wool from the sheep as G-d has chosen him from amongst your tribes to serve Him.

Fourth Aliyah

- The [Kohanim who are] Levites are to set up shifts and rotations of service in the Temple and they may eat portions of the Sacrifices that are designated for them.

5. **Mitzvot relating to not resemble the Canaanite nations:**
   - Upon entering the Promised Land you shall not learn from their abominations.
   - <u>Idolatry of Moleich</u>: You shall not pass your sons and daughters through the fire.
   - <u>Divination and witchcraft</u>: You shall not practice Kesima/divination, Meonein, superstitions, or sorcery. You may not perform Chaver/Charms. You may not seek the service of an Ov. Not to seek the service of a Yidoni. You may not consult the dead. All the above are abominations for which the nations were banished from the land. Be wholehearted with G-d.

Fifth Aliyah

6. Mitzvot relating to a Navi:

- The gentile nations need to turn to Meoninim and Kosmin for future guidance. However, G-d gave the Jewish people the prophets in their place [as the Shekhinah resides on the prophets and the Urim Vetumim]. G-d will bring to you a prophet from your midst who is similar to me, and you shall listen to him.

- You asked G-d by Horeb not to hear G-d's voice directly lest you die. G-d agreed with you and told me that He would establish for you a prophet through whom I shall speak. One who does not listen to the words of the prophet who speaks in My name, I shall hold him accountable.

- <u>A false prophet</u>: A prophet who speaks not in My name, and one who speaks in the name of idolatry, is to be killed.

- <u>How to tell if one is a false prophet</u>: Now, if you ask yourselves how will you know who is a false or true prophet, if the matter that he predicted does not come true, he is a false prophet. Do not fear him.

Chapter 19

7. Mitzvot relating to city of refuge:

- Upon arrival to Israel and the eventual conquest and inheritance, three cities of refuge [i.e. Arei Miklat] are to be established. Each city is to be placed in an equal distance from each other and spread out in the land for a murderer to seek refuge in. The refuge city is meant for an accidental murderer, such as one who accidently killed while wood chopping. He is to seek refuge from the relative of the victim who may kill him.

- <u>Building an additional three cities</u>: When G-d expands your borders, you are to build another three cities.

- <u>An intentional murderer</u>: An intentional murderer cannot seek refuge in the city and he is to be extradited and killed. You are not to have mercy on him.

Sixth Aliyah

8. Miscellaneous Mitzvot:

- <u>Stealing property</u>: Do not steal another's property by changing the line of the border.

- <u>Witnesses</u>: One may not accept the testimony of a single witness for any sin. Testimony is to be accepted only with two to three witnesses.

- <u>Eid Zomeim-False witnesses</u>: If false witnesses testify against someone and the judges discover their falsehood, one is to do to the witnesses just like they desired to do to their victim.

Chapter 20

9. Laws relating to war:

- <u>Not to fear the enemy during war</u>: When you leave to war and see horses and a great nation, do not fear them, as G-d is with you.

- <u>The speech of the war appointed Kohen</u>: The appointed Kohen is to talk to you and encourage you not to fear the enemy, as G-d will wage battle for you.

- <u>Exemptions from battle</u>: The officers are to speak and announce to the children of Israel that all those who are engaged to be married, built a home, or planted a vineyard, are to return. They are to also say that those who fear [the battle or their sin] are to return home and not cause the hearts of their comrades to be fearful as well.

Seventh Aliyah

- <u>Offering ultimatum of peace</u>: When you approach a city to wage war against them, you shall offer them the option of surrender and peace. If they agree, they will be subjugated to you for a tax and slavery.
- <u>If they refuse peace</u>: If they should refuse the offer of peace, every male is to be killed and only the women and children and cattle are to remain. However, from the Canaanite nations, not one soul is allowed to survive.
- <u>Not to destroy fruit trees</u>: One may not destroy a fruit tree even when placing siege onto a city, as man is a tree of the field.

Chapter 21

10. The Mitzvah of Egla Arufa:

- If a murder victim is found on your land and it is unknown who killed him, the elders and judges must go out and measure to which city it is closest in distance.
- <u>The calf</u>: Whichever city is closest, the elders of that city must bring a calf who has never done work or been pulled with a yoke, to a valley that has never been cultivated. The back of calf's neck is to be broken in the valley.
- All the elders of that city are to wash their hands over the calf in the valley, and state that they were not involved in the murder and did not witness it. They are to pray to G-d to atone for the spilled blood.

Parashat Ki Teitzei
Verses: 110 [Siman:עלי]
Haftorah: Isaiah 54:1-10

Number of Mitzvot:
There are a total of **Seventy-Four** Mitzvot in Parashat Ki Teitzei; **Twenty-seven** positive commands and **Forty-seven** negative commands. The following are the commands in the order listed by the Sefer Hachinuch.

A. Positive:
1. **Mitzvah 532/Positive 218:** To act with the Yefat Toar according to the instructions given in the Torah.
2. **Mitzvah 535/Positive 219:** To hang those who are liable for capital punishment of death by hanging.
3. **Mitzvah 537/Positive 220:** To bury those hung on the same day.
4. **Mitzvah 538/Positive 221:** To return lost objects to their rightful owner.
5. **Mitzvah 540/Positive 222:** To help load one's friend's animal.
6. **Mitzvah 545/Positive 223:** The Mitzvah of Shiluach Hakein, to send away the mother bird.
7. **Mitzvah 546/Positive 224:** To make a fence around a roof and remove any danger from others.
8. **Mitzvah 552/Positive 225:** To be Mikadesh/consecrate a woman prior to marriage.
9. **Mitzvah 553/Positive 226:** To remain married forever to a wife whom one was Motzi Shem Ra.
10. **Mitzvah 555/Positive 227:** To stone one who had relations with a Naarah, girl who is engaged to be married.
11. **Mitzvah 557/Positive 228:** That a rapist of a young virgin [i.e. Naarah Betula] must marry her and give her father money.
12. **Mitzvah 566/Positive 229:** To designate an area for doing one's needs at a time of battle.
13. **Mitzvah 567/Positive 230:** For every soldier to carry a shovel with which he can dig and cover when he does his needs.
14. **Mitzvah 573/Positive 231:** To take interest from gentiles when giving them a loan.
15. **Mitzvah 575/Positive 232:** To fulfill one's vows.
16. **Mitzvah 576/Positive 233:** To allow a worker to eat the food that he is working with.
17. **Mitzvah 579/Positive 234:** To divorce one's wife with a document of divorce.
18. **Mitzvah 582/Positive 235:** To rejoice one's wife for the first year of marriage and not go to war.
19. **Mitzvah 587/Positive 236:** To return a collateral to the owner when he needs it.
20. **Mitzvah 588/Positive 237:** To pay a worker on time.
21. **Mitzvah 592/Positive 238:** To leave a forgotten bundle in the field for the poor.
22. **Mitzvah 594/Positive 239:** To give lashes for certain sins.
23. **Mitzvah 598/Positive 240:** The Mitzvah of a levirate marriage.
24. **Mitzvah 599/Positive 241:** The Mitzvah of Halitza.
25. **Mitzvah 600/Positive 242:** To kill a potential murderer.

26. **Mitzvah 603/Positive 243:** To remember the acts of Amalek.
27. **Mitzvah 604/Positive 244:** To destroy Amalek.

B. Negative:
1. **Mitzvah 533/Negative 315:** Not to sell a Yefat Toar.
2. **Mitzvah 534/Negative 316:** Not to make a Yefat Toar work in slavery.
3. **Mitzvah 536/Negative 317:** Not to allow one who was hung to remain on the tree.
4. **Mitzvah 539/Negative 318:** Not to ignore the return of a lost object.
5. **Mitzvah 541/Negative 319:** Not to ignore helping the fallen animal of a friend.
6. **Mitzvah 542/Negative 320:** The prohibition for a woman to wear the clothing of a man [i.e. Beged Ish].
7. **Mitzvah 543/Negative 321:** The prohibition for a man to wear the clothing of a woman [i.e. Beged Isha].
8. **Mitzvah 544/Negative 322:** Not to take the birds with its chicks or eggs.
9. **Mitzvah 547/Negative 323:** Not to ignore a public safety hazard and rather to get rid of it.
10. **Mitzvah 548/Negative 324:** Not to plant a mix breed of grains and grapes.
11. **Mitzvah 549/Negative 325:** Not to eat a mix breed of grains and grapes.
12. **Mitzvah 550/Negative 326:** Not to plow using two different animals.
13. **Mitzvah 551/Negative 327:** Not to wear a mix breed of wool and linen.
14. **Mitzvah 554/Negative 328:** Not to divorce a woman who one slandered.
15. **Mitzvah 556/Negative 329:** Not punish one who was forced to sin.
16. **Mitzvah 558/Negative 330:** Not to divorce a woman whom one raped and then married.
17. **Mitzvah 559/Negative 331:** The prohibition for one with damaged reproductive organs to marry a Jewess.
18. **Mitzvah 560/Negative 332:** The prohibition for a Mamzer to marry a Jewess.
19. **Mitzvah 561/Negative 333:** The prohibition for an Amonite/Moabite male convert to marry a Jewess.
20. **Mitzvah 562/Negative 334:** Not to ever make peace with Amon/Moab.
21. **Mitzvah 563/Negative 335:** Not to prevent an Edomite convert from marrying a Jewess in the third generation.
22. **Mitzvah 564/Negative 336:** Not to prevent a third-generation Egyptian convert from marrying a Jewess.
23. **Mitzvah 565/Negative 337:** The prohibition for an impure person to enter into the Levite encampment.
24. **Mitzvah 568/Negative 338:** Not to force a run-away slave to return from Israel to his master in the Diaspora.
25. **Mitzvah 569/Negative 339:** Not to oppress a slave who ran away to Israel.
26. **Mitzvah 570/Negative 340:** Not to have relations with a woman without Chuppah and Kiddushin.
27. **Mitzvah 571/Negative 341:** Not to offer an offering that was the payment of a harlot, or that was given in exchange of a dog.
28. **Mitzvah 572/Negative 342:** Not to give/take interest by a loan between Jews
29. **Mitzvah 574/Negative 343:** Not to delay bringing a voluntary offering.
30. **Mitzvah 577/Negative 344:** The prohibition for a worker to take more food than

allowed under law.

31. **Mitzvah 578/Negative 345:** The prohibition for a worker to eat on the job.
32. **Mitzvah 580/Negative 346:** Not to remarry an ex-wife who remarried.
33. **Mitzvah 581/Negative 347:** The prohibition for a groom to leave home the first year of marriage.
34. **Mitzvah 583/Negative 348:** Not to take food vessels as collateral.
35. **Mitzvah 584/Negative 349:** Not to remove the skin rash of Tzara'at from the area.
36. **Mitzvah 585/Negative 350:** Not to enter the home of a debtor to take collateral from him.
37. **Mitzvah 586/Negative 351:** Not to abstain from returning the collateral to the debtor upon him needing it.
38. **Mitzvah 589/Negative 352:** Not to accept testimony of a relative.
39. **Mitzvah 590/Negative 353:** The prohibition for a judge to twist the judgment of an orphan or convert.
40. **Mitzvah 591/Negative 354:** The prohibition to take collateral from a widow.
41. **Mitzvah 593/Negative 355:** Not to take the forgotten bundles left in the field.
42. **Mitzvah 595/Negative 356:** Not to give more lashes than instructed.
43. **Mitzvah 596/Negative 357:** Not to muzzle an animal while it works in the field.
44. **Mitzvah 597/Negative 358:** The prohibition for a Yevama [widow of deceased brother] to marry anyone else other than her Yavam [i.e. brother in-law].
45. **Mitzvah 601/Negative 360:** Not to have mercy on a potential murderer.
46. **Mitzvah 602/Negative 361:** Not to own false weights and measurements.
47. **Mitzvah 605/Negative 362:** Not to forget the actions of Amalek

First Aliyah

1. **The laws of a Yefas Toar [i.e. beautiful captive of war]:**
   - When you go to war against your enemies and G-d gives them into your hands and you capture a captive, the following laws are to be followed:
   - <u>Shave head, grow hair, and mourn</u>: If you see a beautiful woman during war that you wish to take as a wife, you are to bring her into your home and shave her head and have her grow her nails. She is to remove her [beautiful] clothing that she wore when taken captive. She is to sit in your home and mourn her parents for a month.
   - Afterwards, you may be intimate with her and take her as a wife. If, however, you do not desire her, then she is to be sent out free. She may not be sold, or work, as a slave.

2. **Inheritance of a firstborn -The son of a beloved wife versus the son of a hated wife:**
   - If a man has two wives, one loved and the second hated, and each begot him a son, the eldest son, the firstborn, is to receive a double portion of the inheritance. One may not remove the double portion from the firstborn son born to the hated wife, and instead grant it to the younger son born to the beloved wife.
   - The firstborn is to receive a double portion of all one's assets, as he is the first of his father's strength and that is his right as firstborn son.

3. **Ben Sorer Umorer-The rebellious son:**
   o If a man has a son who is rebellious and does not listen to his father or mother despite being disciplined by them, then the son is to be brought by the parents to the city gates, to the city elders. The son is to be stoned by the entire city.

Second Aliyah

4. **Miscellaneous Mitzvot:**
   - <u>Hanging and Burying a corpse</u>: If a man received the capital punishment of hanging, his corpse is not to be left hanging on the tree [past sundown]. He is to be buried that day.

Chapter 22

   - <u>Returning lost objects</u>: If you see a lost animal, or garment, or any lost item of a friend, you shall not overlook it and rather you are to return it to the owner. If you do not know the identity of its owner, it shall remain by you until its owner is discovered.
   - <u>Helping load the donkey of a friend</u>: Do not ignore the fallen donkey or ox of your friend, rather you are to help lift him.
   - <u>Beged Isha/Ish-Crossdressing</u>: A woman may not wear the garments of a man and a man may not wear the garments of a woman. It is an abomination to G-d.
   - <u>Sending away the mother bird</u>: If you happen upon a nest with a bird and chicks or eggs, and the mother is crouching over them, then do not take the mother with the children. Rather, send the mother away and then take the children. G-d will grant you long life for fulfilling this command.

Third Aliyah

5. **Miscellaneous Mitzvot:**
   - <u>Fences</u>: When you build a new home, you are to make a fence around the roof and not cause blood to spill in your home.
   - <u>Kilayim-Hybrids & crossbreeds</u>: Do not crossbreed your vineyard by sowing the grapes and grains in close proximation to each other. Do not plow with [two different species of animals, such as] an ox and donkey. Do not wear Shatnez, which is wool and linen woven together.
   - <u>Tzitzis fringes</u>: Tie for yourselves Tzitzis fringes on the four corners of your garments.
   - <u>False claims of adultery-Motzi Shem Ra</u>: If a man marries a woman and despises her and falsely slanders his wife saying that she committed adultery, then after the matter is verified to be false, he is to be fined 100 Kesef and cannot ever divorce his wife.
   - <u>Adultery</u>: If, however, it is true that she committed adultery, then both her and the adulterer are to be killed. If she was a young married girl, then she is to be stoned by the entrance of her father's home. You are to eradicate the evil from amongst your midst.
   - <u>Seduction</u>: If a young Halachically engaged virgin [i.e. Naarah Meurasa] was found in the city by a man and he laid with her [and she did not protest, despite having ability to do so, without being harmed] then both he and the girl are to be killed through stoning.
   - <u>Rape</u>: If, however, the married girl was found in the field and was overcome and raped by a man [against her will, without ability to protest] then only he, the rapist, is killed. If, however, the young girl whom he raped was single, then the rapist is to give her father fifty silver Shekalim and he is to marry her, and cannot divorce her for all his days.

Chapter 23

- <u>Forbidden relations and marriages-Fathers wife, Saris, Mamzer, Amoni</u>: One may not marry his father's wife. A person with an injury in the reproductive system [i.e. Saris/impotent] may not marry into the congregation of G-d [a Jewess]. A Mamzer may not marry into the congregation of G-d [i.e. a Jewess] even in the 10th generation. An Amonite/Moabite convert may not marry into the congregation of G-d [i.e. a Jewess] even in the 10th generation, forever. This is because they did not offer you bread and water when you were traveling from Egypt, as well as because they hired Balaam to curse you. G-d did not listen to Balaam and turned the curse into a blessing, as G-d loves you.

- You may not make peace with Amon/Moab all your days.

Fourth Aliyah

6. **Miscellaneous Mitzvot:**

- <u>Edomites and Egyptian</u>: Do not abhor Edomites as they are your brother, and you are not to abhor Egyptians as you lived in their land. The children of a 3rd generation Edomite or Egyptian convert may enter the congregation of G-d [i.e. marry a Jewess].

- <u>An impure person may not enter into the Levite encampment</u>: One who is impure due to nocturnal emission must exit the camp. Towards evening he is to immerse in water and may then enter the camp after sundown.

- <u>Tzoa and Erva-Burying one's excrement</u>: A set place outside the camp is to be established for one to do his needs. Every soldier is to carry a shovel with his weaponry which will be used to cover his needs that were made outside of the camp. G-d is found within the encampment and it therefore must remain holy. He should not see a shameful matter [i.e. Erva] and turn away from you.

- <u>Slaves</u>: One is not to force a run-away slave to return [from Israel] to his master [in the Diaspora]. One is not to oppress a slave [who ran away to Israel].

- <u>Prostitution</u>: A man or woman may not be promiscuous [and work as a prostitute]. You shall not offer an offering that was the Esnan payment of a Zona, or was in exchange of a dog. Both are an abomination to G-d.

- <u>Interest</u>: You may not take interest from a loan to a Jew so that G-d can bless you in all your work. However, you may take interest from a loan to a gentile.

- <u>To fulfill vows</u>: When you make a vow to G-d, you shall not delay paying it, as G-d will demand it from you and you will carry iniquity. If, however, you abstain from making a vow, you will not have a sin. You are to guard your word.

Fifth Aliyah

7. **Miscellaneous Mitzvot:**

- <u>Feeding workers on the job</u>: When a worker comes to harvest the grapes, he may eat from it as he desires, but he may not fill up vessels with it. Likewise, when a worker comes to harvest the grains, he may eat from it with his hands, but he may not cut it with a sickle.

Chapter 24

- <u>Divorce</u>: When a man takes a woman in marriage, and he dislikes her due to discovering a shameful matter, then he is to write her a bill of divorce. She is to leave his home and may marry another man. If the other man hates her and also divorces her, or if he dies, her first husband may not remarry his ex-wife, being she became defiled with another man. This is an abomination to G-d.

Sixth Aliyah

8. **Miscellaneous Mitzvot:**
   - First year of marriage: When a man marries a new wife, he is to be with her for the first year and is not to be conscripted into the army. He is to rejoice with his wife which he married.
   - Collateral: One may not take food vessels as collateral.
   - Kidnappers: If a kidnapper of Jews is found, and he enslaves and sells the victim, he is to be killed.
   - Guarding the Tzara'at: "Guard the Tzara'at very much and follow all the directives of the Kohanim, the Levites, as I have commanded. Remember what G-d did to Miriam when she left Egypt."
   - Laws of collateral: When someone owes you a debt, you may not enter his home to take collateral. You must stand outside, and he is to bring it to you. If he is a pauper, you may not go to sleep with his item (in your possession) and are rather to return it to him prior to sundown.

Seventh Aliyah

9. **Miscellaneous Mitzvot:**
   - Paying a worker on time: Do not cheat a poor employee. You are to pay him the same day, prior to sundown, otherwise he may call to G-d and you will carry sin.
   - Witnesses: Fathers and sons are not to die based on [testimony of] each other.
   - Orphans and widows: A judge is not to twist the judgment of an orphan or convert and one is not to take their garment.
   - Harvest donations to the poor: When you harvest your field and you forget a bundle in the field, do not return to take it. It shall be left to the convert, orphan, and widow in order so G-d bless you in all your actions. When you harvest your olive or grape orchard, do not remove all the olives and grapes from the tree, it shall be left for the convert, orphan, and widow. Remember that you were slaves in Egypt and therefore G-d has commanded you in this.

Chapter 25

- Not to give more lashes than required: When two people have an argument and the guilty is found guilty, then the judge is to give him lashes in accordance to his wickedness. He is to be stricken [close to] 40 times. You may not give him more lashes lest he become degraded before you.
- Muzzling animals: You may not muzzle an ox while it is threshing.
- Levirate marriage: When a brother dies and leaves a wife without children, she shall marry her husband's brother. The child will be born on behalf of his brother who died, and his name will not be obliterated from Israel.
- Halitza: If the brother does not desire to marry his brother's wife, then she is to go to the elders by the gates and tell them that her brother in-law does not wish to marry her and establish a name for his dead brother. The brother is to be summoned and spoken to, and if he does not desire to marry her, he is to proclaim it. His sister-in-law is to then

approach him before all the elders, and remove his shoe from his feet, and spit in front of him, saying that so is done to whom who does not wish to establish a home for his brother. His name will be called amongst Israel "Beth Chalutz Hanaal."

- <u>Woman injures a man</u>: If two men are fighting and the wife of one of the men grabs the other man in his private area, she is to [figuratively] have her palm cut off [by paying a fine].

- <u>Not to own false measurements</u>: You may not own in your pockets measurements stones which are inaccurate. You must have accurate scales, so you live long on the promised land. It is an abomination before G-d to cheat in measurements.

- <u>Remembering Amalek</u>: Remember what Amalek did to you on the journey when he killed the weak amongst you and he did not fear G-d. When G-d clears you of all your enemies and gives you the promised land, you are to obliterate the memory of Amalek. Do not forget!

Parashat Ki Tavo

Verses: 122 [Siman: לְעַבְדִּיי]
Haftorah: Isaiah 60:1-22

Number of Mitzvot:

There are a total of **Six** Mitzvot in Parashat Ki Tavo; **Three** positive commands and **Three** negative commands. The following are the commands in the order listed by the Sefer Hachinuch.

A. Positive:

1. **Mitzvah 606/Positive 245:** To read certain verses when bringing the Bikurim
2. **Mitzvah 607/Positive 246:** To confess before G-d that the tithes were removed from one's food products.
3. **Mitzvah 611/Positive 247:** To emulate G-d in all our actions.

B. Negative:

1. **Mitzvah 608/Negative 363:** Not to eat the second tithe [i.e. Maaser Sheiyni] in a state of Aninus mourning.
2. **Mitzvah 609/Negative 364:** Not to eat the second tithe [i.e. Maaser Sheiyni] in a state of impurity.
3. **Mitzvah 610/Negative 365:** Not to spend the money of the second tithe [i.e. Maaser Sheiyni] for non-food purposes.

Chapter 26
First Aliyah

1. **First fruits [i.e. Bikurim]:**
   - When you enter Israel and settle in the land, you shall take all the first fruits of the land in a basket to the area that G-d chose to dwell [i.e. Jerusalem] and bring it to the Kohen. The Kohen is to take the basket and place it before the altar of G-d.
   - The declaration of the pilgrim: He is to declare before the Kohen "An Aramean would have destroyed my father and we descended to Egypt few in number and then became a great nation. The Egyptians enslaved our ancestors and afflicted us with hard labor. We screamed to G-d our G-d and G-d saw our suffering and heard our screams. He took us out of Egypt with a mighty hand, with miracles and wonders and brought us to this land, a land of milk and honey. Now, I have brought the first fruits of the land which G-d has given me." You shall place it before G-d and bow to Him. You shall rejoice with all the good that G-d has granted you, you and the Levite and convert amongst you.

Second Aliyah

2. **Mitzvat Viduiy Maaser-Confessing the Maaser tithing:**
   - When you complete the tithing of all your produce in the third year of Maaser, you are to distribute [the tithes] to the convert, the orphan and widow, and they are to eat and be satiated. You shall confess before G-d and say "I have removed the Maasros from the home and distributed it to the Levi, convert, orphan and widow, just as you commanded

me. I have not transgressed your command and have not forgotten. I have not eaten it in a state of Aninus mourning or impurity. I have listened to the word of G-d and did all that He commanded. Gaze down from your Holy abode, from heaven, and bless Israel and the promised land that you have given us."

Chapter 27
Third Aliyah
3. Moses encourages the children of Israel to follow the Mitzvot:
- On this day, G-d has commanded you to perform all of his commands, and you are to guard it with all your heart and soul. You have chosen G-d today as a G-d for you and G-d has distinguished you from amongst all the other nations, to follow his Mitzvot and to make you highest above all the other nations, a Holy people.

Fourth Aliyah
4. Instructions to write the Torah on stones and build an altar of stone:
- Moses and the elders of the Jewish people commanded the nation to guard the Mitzvot. On the day that you pass the Jordan to the promised land, you are to set up large stones [by the Jordan] and cover them with plaster and write the entire Torah on them. [A second set of] stones are to be erected by Mount Ebal. You are to build there an altar for G-d. The altar is to be built of whole stones and is to be used for sacrifices. Iron is not to be used to hew the stones. You are to offer sacrifices there and rejoice there before G-d your G-d. You are to write on the stones the entire Torah, well clarified.

Fifth Aliyah
5. The blessings and curses on Mount Gerizim and Mount Ebal:
- <u>The tribes on Mount Gerizim for blessing</u>: Moses commanded the Jewish people that day saying: After passing the Jordon, on the side of blessing on Mount Gerizim will stand Simeon, Levi, Judah, Issachar, Joseph and Benjamin.
- <u>The tribes on Mount Ebal for curses</u>: On the side of curse on Mount Ebal will stand Reuben, Gad, Asher, Zebulun, Dan, Naftali.
- The Levites are to stand and proclaim to the Jewish people in a loud voice, the following:

6. The curses:
- Cursed is the man who makes idols. The entire nation is to answer Amen.
- Cursed is the man who degrades his parents. The entire nation is to answer Amen.
- Cursed is the man who moves back the boundary of his friend's property. The entire nation is to answer Amen.
- Cursed is the man who fools the blind. The entire nation is to answer Amen.
- Cursed is the man who perverts the judgement of an orphan or widow in a court case. The entire nation is to answer Amen.
- Cursed is the man who sleeps with his father's wife. The entire nation is to answer Amen.
- Cursed is the man who sleeps with an animal. The entire nation is to answer Amen.
- Cursed is the man who sleeps with his sister. The entire nation is to answer Amen.
- Cursed is the man who sleeps with his mother in-law. The entire nation is to answer Amen.
- Cursed is the man who discreetly hits his friend. The entire nation is to answer Amen.

- Cursed is the man who takes money to kill the innocent. The entire nation is to answer Amen.
- Cursed is the man who does not fulfil the Torah. The entire nation is to answer Amen.

Chapter 28

7. The blessings

- If you listen and follow all of G-d's commands He will elevate you from amongst all the nations of the world and you will receive all the following blessings:
- You will be blessed in the city and field.
- Your children and animals and land will be blessed.
- Your fruits and dry goods will be blessed.
- You will be blessed when you enter and when you leave.

Sixth Aliyah

- Your enemies will flee from you. They will approach you on one road and flee in seven directions.
- G-d will bless the storehouses and all your actions.
- All the nations will see that the name of G-d hovers over you and they will fear you.
- The heavens will give rain at their proper time.
- You will lend the nations and will not need to borrow from them.
- G-d will place you at the head and not the tail, and you will be only on top and not on bottom.

8. The curses:

- If you do not listen to G-d and his Torah, all the following curses will befall you:
- You will be cursed in the city and field.
- Your fruits and dry goods will be cursed.
- Your children and animals and land will be cursed.
- You will be cursed when you enter and when you leave.
- You will be stricken with curse in everything you do until you are destroyed.
- You will be stricken with disease until you are destroyed.
- You will be stricken with fever and illness until you are destroyed.
- The heavens will be like copper and the earth like iron.
- The heavens will rain dust and ash until you are destroyed.
- You will flee from your enemies in seven different directions.
- Your corpses will be food for the birds and animals.
- You will be stricken with Egyptian boils and hemorrhoids that cannot be healed.
- You will be stricken with insanity.
- You will be like a blind man who can't see and nothing you do will be successful.
- You will be robbed and swindled without anyone to help you.
- You will marry, and another man will take your wife.
- You will build a house and vineyard and another man will live there.
- Your cattle will be taken by the enemy.
- Your children will be taken captives by other nations.

- Other nations will capture all your work and use it.
- You will go insane from witnessing all this.
- You will be struck with boils throughout your entire body.
- You will be taken captives by other nations and serve idolatry there.
- You will be a mockery amongst all the nations.
- Locusts will eat your produce.
- Worms will eat your vineyard.
- Your olives will fail to produce oil.
- Your children will not be yours as they will be taken captive.
- Your trees and produce will be inherited by locusts.
- The nations will be elevated, and you will be demoted.
- You will borrow from them and they will not borrow from you.
- You will be a tail and they will be a head.
- You will receive all these curses until you are destroyed.
- This is all coming upon you due to the fact that you did not serve G-d with joy of all the abundance that you have.
- You will work hard for your enemy.
- G-d will bring upon you a foreign nation who has no mercy.
- They will take all your crops and belongings.
- Your fortresses will be taken down.
- You will eat the flesh of your children.
- The pampered amongst you will have to do the most gross of acts.
- You will be stricken with other illnesses and tragedies not written in this book.
- You will remain very few instead of the many that you once were, being you did not listen to G-d. Just as G-d rejoiced by doing good to you, so too He will rejoice to destroy you.
- You will be scattered across the earth and serve other gods. You will not be tranquil there. In the morning you will say, "If only it was the night before" and in the evening you will say "If only it was the morning."
- You will be returned to Egypt on ships and sold as slaves, but no one will buy you.
- These are the words of the covenant that G-d commanded Moses to make with the Jewish people, aside for the covenant that was made in Horeb.

Chapter 29
Seventh Aliyah
9. Moses recounts the miracles witnessed by the children of Israel:
- Moses called to the Jewish people and said to them "You have seen all that G-d has done to Egypt, and to Pharaoh, his servants and all his land. You saw all the great miracles and wonders. You have not been given by G-d a heart to know and an eye to see and an ear to hear until this day. You have traveled the desert for 40 years and saw that your clothing and shoes did not get worn out. You did not eat bread, and wine and beer you did not drink, [and rather you lived off the Mun].
- Sihon the king of Cheshbon, and Og the king of Bashan, came against us in war and we smote them. We took their land and gave it as an inheritance to Reuben, Gad, and half of Manasseh. You are to guard this covenant in order so you will succeed in all that you do.

Parashat Nitzavim

Verses: 40 [Siman:לבבו]
Haftorah: Isaiah 61:10-63:9

Number of Mitzvot:
There are no Mitzvot in Parashat Nitzavim.

The Portion Theme:
Moses enters the Jewish people into a covenant with G-d and warns them of the dangers of getting involved in sinful behavior.

First Aliyah

1. **The covenant:**
   - All the Jewish people are present: [Moses gathered the Jewish people before G-d on the day of his passing and told them] You are all standing before G-d today to pass into a covenant of G-d and His oath. All the Jewish people are here including your heads, tribes, elders, officers, children, wives, converts, wood choppers and water carriers, in order to enter the covenant that G-d will make with you today.

Second Aliyah

   - Purpose of the covenant: The purpose of the covenant is for you to become G-d's nation and G-d become your G-d as he promised your forefathers, Abraham, Isaac and Jacob.
   - Applicable forever: The covenant and oath are binding and applicable not just to those present, but for all future generations, even those not here today.

Third Aliyah

2. **Moses warns the children of Israel against breaking the covenant:**
   - [Moses said to the nation:] "You know what it was like to live amongst the Egyptians, and you passed through other nations [and saw their ways of living]. You saw their abominations, and detestable idols of wood, stone, silver and gold."
   - A warning for the careless sinner: "Perhaps you have amongst you today a man or woman, family or tribe, whose heart swerves from G-d and desires to go serve the idols of the gentiles. Perhaps you have a miscreant growing amongst you who even after hearing these words will say to himself that he can do whatever his heart desires and peace will remain upon him. So, I tell him today, no, I will add to your punishment. G-d will not forgive him, and His wrath and vengeance will smoke against the man, and all of the oaths written in this book will befall him. G-d will obliterate his name from under the heavens. He will be set aside from all of Israel for evil and will receive all the curses written in this book."
   - The curses for not obeying the covenant: Your children and the nations who visit the land will see that the land is plagued and affected with illnesses by G-d. The earth will be scorched with sulfur and salt and will not be able to be sowed or grow produce, just as occurred with Sodom and Gomorrah, Adma and Tzevoim which G-d overturned in His

anger. All the nations will ask why G-d destroyed the earth with such anger and they will be told it is because the Jewish people left the covenant G-d made with their ancestors when He took them out of Egypt. They went and served foreign gods, and therefore He went and brought upon them the curses written in this Sefer. G-d will throw them off their land in anger and fury and displace them into foreign territory.

- The hidden is to G-d while the revealed is to man and his descendants forever, to perform this Torah.

Chapter 30
Fourth Aliyah (Third Aliyah when combined with Vayeilech)

3. G-d comforts the children of Israel that He will return them from exile:
- The children of Israel will do Teshuvah: "After experiencing all the blessings and curses you will take to heart all that has happened and return to G-d and follow His will with all your heart and soul."
- Gathering of exiles: "G-d will then have mercy on you and return you from the exiles, gathering you from all the nations to which you were dispersed. Even if you were dispersed to the end of the heavens, He will gather you and take you from there. He will bring you back to Israel, to the land your ancestors inherited, and you shall inherit it."
- The blessings upon the return from exile: "G-d will benefit you and make you multiply more than your forefathers. G-d will circumcise your hearts and the hearts of your descendants, so you can love Him with all your heart and soul."

Fifth Aliyah (Third Aliyah when combined with Vayeilech)
- The curses that will befall our enemies: G-d will place all the curses of this book onto your enemies who pursued you.
- More blessings: "You will repent and listen to the voice of G-d and perform all of his commands. G-d will make you successful in all your activities, in having children and cattle, and produce. G-d will return to rejoice in you for good, just as He rejoiced with your forefathers."

Sixth Aliyah
4. G-d encourages the children of Israel to keep the Mitzvot:
- "The Torah and Mitzvot are not distanced from you. It is not in the Heavens or across the sea that you need to ask someone to reach there to bring it to you. The Torah is very close to you, to your lips and to your heart to perform it."

Seventh Aliyah (Fourth Aliyah when combined with Vayeilech)
- Freedom of choice to choose life or death: "G-d has given you today [the choice between] good and life and evil and death. If you choose to love Him and follow His will and guard His Mitzvot then you will live and receive His blessings. But, if you lead your heart astray and disobey His commands and serve idolatry, you shall know now that you will be eradicated. You will not last long on the land of inheritance. I call the heaven and earth to witness today that I have given you the path of life and death, blessing and curse, and I instruct you to choose life, so you and your descendants shall live."

Parashat Vayeilech

Verses: 30 [Siman:אנינה]
Haftorah: Isaiah 61:10-63:9
Shabbat Shuva Haftorah: Hosea 14:2-10[1]; Micah 7:18-20

Number of Mitzvot:

There are a total of **Two** Mitzvot in Parashat Vayeilech; **Two** positive commands and **Zero** negative commands. The following are the commands in the order listed by the Sefer Hachinuch.

A. Positive:
1. **Mitzvah 612/Positive 247:** The mitzvah of Hakhel
2. **Mitzvah 613/Positive 248:** To write a Sefer Torah.

Chapter 31
First Aliyah

1. Moses's last day, instructions not to fear conquering Canaan:

- Moses informs that he must step down from leadership: Moses went and spoke the following words to all of the children of Israel: "I am 120 years old today, and I am no longer able to enter and exit [to the Jewish people], and G-d has informed me that I will be unable to cross the Jordan river.

- Conquering the nations of Canaan: G-d will pass before you [to Canaan] and He will destroy the nations from before you, and you shall inherit them. Joshua will lead you into Israel, as G-d has spoken."

Second Aliyah

- "G-d will do onto the nations as He did to Sihon and Og, the Amorite kings, and their land, which He obliterated. G-d will deliver these nations to you, and you shall do with them that which I commanded.

- Not to fear: Be strong, do not fear the gentile's nations as G-d your G-d will be leading you and will not forsake you."

Third Aliyah (Fifth Aliyah when combined with Nitzavim)

- Moses appoints and encourages Joshua: Moses summoned Joshua and said to him in front of all the Jewish people to be strong, as he will lead the Jewish people into the promised land and conquer it. "G-d will lead you and be with you and will not forsake you. Do not be afraid."

2. Moses gives a Torah scroll to the tribe of Levi:

- Moses wrote this Torah and gave it to the Kohanim who carry the Aron, and to all the elders of Israel.

---

[1] So is followed by Sepharadi and Chabad communities. However, Ashkenazi communities read also from Yoel 2:11-27 and only then read from Micah 7:18-19.

Fourth Aliyah

3. The Mitzvah of Hakhel:

- Moses commanded them as follows: "At the end of the seventh [i.e. Shemita] year, during Sukkot, when all of the children of Israel come [to Jerusalem] to visit G-d, you are to read this Torah before them.
- Gather the men, women, children and converts so that they hear and learn and install fear of G-d in their hearts to perform all of the Torah commands. Their children who are ignorant will hear and learn to fear G-d throughout all the days that you live on earth, on the land that you will inherit."

Fifth Aliyah (Sixth Aliyah when combined with Nitzavim)

4. G-d instructs Moses before his death:

- G-d summons Moses and Joshua: G-d said to Moses: "Your days are limited, and you will soon pass away. Summon Joshua and you and him should stand before Me by the Tent of Meeting and I will command you." Moses and Joshua did as instructed and stood before the Tent of Meeting. G-d appeared in the Tent of Meeting in a pillar of cloud.
- G-d tells Moses the future sins of the Jewish people and their punishments: G-d told Moses that he will soon pass away and the Jewish people will stray after Moses's passing. "They will stray after the foreign deities and they will leave Me and annul My covenant which I made with them. I will be very angry on that day and will forsake them and hide My face from them. They will become prey, and much evil and suffering will befall them. On that day it will be said "All this tragedy is happening to me because I do not have G-d found within my midst." I, G-d, will hide My face from them on that day due to all the evil they did, as they turned to other Gods."

5. G-d commands Moses to write the song of Haazinu:

- "Now, you shall write for yourselves this song and teach it to the Jewish people. Place it on their mouths in order so this song serve as a testimony to them."

Sixth Aliyah (Seventh Aliyah when combined with Nitzavim)

- "I will bring the Jewish people to the promised land, the land of milk and honey, and they will eat to satiation and stray after other gods, breaking My covenant. When tragedy befalls them, this song will be their testimony. This song shall never be forgotten from their offspring." [It will serve as testimony that I forewarned regarding the punishments if they do not guard my words.]
- Moses wrote the song on that day and taught it to the children of Israel. So it was that Moses completed the writing of the Torah until its end.

Seventh Aliyah

6. **Moses instructs the Levites to place the Sefer Torah in the Aron:**

- Moses instructed the tribe of Levi who carry the Aron as follows: "Take this Sefer Torah and place it at the side of the Aron as a testimony. I know the nation's rebellious nature and stubbornness as I witnessed during my leadership and as will occur after my death."

7. **Moses summons the leaders to gather before him and teaches them the song of testimony:**

- Moses asked for all the elders of Israel to gather before him for him to teach them all these words, and called the heaven and earth to bear witness. "I know that the Jewish people will become corrupt after my death and stray away from the commands, and tragedies will befall them in the end of days."
- Moses told this song to all of the Jewish people, until its conclusion.

Parashat Haazinu
Verses: 52 [Siman: כלב]
Haftorah:[1] Samuel 2 22:1-51

Number of Mitzvot:
There are no Mitzvot in Parashat Haazinu.

Chapter 32
First Aliyah

1. The song of Haazinu:
[Moses taught the children of Israel the Haazinu song which consisted of the following points:]
- The heavens and earth are to hear [and bear witness] of my words.
- May my teachings be like rain and dew.
- Praise G-d: When I call the name of G-d bring greatness to His name.
- G-d's Justice: G-d is perfect in His work and all His actions are justified. He is not corrupt.
- Admonishment: How can you act crookedly towards your father who acquired you, who made you and established you?

Second Aliyah
- Remember the days of old and contemplate the past generations. Ask your father and grandfather how G-d separated the nations according to the people of Israel.
- G-d's love for the Jewish people: A portion of G-d is His people and Jacob is the rope of His inheritance. He found him in the desert and guarded him like the pupil of His eye. He acted like an eagle protecting his children. G-d alone did this without any other god.

Third Aliyah
- G-d carried him over the high mountains and fed him the produce of the earth, nursing him with honey and oil from the rocks. Cattle and flock, milk, meat of various animals, and the blood of grapes were given to them.
- Jewish rebelliousness: The Jewish people became fattened and rebelled and deserted G-d. They provoked Him with abominations, slaughtering to demons and foreign entities. You ignored the Rock who gave birth to you and the G-d who brought you out.

Fourth Aliyah
- G-d's punishments to the Jews: G-d will become angry at what He sees, and He will hide His face from them. "Just as they angered Me with a foreign god so too I will anger them with a foreign nation. Fire will burn through My nostrils and consume the land and its produce. Bloated by famine, they will have the teeth of animals sent against them. Outside there will be the sword [of war], and inside will be fear. I will scatter them amongst the nations and obliterate their memory from man. The nations will think this is their doing and not that of G-d. They are a nation bereft of council or understanding.

---

[1] This only applies if Haazinu falls between Yom Kippur and Sukkos, otherwise the Haftorah of Shabbos Shuva is read

Fifth Aliyah

- If they were bright they would understand that it is not possible for one person to chase a thousand, and two people 10,000, unless G-d has sold them.
- Where are the gods whom they worshiped and trusted in, why did they not save them? I am G-d and no other god is with Me. I put to death and bring life and I strike down and heal."

Sixth Aliyah

- G-d's punishments to the gentiles: "I will return vengeance upon My enemies and to those who hate Me. My arrow will become drunk with blood. Let all the nations sing the praise of the Jewish people as He will avenge the death of His servants. He will bring retribution to His enemies and appease His land and His people."

Seventh Aliyah

2. **Moses teaches the song to the Jewish people:**

- Moses came and spoke the words of this song to the Jewish people, him and Joshua Ben Nun. After its conclusion, Moses told the Jewish people to pay close attention to these words of testimony said today, to guard all the words of the Torah. "The Torah is not empty for you, as it is your very life and with it you will lengthen your days on the land that you will inherit."

3. **G-d instructs Moses to ascends the mountain of Nebo:**

- G-d spoke to Moses on the essence of this day saying that he should ascend the mountain of Avarim, mountain of Nebo, which is in the land of Moab, facing Jericho. He should gaze at the land of Canaan which will be given to the children of Israel as an inheritance. "You will die on this mountain, just as Aaron your brother died due to that you transgressed against me with the story of Mei Meriva in Kadesh, and did not sanctify Me amongst the Jewish people. You will see the land but not enter it"

Parashat Vezot Haberachah
Verses: 41[Siman: גאואל]
Haftorah: Joshua 1:1-18

Number of Mitzvot:
There are no Mitzvot in Parashat Vezot Haberachah.

Chapter 33
First Aliyah

1. **The blessing of Moses prior to his death:**
   - The following is the blessing that Moses, the man of G-d, blessed the Jewish people prior to his death.
   - <u>Singing the blessings of all the Jewish people</u>: G-d came from Sinai and gave you the fire of his law [i.e. the Torah]. He has loved the Jewish people. The Torah that Moses commanded is the inheritance of the congregation of Jacob. G-d became king over the Jewish people when their tribes are gathered together.
   - <u>Blessing of Reuben</u>: May Reuben live and multiply to many numbers.
   - <u>Blessing of Judah</u>: May G-d listen to the voice of Judah, and help him against his enemies.

Second Aliyah

- <u>Blessing of Levi</u>: Your Urim and Tumim have been given to the man of kindness whom You have tested. They have guarded your covenant and preserved your command. They will teach the laws to Jacob and its statutes to the Jewish people. They will bring You the Ketores incense and sacrifices. G-d shall bless his possessions and bring success to his work. He will destroy his opponents and not allow his enemies to rise.
- <u>Blessing of Benjamin</u>: Benjamin is a friend of G-d, may he dwell securely by Him. He protects him all day and dwells between his shoulders.

Third Aliyah

- <u>Blessing of Joseph</u>: Joseph's land is blessed by G-d with the delicacies of the heavens, with dew and the depths of waters. With delicacies of the sun and moon, and the mountains and hills. He is a firstborn, an ox, glorified with the horns of a Reim. He will gore the nations.

Fourth Aliyah

- <u>Blessing of Zebulun and Issachar</u>: Zebulun should rejoice in his outings [of business] and Issachar in his tents [of Torah learning]. They will slaughter together offerings on the mountain and benefit from the treasures of the sea and sand.
- <u>Blessing of Gad</u>: Gad dwells like a lion and tears the head and arm of the enemy. He took the first portions [of the land of Sihon and Og] as there is buried the lawgiver [Moses].

Fifth Aliyah

- Blessing of Dan: Dan is a lion cub who springs forth from the Bashan.
- Blessing of Naftali: Naftali is satiated [with all his land desires] and is filled with the blessing of G-d. He inherits the sea and the south.
- Blessing of Asher: Asher is blessed with sons and is pleasing to his brothers. He dips his foot in oil. His locks are iron and copper.
- Praising G-d and Israel: There is no one like the G-d of Yeshurun who rides the heavens.

Sixth Aliyah

- He destroyed the enemy from before you and secures the dwelling of the Jewish people in a land of grain and wine which drips dew. Praised are you Israel, who is like you, a people delivered by G-d who was your shield and sword.

Seventh Aliyah

2. **Moses is shown the land of Israel and the future times:**
   - Moses ascended from the plains of Moab to the summit of the mountain of Nabo. G-d showed him the entire land, from Gilad until Dan, Naftali and the land of Ephraim and Manasseh, the entire land of Judah until the western sea [and until the last day of the resurrection]. He showed him the south and the valley of Jericho, the city of date palms, as far as Tzoar.
   - G-d told Moses that this is the land that was promised to Abraham, Isaac and Jacob be given to their descendants. You saw it with your eyes but you will not enter there.

Chapter 34

3. **Moses passes away:**
   - Moses the servant of G-d passed away in the land of Moab by the mouth of G-d.
   - The burial: G-d buried him in the gorge of the land and no one is aware of his burial place until this very day.
   - His age: Moses was 120 years of age at his passing. His eye did not dim, and his moisture did not leave him.
   - The mourning: The Jewish people mourned Moses's passing in the plains of Moab for thirty days.
   - Joshua the new leader: Joshua Ben Nun was filled with wisdom, as Moses leaned his hands on him and the Jewish people listened to him and followed the instructions G-d commanded Moses.
   - None like Moses: There has never been a prophet amongst the Jewish people like Moses to whom G-d had made Himself known face to face. For all the miracles and wonders which G-d sent him to perform in Egypt, against Pharaoh and his servants, and all his land, and for all the miracles that Moses performed before the eyes of all Israel.

Chazak Chazak Vinitchazek!

Our other Sefarim available on shulchanaruchharav.com, Amazon.com and selected book stores

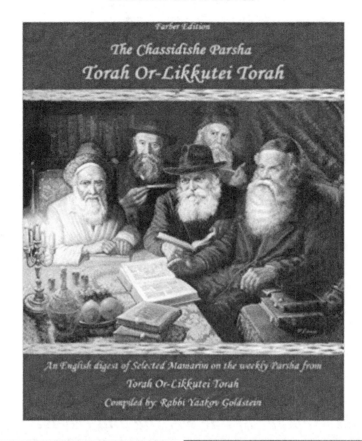

Between Pesach and Shavuos

וספרתם לכם ממחרת השבת

The laws and customs of Counting the Omer, The
Mourning Period, Pesach Sheiyni & Lag Baomer

Compiled by Rabbi Yaakov Goldstein

The Laws & Customs of Shavuos

לקבלת התורה בשמחה ובפנימיות

An English compilation of Halacha, Midrash,
Chassidus & Kabala on the Holiday of Shavuos
Based on Shulchan Aruch Harav Chapter 494 and Chabad Custom
Includes summaries and Hundreds of practical Q & A
Rabbi Yaakov Goldstein

The Laws & Customs of
Rosh Hashanah

An English compilation on the Holiday of Rosh Hashanah based on
the Shulchan Aruch Harav, Chabad custom & Chassidic teachings
Includes Summaries & Hundreds of Practical Q&A
Rabbi Yaakov Goldstein

The Laws & Customs
of Yom Kippur

A digest of laws, customs, Chassidus
& Kabala on the Holiday of Yom Kippur

Compiled by Rabbi Yaakov Goldstein

היה קורא פרק שני ברכות יז.

ולא פריה ורביה ולא משא ומתן ולא קנאה ולא שנאה ולא תחרות אלא צדיקים יושבין ועטרותיהם
בראשיהם ונהנים מזיו השכינה שנאמר יויחזו את האלהים ויאכלו וישתו: גדולה הבטחה שהבטיחן
הקב"ה לנשים יותר מן האנשים שנא' ינשים שאננות קומנה שמענה קולי בנות בוטחות האזנה אמרתי
א"ל רב לר' חייא נשים במאי זכיין יבאקרויי בנייהו לבי כנישתא ובאתנויי גברייהו בי רבנן ונטרין לגברייהו
עד דאתו מבי רבנן. כי הוו מפטרי רבנן מבי ר' אמי ואמרי לה מבי ר' חנינא אמרי ליה הכי עולמך תראה בחייך
ואחריתך לחיי העולם הבא ותקותך לדור דורים לבך יהגה תבונה פיך ידבר חכמות ולשונך ירחיש רננות
עפעפיך יישירו נגדך עיניך יאירו במאור תורה ופניך יזהירו כזוהר הרקיע שפתותיך יביעו דעת וכליותיך

Rav said to Rav Chiya
*"With what do women receive merit [of learning Torah]? Through escorting their children to
the Talmud Torah, and assisting their husbands in learning Torah, and waiting for their
husbands to return from the Beth Midrash"*

*This Sefer is dedicated to my dear wife whose continuous support and sharing of
joint goals in spreading Torah and Judaism have allowed this Sefer to become a
reality.*

*May G-d grant her and our children much
success and blessing in all their endeavors*

שיינא שרה ליבא בת חיה ראשא
&
מושקא פריידא
שניאור זלמן
דבורה לאה
נחמה דינה
מנוחה רחל
חנה
שטערנא מרים
שלום דובער
חוה אסתר
בתשבע

In memory of our dear and beloved father

Eliezer Goldstein

אליעזר בן יעקב ישראל ז"ל

Aba always wanted to spread words of truth and Torah to the four corners of the earth! May this book authored by your son and my brother reach as many people as possible. We all miss you and love you and know that you are very proud of us, as you smile down on us from heaven.

May his soul be bound in the bonds of eternal life and his memory ever be for a blessing

ת.נ.צ.ב.ה

Dedicated with much love by his son,
Abraham (Avi) David Goldstein

In memory of

Gladys Szerer

שרה בת שלום ז"ל

May her soul be bound in the bonds of eternal life and her memory ever be for a blessing

ת.נ.צ.ב.ה

Dedicated by
Rabbi Roberto and Margie Szerer, New York

Dedicated by the Trestman Family in memory of

פריידל באשה בת חיים שלמה
Friedel Basha bas Chaim Shlomo

משה בן שלמה
Moses ben Shlomo

May their souls be bound in the bonds of eternal life

ת.נ.צ.ב.ה.

Dedicated in memory of

מרדכי בער בן בנימין
Mordechai Ber Ben Benjamin

שרה בת יעקב
Sarah Bas Jacob

נחום ליב בן יצחק
Nachum Leib Ben Isaac

May their souls be bound in the bonds of eternal life
ת.נ.צ.ב.ה

Dedicated by Mr. & Mrs. Andrew Bales in honor and deep appreciation of the

Lubavitcher Rebbe
Rabbi. M.M. Schneerson OBM

&

In the merit of all the extended Bales Family

Dedicated in honor of the beloved Grandmothers

Bessie Goldstein
In honor of her 93rd Birthday

&

Jeanne Finkelstein
In honor of her 90th Birthday

May they merit a healthy long life with many more years of love, prosperity, and happiness, from their children, grandchildren, and great grandchildren

Rabbi & Mrs. Goldstein
The Goldstein and Kaplan Grandchildren

Dedicated in honor of all the members and subscribers of Shulchan/Tablearuchharav.com who help support our work

To become a member and help support our work-Visit our site at shulchanaruchharav.com

Dedicated by Mr. & Mrs. Tzvi Meir & Basha Hacohane Cohn

In honor of their beloved children

Daniel Menachem Mendel HaCohane

Abraham Schneur Zalman HaCohane

Dedicated by the Goldstein Family in memory of the beloved Grandparents of the Author

אברהם בן יהודה
Abraham [Albert] Ben Judah
נלב"ע ו' תמוז תש"מ

שמחה בת יצחק
Simcha [Arlete] Bas Isaac
נלב"ע א' אדר א' תשע"ד

May their souls be bound in the bonds of eternal life
ת.נ.צ.ב.ה

Dedicated by Mr. Tzvi Shochat

In loving memory of his Grandfather

Moses Ben Zalman Tzevi
Passed away on 8ᵀᴴ Nissan 5778

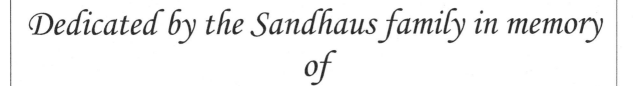

Dedicated by the Sandhaus family in memory of

יוסף יהושע בן יבלח"ט צבי אלימלך
Joseph Joshua z"l
Ben Tzevi Elimelech [May he live long years]

May his soul be bound in the bonds of eternal life
ת.נ.צ.ב.ה

Made in the USA
Coppell, TX
21 January 2025

44634709R00168